*"Why should not the New Englander
be in search of new adventures?"*
THOREAU: *Walden*

Country Inns and Back Roads

VOLUME XV

BY THE BERKSHIRE TRAVELLER

Norman T. Simpson

THE BERKSHIRE TRAVELLER PRESS

Stockbridge, Massachusetts 01262

THE BERKSHIRE TRAVELLER TRAVEL SHELF

Country Inns and Back Roads, North America (1980)
Country Inns and Back Roads, Britain and Ireland
Country Inns and Back Roads, Europe
Farm, Ranch, and Country Vacations
Adventure Travel (1980)
Country Bed and Breakfast in Canada
The Inn Way . . . Switzerland (Revised 1980)
The Inn Way . . . Caribbean
A Guide to Music Festivals in America
A Guide to Music Festivals in Europe and Britain
A Guide for Solo Travel Abroad

(See last page for information
for other Berkshire Traveller Press titles)

6 5 4 3 2
COVER PAINTING: Shelia Granda
BOOK DESIGN AND DRAWINGS: Janice Lindstrom

Library of Congress 79-615664
ISBN 912944-57-9

A Brief Backward Glance at Matters Personal and Public:

In 1966, when I wrote the first edition of *Country Inns and Back Roads,* I never for a moment envisioned it as it is today, fifteen editions later. That first edition, by the way, was sixteen pages long and had the account of visits to twelve inns by a man called "The Berkshire Traveller."

I discovered almost at the start that country innkeepers lacked one important ingredient in their lives, a forum or seminar in which to exchange ideas and solutions to problems. I brought them all together at a dinner, and it was such a success that the idea of an association became a reality.

Today, the Independent Innkeepers Association is an important factor in the continuity and growth of *Country Inns and Back Roads.* Large, annual, three-day meetings have been augmented by many shorter regional meetings during the year, so that innkeepers in this book have ample opportunity to get together and exchange ideas, solve problems, and enjoy talk about inns. Furthermore, as a result of my writing a book about European inns and small hotels, our gatherings are enriched by visits from several of those innkeepers each year. In 1979, we had a number of German hoteliers, and in 1980, a group from the United Kingdom.

By 1976, I felt that I had learned my trade sufficiently, so I made the first of several trips to Europe. This resulted in *Country Inns and Back Roads, Europe,* which has since been enlarged and revised. In May of 1980, we will be publishing *Country Inns and Back Roads, Britain and Ireland,* to be followed by *Country Inns and Back Roads, Spain and Portugal,* in November, 1980.

Bill Winterer, the innkeeper of the Griswold Inn in Essex, Connecticut, reminded me a couple of years ago that I had almost singlehandedly created a new, thriving business: "Country Inn-keeping." That was a generous thought on his part, and I'm very happy if *CIBR* has made travelers more aware of these delightful accommodations. A year or so later, Bill said, "I think you've also added *another* business to the American scene—writing books about country inns!" We both had a good laugh at this, and I believe he quoted the classic phrase about imitation being the sincerest form of flattery. Yes, there are other books, and whether they be imitators or not, I welcome honestly-researched, carefully written books and articles which call favorable attention to country inns. I believe, however, that *CIBR* is still the only *single* volume that is revised and rewritten every year by one person, who travels throughout North America.

I have had a lot of help along the way, and in the beginning much came from my wife, the late Nancy Simpson, who designed and created the covers and some illustrations for a few years before her passing in 1972. Some of her early covers are now being encored.

For ten years, the art director and frequent cover artist has been Jan Lindstrom, an invaluable asset to all that we are doing. Jan creates the attractive drawings seen in all *CIBR* books.

Still another source of assistance has been the innkeepers themselves, to whom I owe so much of my inn-education and appreciation of just what is involved in keeping an inn. My association with them has been most rewarding and I number dozens of good friends among them.

The Studley Press in Dalton, Massachusetts has been my printer since the beginning. Not only have they provided me with much useful advice, but many times they worked overtime to meet demanding deadlines. It has been a wonderful association with the Reardon family.

Mention should be made of my friend and longtime sales representative, Roger Wunderlich, who ten years ago appeared at my office in Stockbridge and suggested that instead of my offering books by direct mail, he could sell them to bookstores. Roger's counsel, wisdom, and persistence have been one of the main reasons that we became a bona fide publishing house now offering many other titles, with sales representatives all over North America and in Britain.

Perhaps the biggest single media break came when I met Pete Johnston, then of the *New York Times,* and now on the faculty of the Columbia University School of Journalism. The result, early in 1972, was a blockbuster of an article in the Sunday *Times* which called the attention of a vast readership to a new-old thing called "Country Inns."

Since that time, I've been pleased to have excerpts from *CIBR* run in several national magazines and also to be mentioned favorably (and sometimes unfavorably) on national TV. (As Jane Ace used to say, "You've got to take the bitter with the better.")

One of the most rewarding experiences was the recognition in 1978 by the Cornell University Hotel School for the contributions made by *CIBR* to the accommodations business. After my short talk to the entire student body, I was delighted to have a reunion with four students who were sons and daughters of innkeepers in *CIBR*.

Perhaps the single, most helpful source for learning of potential inns to visit are the letters from readers which pour in constantly. Many of these correspondents have become very good friends over the years, as well.

In spite of the fact that between 1966 and the present many new inns came into being, I decided early-on to keep *CIBR* to one volume with one writer . . . me. When inns change ownership they are not included in the next edition, and about the same number of newly-included inns are added to replace them. This means traveling thousands of miles each year visiting inns for the first time and re-visiting those already included.

For me it is a great thrill knowing that wherever I go there may be a country inn beyond the next hill!

Norman T. Simpson
Stockbridge, Massachusetts
February 29, 1980

Contents

UNITED STATES

Michigan

Minnesota

Mississippi

Missouri

New Hampshire

CANADA

MONTREAL

North Hero House, *North Hero*

Inn on the Common,
Craftsbury Common

■ BURLINGTON

Edson Hill Manor,

Philbrook Farm, *Shelburne*

Spalding Inn,

ST. JOHNSBURY ■   *Whitefield*

Dana Place Inn, *Jackson*

Lovett's, *Franconia*

NORTH CONWAY

Rockhouse Mountain Farm, *Eaton Center*

V E R M O N T   Stafford's-In-The-Field,
Chocorua

Blueberry Hill Farm, *Goshen*   Lyme Inn, *Lyme*

■ RUTLAND   ■ HANOVER

Hickory Stick
Farm, *Laconia*

Kedron Valley Inn,
South Woodstock

Village Inn, *Landgrove*

Chester Inn, *Chester*   Dexter's Inn, *Sunapee*

Barrows House, *Dorset*   N E W   ■ CONCORD

H A M P S H I R E

Colby Hill Inn, *Henniker*

John Hancock Inn, *Hancock*

Inn at Sawmill Farm,
West Dover

Woodbound, *Jaffrey*

Northern
New England

Eastern Time Zone

MAINE

CALAIS ■

■ BANGOR

- Waterford Inne,
  E. Waterford

Asticou Inn,
Grey Rock Inn,
Northeast Harbor

Whitehall Inn, *Camden*
- Pilgrims Inn, *Deer Isle*

Jordan Pond House,
Seal Harbor

Squire Tarbox,
Westport Island

Claremont Inn,
Southwest Harbor

Homewood Inn,
Yarmouth •

PORTLAND ■

- Black Point Inn, *Prouts Neck*
  Captain Lord, Old Fort Club, *Kennebunkport*
- Whistling Oyster, *Ogunquit*

Dockside Guest Quarters, *York*

New Hampshire

COLBY HILL INN
Henniker, New Hampshire

"As far as we have been able to discover, the original building was built in 1821 by John S. Bartlett on 75 acres of land." Don Glover was explaining some of the interesting history of the Colby Hill Inn. "He developed it into a good farm to provision his tavern. It consisted of what is now the two-story house and an addition to the north of only one story. This new section was all in one room and called 'Bartlett's Hall.' It was used for dances and meetings of various sorts. Several times it sheltered a private school. After the burning of the second meeting house of the Congregationalists in Henniker in the winter of 1883, the church hired Bartlett's Hall in which to hold Sunday services.

"In 1836, it was sold to Oliver Pillsbury and ceased to be a tavern. The Pillsburys were excellent farmers and held possession through their son until about 1866, when it was purchased by Lewis Colby. The road from which the present inn takes it name ran up to Colby Hill in those days.

"George Rice and his son Elmer, the next owners, continued to farm for a number of years and also ran a retail milk route in the town. Subsequent proprietors continued it as a farm until 1959, when it was restored as a place of entertainment."

This New Hampshire village, home of New England College, with its white clapboard houses and its church spires rising in the blue sky, is an ideal location for this trim little inn which is now owned by the Glover family, including the senior members, Don and June, classmates of mine at Bucknell University, and their son Don, Jr., who is now the manager and chef. They acquired it a few years ago from my good friend Bettie Gilbert who now lives right across from the inn in a beautiful red house.

A letter I received from a reader says: "The inn was just as you described it. The house, the furniture, the paintings, the wide floorboards were all a feast for the eyes. We especially enjoyed looking out the dining room window and watching two large birds roosting in the doorway of the barn. We realized they were live turkeys.

"After dinner I took a swim in the pool next to the barn, while my wife watched the sunset behind the mountains."

The inn is rather small and the dining room, with its pewter serving plates and gay linen, is a popular meeting place for people from the surrounding countryside and villages. It has many country antiques, a group of old post office boxes, and a solemn grandfather's clock.

Don, Jr., brought a wealth of experience to the kitchen of the inn, and besides the freshly baked bread there are such interesting menu items as beef kabob Teriyaki, fresh seafood, crab Imperial, shrimp Scampi, and usually a fresh fish of the day. June Glover has her own little baking corner and does the chocolate cakes, the cinnamon buns, the biscuits, and the applesauce. Their garden provides some interesting things for the table, such as juice from their tomatoes, and jelly made from wild grapes that grow out behind the barn.

"I shall certainly always be grateful to George W. Rice," said Don. Puzzled, I inquired just why. "Because he's the man who built the beautiful barn in 1893. We have more people stop and want just to run their hands over the old barn wood and roam around inside. For barn lovers, it is really a monument."

Colby Hill Inn has been included in *CIBR* since 1974.

COLBY HILL INN, Henniker, N.H. 03242; 603-428-3281. An 8-room inn on the outskirts of a New Hampshire college town. European plan. Some rooms with shared baths. Breakfast served to houseguests only. Dinner served to travelers Tuesdays through Sunday, except Thanksgiving, Christmas, and New Year's Day. Open year-round. No children under 6. No pets. Swimming pool on grounds. Tennis and xc skiing one short block; alpine, 3 mi., golf, canoeing, hiking, bicycling, and fishing nearby. The Glover Family, Innkeepers.

Directions: From I-89, take Exit 5 and follow Rte. 202 to Henniker. From I-91, take Exit 3 and follow Rte. 9 through Keene and Hillsborough to Henniker. At the Oaks, W. Main St., one-half mile west of town center.

DANA PLACE INN
Jackson, New Hampshire

I was in the hammock strung between two birch trees on the bank of the Ellis River in back of the Dana Place Inn. The corn was up, but not quite in tassel, and I could look across the vegetable garden with its crop of summer squash, zucchini, lettuce, Brussels sprouts, and cucumbers.

Over my other shoulder, I could just see the tip of Mount Washington towering above the steep sides of the valley. It seemed impossible that in just a few months there would be at least two feet of snow on the ground and I could almost hear the shouts of the cross-country skiers as they skied up from Jackson to have lunch here at the inn.

I heard a footstep behind me and a firm hand lifted up one side of the hammock and then dumped me out on the ground. Sure enough, there was Betty Jennings, eyes smiling gaily from a face browned by the New Hampshire sun. "Up you slugabed, it's time for our annual walk along the river."

Vowing somehow or other to even the score, I fell into stride with her as we walked down through the fields past her extensive flower garden. "Tell me, Mrs. Burbank, what are the names of all of the flowers?"

She gave me a sidelong glance and then ticked them off on her fingers: "We have nasturtiums, ivy geraniums, lobelia, and sunflowers. This is my cutting bed. Everything I put in it, I can use in the dining room."

The Dana Place has been an inn since the late 1800s. At one time it was a farm, as evidenced by the many apple trees. Like so many New England dwellings, it has been through additions, with buildings snuggled up against each other. Now, it's L-shaped and has many comfortable, homey bedrooms of different sizes and shapes.

The location in the White Mountains National Forest offers opportunities for mountain climbing, hiking, walking, and has some access to alpine trails above the timberline for the avid and experienced climber. The lower mountains invite those who prefer easier walking and enjoy the pleasure of beautiful woodland paths and, in the winter, cross-country skiing. Guests can order picnic lunches for walks or drives through the countryside or into the mountains.

Our walk brought us to the edge of the river, and pointing to a shallow place, Betty said, "Next year, Mal is going to build a small sluiceway right about there so that our guests can pan for gold." I must have looked incredulous, so she continued, "We understand the Ellis River may well contain a small amount of gold, and picking up a bit of gold dust or semi-precious stones would be a nice way to spend a few hours. After a hard day's work panning for gold, the guests could flop in our hammock for a snooze before dinner.

"Incidentally, we have already made plans to start making our own apple cider. With all the apple trees, it seems a shame not to take advantage of them since we serve so much hot mulled cider during the fall and winter months.

"We have a guest from New Britain, Connecticut, Mr. Hannon, who told Mal that he was able to identify practically every fall warbler in the guidebook. It's the combination of the old apple trees and the thickets bordering the meadow that makes the area a perfect place for migrating birds, and for observing them. Our chef spotted a great grey owl; they are very rarely seen south of Canada."

I started thinking about dinner and asked Betty what was on the menu. "Well, we're sort of country gourmet," she said. "Our guests enjoy things like our veal and ham in a casserole, and chicken Gloria. I still do all the desserts, including a cranberry torte pie which is just wonderful, even if I do say so myself. I also do the cheesecake and French chocolate custard served with whipped cream."

We turned past the swimming pool and walked back by the orchard. I noticed a new edging of naturtiums in front of the white clapboard wall of the inn. The color reminded me of something she had said. I stopped. "Panning for gold?" I asked. "are you really serious?"

"Certainly I'm serious," she said. "But bring your own pans."

And that's how the great Jackson, New Hampshire gold rush began.

DANA PLACE INN, Route 16, Pinkham Notch, P.O. Box 157-B, Jackson, N.H. 03846; 603-383-6822. A 14-room resort inn, 5 miles from Jackson, N.H. in the heart of the White Mountains. Rates include lodging and full breakfast. Lunches served on winter weekends only. Dinners served to travelers daily from late May to late October and from mid-December to late April. Closed Thanksgiving Day. Two tennis courts, natural pool, trout fishing, xc skiing, bird watching, panning for gold(?) on grounds. Hiking trails, indoor tennis, 5 golf courses, downhill skiing nearby. Malcolm and Betty Jennings, Innkeepers.

Directions: Follow Rte. 16, north of Jackson Village toward Pinkham Notch.

DEXTER'S INN AND TENNIS CLUB
Sunapee, New Hampshire

There was a light mist (euphemism for rain) in Sunapee, New Hampshire. The guests at Dexter's Inn were dividing into two groups. Some were out antiquing and taking back road tours or perhaps visiting nearby Hanover, the home of Dartmouth College. Another group was seated inside watching the tennis tournaments on television, already dressed in their tennis togs ready to run outside in case the weather should let up again. I walked across the lawn to the tennis courts which were wet and then past the swimming pool, the rose garden, the horseshoe pits, and across the grass to a nice hammock strung out for somebody to use, and yellow umbrellas which were folded until after the rain had stopped. The mountains were slightly obscured by mist, but there was an air of expectancy and an occasional movement of the clouds overhead.

Tennis and cross-country skiing are really the watchwords here at Dexter's Inn. There are nine-and-a-half miles of cross-country ski trails which are used for walking in the summer and fall. Three all-weather courts are constantly in use with the active tennis program. Incidentally, the last week in September is one of the best times to visit New Hampshire; the leaves are already turning, and it's not crowded.

The lodging rooms at Dexter's are fun. The accent is on very bright and gay colors in wallpaper, curtains, and bedspreads. Ten rooms in the main house are reached by funny little hallways that zigzag around the various wings.

The front parlor has a baby grand piano, a lovely old antique desk loaded with copies of newspapers and magazines, a very inviting fireplace, and lots and lots of books. There's also a little gift shop.

There are other bedrooms with a rustic flavor located in barns

across the street. These I visited briefly noting the country wallpaper which makes an interesting contrast with the barn siding. The newly decorated rooms were very attractive.

Recreation for the younger set during rainy days or after tennis or skiing is provided in the recreation room in this barn which has a small pool table, a television set, and other games. "I think that kids need an area like this when they're on vacation," was the way Frank Simpson put it.

It was on this visit that I met Norman Arluck, a gentlemen of some seventy-two years who plays tennis with tremendous zest and skill and is also ready to play any type of card game. Norman has been coming to Dexter's for many, many years, and the recreation hall has been named in his honor because of his good humor and high spirits.

Among the other interesting small but important touches at Dexter's is the fact that morning coffee and juice are brought to the guest rooms, if desired. A Boston morning paper is provided for guests in the dining room and, a little later, the *Wall Street Journal.* Guests may feel free to pick flowers for their rooms if they like, and there are, also, wonderful wild strawberries, raspberries, and black-berries to be picked and eaten on the spot and/or brought into the kitchen and served in a bowl.

Just a word or two about the menu. The specialties are french market soup, the base of which is a baked onion, homemade fresh bread and rolls every day, meringues that melt in the mouth, and apple crisp.

I was looking at the latest copy of the *Smithsonian* when one of the guests came running in from the outside, yelling, "The sun, the sun!" Immediately all was activity as tennis players made a beeline for the doorway in a flurry of tennis rackets and ball bags. There was a brief moment when six people were trying to get through the door at the same time.

The principal summertime activity at Dexter's Inn was again underway.

DEXTER'S INN AND TENNIS CLUB, Box R, Stagecoach Rd., Sunapee, N.H. 03782; 603-763-5571. A 17-room country inn in the western New Hampshire mountain and lake district. Mod. American and European plans available. Breakfast, lunch, and dinner served to travelers by advance reservation. Lunches served only July, Aug.; Dec., Feb. Open from early June to mid-October; December 26th through mid-March. Closed Thanksgiving and Christmas Day. Pets allowed in Annex only. Limited activities for children under 12. Three tennis courts, pool, croquet, shuffleboard, 12½ mi. of xc skiing on grounds. Downhill skiing and additional xc skiing nearby. No credit cards. Frank and Shirley Simpson, Innkeepers.

Directions: From North & East: Use Exit 12 or 12A, I-89. Continue west on Rte. 11, 6 mi.-just ½ mi. past Sunapee to a sign at Winn Hill Rd. Turn left up hill and after 1 mi., bear right on Stagecoach Rd. From west: use Exit 8, I-91, follow Rte. 103 east into N.H.-through Newport ½ mi. past Junction with Rte. 11. Look for sign at "Young Hill Rd." and go 1½ mi. to Stagecoach Rd.

HICKORY STICK FARM
Laconia, New Hampshire

I carefully separated the first bite of my first breast of roast duckling at Hickory Stick Farm, and prepared to transfer it to my expectant mouth. I could plainly see the succulent textures and colors. The outside was crisp and beautifully browned, and the meat underneath the skin was moist with just enough juice. I placed the tender morsel in my mouth and was immediately transported.

I take a lot of ribbing among the many innkeepers of my acquaintance for having a penchant for roast duckling. I've eaten it everywhere, from Longfellow's Wayside Inn in South Sudbury, Massachusetts, on New Year's Eve, to the Inn at Rancho Santa Fe, California. Now, I was in the Shangri-la of the world of roast duckling, the place where other roast duckling specialists want to go when they have roasted their last duckling—Hickory Stick Farm in Laconia, New Hampshire.

It's located on the top of a hill outside of Laconia, (see directions below) in a very busy section of the resort area of New Hampshire, dominated by Lake Winnipesaukee.

The entrance to this old converted farmhouse is through a lovely old-fashioned door leading into a beamed, low-ceilinged room with a brick fireplace which, at the time I was there, had some antiques on display. The floors are of brick or stone and there are antiques and gift items scattered about in several rooms which precede the entrance to the restaurant itself. The stenciling on some of the walls was done by Mary Roeder and is after the manner of Moses Eaton, Jr., who used to travel around southern New Hampshire in the early 1800s as a journeyman stencil artist. I believe some of his original work is in the Hancock Inn in Hancock, New Hampshire.

Mary and Scott Roeder (his brother Steve is at the Dockside Restaurant in York, Maine) showed me to a table with a most pleasant view of the fields, woods, and valleys with Mount Kearsage, Ragged Mountain, and Cartigan in the distance. Outside, the lilac and forsythia bushes were augumented by maple, butternut, apple, and locust trees, and I noticed several birds fluttering about in the branches.

Besides the duckling, the menu had many other items on it such as veal a la Hickory Stick, seafood, and steaks, but it was to the duckling section that my eye was immediately drawn. I could have ordered a quarter of a roast stuffed duckling, a half, or a whole one for two, three, or four. They are all served with a country herb dressing and orange sherry sauce. Scott Roeder asserted that at least seventy-five percent of all of his entrées served are for roast duckling.

As the duckling on my plate disappeared, Scott went on to elaborate on the message that can be found on each table about how the ducklings are cooked. "This process involves roasting at a low temperature for about eight hours, which extracts about a pound of grease from each bird," he explained. "The ducks are then refrigerated, and as orders are received from the dining room, they are placed in a very hot oven for fifteen to twenty minutes. This final roasting extracts even more grease and produces a duckling which is golden brown.

"It is now possible for us to ship our duckling anywhere in the United States. We pack the frozen ducks in dry ice and they're shipped air freight right from our little plant next door to the inn. If your readers drop us a line, we'll be very happy to put them on our mailing list."

Filled with duckling, dessert, and good will, I staggered out to the lawn to take a constitutional and enjoy the view. For some reason, that obscure one-liner by the late Joe Penner kept running through my mind: "You wanna buy a duck?"

You bet I do.

HICKORY STICK FARM, R.F.D. #2 Laconia, N.H. 03246; 603-524-3333. A hilltop country restaurant (no lodgings available) 4 mi. from Laconia in the lake country of New Hampshire. The Shaker Village in Canterbury is nearby, as well as the Belknap recreational area and other New Hampshire attractions. Open from Memorial Day to Columbus Day. Luncheons served in July and August only from 12 noon to 2 p.m. and dinners from 5:30 to 9 p.m. Sunday dinner served all day from noon to 8 p.m. CIBR Readers may be able to be accommodated for lunch during the fall foliage season, but prior arrangements must be made in advance. Scott and Mary Roeder, Innkeepers.

Directions: Use Exit 20 from I-93. Follow Rte. 3 toward Laconia approximately 5 mi. over bridge over Lake Winnisquam. A short distance past this bridge on the right is a drive-in restaurant (Double Decker), turn right on Union Road immediately past Double Decker and follow Hickory Stick signs 1½ mi. into the woods. If you do not turn onto any dirt roads, you are on the right track.

JOHN HANCOCK INN
Hancock, New Hampshire

I remember very well the first time I met Pat and Glynn Wells. We had lunch together in the sunny courtyard of the Red Lion Inn in Stockbridge. They had driven from New Jersey to talk to me about buying a country inn. Like so many of today's budding innkeepers, they had visited several country inns, and felt that they would prefer to leave their present careers and devote their experience and enthusiasm to becoming country innkeepers.

As it developed, they found the John Hancock Inn, which is New Hampshire's oldest operating inn, located in one of the prettiest

towns in the Mount Monadnock region. The town is not very big, but what there is of it is honest and true. It is a community of white clapboard houses, a broad village green with a bandstand and churches around it. The people are very friendly as I have learned in the course of many visits.

And how are Glynn and Pat Wells and their children, Susan and Andrew, doing with their country inn? I think the best thing I can do is to quote from a letter Pat wrote to me.

"People—that's our great blessing! Let me explain. Last night we were sitting in the Carriage Room at one of the bellows tables in front of a cheerful fire. I looked around and there were two couples who were strangers an hour before, talking like old friends, having just discovered to their mutual wonder that though they came from opposite sides of the continent, they shared common roots in the Midwest.

"In one corner, there was a couple who had arrived a little earlier amid clanging cans and flying balloons, with 'just married' written in shaving cream across the back of the car. They were staying in the Mural Room with its pastoral scene, which we believe was created by Moses Eaton in the 19th century. By the way, it's been redecorated and has a four-poster topped with a beautiful canopy.

"A gust of cold air heralded some new arrivals. Andrew was quick to move to the lobby—he enjoys the role of front desk clerk when opportunity presents itself. Susan enjoys the innkeeper's role at times, too. Tonight, she was toasting marshmallows in the fire, ready to share them with any whose memories include the yummy taste of 'blackened outside, squishy inside.' A few days ago, she helped me serve breakfast to some of our local preschoolers who wanted to practice their 'social skills' by eating in a restaurant! They had a great time and according to Susan, *she* had a ball.

"I heard Glynn's laugh from the living room. He was hosting and enjoying the conversation with a family from Hancock who were entertaining visitors from Australia. The Orient was represented also by a group of Japanese engineers who were visiting the facilities of our area's fine industries.

"It's been a few years since our talk in the Red Lion courtyard and we always seem to have something planned or in progress. We are blessed in being located in the woods not far from wonderful things for our guests to enjoy in all seasons of the year. I just can't imagine being anything other than an innkeeper!"

The John Hancock Inn has been included in *CIBR* since 1972.

THE JOHN HANCOCK INN, Hancock, N.H. 03449; 603-525-3318. A 10-room village inn on Rtes. 123 and 137, 9 mi. north of Peterborough. In the middle of the Monadnock Region of southern N.H. European plan. Breakfast, lunch, and dinner served daily to travelers. Closed Christmas Day and one week in spring and fall. Bicycles available on the grounds. Antiquing, swimming, hiking, Alpine and xc skiing nearby. Glynn and Pat Wells, Innkeepers.

Directions: From Keene, take either Rte. 101 east to Dublin and Rte. 137 north to Hancock or Rte. 9 north to Rte. 123 and east to Hancock. From Nashua, take 101A and 101 to Peterborough. Proceed north on Rtes. 202 and 123 to Hancock.

LOVETT'S BY LAFAYETTE BROOK
Franconia, New Hampshire

Lovett's (as it is known locally) is a sophisticated country inn with a spectacular view of Cannon Mountain with its many ski trails. There is considerable emphasis on excellent food and service, and the inn is well into its second generation of one-family ownership. Many of the guests have been returning for years; their fathers and mothers having come before them. "It is," one guest remarked, "almost like a club."

Summer in Franconia has many delights—antiquing, horse shows, summer theatre, flower shows, auctions, and country fairs. Most of the ski areas run their lifts during the summer and autumn. Shopping seems to intrigue Lovett's guests, and there is a sprinkling of country stores and craft shops throughout the mountains.

On the campus-like grounds of the inn there are small chalets with mountain views and living rooms, many of them with fireplaces. There are also poolside chalets, as well as several bedrooms in the main house and in two nearby houses.

Of the two swimming pools, one has rather chilly mountain

water that comes right off nearby Cannon Mountain, and the other has a solar heater; one of the first in the area, I am sure.

With Lovett's impressive reputation for its food, it is difficult to make a choice from the tempting menu.

When I pressed Charlie Lovett to tell me which dish was most favored, he had this to say, "We're particularly proud of our cold bisque of native watercress, our eggplant caviar, and our pan-broiled chicken in brandy, herbs, and cream. People also tell us they enjoy our braised sirloin of beef Beaujolais, and lamb served with our own chutney."

The most exciting news in recent months has been the research and work to comply with the requirements for Lovett's nomination to the National Register of Historic Places. "This was both exciting and tedious," said Charlie Lovett. "Now, the outside colors are the same as the original farmhouse, and matching the red color was an achievement. It meant taking an original clapboard to a learned Boston colorist. She peeled back 190 years of paint to the first color and we had the red!

"Outside the front door we have made an old-fashioned herb bed; the 37 specimens are labeled.

"We discovered that Lovett's was constructed around 1784 and was built in Franconia's early days. Its original owner was active in the development and history of the town. In October, 1790, Nicholas Powers, the original homesteader and builder, was the petitioner to the State asking for aid to build a road through Franconia Notch. He was also one of the surveyors."

Today, Lovett's is a fine example of an early American farmhouse. It retains its original colonial country charm although there are many additions. Once again the building, the Nicholas Powers' House, is used as a stop-over for weary and hungry travelers.

LOVETT'S BY LAFAYETTE BROOK, Profile Rd., Franconia, N.H. 03580; 603-823-7761. A 32-room country inn in New Hampshire's White Mountains. Modified American plan omits lunch, although box lunches are available. Breakfast and dinner served by reservation to travelers. Open daily between June 29 and Oct. 8 and Dec. 26 and April 1. No pets. Two swimming pools, xc skiing, badminton, lawn sports on grounds. Golf, tennis, alpine skiing, trout fishing, hiking nearby. Mr. and Mrs. Charles J. Lovett, Jr., Innkeepers.

Directions: 2½ mi. south of Franconia on N.H. 18 business loop, at junction of N.H. 141 and I-93 South Franconia exit. 2¾ mi. north of junction of U.S. 3 and 18.

LYME INN
Lyme, New Hampshire

The Lyme Inn is a precise, antique-laden gem. Lodging rooms, parlors, and dining rooms are meticulously furnished with wall coverings, fabrics, and paintings chosen to complement this most New England of settings.

The inn rests on the end of a long New England common, and although the village feels quite remote, it is nonetheless just ten miles from Hanover, New Hampshire, the home of Dartmouth College, and inn guests have the opportunity to share some of the sporting and theatrical events taking place there. It is just a few minutes from the Dartmouth Skiway, and there's plenty of cross-country skiing nearby.

Bedrooms have poster beds, hooked rugs, handstitched quilts, wide pine floorboards, stenciled wallpaper, wingback chairs, and all kinds of beautiful antiques which guests frequently become very attached to and purchase.

On a recent visit, Fred and Judy Siemons showed me the third dining room which has been completely redecorated. Fred built a series of room dividers so it can be used for different purposes. "We have had a number of weddings on the porch," Judy commented, "and the receptions have been held in this room. As you see, we have added more old maps and larger farm tools to give the room a character all of its own."

Judy had news about the three Siemons sons who have been very much involved at the inn: "Rick is working as an assistant to the golf pro at Lake Marey across the river," she said. "He is a full-fledged hotel student at the University of New Hampshire and loves it. Gary, our second son, is really the automobile mechanic and on weekends helps out here at the inn. Our youngest son has been busy splitting wood for our new Garrison stove in the lobby. Incidentally, it's a wonderful place for our guests to gather around. By the way, Fred still does the breakfast and all the rolls and breads."

Speaking of breakfast, the Lyme Inn is well-known in that particular department. Besides an à la carte breakfast, there are at least eight other full breakfasts with everything from cheese omelets, poached eggs, English muffins, and French toast, to a north country breakfast featuring pancakes.

The main dishes on the dinner menu include hasenpfeffer, weiner schnitzel, rack of lamb, and hunter-style veal.

I would estimate that it takes about three days really to enjoy this part of New Hampshire. The Dartmouth College Theatre, the backroads, local shops, fairs, auctions, and the great emphasis on handcrafts in the area, plus the skiing, both cross-country and downhill, would encourage many guests to extend their holidays.

The Lyme Inn is small and intimate. It has nine rooms with private baths, and five rooms with shared baths. I feel certain that children would not be comfortable, because there is no entertainment particularly designed for them.

In keeping with its austere New England setting, the inn has only one television set located in a side sitting room. However, there are loads and loads of books. Fred and Judy encourage guests to take home partially-read copies and return them when finished.

The Lyme Inn has been included in *CIBR* since 1971.

LYME INN, on the Common, Lyme, N.H. 03768; 603-795-2222. A 15-room village inn, 10 mi. north of Hanover on N.H. Rte. 10. Convenient to all Dartmouth College activities, including Hopkins Center, with music, dance, dramas, painting, and sculpture. European plan year-round. Some rooms with shared baths. Breakfast and dinner served daily to travelers, except dinner on Tuesdays. Closed three weeks following Thanksgiving and three weeks in late spring. No children under 8. No pets. Alpine and xc skiing, fishing, hiking, canoeing, tennis, and golf nearby. Fred and Judy Siemons, Innkeepers.

Directions: From I-91, take Exit 14 and follow Rte. 113A east to Vermont Rte. 5. Proceed south 50 yards to a left turn, then travel 2 mi. to inn.

PHILBROOK FARM INN
Shelburne, New Hampshire

The Philbrook Farm Inn *is* New Hampshire. There's New Hampshire everywhere I looked: New Hampshire prints, paintings, and photographs—some of them really irreplaceable. There were some tints of old prints, hooked rugs and many, many books about New Hampshire. A whole library of books is just on the White Mountains. Some have been written by former guests.

Another fun activity is looking at the albums, photographs, and mementos of the farm that go back over the years. In one of them I found a copy of a 1952 edition of *White Mountain Echos* which, among other things, had a story about the inn and a photograph showing all of the elm trees in the front. Even in 1952, the headline said, "Philbrooks of Shelburne have played host for generations because innkeepers run in their family."

In 1980, guests at the farm in all seasons will be able to sharpen up their games on a new-old pool table, vintage 1918, which innkeepers Connie Leger and Nancy Philbrook discovered in an old pool parlor which went out of business. "We purchased the works," said Connie, "the lights, markers, cues, and everything. It took five hours to move it. It's a beauty."

Wintertime is waking up in the morning to snowstorms, or brilliant sunshine, seeing Mount Washington over the hill in the distance, and also looking at the cross-country ski wax thermometer which gives advice on the correct wax to use. It's looking out over the snow-filled fields, which in summertime have Herefords standing knee deep in the lush grass. Summer and fall are a pure delight.

All of this outdoor activity in all seasons encourages the kind of appetites that most people forgot they had. Consequently, food is on

everybody's mind at least three times a day. "It is all homemade with no mixes," said Connie. "There is one main dish each night, and the dinner usually consists of a homemade soup, some type of pot roasts, pork roast, or roast lamb. The vegetables are all fresh and we try to stay away from fried foods. Most of the guests enjoy roast, because these days they are not served as much at home. All the desserts are homemade. There's pie, ice cream, and pudding.

"For lunches, we serve salads, chowder, hot rolls, hash, macaroni and cheese, and things like that. We always serve a full breakfast with a choice of juice, hot or cold cereal, eggs, bacon, toast or muffins. On Sunday morning, we have New England fish balls and corn bread. On Saturday night, we have a New England baked bean supper. We almost always have roast chicken dinner at Sunday noon."

On the morning of my departure, we were all together in the great farm kitchen of the Philbrook Farm Inn.

First, there was Maxine McKay who is really, as innkeeper Connie Leger says, "the pulse of the kitchen. She has been here for so many years." Then there was Cilla, the morning waitress, who is the fourth generation of her family to work at the inn. Nancy, along with a few other assorted neighbors, rounded out the gathering. Nancy said, "Come on in, I think we're having a mini-town meeting."

Everybody sat around on stools or leaned up against the counters drinking coffee, joking, and telling stories about the old days. Through the outside door came a very hearty man who has been plowing the town roads since the days when they were rolled instead of cleared. He was retiring after the winter, and everyone laughingly attempted to dissuade him from leaving his job.

Most of the heat in the kitchen came from the ten-burner *woodburning* range built by the Magee Furance Company of Boston during the 1890s. "Yes," said Nancy, "we do almost all of our cooking

31

and baking on this range. We only use the electric stove in case of emergencies or to keep things warm." Imagine, a country inn where almost all of the cooking is done on a woodburning range!

PHILBROOK FARM INN, North Rd., Shelburne, N.H. 03581; 603-466-3831. A 20-room country inn in the White Mountains of northeastern N.H., 6 mi. from Gorham and just west of the Maine/N.H. line. American, mod. American, & European plans available. Breakfast, lunch, and dinner served daily to travelers. Open May 1st to October 31st; December 26th to April 1st. Closed Thanksgiving, Christmas. Pets allowed only during summer season in cottages. Shuffleboard, horseshoes, badminton, ping-pong, croquet, pool, hiking trails, xc skiing, snowshoeing trails on grounds. Swimming, golf, hiking, back roading, bird watching nearby. No credit cards. Nancy C. Philbrook & Constance P. Leger, Innkeepers.

Directions: The inn is just off U.S. Rte. 2 in Shelburne. Look for inn direction sign and turn at North Rd., cross r.r. tracks and river, turn right at crossroad, and the inn is at the end of road.

ROCKHOUSE MOUNTAIN FARM
Eaton, Center, New Hampshire

Betsi set the delicious piece of apple pie down in front of me and said; "Now that I have been elected selectman in Eaton Center, I hope that I will finally receive from you the respect that I deserved all along!" I sprang up from my chair and made a deep bow. "Madame, henceforth I shall certainly give you all the respect you deserve." Betsi and I have had a wonderful kidding-insulting relationship since my first visit several years ago. It is her father and mother, John and Libby Edge, who started Rockhouse Mountain Farm, as Libby says, "a thousand years ago." They were joined subsequently by Betsi's brother, Johnny, to make it a continuing family affair. In the course of time, Betsi Edge became Mrs. Betsi Ella, but she still does all of the cooking at the inn.

Guest-friends have been returning to this farm-inn for the tenth, fifteenth, twentieth, and even thirty-second season. "It's a continuous stream all summer," said Johnny, when I joined him down at the barn where he was taking care of the stock. "Life is a continual round of arrivals and departures. As you know, when guests leave, we all gather around the front door and ring bells." I was reminded of a similar ceremony at the Milford House in Nova Scotia.

It was a beautiful August morning, and Johnny put out the feed for the horses which were down across the road in the meadow. He whistled sharply and soon they all came galloping up and through the

gate and began to enjoy their morning repast. Three German shepherd dogs added to the excitement by barking and chasing each other. What a wonderful experience to be so close to farm animals!

The horses are just a part of the completely self-contained farm environment. They're used for trail rides which are conducted by Johnny. There are also cows, ducks, geese, chickens, pigs, piglets, ponies, and guinea hens. Believe it or not, they all have their own names. The great barn is filled with hay in which the younger guests burrow tunnels and play circus on rainy days.

Besides the fun of being on a farm where guests can milk the cows, feed the calf, help with the haying, hike up to the Indian cave, go on cook-outs, and use the canoes and sailboats at Crystal Lake, there is tennis, golf, soaring, bicycling, hiking, fishing, summer theater, antiquing—lots of things for guests of all ages to enjoy.

Suddenly, I was startled by a caterwauling immediately behind me. When I jumped, Johnny put his hand on my shoulder and said, "Oh, don't worry. That's just our Bourbon Red turkey gobbler from Michigan. He scares everybody."

Since Rockhouse Mountain Farm is open from June 15 through October, I remarked to Johnny that he probably had plenty of chances to take it easy during the wintertime when Betsi returns to being a full-time housewife and his mother and father, John and Libby, go to Florida.

"People are always asking me that," he said, with a twinkle in his eye. "Running a farm as well as an inn puts a double load on the work. Fences have to be taken down, wood has to be cut and split, water has to be drained, and generally speaking, the establishment has to be put to bed for the winter. The stock still has to be taken care of and there seems to be as much to do in the winter as there is in the summer when we have all the guests here."

RMF is informal, rustic, and gregarious. The happiest guests are those willing to lend a hand with the chores, "do" the dozens of White Mountain things together, and sit talking around the table long after the remains of one of Betsi's wonderful dinners—lobsters or roasts and pies—have been cleared away.

ROCKHOUSE MOUNTAIN FARM INN, Eaton Center, N.H. 03832; 603-447-2880. A complete resort in the foothills of the White Mountains, (6 mi. south of Conway), combining a modern 18-room country inn with life on a 350-acre farm. Some rooms with private bath. Mod. American plan. Open from June 15th through October. Own saddle horses, milk cows, and other farm animals; haying, hiking, shuffleboard; private beach on Crystal Lake with swimming, rowboats, sailboats, and canoes—canoe trips planned; stream and lake fishing; tennis and golf nearby. No credit cards. The Edge Family, Innkeepers.

Directions: From I-93, take Exit 23 to Rte. 104 to Meredith. Take Rte. 25 to Rte. 16, and proceed north to Conway. Follow Rte. 153, 6 mi. south from Conway to Eaton Center.

SPALDING INN CLUB
Whitefield, New Hampshire

The Spalding Inn Club is an excellent example of the entertainment and hospitality that can be provided for a family with many different preferences. For example, on the inn grounds there are four clay tennis courts, a swimming pool, a nine-hole par-three golf course, two championship lawn bowling greens, and shuffleboard. Five full-size golf courses are fifteen minutes away, and there is plenty of trout fishing, boating, canoeing, and many enticing back roads for motoring. The Appalachian Trail system for mountain climbing is a short walk from the inn.

I personally prefer to have a balance of vigorous outdoor activity plus some quiet times, so I was pleased to find the extensive library, a card room, and a fine collection of jigsaw puzzles. I also enjoyed quiet walks in the nearby woods among the beautiful maple, birch, and oak trees native to northern New Hampshire. There are over four hundred acres of lawns, gardens, and orchards. Ted explained somewhat ruefully that it takes a staff of nine gardeners to keep everything up to snuff!

I like good food, so I was in seventh heaven with a menu reflecting both the mountains of New Hampshire and the seacoast of Maine which is just a few hours away. Delicious clam chowder, oyster stew, lobster bisque, cod fish drops, broiled scrod, and poached salmon are some of the seafood offerings. Pork chops, roast

stuffed duckling, roast tenderloin, sweetbreads, Indian pudding, and hot mince pie are a few of their other specialties. They do their own baking, make their own soups and sauces, and even raise some of their own fruits and vegetables.

This lovely old place is a second and third generation destination resort with an air of quiet dignity. You wouldn't think of going in to dinner without a jacket or tie, and during my trips there I saw some extremely attractive dinner and sports outfits on the guests. Elegant touches include finger bowls and turn-down service.

There are real country inn touches everywhere. The broad porch is ideal for rocking, and the main room has a big fireplace with a low ceiling and lots of books and magazines, a jar of sour balls, apples in baskets, and a barometer to tell you tomorrow's weather.

The inn also maintains completely furnished and equipped cottages. They are available for rental periods of three days or longer from December to April. This makes winter activities, including downhill and excellent cross-country skiing as well as snowmobiling and snowshoeing, available during the beautiful New Hampshire winter.

SPALDING INN CLUB, Mountain View Road, Whitefield, N.H. 03598; 603-837-2572. A 70-room resort-inn in the center of New Hampshire's White Mountains. American plan only from late May to mid-October when breakfast, lunch, and dinner are served daily to travelers. Housekeeping cottages only from mid-December to April. Heated pool, tennis courts, 9-hole par-3 golf course, 18-hole putting green, two championship lawn bowling greens, and shuffleboard on grounds. Also guest privileges at 5 nearby golf clubs. Trout fishing, boating, summer theater, and backroading nearby. Ted and Topsy Spalding, Innkeepers.

Directions: From New York take Merritt Pkwy. to I-91; I-91 to Wells River, Vt. Woodsville, N.H. exit; then Rte. 302 to Littleton, then Rte. 116 thru Whitefield to Mtn. View Rd. intersection—3 miles north of village. From Boston take I-93 north thru Franconia Notch to Littleton exit; then Rte. 116 thru Whitefield to Mtn. View Rd. intersection—3 miles north of village. From Montreal take Auto Route 10 to Magog; then Auto Route 55 and I-91 to St. Johnsbury, Vt.; then Rte. 18 to Littleton, N.H. and Rte. 116 as above. The inn is situated 1 mi. west on Mountain View Rd.

STAFFORD'S IN THE FIELD
Chocorua, New Hampshire

I'd like to share a letter that was written about a visit to Stafford's in the Field. "I have just returned from the most fantastic experience at Stafford's in the Field, Chocorua, New Hampshire. It was almost unbelievable to me that in today's commercial world, it can still be possible to find a haven so well-run by such a beautiful family.

"From the moment we left the highway and saw Stafford's, I knew this vacation would be something special. Fred and Ramona Stafford are incredible when it comes to hospitality. And, as you stated in your book, Ramona is a superb gourmet cook. Our stay brought back memories of visiting my grandparents long ago in their big-old country home on the farm. This inn is an experience that I will long remember and I will make every effort to go back as soon as possible."

That letter was written in 1972, the first year I included

Stafford's Inn in *CIBR*. Since that time, many things have been happening at this inn which have made it an even more enjoyable experience.

The summer of 1980 will see the new tennis court put to good use.

Ramona's gourmet meals continue to surprise and delight all the guests. The lamb curry, served with her own combination of condiments, and the spare ribs cooked with maple syrup, are two of my favorites. Others are chicken breasts in a marinated sauce, and fish crepês served with a spinach soufflé.

In recent years, Fred and Ramona's daughter Momo has become, under her mother's instruction, an excellent cook who particularly excels in desserts. I can remember on one visit she had just finished a Black Forest cake, and we each ate a piece while sitting in the kitchen.

All three young Staffords, Momo, and her two brothers Hans and Fritz, have beautiful voices. They've appeared many times in local shows and operettas and they've also made yearly appearances at the inn's big barn, which has offered Gilbert and Sullivan during the past few summers. The barn is the scene for square dances and other summer entertainment.

Accommodations in the main house are comfortable rooms that have been furnished with country antique furniture. Hans and Fritz did a handsome stenciling job in one of the bedrooms, and Ramona tells me that they are planning to do even more rooms. Other accommodations are in cottages.

As the letter mentioned, Fred and the guests sit together evenings, and I think this is when the dinner party atmosphere is particulary enjoyable for everyone. Many guests enjoy a stroll through the open fields before dinner, walking down the shady paths in the woods surrounding the inn. Winter transforms these paths into ski trails and guests often spend the whole day out on skis with a picnic lunch that is prepared for them by Ramona.

In March, it's maple syrup time, and anyone who wants to help, can. I think it adds to the flavor of the blueberry waffles if one has had a first-hand knowledge of the source of the syrup!

STAFFORD'S IN THE FIELD, Chocorua, N.H. 03817; 603-323-7766. An 8-room resort-inn with 5 cottages, 17 mi. south of North Conway. Modified American plan at inn omits lunch. European plan in cottages. Some rooms in inn with shared baths. Meals served to guests only. Closed Apr. and May, Nov. and Dec. No pets. Bicycles, square dancing, tennis, and xc skiing on the grounds. Golf, swimming, hiking, riding, tennis, and fishing nearby. The Stafford Family, Innkeepers.

Directions: Follow N.H. Rte. 16 north to Chocorua Village, then turn left onto Rte. 113 and travel 1 mi. west to inn. Or, from Rte. 93 take Exit 23 and travel east on Rtes. 104 and 25 to Rte. 16. Proceed north on Rte. 16 to Chocorua Village, turn left onto Rte. 113 and travel 1 mi. west to inn.

WOODBOUND INN
Jaffrey, New Hampshire

"In the summertime we have a very full program of activities for our guests." Jed Brummer and I were having dinner on Saturday night at the Woodbound Inn. Earlier, Jed had introduced the staff members including the cook and the hostess, to the assembled guests, and everyone was made very welcome and all the activities for the coming week were carefully explained.

"During July and August, our minimum length of stay is one week, which starts on Saturday and ends the following Saturday. There is a constant program going on every day, including something for both adults and children. For example, on Monday we have craft courses in basket-weaving, candlemaking, and jewelry-making, and in the evening, a gentleman from the area comes in and runs a card party. There are games for children at night, as well. Tuesday is beach-luncheon day. In the evening, there is outside entertainment, either a magician or a puppet show.

"On Wednesday, we always have a golf tournament, and a cookout and a softball game at night.

"Thursday, we continue the crafts during the day, and square dancing at night. On Friday, we have a farewell party and give commemorative plates to guests who have been returning to Woodbound each year for either 20, 25, 30, or 35 years. We've had young people who came here before they were one year old, and now are bringing *their* children to Woodbound."

We talked about the children's program, and Jed explained that their program actually goes on all day long, with time out for lunch in the summertime. There is an early supper for small children, and after-supper activities for the younger set, so the parents can be free to socialize.

He handed me a very attractive basket. "These baskets are made in West Rindge and decorated by a local artist. We fill them up with picnic lunches which our guests can take to their cottages or to the beach or hiking or even backroading. They are much enjoyed.

"In the winter we find the cross-country touring is very popular, especially since we have 27 miles of trails. We also have special rates which are attractive to families during the winter, and the program includes sleigh rides, cookouts during the day, and square dancing and other such entertainment in the evening."

The Woodbound is a genial, family-resort inn. Ed and Peg Brummer started it all; their son, Jed, continued, along with his wife, Mary Ellen; and there is a third generation of Brummers doing the inn chores as well. For guests who like outdoor activities, it is a delight. The lake, the sailboat, canoes, and swimming are just a step away. The inn has its own golf course and tennis courts. Shuffleboard, hiking, and walking in the deep woods are other activities.

"Let's take a stroll over here where dad has been working on a display of historical sites. We have some foundations of old farmhouses, schoolhouses, and extinct mines. He's having a great time and I'm sure our guests will find it very interesting."

WOODBOUND INN and COTTAGES, Jaffrey, N.H. 03452; 603-532-8341. A 40-room resort-inn on Lake Contoocook, 2 mi. in the woods from West Rindge or Jaffrey. Within walking distance of Cathedral of the Pines. Both American and Mod. American plan available. Overnight European plan available in May, June, and late fall. Special rates for retirees in June and fall. Breakfast, lunch, and dinner served daily. Open from May 26 to 30; June 9 to Oct. 10; Dec 26 to March 12, with some closed periods. Par 3 golf course, swimming beach, sailing, water skiing, tennis, hiking, children's programs, ski area, touring trails, tobogganing, and skating on grounds. Ed and Peggy Brummer, Jed and Mary Ellen Brummer, Innkeepers.

Directions: From Boston, follow Rte. 2, then Rte. 119 to Rindge where there are directional signs to inn. From New York, follow I-91 to Bernardston, Mass. Proceed on Rte. 10 to Winchester, then Rte. 119 to Rindge and watch for signs to inn.

Vermont

BARROWS HOUSE ·
Dorset, Vermont

Let me share with you a letter I received recently from Charlie and Marilyn Schubert at the Barrows House: "We have recently discovered another way to add warmth and originality to our guest rooms. A young woman named Joan Stuart Agard provides us with a quantity of her calico appliqué pictures. They are designed and created in her Patchcroft Studio in Dorset, and consist of colorful country scenes meticulously stitched together from tiny pieces of carefully selected old-fashioned calico prints. Each picture is framed with contrasting fabric, and is hung like a painting."

It is difficult for me to realize that the Schuberts have been at the Barrows House for eight years. It's been ten years since I first met Charlie and his father when they stopped and paid me a short visit in Stockbridge while on their way to Vermont to look at country inn property. The Barrows House was for sale at that time and the Schuberts, including their son Carlie (who has just completed the seventh grade at Pine Cobble School in Williamstown), have been hard at work ever since.

In the intervening years, Charlie and Marilyn who, by the way, is a former airline stewardess, have added considerably to the on-the-ground facilities, including a swimming pool and tennis courts. They also have a very vigorous cross-country ski program with a well-stocked shop, just a few paces to the rear of the inn.

"I think we've become a sort of mini-resort-inn," said Charlie.

"Many of our guests spend a great deal of time right here, but when the spirit moves them, they can go antiquing in the little villages like Pawlet and Wells up and down the Mettowe River, or they can drive into the mountains to Weston and perhaps have lunch at the Chester Inn. Sissy can pack a lunch if they like. In the winter, it's just a short drive to Bromley or Stratton Mountain for downhill skiing."

The Barrows House is a traditional New England white clapboard building with black shutters, set considerably back from the main road of the village. It has a rather large English garden on the east side with many varieties of annuals including phlox, lilies, iris, tulips, and peonies. The entire setting is like a small park with elm trees, sugar maples, birches, locusts, and various evergreens.

One of the two front parlors has a welcome fireplace and a whole wall of books. There are several different couches and comfortable chairs. Even in February, the Christmas plants were still in bloom. I found myself a nice Boston rocker and toasted my toes.

In the other parlor which also serves as the reception area, there were some American primitive-style paintings of both the village of Dorset and the inn. Two young boys were seated on the floor playing with Lincoln logs, and there were all kinds of games on the shelves lining the room.

Upstairs, there are a group of old-fashioned bedrooms with flowered wallpapers, early-attic country furniture, and lots of books and magazines.

Barrows House has been included in *CIBR* since 1974.

BARROWS HOUSE, Dorset, Vt. 05251; 802-867-4455. A 26-room village inn on Rte. 30, 6 mi. from Manchester, Vt. Modified American plan omits lunch. Breakfast and dinner served daily to travelers. Swimming pool, sauna, tennis courts, paddle tennis, bicycles, skiing facilities, including rental equipment and instruction on grounds. Golf, tennis, trout fishing, and Alpine skiing nearby. No credit cards. Charles and Marilyn Schubert, Innkeepers.

Directions: From Rte. 7 in Manchester, proceed 6 miles north on Rte. 30 to Dorset.

BLUEBERRY HILL
Goshen, Vermont

I first visited Tony and Martha Clark at Blueberry Hill in midsummer of 1972, when the idea of opening up an inn exclusively for cross-country skiers was just taking shape in their minds. I followed up with a mid-December trip that same year, and already there was a great deal of progress.

In the 1973 edition, I wrote of that visit: "Here in the beautiful Green Mountains of Vermont, cross-country skiing is just about everything. On the day of my visit, it was cold; I mean *really* cold. Nevertheless, the inn guests were out on the trails in full force, and every once in a while, a little group of them would ski to the rustic lodge where Martha keeps two tremendous kettles of soup on the potbellied stove for anyone who needs to be warm. Most everyone did.

"The inn is very definitely family-style. Everyone sits around the big dining room table and there is one main dish for each meal, which Martha cooks in the farmhouse kitchen. This main dish is likely to be something quite unusual, as she is sort of a country cook with gourmet tendencies.

"The bedrooms are plain and simple with hot water bottles on the back of the door and handsome patchwork quilts on the beds. It truly is visiting a Vermont farm in the Vermont mountains."

Well, things have really happened since 1972, and Blueberry Hill inn has become nationally famous. Tony is a recognized authority on cross-country skiing, and most avid on the subject of safety. The reservation book for winter opens on September first, and it's only fair to say that all the weekends are fully booked almost immediately. The rustic warm-up lodge has been replaced by a large ski-touring center.

I'd like to share with you a letter from Martha, telling about *summer* at Blueberry Hill: "We're now open from June through October as well as from December through March for skiing. Summertime here in the Green Mountains is just fabulous. My vegetable and flower gardens are the best they've ever been. Guests gave a hand to Tony while he took down two nearby barns. Our little restaurant went off very well, with Elsie doing a super job with busy crowds on Saturday nights. Tony, by the way, does the omelets on Sunday nights.

"There's great fishing in our streams, hiking, and biking, and nearby tennis, and always a refreshing dip in the pond (I'll bet you didn't even know we had one!). Many guests who don't have their own gardens enjoy helping us pick the vegetables from ours. They can even help clear trails."

Besides being one of the oldest and best-known ski touring centers in Vermont, Blueberry Hill is now very popular with summer and fall back-packers and hikers. Having done a little of that in Vermont a few years ago, I know it's a great deal of fun. There are many, many trails, most of which are used for cross-country skiing in the wintertime. It's possible to use the inn as a central point for such activities or to include it on an itinerary. It's always important to phone ahead for reservations and information.

By the way, on this subject, especially since hiking is getting to be an increasingly popular pastime: whether it be Vermont or any other place, do not go into the woods without careful planning and all of the information available.

A few important observations about Blueberry Hill: there are no babysitting facilities for young children. Reservations for winter accommodations should be made as early as possible, as the inn is often booked solid for weeks at a time for winter.

BLUEBERRY HILL, Goshen, Vt. 05733; 802-247-6735. A mountain inn passionately devoted to cross-country skiing, 8 mi. from Brandon. Modified American plan omits lunch. All rooms with private baths. Meals not served to travelers. Open from June to November; December to April. Closed Christmas. Swimming, fishing, and xc skiing on the grounds. Tony and Martha Clark, Innkeepers.

Directions: At Brandon, travel east on Rte. 73 through Forest Dale. Then follow signs to Blueberry Hill.

CHESTER INN
Chester, Vermont

"What in the world is that?" I asked Betsy Guido, with whom I was sitting by the pool at the Chester Inn on a very warm July day. There were several other inn guests enjoying the warm weather, reading, chatting, or simply basking in the sun.

"That is a genuine Nubian goat," she responded. "We have added them to our menagerie. They are friendly and doglike, craving human attention to the point of walking right out through the electric fence to greet our guests. We also have a kid-proof pony who pulls our sulky. I love to take our young guests in it on rides through the village.

43

"There are many more young people traveling today, and they are bringing their children. Tom and I adapted some of the rooms to meet these families' needs, and we now have two 'bunk' rooms, and we supply baby sitters when requested." She laughed and continued, "There are certainly enough diversions here to make us a point of destination rather than an overnight stop: the pool, tennis courts, the children's outdoor play area, the log cabin tree-house —reachable only by a rope ladder and with a sign that says 'no grown-ups.' We also have bicycles and cross-country ski rentals."

The Chester Inn is located in an old central Vermont village with many nineteenth-century homes and buildings, including a striking group of stone houses at the eastern end of the town. It has one of the longest main streets of any village I've ever visited.

Dominating the center of Chester is a Victorian building that reflects many architectural influences. The porch runs across the entire first floor and there is a second balcony over the center section. This is the Chester Inn.

The innkeeper-owners for the last four years have been Tom and Betsy Guido who moved to Vermont from Cleveland, Ohio. They hosted a meeting of other *CIBR* innkeepers from northern New England in March, 1980.

Meanwhile, back at the pool, Betsy talked enthusiastically about Tom's culinary skills. "He's really the head chef," she said, "and I'm very proud of his expertise and accomplishments. Oh, there he is now." She waved to a handsome man with a black beard who was picking his way towards us through the sunbathers.

"I was just telling Norman how well you were doing, but maybe you could tell him about some of your specialties."

Tom and I shook hands warmly and he launched right into the subject. "The menu is largely French, although we have many other things as well. We've always been well-known for our veal dishes, and for entrées such as roast duck with peaches, French lemon sole and beef Bourguignonne. On sufficient notice, we can do 'grande cuisine' too." He laughed and reached over to pat his young son Zachary, who was just learning how to swim.

"The soups and French bread are made fresh every day. We also make our own desserts, and the one I just finished is a chocolate log—that's a chocolate roll filled with mocha cream, iced in a deep rich chocolate, and covered with fresh whipped cream. You'd better have some tonight."

"Innkeeping, contrary to appearances, is not all work," said Betsy. "Perhaps the most rewarding aspect is talking with and getting to know our guests. Many of these lovely people have become very dear friends who have even brought presents to our children during the holidays."

The Chester Inn has been in *CIBR* since 1970.

CHESTER INN, Chester, Vt. 05143; 802-875-2444. A 30-room village inn on Rte. 11, 8 mi. from Springfield, Vt. Convenient to several Vt. ski areas. Lodgings include breakfast. Lunch and dinner served to travelers daily except Mondays. Closed from late October to mid-November and April to mid-May. No children under 4 in dining room. No pets. Pool, tennis, and bicycles on grounds. Golf, riding, Alpine and xc skiing nearby. Tom and Betsy Guido, Innkeepers.

Directions: From I-91 take Exit 6. Travel west on Rte. 103 to Rte. 11.

EDSON HILL MANOR
Stowe, Vermont

There were five of us. Four ladies from Quebec and me. Joyce, Betty, Gisele, and Lisette—two English and two French—enjoying the midday sunshine on the terrace at Edson Hill Manor. It was late March and the snow was still very deep on the slopes of Mount Mansfield. The inn looked very story-bookish with snow piled very high on the roof. There were some early-returning birds who didn't know that Vermont has a very late winter. The cross-country ski trails were the same bridle trails that I had taken on horseback during the previous autumn. The Edson Hill touring center was very busy that morning renting skis, applying wax, and giving advice.

On my last visit, Liz Turner had invited me to "meet the horses" and we had walked down the mountain from the main house past the

sunlit terrace, flagstone swimming pool, the putting green, and the trout pond with the rowboat. The air at fifteen hundred feet was clear and sharp. The same robins and chickadees chattered noisily among the many varieties of trees to be found in the high Vermont forest — most of which already had some brilliant autumn shades.

Innkeeper Liz Turner remarked that she was glad I was there. "The fall colors are almost at their height; it's one of the very best times of year."

The barn was busy with horses stamping and snorting and guests getting ready for a morning ride. "We try to fit our riding program to the horsemanship of our guests," she said. "We can accommodate first-time riders or people who really want to improve their riding technique. I've been teaching advanced riding for quite a few years. During the winter our entire stable is turned into a cross country ski shop where our guests can rent all the equipment they need. We have miles and miles of trails on our own property and good instructors."

Horseback riding and cross-country skiing are just two of the outdoor activities available at Edson Hill. There is golfing, fishing, tennis, and hiking nearby. For the guests who might be in a more contemplative mood, there's a beautiful view of the valley and mountains beyond, dozens of places to curl up quietly with a book, and it takes just about thirty seconds to be on one of the walking trails into the woods.

Vermont backroading in the area is some of the best. The inn has a road and tour map for all of them. In the summertime, almost everybody rides up to the top of Mount Mansfield on the gondola.

As might be expected, the view is just tremendous.

Edson Hill Manor is a gracious and luxurious home. The atmosphere is low-key, informal, and simple. In the living room is a beautiful oriental rug, a spacious fireplace flanked by comfortable divans, and pine-paneled walls hung with paintings—some by owner Larry Heath's mother. There are floor-to-ceiling windows with elegant draperies. Bookshelves full of books are everywhere. The same sense of casual luxury extends to the bedrooms, many of which have fireplaces, private baths, and spacious closets.

It was in the 1978 edition that I shared my first adventures at Edson Hill Manor, and I received several letters from readers who expressed gratitude for the information that there were horses available in the summertime.

Now, Gisele, who had such pretty blue eyes, turned from her conversation with the other girls, and said, "We have a wonderful idea. We've done enough skiing for today and we must return to Montreal late this afternoon. Why don't we all go up to the top of Mount Mansfield in the gondola and look at the view."

I'll never get a better offer.

EDSON HILL MANOR, Edson Hill Rd., Stowe, Vt. 05672; 802-253-7371. A 16-room resort-inn about 6 mi. from the center of Stowe, high in the Mt. Mansfield area. Mod. Amer. plan, winter; European plan, summer. Breakfast, lunch, and dinner served to travelers, winter only. Open mid-December to mid-April; mid-June to end of October. Closed Memorial Day. No pets. Children welcome. Horseback riding, swimming, practice golf, xc skiing, fishing on grounds. Mountain climbing, downhill skiing, back roading nearby. No credit cards. Laurence P. and Dorothy Heath, Owners. Elizabeth Turner, Innkeeper.

Directions: Exit I-89 at Waterbury/Stowe. Follow Rte. 100 north to Stowe village; turn left on Rte. 108 north, turn right on Edson Hill Rd. immediately past Buccaneer Motel.

INN AT SAWMILL FARM
West Dover, Vermont

It was three o'clock on a bright winter's afternoon when I drove from Wilmington, Vermont, to West Dover on the twisting, winding road that ascends into the mountains alongside the creek which now was frozen over with ice formations that created weird and wonderful ice-sculptures. Although there had been lots of snow, the efficient state road crews had cleared the way, and other cars with racks of cross-country and alpine skis were proceeding on their

expectant ways. Passing through West Dover, the Congregational Church was on the right, and I could see the snow-covered tennis courts and buildings of the Inn at Sawmill Farm. I drove over the bridge into the parking lot and once again was ready for a pleasant visit at this very popular Vermont country inn.

This time I noticed that the old barn which had stood across from the front door of the inn since long before my first visit had been moved down to the edge of the trout farm. It is now known as the "Blacksmith Shop," and has a large living room/bedroom with a high studio ceiling, a fireplace, and a large window over a private terrace overlooking the pond. It has the customary tasteful furnishings that mark the other Sawmill Farm lodgings, plus the addition of a large dressing room and bath. The private terrace has a new three-tier flower garden.

The Resident's Lounge (usually found in British country house hotels) has a handsome view of Vermont hills and Mount Snow to the north. There are many books and magazines, copies of *Antiques Magazine, Architectural Digest, History of Art,* and *Architectural Record.* In one corner are some beautiful duck decoys and on the walls are traditional and contemporary watercolors and oils of outdoor scenes. All of these reflect the Williams family's continuing interest in the beautiful things of the world. A checkerboard beckons from one corner; in another is a table for bridge, and there are other games in profusion.

Lodging rooms have been both added and redecorated, and again I was smitten with the beautiful quilted bedspreads, the bright wallpaper and white ceilings, the profusion of plants in the rooms, and all of the many books and magazines which add to the guests' enjoyment. There were several new suites. One had an extremely attractive summery wallpaper with a matching quilt, and overlooked the swimming pool. I took a walk outside, before the December sun set completely. The swimming pool was now dormant, but in a few months it would be the scene for more good times. I walked to the brow of the little hill overlooking the pond. The view of the village, usually obscured by the apple orchard, was clear and idyllic. I could see some cross-country ski trails stretching out beside the banks above the Sawmill River.

Some of the guests, having finished skiing at Mount Snow, were now gathering in the big living room, eagerly awaiting dinner. I looked at the evening menu and noted that among other things there were dried, cured, Irish smoked salmon, escargots, backfin crab-meat, and clams casino. Some of the entrées were veal and peppers, braised duck, roast duck, frogs' legs Provencal, fresh oysters, Icelandic lobster tails, rack of lamb for two, steak au Poivre flambe, and sweetbreads.

Warming myself in front of the fire, I had a conversation with another guest who had visited many other inns. "Of course they're all different," he said, "and I enjoyed them all very much. But, for me, this is a very special place. In fact, I think it's a model for all country inns."

INN AT SAWMILL FARM, Box 8, West Dover, Vt. 05356; 802-464-8131. A 19-room country resort-inn on Rte. 100, 22 mi. from Bennington and Brattleboro. Within sight of Mt. Snow ski area. Modified American plan omits lunch. Breakfast and dinner served to travelers daily. Closed Nov. 7 through Dec. 7. No children under 8. No pets. Swimming, tennis, and trout fishing on grounds. Golf, bicycles, riding, snowshoeing, Alpine and xc skiing nearby. No credit cards. Rodney, Brill and Ione Williams, Innkeepers.

Directions: From I-91, take Brattleboro Exit 2 and travel on Vt. Rte. 9 west to Vt. Rte. 100. Proceed north 5 mi. to inn. Or, take U.S. 7 north to Bennington, then Rte. 9 east to Vt. Rte. 100 and proceed north 5 mi. to inn.

THE INN ON THE COMMON
Craftsbury, Vermont

The village of Craftsbury Common, Vermont, was founded in 1789 by Ebeneezer Crafts. For a long time, it was the northernmost part of New England occupied by settlers. "Ebeneezer himself," said Penny Schmidt, "has a most remarkable history. He owned the

Publick House in Sturbridge, Massachusetts, and at the outbreak of
the Revolutionary War joined Washington's army, and afterwards
was involved in Shay's Rebellion. After being bankrupted by taxes
and debts, he decided to bring a number of his fellow townsmen
from Massachusetts up here to the northern kingdom of Vermont on
land which he had purchased earlier."

Aside from Colonel Crafts' bankruptcy, I found an interesting
parallel between this vigorous man and Penny and Michael Schmidt,
who left New York city early in the 1970s and decided to start an
entirely new way of life by opening an inn in this beautiful Vermont
hilltown.

They had been summering in this section of Vermont for many
years so the area was most familiar. The house dates from about
1805 and was built by Samuel French, one of the original incorp-
orators of Craftsbury. It is a graceful example of Federalist
architecture and, in a community where everyone is particularly
proud of gardens, the Schmidts have carefully maintained one of the
most impressive formal gardens that I have seen in North America.

Penny and Michael, who are extremely well-informed on the
subject of antiques have furnished the inn with love and care. Each
guest room has its own individual personality and is enhanced with
fresh flowers or plants. Guests in rooms that use the bath "down the
hall" are supplied with terry cloth bathrobes.

Recognizing that more and more guests are enjoying longer
stays, Michael and Penny have in recent years provided an expanding
program of outdoor recreation which includes a swimming pool,
tennis courts, and English croquet in summer; and cross-country
skiing and snowshoeing in winter.

At dinner, guests sit at two oval tables, one hosted by Michael and the other by Penny. The menu includes such delicious offerings as lamb in sorrel sauce; veal sliced very thin in a sauce made from creamed wine, ham, and anchovies; carrots sautéed until just done and then served with butter and capers; and ratatouille, an eggplant dish from southern France which can be served hot or cold. Breakfasts are quite elaborate and feature many different types of omelets.

The most exciting news for 1980 is the development of the Craftsbury Sports Center, which during the winter is the Nordic ski facility and was used as the training site for the U.S. ski team and Dartmouth and Middlebury colleges.

"Summer at the center has taken on great new dimensions," said Penny. "The first event is a sculling camp for adults. Lake Hosmer is particularly well-suited to this as it is long, deep, narrow, and shielded from the wind. There will also be a running camp for adults, a soccer camp for teens, and kyaking and canoeing, as well. Our guests are invited to be spectators at various events during the summer, if not actually participating, and they have access to a superb lake, excellent dock facilities, and a sports-minded staff. They may even get involved in some excellent sports that may be new to them."

May I add that if all of this sounds a bit too vigorous for some of our readers, there is ample opportunity for sitting in the inn garden, watching sunsets, walking on country roads, reading books, and enjoying the peace and quiet of the countryside.

I'm sure that the innkeeper in Ebeneezer Crafts would be mightily pleased with both the atmosphere and the hospitality now offered at the Inn on the Common, which has been in *CIBR* since 1976.

THE INN ON THE COMMON, Craftsbury Common, Vt. 05827; 802-586-9619. An 11-room inn in a remote Vermont town 35 mi. from Montpelier. Shared baths. Modified American plan omits lunch. Breakfast and dinner served to houseguests only. Open from May 15 to Oct. 20 and Dec. 20 to Mar. 31. Attended pets allowed. Swimming, tennis, croquet, lawn bowling, xc skiing, snowshoeing, on grounds. Golf, tennis, swimming, sailing, horseback riding, canoeing, fishing, xc and downhill skiing, skating, hiking, and nature walks nearby. Michael and Penny Schmidt, Innkeepers.

Directions: From Exit 7, I-89N, take Rte. 2 east to Rte. 14 north until 8 mi. north of Hardwick. Watch for marked right hand turn, go 2 mi. to inn. From Canada and points north, use Exit 26 on I-91 and follow Rte. 58W to Irasburg. Then Rte. 14 southbound 12 mi. to marked left turn, 3 mi. to inn.

KEDRON VALLEY INN
South Woodstock, Vermont

I'd like to share with you some of the history and heritage of the Kedron Valley Inn, which is recounted on the back of the menu. The valley is named after the brook which flows right through the community. Actually, very little has changed in South Woodstock since its original settlement. According to this account, "The beautiful meadows, pasture, uplands, and timbered hills are natural and unspoiled by most civilized 'improvements'. The fields and forests are rich in many varieties of flora and fauna. Should any early pioneer of Kedron Valley rise from his resting place to have a look around, it is doubtful that he would find very much different than when he was alive and well. The citizens of South Woodstock are still country people at heart. We still look up when a plane flies over. And we don't have to look both ways before crossing the road, except during the tourist season. And we, the Kendall family, owners and proprietors of the Kendron Valley Inn, are very proud of the fact that the Kendalls were here from the beginning. Running in a single blood stream, our children are the seventh generation to live in the Kedron Valley."

The present Kendall family is composed of Paul and Barbara and their two sons, Dane, 21, and Chip, 22. In addition, Paul's mother is still very active in the inn, and I've written several times about her wonderful pies.

The inn, as well as its annex, is built of beautiful dark red brick with very white mortar and has been in continuous operation since 1822. The annex was for many years the store and post office of South Woodstock. The old safe is still built into the wall.

Many of the rooms are in the main house, and are in the traditional country inn, early-attic style. Some motel-type lodgings in a Vermont log house are a few steps away.

During the winter, there is excellent cross-country and downhill skiing, and lots of horse-drawn sleigh rides. The cross-country ski activities are aided by a complete ski shop with rentals and supplies, and several miles of well-marked and maintained trails. Instruction is also available. Other outdoor winter activities include paddle tennis and ice skating on the pond.

In the spring, everyone at the inn becomes involved with maple sugaring. Much of this is done in the old-fashioned way, using a team of horses and a sled for gathering the sap. Then it's taken to the "sugar house" for boiling down to syrup for canning and shipping. It's wonderful to visit there in the late winter and see how it's done, from tapping the trees, to gathering, boiling, and best of all, tasting.

In the summertime, it's a very active place for people who enjoy horses. There are trail rides and surrey rides. Many guests have received their first riding instruction at KVI. The pond and sandy beach provide a respite for warm summer days.

The Kedron Valley Inn is a traditional Vermont inn that reflects the changing vacation interests and enthusiasms of America. Many guests who visit and revisit enjoy the quiet atmosphere, beautiful mountain scenery, and an opportunity to sit in the rockers on the front porch and watch an occasional car pass by.

Kedron Valley Inn has been in *CIBR* since 1968.

KEDRON VALLEY INN, Rte. 106, South Woodstock, Vt. 05071; 802-457-1473. A 34-room rustic resort-inn, 5 mi. south of Woodstock. Near Killington, Mt. Ascutney ski areas. European plan and modified American plan offered. Breakfast, lunch, and dinner served daily. Closed Sunday evenings November to May. Closed Christmas Day. Swimming, riding, sleigh rides, carriage rides, paddle tennis, hiking, and xc skiing on the grounds. Tennis, golf, and bicycles nearby. Paul and Barbara Kendall, Innkeepers.

Directions: Take Exit 1 from I-89 and follow Rte. 4 to Woodstock. Proceed south on Rte. 106 for 5 miles. Or, take Exit 8 from I-91 and follow Rte. 131 for 8 mi. Proceed North on Rte. 106 for 12 mi.

NORTH HERO HOUSE
North Hero, Vermont

I opened the envelope postmarked "Flemington, New Jersey" with expectant fingers. In it was a long letter from Caroline Sorg, and an errant piece of paper fluttered to the table. It proved to be a photograph of Tom and Michelle's wedding which took place on the steamship dock in front of the North Hero House on July 21, 1979.

Tom is the maitre d' and Michelle is the assistant manager, and they had met at the inn a few summers ago. Caroline's letter said that the day was magnificent and the wedding, beautiful. "All who were there were deeply impressed (we had two weddings on the dock later on in the summer)."

For twelve weeks of every summer, innkeepers Roger and Caroline Sorg and their children, David and Lynn, open their inn on the island of North Hero in Vermont's Lake Champlain. Roger had spent several summers on the island as a boy, and even in those early days had dreamed of becoming the owner of the North Hero House. For nine months of the year, Roger practices dentistry in Flemington.

On my first visit, in 1972, I realized that the Sorgs were builders and "inn-ovators" (new word!), and every visit since then, I have found something new and exciting, either on the drawing board or in the final phases of completion. For example, in 1979, I enjoyed lunch with the Sorg family in the beautiful new greenhouse-dining room which has been set aside for non-smokers. The glassed-in walls and ceiling bring the entire outdoors inside, and the room is even further beautified by baskets of hanging flowers. The room is air conditioned and cleverly arranged so that there is no direct sunlight on any of the tables.

Caroline's letter mentioned some of the latest specialties on their menu: duckling with plum sauce, stuffed pork chops, seafood Thermador, Weinerschnitzel, and fish Florentine. "Many of our guests are staying for additional nights so we keep the menu as varied as possible.

"The new waterside accommodation, the Cobbler's Room," her letter continued, "was a great success, and the new shuffleboard court at water's edge was in constant use. It has a magnificent view of

Lake Champlain, Mount Mansfield, and the towering Green Mountains to the east."

Vacation activities at or near the inn include boating, water skiing, snorkeling, fishing, tennis, sailing, bicycling, and horseback riding. The inn is also in a great location for backroading, antiquing, and just simply rocking on the porch and looking out over Lake Champlain. Lodgings are in country-innish rooms in the building of the inn, which dates back to the late nineteenth century, and also in a series of waterside cottages which have been attractively modernized by the Sorgs over the years. It has become a wonderful place for families to visit. Many of the same guests have been returning year after year.

So 1980 will bring still another summer season to the North Hero House, and I'm looking forward to wading out into the natural sand-bottom beach where the water is so clear that even when it's up to my shoulders, I can see my toes wiggle. Perhaps Mr. Goodspeed will take me for another spin around the lake on the float boat, and I can fly my kite from the steamship dock, even if I did miss the wedding!

North Hero House has been included in *CIBR* since 1972.

NORTH HERO HOUSE, Champlain Islands, North Hero, Vt. 05474; 802-372-8237. A 22-room New England resort-inn on North Hero Island in Lake Champlain, 35 mi. north of Burlington and 65 mi. south of Montreal. Modified American plan. Breakfast, lunch, and dinner served daily to travelers. Open from late June to Labor Day. No pets. Swimming, fishing, boating, waterskiing, ice house game room, sauna, bicycles, and tennis on grounds. Horseback riding and golf nearby. No credit cards. Roger and Caroline Sorg, Innkeepers.

Directions: Travel north from Burlington on I-89, take Exit 17 (Champlain Islands) and drive north on Island Rte. 2 to North Hero. From N.Y. Thruway (87 north), take Exit 39 at Plattsburg and follow signs "Ferry to Vermont." Upon leaving ferry, turn left to Rte. 2, then left again to North Hero. Inn is 15 min. from ferry dock on Rte. 2.

THE VILLAGE INN
Landgrove, Vermont

"Happiness is children riding our pony cart." Kathy Snyder and I were taking a walk on the Vermont dirt road that runs in front of the Village Inn, when we caught sight of some of the younger inn guests enjoying an outing on the pony cart. "We just love families with

children," she went on, "and I think they like us because we really have a number of activities that children enjoy. There's horseback riding, cross-country skiing, tennis, rides on the Bromley chair lift and the Alpine slide."

I reflected that, in my opinion, one of the reasons the young people like to visit the Village Inn is because of the wonderful Rafter Room. It is a recreation room with a big fireplace, log beams across the low ceiling, and plenty of games like ping-pong, skittles, and bumper pool. "Yes, that's true," she responded. "It's all very well and good to think children are happy during the wintertime on our cross-country ski trails or perhaps downhill skiing, but there comes a time at the end of the day when they all gather back here at the inn. That's why we took particular pains to have an area where they can really have a good time, and we found that with games and other diversions, they could work off what seems to be their unending supply of energy. In winter, we have a couch in front of the fireplace that holds twelve kids."

My most recent visit was at the height of the summer activities and everybody was enjoying the swimming pool. The tennis court sign-up sheet indicated that it was also a very popular activity.

"There are quite a few guests backroading today," Kathy added. "We give them maps and a box lunch, if they wish."

The Snyders have been at the Village Inn for nineteen years. During this time, their two children, Heidi, who is now ten years old and in the fifth grade, and Kimberly, who is twelve and in the seventh grade, have become quite familiar to inn guests. "Heidi likes to ride one of her Shetland ponies over to the inn from where we live nearby," explained Kathy. "She frequently gives the children a ride. Kimberly is a regular innkeeper. She does all kinds of things to help out." To further engender the family feeling, Jay's parents, Don and Else, moved to Vermont in 1977 and are both quite active at the inn.

There's a great deal of emphasis on Vermont-style home-cooking with dishes like roast beef, leg of lamb, baked potatoes, summer salads, strawberry shortcake, apple and blueberry pies, and similar hearty country fare. Fresh vegetables come from the inn garden.

The guest rooms at the Village Inn span a wide variety of tastes. Because the inn is family-oriented, there are several rooms that would be adaptable for whole families, as well as bunk rooms. There are also rooms in a newer section which are furnished in a more contemporary style. Lodgings include a hearty breakfast.

"Before I forget," exclaimed Kathy, "we had a wonderful time at Christmas. Among others, there were two very large families gathered from all over the country. It was delightful, and their stockings covered the fireplace mantel."

This inn high in the Vermont mountains in Landgrove is the place where both adults and children can have a beautiful country inn experience.

THE VILLAGE INN, Landgrove, Vt., 05148; 802-824-6673. A 21-room rustic resort-inn in the mountains of central Vermont, approximately 4½ mi. from Weston and Londonderry. Lodgings include breakfast. Breakfast and dinner served to travelers by reservation during the summer except Wed. dinner. Open from Nov. 23 to April 15; July 1 to Oct. 17. Children most welcome. No pets. Swimming, tennis, volleyball, pitch and putt, xc skiing, fishing on grounds. Downhill skiing, riding, indoor tennis, paddle tennis, antiquing, backroading, Alpine slide, golf, summer theatre nearby. Jay and Kathy Snyder, Innkeepers.

Directions: Coming north on I-91 take Exit 2 at Brattleboro, follow Rte. 30 to Rte. 11 and turn right. Turn left off Rte. 11 at signs for Village Inn. Bear left in village of Peru. Coming north on Rte. 7 turn east at Manchester on Rte. 11 to Peru. Turn left at signs for Village Inn. Bear left in village of Peru.

Maine

BLACK POINT INN
Prouts Neck, Maine

The sun, although still bright in the sky, cast long shadows across the Black Point Inn swimming pool. I stood for a quiet moment at the head of the flagstone terrace and looked out over the waters of the bay. I spotted the bobbing markers for the lobster pots,

and in the distance I could see a sailboat beating around the point. Two or three ocean swimmers had made their last dash into the water and were now toweling off, headed back up the steps toward the inn. The flags at poolside, Canadian and American, were now hanging somewhat listlessly as the late afternoon breeze had not yet freshened. I returned to my room through the new rose garden.

Earlier, the lunch served here at poolside can best be described as "bounteous." There were several different kinds of salads and a special plate of corn beef hash which innkeeper Norm Dugas insisted "was not from the can." A small orchestra played very lightly at one end of the inn terrace. It was like a scene from a Fitzgerald novel.

The Black Point Inn is one of the few remaining American plan hotels that were so numerous on the New England coast sixty and seventy years ago. It has quiet dignity, personal service, and attention to details.

For the active sports-minded, there's just about everything: a good 18-hole golf course, tennis courts, sailing, fishing, swimming, beach walking, and clambering over rocks.

It was in the late sixties that I first visited this inn which, like the Asticou in Northeast Harbor, the Spalding Club Inn in Whitefield, New Hampshire, Hound Ears in Blowing Rock, North Carolina, and the Brazilian Court in Palm Beach, provides some of the last remaining intimate resort experiences.

I noticed that along with the Rolls Royces, Cadillacs, and Lincolns in the parking lot, there was a sprinkling of Porsches, Audis, and VWs. The younger people are also enjoying themselves at the Black Point Inn.

One hundred years ago, a young Winslow Homer, the American painter, found in this section of the rocky Maine coastline the inspiration and atmosphere in which to create some of his greatest works. In fact, he walked these sandy shores and climbed these same rocks.

Prouts Neck became popular as a summer resort at the end of the nineteenth century, and time has brought few changes to this lovely neck of land which stretches out into the Atlantic. The sea, birds, water, sky, and trees, all of which go to make such desirable tranquillity, are still here today.

The Black Point Inn and all of the beautiful summer homes at Prouts Neck are privately owned. The same families have been coming here for generations and the beauty is well protected.

The inn fits perfectly into the ambience of the community. Gentlemen wear coats, and ladies don colorful dresses for dinner. The same small orchestra plays for dancing in the evening. Families with children over the age of twelve find the inn rewarding; however, younger children may be bored, as the inn has no junior hostess or children's activities or facilities.

Black Point Inn has been included in *CIBR* since 1969.

BLACK POINT INN, Prouts Neck, Me. 04070; 207-883-4311. An 80-room luxury resort-inn on Rte. 207, 10 mi. south of Portland. American plan. Breakfast, lunch, and dinner served to travelers. Open early June to mid-Oct. No children under 12 between July 15 and August 15. No pets. Pool, bicycles, sailing, dancing, golf, tennis, and ocean bathing all within a few steps. Normand H. Dugas, Innkeeper.

Directions: From Maine Tpke., take Exit 7. Turn right at sign marked Scarborough and Old Orchard Beach. At second set of lights turn left on Rte. 207. Follow 4.3 miles to Prouts Neck.

MAINE'S OXFORD HILLS

If I were lost before I arrived at this fantastic signpost, I certainly was totally lost now. The post, with dozens of small signs, said: "Norway-14 mi., Paris-15 mi., Denmark-23 mi., Naples-23 mi., Sweden-25 mi., Poland-27 mi., Mexico-37 mi., Peru-46 mi., China-94 mi." It was crazy, but it was wonderful, and it was in the southwest corner of the State of Maine in the Oxford Hills. Someone with a great sense of Maine humor decided to have a lot of fun. (These are all actual towns in Maine.)

Right now, and for an unpredictable length of time, the Oxford Hills are relatively undiscovered. It's one of those, "You can't get there from here" places, which has to be approached from the north near Bethel, or from the south from Conway, New Hampshire, or

Fryeburg, Maine. I was searching for Waterford, where I had good reason to believe a fine country inn was located, and in the process of searching I found some most delightful scenery and panoramic views.

There were heavily forested areas, and open rolling fields with the inevitable stone walls built long ago by the early settlers. One of the great points of scenic interest was Snow's Falls, which may be seen from many different angles as the river winds a dynamic course down a steep, narrow gorge. The Oxford Hills, I subsequently learned, are famous for their rare minerals and unique crystals. Many abandoned mines can be discovered in the woods, and Mount Mica is reputed to have been the largest tourmaline mine in the world.

There are numerous lakes, some with long Indian names. While roaming about the area, I found there were such interesting cultural attractions as the Celebration Mime Theater, located in an old barn on Paris Hill, and an excellent baroque ensemble developed at Hebron Academy. The Deer Trees Performing Arts Festival, located in Harrison, has theater, opera, and concerts ranging from The Fantasticks *to* The Marriage of Figaro.

The little town of Waterford is located in a place where several pastoral roads come together. There are four or five white clapboard New England homes and a post office, as well as the L.R. Rounds General Store. The church, instead of having a conventional steeple, has a round turnip-top dome. The beach and lake are just up the road a piece.

There are also some excellent antique and craft shops, and the Fryeburg Fair has been going for 129 years between October 1st and 8th.

THE WATERFORD INNE
East Waterford, Maine

Yup, there was Springer's General store, and right next to it the sign for the inn pointing up the hill. It was only a short distance on the narrow road, and there was the large yellow house with a second-floor porch and a big red barn.

A big English sheepdog came bounding out, followed by a little poodle, but the resident cat on the porch rail, just opened one eye and went back to sleep. As I pulled into the little parking area, two attractive women left their rockers and came down off the porch: "Hi, I'm Barbara Vanderzanden and this is my mother, Rosalie. Welcome to the Waterford Inne!"

Thus began a pleasant first-of-many visits to this very comfortable and accommodating inn high in the Oxford Hills of western

Maine. There are no end of things to delight the devotee of country inns. The original house had been built in 1825 and had five upstairs bedrooms that stepped out of the nineteenth century. These have been augmented by four additional rooms which had been created in a wing leading out to that tremendous barn which itself has many pleasant surprises. My room in the wing was called the Strawberry Room, and had strawberry wallpaper, strawberries on the quilt, and strawberry-shaped soap!

Barbara and Rosalie were filled with enthusiasm for what is for them a brand-new career. Both had been schoolteachers from Oradell, New Jersey. "Mother is the real creative force in the kitchen," said Barbara, as we all settled down in the main living room with its warm barn boards and views of the hills in two directions. "She has some wonderful recipes and does all the cooking. I do the serving, and the two of us pitch right in and take care of all the other chores in the house.

"We serve a fixed-price dinner every evening for both house-guests and visitors. We do all our own baking, and in season use only fresh vegetables from our own garden. Actually, we are a very comfortable place for children and see a lot of them during the summer and also during the winter holidays. We're planning to have some farm animals including chickens, sheep, and a pig. The farm pond is going to be cleared for boating and swimming on a limited scale. As you'll see when we get to the barn, there's plenty of room for rumpusing around on rainy days. We also have badminton, horse-shoes, and croquet."

"Cross-country skiing is very popular here," said Rosalie. "We have some trails leading from our own property into the woods and beyond. People also bring their own snowshoes."

Rosalie excused herself to run into the kitchen and Barbara went out to greet some new guests, leaving me the opportunity to contemplate the many books and periodicals that were available.

There was a whole shelf filled with parlor games, as well as backgammon, checkers, and chess. A coffee table carved out of natural wood was also a cribbage board, and in one corner an old buggy seat was piled high with magazines.

Rosalie returned, saying, "Oh, it has just been wonderful moving up here, and our neighbors are so very nice. By the way, we're having baked ham with a peach glaze tonight. The dessert is angel cake filled with fresh strawberries and cream. I also make cream cheese pie with a fruit topping, and lots of different types of mousses and homemade cakes."

The new arrivals came clumping into the room filled with great expectations for a good time. This was their third visit and they were already making plans and joking about having the honeymoon room upstairs.

I could see that it was going to be great fun at the Waterford Inne.

THE WATERFORD INNE, Box 49, East Waterford, Maine 04233; 207-583-4037. A 9-room farmhouse-inn in the Oxford Hills section of southwest Maine, 8 mi. from Norway and south of Paris. Open every day in the year. Breakfast and dinner served to travelers by reservation. European plan. Within a short distance of many recreational scenic and cultural attractions in Maine and the White Mountains of New Hampshire. Cross-country skiing and badminton on grounds. Lake swimming, golf, rock hunting, downhill skiing, hiking, canoeing nearby. No credit cards. Alcoholic beverages not served. Well-behaved pets welcome. Rosalie and Barbara Vanderzanden, Innkeepers.

Directions: From Maine Turnpike: use Exit 11, follow Rte. 26 north approximately 28 mi. into Norway, then on Rte. 118 west for 8 mi. to Rte. 37 south (left turn). Go ½ mi., turn right at Springer's General Store, up the hill ½ mi. From Conway, New Hampshire: Rte. 16 to Rte. 302 east to Fryeburg, Me. Take Rte. 5 out of Fryeburg to Rte. 118. After Papoose Pond camping area, watch for right turn onto Rte. 37 south. Go ½ mi. to Springer's General Store. Take immediate right turn, ½ mi. up hill.

ASTICOU INN
Northeast Harbor, Maine

The Asticou is a luxurious summer resort-inn in the now-rare tradition that was popular for so many years in the White Mountains of New Hampshire, the Berkshires, the Maine coast, and certain resort areas in West Virginia, South Carolina, and Palm Beach.

There were the small, extremely well-run resorts where guests would spend a great deal of the summer, reaching them by train and making a trip back to the city at the "end of the season." Now, there are very few of these medium-sized resort-inns that have the many little touches that make them so special, such as beautiful table linen, fresh flowers, and turn-down service. Even today, many guests stay for as long as three or four weeks, but just a few for the entire season. In *Country Inns and Back Roads* I think these beautiful little jewels are typified by the Asticou, the Black Point, the Spalding Inn Club, and the Brazilian Court.

George Stiles, the innkeeper, and I were seated on the outer deck overlooking the harbor with its tremendous sweep and panorama. "We have had the same people coming back here for many years," he said, "and now their children and grandchildren are returning. The Asticou is growing with the times. For example, in former days the guests would go swimming in the cool waters of the harbor, but today's guests enjoy our swimming pool because it's just a few steps away. The tennis courts, which are brand new, are also very popular.

"Today's guests at the Asticou are much more active. We have so many things here on Mount Desert that attract outdoor-minded people who are concerned about ecology and nature. Our guests stay here on the modified American plan which omits lunch and allows everyone to enjoy the one hundred different activities on Mount Desert Island."

Although the Asticou was for many years a "carriage trade" accommodation, there is a most informal feeling here, with the head waiter, the chef, Allen Weigman, and the front desk personnel all very helpful and friendly. I was particularly impressed with Geneva

Wilcox, who seemed to have patient answers to all of the guests' questions.

There are changes at the Asticou, but it is the enduring tradition and the beautiful situation of the inn which make it such a joy. For the most part, because this is an older building, the bedrooms are larger than usual and many of them have a view of the harbor which is one of the most exciting and dramatic in the Bar Harbor area. Most have twin beds as well as double beds.

The furnishings in the dining room and the various sitting rooms are very gay with bright summer colors that offer an immediate holiday atmosphere. The inn is a friendly and relaxing place with backgammon, jigsaw puzzles, many books, and perhaps best of all, the sundeck which offers everyone an opportunity to sit outside and enjoy the panorama of sky, water, and trees.

The Asticou Inn has been included in *CIBR* since 1974.

ASTICOU INN, Northeast Harbor, Me. 04662; 207-276-3344. A 60-room elegant resort-inn on the northern coast of Maine. Near Acadia National Park, Cadillac Mountain, Abbey Rockefeller Gardens, Thuya Lodge˙ and Gardens, and Jackson Laboratory. Modified American plan omits lunch. Breakfast, lunch, and dinner served daily to travelers from late June to mid-September. Swimming pool and extensive gardens on the grounds. Bicycles, golf, tennis, sandy beaches nearby. George M. Stiles, Innkeeper.

Directions: Exit Maine Tpke. (Rte. 95) at Bangor. Follow Alt. Rte. 1 to Mt. Desert Island.

THE CLAREMONT HOTEL and COTTAGES
Southwest Harbor, Maine

It was September 11, 1979, the day of the opening round of the Annual Claremont Croquet Classic which starts every year on the Thursday after Labor Day.

"Well, we're certainly into croquet here," said Jay Maderia, the innkeeper of the Claremont. "We have croquet all summer in which people play a series of challenge matches leading up to our tournament. Many of our local friends participate. Guests at the hotel automatically qualify. Last summer, we had Robert Liberman, the author of the book *Croquet,* who stayed with us about five days and played quite a bit. By the way, we're putting in all new official equipment for 1980."

Jay and I were seated on the lawn of the Claremont which has been a resort inn for almost a hundred years. It is the oldest continuously operating hotel on the island. In recent years, the

McCue family has added attractive cottages which are nestled in the trees with a view of the water. "There have been more visitors from Europe," he said, "particularly from England. Many people fly to Bangor which is fifty miles away, or to Bar Harbor, which is eleven, and we pick them up. Many of our guests are coming in the early or late season, and we've adjusted our schedule for people who might enjoy Mount Desert Island when almost no one but year-round residents are here."

The inn first opened in the summer of 1884, and grandmothers, grandfathers, and great-grandfathers have been coming ever since. The Claremont has known only three owners in all of its years, which in itself is most unusual.

There are twenty-two rooms in the three-story main building with additional rooms in the Phillips House, the Clark House, and other cottages.

One of the reasons for its continuing popularity is the extensive menu prepared by chef Billie McIntire. Besides the lobster, scallops, steak, and coq au vin, Billie prepares fresh seafood dishes to order, and the desserts are fabulous. Many a resolve goes out the window when guests see something being served at the next table.

Ever since my first visit here, I've been struck by the wide variety of entertainment and recreation that the Claremont guests can enjoy. For example, the location on Mount Desert Island puts all of the wonderful attractions of the area within a very convenient distance. In addition, the inn's launch is available for guests to cruise the intricate and fascinating waterways of the area.

The Claremont, now on the National Register of Historic Places, approaches its one hundredth year with great anticipation.

THE CLAREMONT HOTEL AND COTTAGES, Southwest Harbor, Me. 04679; 207-244-5036. A 22-room rambling summer hotel with rooms also in two adjacent guest houses; on Somes Sound, Mt.

Desert Island, 20 mi. south of Ellsworth. Modified American plan omits lunch. Some rooms with shared baths. Hotel open June 20 to Sept. 16. Guesthouse rooms available year-round. Eight house-keeping cottages on grounds open Memorial Day weekend to Columbus Day weekend. Dining room open Memorial Day weekend to Sept. 30, serving breakfast and dinner daily to the public as well as guests. Tennis, rowboats, croquet, badminton, dock, and deep water moorings on grounds. Fresh water swimming, golf, bicycles, riding, boating, and sailing rentals nearby. No credit cards. Personal checks accepted. The McCue Family, Owners; John Maderia, Jr., Innkeeper.

Directions: From Maine Tpke., exit at Augusta and proceed east on Rte. 3 to US #1. At Ellsworth, pick up Rte. 3 again and follow Rte. 102 on Mt. Desert Island to Southwest Harbor. Follow inn signs approaching and in Southwest Harbor.

JORDAN POND HOUSE

Many readers will no doubt notice the absence from these pages of the Jordan Pond House, a most distinguished restaurant on Mount Desert Island. I regret to report that it was destroyed by fire in 1979 but, according to my most recent letter, Mr. David Rockefeller spearheaded a committee of interested citizens which was formed to raise part of the funds necessary for the rebuilding of this truly international institution. I understand that the National Park Service is committed to the rebuilding of the Jordan Pond House, complete with its former ambience, traditions, and all of the essentials intact. The construction will probably continue through 1980, but we are all looking forward to its reopening in 1981.

GREY ROCK INN
Northeast Harbor, Maine

"June is a wonderful month to come here," said innkeeper Janet Millet, as we walked down the short path from the main house at Grey Rock with its broad veranda and cathedral of trees. "This is the time when so many flowers are in great profusion like lady's-slippers, begonias, tiger lilies, wild columbine, wild lupin, alpine flowers, bayberries, red cranberries, and bluebells. Over there is a linden tree and very soon it will be covered with blossoms."

Grey Rock sits on a rocky promontory overlooking a corner of Northeast Harbor bay and yacht basin. It was built as a private estate in the early 1900s and the large and comfortable bedrooms are replete with wicker furniture and iron bedsteads, big deep bathtubs,

lovely fluffy towels, and everything is clean, bright, and shiny. There are lots of books, good bedlamps, and vases of flowers in the rooms. Each bedroom, facing out and with its own bath, is cool and shady in the summertime and pleasantly decorated with many delightful family touches.

"I'm so glad that we now have 'Treetops,'" Janet continued, "the guests just love it." 'Treetops' is an English-style cottage which is on one corner of the Grey Rock property. It has a beautiful living room with a fireplace, two bedrooms, and a full kitchen. It is adaptable for either one couple or two, and also for families traveling with children. It is available for a four-day minimum stay. "Guests can join the rest of us in the main house for afternoon tea or a fireside chat in the evenings, which is a wonderful opportunity to get to know each other." Being English, afternoon tea is one of Janet's specialties.

It just so happened that on the morning I was at Grey Rock, the dining room was filled with people who were there for their second, third, and even fourth visits! Some had met each other on earlier visits, and naturally the talk turned to country inns both in America and Europe. One guest said that in all her travels she had never found a place at all like Grey Rock. "Everything adds up to a wonderful experience," she said. "We have stayed here several times and have had different rooms, and I think all of the bedrooms are wonderfully large and comfortable."

Many of the guests stay on for additional days because after they get to Mount Desert Island they find so many things to do. There are quiet places to have dinner, including the Claremont and the Asticou. I have always enjoyed the Northeast Harbor shops; they are small and personal.

In one corner of the reception area there is a most interesting arrangement of furniture in front of the fireplace—a loveseat, a platform rocker, a wing chair, and floor lamp—all in wicker! On the fireplace there is a little plaque which reads:

> "Stand firm Grey Rock
> Tough weathered beams hold fast!
> Staunch walls, proud root,
> Repel the marring blast.
> Glow warm deep hearth
> Against the winter's chill;
> Clear flame of love,
> Burn brighter, warmer still!"

GREY ROCK INN, Harborside Rd., Northeast Harbor, Me. 04662; 207-276-9360. A 12-room village inn in the town of Northeast Harbor, Me. adjacent to Acadia National Park and all of the attractions of this unusual region. European plan. Continental breakfast served to houseguests only. No other meals served. Small cottage available for minimum 4-night stay. Season from early spring to Nov. 1. Children 14 yrs. and older preferred. No pets. No credit cards. Janet Millet, Innkeeper.

Directions: Located on the right-hand side of Rte. 198 approaching the town of Northeast Harbor. Note sign for inn. Do not try to make a right-hand turn at this point, but proceed about one block, turn around and approach the inn on the left up the steep hill.

PILGRIM'S INN
Deer Isle, Maine

It was a lively, stormy night; the remnants of Hurricane David were being felt on the Maine coast, bringing with them a foretaste of the winter to come.

I turned off coastal Route #1, turning into the Blue Hill Peninsula on Route #15 and headed across the Eggemoggin Reach on the old suspension bridge to Little Deer Isle. Following the snaking causeway to Deer Isle, I soon pulled up to the Pilgrim's Inn.

Hurrying inside, I was given a warm greeting by Elli Pavloff, who suggested that I immediately go downstairs to the Common Room where Rebekah would have something to warm me up. "We've saved a place by the fire for you," she said. Rebekah, a gentle-eyed Tennessee lass, provides the inn with baked breads, pastries, and charming watercolors throughout the summer.

Sure enough there were the happy guests, all assembled and nibbling on cheese and biscuits, and eager to share the day's

experiences. Outside, the wind and storm still beat against the windows. One man remarked, "This is the best kind of night to be at a country inn."

Later, Elli collected me for a tour of the upper stories, and she proudly showed me the newly furnished and tastefully redecorated bedrooms, many with broad pine floorboards. "We now have twelve small cast iron wood stoves scattered throughout the bedrooms," she said, "and we have twelve cords of wood stacked out in back." Most of the eleven guest bedrooms are quite large and have remained unchanged since the Colonial days of Squire Haskell, who floated the building in sections over from the mainland in 1793.

"We usually come up and turn the beds down at night," Elli said, as we crisscrossed the hallways visiting the Pumpkin Room, the Cranberry Bog Room, and the Blue Room.

Up on the fourth floor of this gambrel-roofed house are some newly created rooms, one of which overlooks the millpond. Everything is very cozy and trim with lots of books and magazines. The baths are semi-private and Elli says, "Six are a lot more than they had in 1793! We recognize an occasional guest will be taken aback by the fact that we do not have private baths, telephones, television, air conditioning, room service, and other conveniences of a hotel or motel."

It was still summertime, so all of the guests repaired to the attached barn where dinner was served. We were entertained by two guitar-playing singers who offered pleasant folk songs in many languages. "We have gifted musicians here quite frequently," Elli commented. "The Deer Isle area attracts people of many talents."

The electricity did flicker and go out a few times during dinner, but we hardly noticed it since the candles were unaffected, and the musicians never missed a beat.

At the conclusion of dinner, we walked back through Elli's kitchen where preparations for the next day's meal were already being discussed and planned. We lingered for a moment in the low-ceilinged Tap Room which also has a huge fireplace.

"Doing nothing pleasantly is at the top of the list of suggested activities. This is not the place for anyone in a hurry," says George. "We want people to stay for a week or two to savor the inn and island, and to go away really refreshed with new friends and, perhaps, a few new pounds, ready for the fray once again."

PILGRIM'S INN, Deer Isle, Me. 04627; 207-348-6615. An 11-room inn, some with shared baths, in a remote island village on the Blue Hill Peninsula on the Maine coast. Modified American plan, May 15 to Nov. 1, includes a hearty breakfast and a gourmet dinner. During the winter, bed and breakfast is offered to the passing pilgrim. In season outside dinner reservations accepted Wednesdays through Saturdays. A 4-day mimimum reservation is required in August. Bicycles, badminton, ping pong, regulation horseshoes, croquet, and an old rowboat for the millpond on the grounds. The Deer Isle area is replete with all types of cultural and recreational advantages including golf, fishing, sailing, hiking, and browsing. George and Eleanor Pavloff, Innkeepers.

Direction: From Boston, take I-95 to Brunswick exit. Take coastal Rte. 1 north past Bucksport. Turn right on Rte. 15 which travels to Deer Isle down the Blue Hill Peninsula. At the village, turn right on Main Street (Sunset Rd.) and proceed one block to the Inn on the left side of the street, opposite the Harbor.

WHITEHALL INN
Camden, Maine

I certainly knew that I was in Camden, Maine. There again were the flowered-decorated lamp posts and the waterfall at the town landing. Also present was green-clad Mount Beattie and the lovely Camden Harbor with its colorful Windjammer sailing fleet. They set sail each Monday morning with the tide.

If ever an inn and a setting were made for each other, the Whitehall Inn and Camden are perfectly matched. The buildings of the inn have a neo-classic design connected by a large porch with plenty of comfortable wicker furniture. The inn sits back from the main street among huge elm and pine trees, and there are many window boxes and arrangements of summer flowers.

On the first floor, there are several parlors and a large lobby, all of which are furnished with Maine antiques. The lounge is furnished

with sewing machines ingeniously converted into tables; chess sets which invite competition; and a large collection of unusual shells which are displayed under glass. Lodgings are country-style.

Innkeeper Ed Dewing met me at the front door and immediately launched into an update of all of the Dewing family activities.

"Chip and Jonathan are both here at the inn this summer, and they are both also planning to return to the Gasparilla Inn in Boca Grande. Heidi is still very happy as the number one pastry baker at the Ritz in Boston."

The Dewing family left Boston and came to Camden in the early 1970s to become keepers of this highly reputable village inn. Because their maturing years were spent working at the inn, all three of the second generation are pursuing careers in the hospitality business.

Ed said that most of the guests still are interested in the Edna St. Vincent Millay Room with its collection of photographs of Miss Millay from the time she was eighteen years old and lived here in Camden. The room has been designed as a tribute to her and contains many volumes of her poems, along with memorabilia that would be of interest to Miss Millay's numerous admirers. It was here at the Whitehall Inn on a warm August evening in 1912 that young Edna first recited her poem, "Renascence."

The inn is located just a short tree-lined walk from the center of the village. An excellent folder provided by the inn has dozens of suggestions about activities in and around this part of Maine, including golf, sightseeing, art exhibitions, boating, swimming, hiking, and fishing.

The Whitehall Inn has its own island reached by the inn launch in nearby Penobscot Bay. As Ed pointed out, "Little Green Island continues to enchant all who visit, and becomes the highlight of their water experience in Maine. It has a lobsterman's shack on it, and is also a game reserve. There are seventeen varieties of wildflowers and many birds in a natural habitat. It's a wonderful place to spend the day in quiet and contemplation."

I believe that a major part of everyone's country inn experience is the food. In reference to the Whitehall Inn, here's a letter I have from a gentleman from Vermont. "Because I have been connected with the food industry most of my life, I instinctively notice the small considerations that lift an establishment head and shoulders above the rest. During the past few years, we have enjoyed quite a few meals at the inn, and this year we were guests for a delightful week. The food is certainly exceptional."

As Ed and I stood on the porch sort of summing things up at the Whitehall, he said, "Actually nothing is new and I think that's why our guests have chosen the Whitehall as their special place. We still don't have any television or air conditioning, no swimming pool, and no disco. We've added new electrical service so that we blow fewer fuses. The Whitehall has been here seventy-seven years and we promise the same beautiful sunrises and sunsets, crisp clean air, days filled with sunshine (a little fog now and then), brilliant fall foliage, picture book villages, friendly neighbors, a bountiful table, and lots of people to look out for everybody's comfort and well-being."

Whitehall Inn has been in *CIBR* since 1973.

WHITEHALL INN, Camden, Me. 04843; 207-236-3391. A 38-room village inn in a Maine seacoast town, 75 mi. from Portland. Modified American plan omits lunch. Breakfast and dinner served daily to travelers. Open, May 25 to Oct 15. Tennis, bicycles, shuffleboard, day sailing, harbor cruises on grounds. No pets. Golf, hiking, swimming, fishing nearby. Jean and Ed Dewing, Innkeepers.

Directions: From Maine Tpke. take Exit 9 to coastal Rte. 95. Proceed on 95 to Rte. 1 at Brunswick. Follow Rte. 1 to Rte. 90 at Warren, to Rte. 1 in Camden. Inn is located on Rte. 1, 1/4 mi. north of Camden.

THE SQUIRE TARBOX INN
Westport Island, Maine

The Squire Tarbox Inn is a very quiet place in a section of the Maine coast sufficiently off the beaten track to be unspoiled and natural. It is an expression of the best of 19th-century ambience and tradition. The original house, constructed about 1763 some distance away, was purchased in 1806 by Squire Samuel Tarbox and moved to its present location. The exposed boards and timbers that remain today are original. About 1825, the Squire built the main house in which the original floors, carvings, moldings, and windowpanes have been preserved.

Lodgings are in the main house and in the attached barn, and both are very cozy in a real upcountry manner.

It has always been one of my principal joys, while visiting the Squire Tarbox, to sit around the dining room table after dinner and enjoy long conversations which frequently move into the sitting room in front of the fire. Innkeepers Anne McInvale and Elsie White have a number of enthusiasms and interests that are reflected by the unusual number of books and magazines to be found throughout the parlors and lodgings of the inn.

"For our guests who want to sample a slice of New England country life," explained Anne, "we have a friendly game of darts in the barn, a walk down the pine-needled path to Squam Creek, the fragrance of wild strawberries in the summer sun, snuggling into a soft chair with a good book, sunning on the open deck overlooking the woodlands, swimming or fishing in Montsweag Bay, or picking blueberries and raspberries.

"For those who desire, there is golf at the Bath Country Club, tennis and swimming nearby. Many people call Wiscasset the prettiest village in Maine, and Boothbay Harbor, which is just a short drive, has many local craftsmen and artists.

"Many of our guests presented weekends at the Squire Tarbox Inn as wedding gifts this year. The result was a steady stream of happy honeymooners. It is comforting to know that we do not have to add tennis courts, a swimming pool, etc., to provide people with the kind of experience they are seeking. Incidentally, we have added lovely quilts handmade by Elsie's mother to all of the beds.

"Our menus include several flounder dishes, as well as scallops and shrimps. We continue to feature fish or seafood as a choice at every dinner. The rest of the menu is set. It includes soup, salad, three vegetables, and dessert. The favorite soup this year seems to have been our own apple soup made from old-fashioned varieties of apples such as Red Astrakhan and Yellow Transparent. The favorite dessert is probably the chocolate mint pie which we call 'sin pie' because of its sinfully rich nature. Our dinner priority is to accommodate our houseguests, but we can usually take four to six other guests.

"As you know, we grow some of our own vegetables, including tomatoes, summer squash, zucchini, green beans, lettuce, and cucumbers. We are also able to get a specially-grown variety of tiny sweet corn. We grew six varieties of lettuce, and our guests found it a real treat to have salad made from all of the varieties, served with our special old-fashioned bacon dressing.

"In 1979, we had many guests who came at the beginning of the season and then returned later on during the summer or fall. One couple from Unionville, Connecticut, were both first and last guests of the year. Other guests sent children, parents, friends, and so forth, to be with us. Many people stayed longer and had more time to explore the area. I think that American vacations are subtly changing in character, perhaps reverting back to the old days, when people stayed longer and really became part of the community."

The Squire Tarbox has been included in *CIBR* since 1974.

THE SQUIRE TARBOX INN, Wesport Island, R.D. #2, Box 318, Wiscasset, Me. 04578; 207-882-7693. A restored Colonial home on Rte. 144 in Wesport, 10 mi. from Wiscasset. European plan. 6 rooms with shared baths; two with private bath. All lodgings include Continental breakfast. Breakfast served to houseguests only. Dinner served to travelers by reservation daily, except Sunday. Open from mid-May to mid-Oct. No pets. Golf, tennis, pool, sailing, exploring, walking nearby. Anne McInvale and Elsie White, Innkeepers.

Directions: From Maine Tpke. take Exit 9 follow Rtes. 95 and 1 to Rte. 144, 8 mi. north of Bath. Follow Rte. 144 to Wiscasset-Westport Bridge. Inn is located 6 mi. south of bridge on Westport Island.

HOMEWOOD INN
Yarmouth, Maine

It was great to be back at the Homewood Inn once again, especially since we were all celebrating Ted Gillette's 80th birthday. Ted and Doris, Fred Webster's mother, were married a few years ago and they've both been having a wonderful time with excursions to all parts of Maine to collect antiques and collectibles for the Homewood Inn shop, which can be found in the Lodge. In fact, Fred has become so interested in antiques, he is planning on taking a course on the subject. Fred and Colleen Webster, who, along with Doris and Ted,

are the co-innkeepers, presided over dinner, during which there was a continual reunion of old friends, not only from the community of Yarmouth, but also the first guests of the season, making this occasion even more festive. Particulary touching were the greetings exchanged by the waitresses with long-time guests.

There was lots of news to catch up on with the Websters, including their trip to the Lamothe House in New Orleans, the Lodge on the Desert in Tucson, and the Rancho de los Caballeros in Wickenburg, Arizona. "We just had wonderful times," said Colleen.

I've been visiting the Homewood Inn since 1972, and each time I've met guests who have returned year after year. It's a very homey, family-type place. Lodgings are in single and double cottages; many have fireplaces and views of Casco Bay. They are set among the junipers, cedars, maples, and Norway pines. Guests are frequently delighted to find they are sharing the waterside environment with dozens of varieties of land and shore birds. It's a great place for children of all ages and there is much activity for them to enjoy on the grounds.

After dinner, we all gathered around the piano in the lounge, where a local history teacher holds forth each weekend. Everyone joins in the old songs. Afterwards, we walked outside, past the swimming pool, the shuffleboard and tennis courts, where there were many marigolds, French and African blue ageratums, and a flower called "the dusty miller" with a very pleasant white blossom.

As we wandered down to the shore, she remarked that the cottage where I would be staying had needed exterior repairs after the blizzard and storm in February 1978. "The waves were very high and did quite a lot of damage," she said.

The next morning before breakfast I took a jog around the beautiful roads of Cousins Island and noted that a few of the guests were already up and about, playing tennis and even dipping an inquiring toe into the swimming pool. It was going to be a beautiful weekend and I imagine many of them would be taking advantage of the sunshine to get an early tan. Some of them were already taking photographs of the water, shore, and sky.

Once again after a hearty Maine breakfast, which was punctuated by lots of joking and good times, I bade goodbye to all of my good friends at the Homewood Inn and took one last lingering look at the splendid Casco Bay shoreline.

Homewood Inn has been included in *CIBR* since 1973.

HOMEWOOD INN, Drinkwater Point, Yarmouth, Me. 04096: 207-846-3351. A 46-room waterside inn in Casco Bay north of Portland. European plan. Breakfast and dinner served to travelers daily except Mondays when Continental breakfast and steak or lobster cookout at night available (by advance reservation). Open June 13 through October 13. (Some rooms and cottages with kitchenettes available from May 15 and after October 13.) Bicycles (incl. tandems), pool, tennis, croquet court, boating, hiking, salt water swimming on grounds. Golf, riding, fishing, state parks, theatre nearby. Fred, Colleen, and Julie Webster, Ted and Doris Gillette, Innkeepers.

Directions: From the south, take Exit 9 from Maine Tpke. (I-95) to Rte. 1-N and follow signs to inn. From the north, take Exit 11 from I-95 at Gray and follow Rte. 115 to Yarmouth. Follow signs to inn.

THE CAPTAIN LORD MANSION
Kennebunkport, Maine

Bev Davis and Rick Litchfield, the personable owners of the Captain Lord Mansion, were filling me in on a few of the intriguing historical details of the building and the town. "During the war of 1812, the British threatened to burn the port if shipbuilding and trade didn't cease. Captain Nathaniel Lord answered the needs of idle carpenters and sailors by engaging them to build this mansion using timbers intended for ships. The carpenters not only topped the house with a cupola, but incorporated hints of their nautical trade throughout the interior.

"Naturally, as the Lord Mansion progressed through several generations of descendents, it acquired all of the trappings and legends that such a building might accumulate. We even have ghosts. One is Sally Buckland, whose portrait hangs in the front sitting room. She has the kind of eyes that actually follow you around, and

you can even feel them looking at you when your back is turned.

"In addition to the cupola, the original structure claims one of the few three-story, unsupported elliptical staircases in Maine. Each window is considerably enhanced by hand-sewn draperies, and each displays its original double Indian shutters and blown glass. The beautiful floors with their original pine boards are a handsome complement to the remainder of the furnishings, most of which are antiques of such great history and pedigree that we have conducted tours for all of our houseguests."

The Captain Lord Mansion is an opportunity to be transported into an elegant era of the nineteenth century. It is a mansion of over thirty-five rooms of many descriptions. Most of the bathrooms have marble sinks. Some have light fixtures that are real silver. One of the sitting rooms has the original French imported wallpaper from 1812, and still another has real gold leaf paper.

During the past year, Bev and Rick have continued their finishing touches. For example, they now have large brass kettles to hold firewood for the seven rooms with working fireplaces. In redecorating each room, they started with big thick towels, and thick carpets which are luxurious to walk on. The handmade afghans and quilts are found in most of the rooms.

They've also purchased "posturepedic" mattresses for each room, and have found some truly beautiful beds, including four-poster, canopy types, cannonball style, brass, and ornately carved Victorian beds.

"We've tried to make the rooms fit the kind of guests who've been visiting us," Rick remarked. "We've had a number of women traveling together this summer. They want twin beds, so a few of the doubles have been replaced by twins. By the way, we've started a collection of old steamer trunks. They are most appropriate as luggage racks, and they store extra blankets and pillows. A few of our guest rooms have working fireplaces."

The subject turned to breakfast, and Bev took over: "We have a variation of breads. There's pumpkin bread, zucchini bread, and cranberry bread, and I also make a lot of different types of coffee cake and cinnamon rolls. We also serve hard boiled eggs, juice, and coffee or tea. Most everybody gathers downstairs in the big kitchen. However, we do serve breakfast in bed in the winter to those who request it. Many of our guests say that they have *never* had breakfast in bed, and it's such a romantic idea!"

After breakfast, Rick conducts a tour of the house and tells about the antiques, the history, and some of the legends. Of course, everybody loves to go up into the cupola which provides such a wonderful view of many of the historic houses of Kennebunkport.

"I've never met Captain Nathaniel Lord," said Rick, "nor, for that matter, any members of the Lord family, but fortunately, so much of his way of life has been preserved in this building for more than a hundred and fifty years that I feel I have a very strong tie with him. I've studied the history of the family and love to tell it to our guests."

Bev had the last word: "It's like acquiring a whole new set of ancestors."

THE CAPTAIN LORD MANSION, Box 527, Kennebunkport, ME 04046; 207-967-3141. A 15-bedroom inn located in a mansion in a seacoast village. Near the Rachel Carson Wildlife Refuge, the Seashore Trolley Museum, The Brick Store Museum, and lobster boat tours. Lodgings include breakfast. No other meals served. Not particularly oriented to children. No pets. Open year-round. Bicycles, hiking, xc skiing, deep sea fishing, golf, and indoor swimming and tennis, nearby. No credit cards. No children under 12. Bev Davis and Rick Litchfield, Innkeepers.

Directions: Take Exit 3 from the Maine turnpike. Turn left on Rte. 35, follow signs through Kennebunk across Rte. U.S. 1 to Kennebunkport. Turn left at the Sunoco station at the traffic light, go over the bridge and then the first right around the monument to Ocean Avenue. Go exactly 3/10 mi., turn left, and the mansion will be on the left on a slight rise. Park at rear entrance.

OLD FORT CLUB
Kennebunkport, Maine

Yale Brass and I had just finished two sets of tennis and were

seated at courtside enjoying the sunshiny weather in mid-June.

"As you know, I'm an airline pilot," he said "and I've seen a great many parts of the world. However, Kennebunkport is really 'home' for us. I guess it's a *second* home to many of our guests who return each year. We have people from all over the United States, but did you know that this part of the Maine coast is also very popular with Canadians? Kennebunkport seems to be the focal point for them; we have people from all over Canada throughout the summer.

"There used to be a hotel on this property, but Marjorie and I had it torn down. We converted one of the buildings into twelve efficiency apartments which include daily maid service, and an enclosed garage. We also converted a portion of the carriage house into Marjorie's antique shop and gallery. In the section overlooking the swimming pool, we built a clubroom with a big fireplace, a large terrace, and a kitchen for entertaining. It makes a nice place for our guests to enjoy lobster and steak cookouts."

The apartments Yale mentioned are meticulously designed in decorator colors with harmonizing draperies, slip covers, and furnishings. All have fully-equipped kitchen facilities. The dimensions are large enough so that people can stay for longer periods without feeling cramped.

"You probably noticed that we planted many new rose bushes, added more flower boxes, and have continued our beautification projects," he said. "Marjorie is planning more art exhibitions in the shop and possibly a fashion show. She's also mentioned a few painting demonstrations.

"Karen and Mario Mesiti are the new resident managers and have already become a part of the family. They make certain that guests are introduced, arrange fishing trips, plan backroading trips, recommend restaurants, and make telephone calls for reservations. They will also make a third and fourth for tennis and, in general, attend to everybody's comfort. One of the things that we're happiest about is that many of our guests have developed 'Old Fort friendships,' and plan to come back when their new friends will also be here."

I like to visit Kennebunkport because it still retains the charm it had when it was the queen of the seas for this part of Maine. The old sea-captains' houses, beautiful streets, and winding river make it a very pleasant vacation experience. The area also has two golf courses, boating, and fishing, and an excellent summer theater is just a few miles away.

Across the pool, the sunlight created a dappled pattern through the trees. Roses climbed the stone wall and the corners of the stone-and-brick garage. Overhead, a few errant clouds chased each other across the blue sky. Yale suggested that we had just about time enough to take a good stroll on the sandy beach. "I think this is really the best time of day," he said, "and then we can work up an appetite for dinner. I've got to fly again tomorrow, but I certainly try to be here as much of every summer as possible."

OLD FORT CLUB, Old Fort Ave., Kennebunkport, Me. 04046; 207-967-2709 or 3980. A 12-apartment resort-inn on Cape Arundel within walking distance of the ocean in an historic Maine town. No meals are served, but a full kitchen is provided with each apartment. Daily maid service. Balconied club room. Open from Memorial Day to Oct. 15. No pets. Heated pool, tennis court, shuffleboard on grounds. Bicycles, golf, salt water swimming and boating nearby. Yale and Marjorie Brass, Innkeepers.

Directions: Use Exit #3 (Kennebunk) from Maine Tpke. Turn left on Rte. 35 to Kennebunkport and follow signs to inn.

THE WHISTLING OYSTER
Ogunquit, Maine

Ogunquit is actually an Indian word which means: "Beautiful place by the sea." For the past 100 years an increasingly favorite spot for many people, Ogunquit is a splendid place where writers, artists, and tourists gather to enjoy the singular delights that are special to this part of the southern Maine coast. I have spent many happy hours strolling the Marginal Way, the natural path that clings to the cliffs high above the sea, where I watched the ocean change its moods quickly and decisively, from a gentle splashing on the sandy beach to

raucous waves breaking high over the rocks, blending green-blue and moody grey hues.

The Whistling Oyster is located in Perkins Cove right on the waters of this sheltered harbor and it has a splendid view of all of the activities of the busy waterway.

The late afternoon sun reflecting the cove waters created dappled patterns on the walls and ceilings of the Whistling Oyster's outer-deck dining room. Lobster boats were coming in under the drawbridge and many smaller boats darted among the moored pleasure craft. John Parella, whom I have called for years, "the best baritone-innkeeper I have ever met," came toward me once again with his hand outstretched. "I'm so glad you could come today," he said. "We've got a lot to talk about."

There is some drama involved with this restaurant which I have been visiting since the late 1960s. I'll touch just briefly on the fact that in late summer, 1976, the original Whistling Oyster was completely destroyed by fire, and during the following winter and spring, a new building was designed and constructed that included some of the best concepts of the original structure. I am happy to say that the Whistling Oyster has indeed been restored, "beyond my fondest dreams," said John. Once again, he gave full credit to the many people who worked so hard during the reconstruction period. "It is all behind us now," he said, "but you'd be surprised at how many people seem so delighted with the *new* Oyster."

This time John was filled with news about how gratifying it was to keep the restaurant open all winter. "Many people enjoy the coast of Maine in the off-season," he said, "and believe me there is nothing quite as beautiful as Perkins Harbor under a fresh blanket of snow. It never gets very deep except for that one bad blizzard in 1978.

"We're continuing with the special events connected with our Oyster Club," he said. "Some of the highlights, in addition to the International Dinners, have been the English Hunt Breakfast, a New

England Harvest Buffet, and the traditional holiday celebrations. We initiated a Christmas carol sing last year."

The International Dinners to which John alluded included a number of different evenings devoted to the cuisine of many different countries—there were English dinners, Italian dinners, Russian, French, and Mardi Gras dinners. These were all the creation of chef Bill Cardwell, who seems to thrive on continuing challenges.

While John and I were holding this animated conversation, waiters brought in bowls of Captain Blight's Delight and Crabmeat Snug Harbor, two of the menu offerings that I have been enjoying ever since my first visit. Other luncheon items included broiled filet of haddock amandine and eggs Benedict. Some of the entrées on the dinner menu included duckling flambé, roast rack of lamb Persillé, and shrimps and mushrooms sautéed in garlic butter.

After lunch I couldn't resist another visit to the famous Whistling Oyster gift shop which now occupies considerably more space than the original.

We lingered for a few moments at the front entrance and John had one final thought: "When you are in our vicinity on a Sunday, be sure and drop in for our champagne lunch—we offer it year around."

The Whistling Oyster has been included in *CIBR* since 1969.

THE WHISTLING OYSTER, Perkins Cove, Ogunquit, Me. 03907; 207-646-9521. A waterfront restaurant in Perkins Cove at Ogunquit. No lodgings. Lunch and dinner served daily. Open throughout the year. Reservations advisable. Nearby CIBR *overnight lodgings include the Capt. Lord Mansion and the Old Fort Club in Kennebunkport; and the Dockside Guest Quarters in York. John Parella, Innkeeper.*

Directions: From the south, take the York exit from I-95. Turn north on Rte. 1 to Ogunquit Square. Proceed south on Shore Rd. for about 1 mi. to Perkins Cove turnoff.

DOCKSIDE GUEST QUARTERS
York, Maine

It was dawn on York Harbor. I awakened when the October sun peeked into my east window and illuminated the trees along the shore—the white pines and firs, native spruces, all of which remain green year around. The yellows and oranges of the maples, the rusty greens of the hickories, and the scarlets of the sumacs and beeches were at the height of their autumn glory.

The sundeck of my room, almost at water's edge, looked most inviting, so with camera and binoculars in hand, I put my feet up on

the rail and settled back to watch the harbor drama unfold.

The tide was on the way in, the sea was calm, and the first of the lobster boats was gliding out of the harbor. Almost immediately, the "resident flock" of mallard ducks, as David Lusty calls them, came quacking into view and hesitated momentarily looking for a handout. They're really quite tame and serve as perfect decoys to bring literally hundreds of migrating ducks to the nearby marsh.

I thought immediately of all the people who write to me saying, "Can you help us find a country inn located directly on the water — preferably in New England?" Well, the Dockside Guest Quarters fills the bill. David Lusty who is a native "state-of-Mainer," complete with a Down-Easter accent, purchased Harris Island, where the DGQ is located, a number of years ago. He hired a young lady whom he had met in college, and fourteen months later, David and Harriette were married at Dockside Guest Quarters. Over the years it has proven to be a very popular place with honeymooners.

The inn has grown to include not only the original 1880s-style New England homestead called the Maine House, but also other multi-unit cottage buildings of a contemporary design each with its own porch and a view of the ocean. Some have a casual studio feeling. In 1979, a new gift shop was added.

At breakfast which is Continental style at the Maine House, David enthusiastically made suggestions to all of us about a foliage tour of the Maine coast. As he said, "I think this is the best time of the year to be here."

A few years ago, David and Harriette added the Dockside Dining Room, now managed by Steve and Sue Roeder, serving luncheon and dinner with a great deal of emphasis on food from the waters of the nearby Atlantic. One of the non-sea offerings is a splendid roast duckling, "a la Hickory Stick," from the famous Hickory Stick Farm restaurant in Laconia, New Hampshire, which is owned by Steve's brother Scott, and is included in *CIBR* for the first time in this issue.

The first order of the day was a guided tour of York Harbor and river in the DGQ launch with the Lusty's son Eric. In his laconic way he said he did it every day, but never got tired of it.

Pointing due east toward the open sea, he said, "Next stop — Spain."

DOCKSIDE GUEST QUARTERS, Harris Island Rd., York, Maine 03909; 207-363-2868. An 18-room waterside country inn 10 mi. from Portsmouth, N.H. Some larger quarters in newer multi-unit cottages. York village is a National Historic District. American plan available. Continental breakfast servecd to houseguests only. Dockside Dining Room serves lunch and dinner to travelers daily except Mondays. Open from Memorial Day weekend in May through Columbus Day. Lawn games, shuffleboard and badminton, fishing, sailing, and boating from premises. Golf, tennis, and swimming nearby; safe and picturesque paths and roadways for walks, bicycling, and jogging. Credit cards are accepted for any amounts under fifty dollars. Personal checks accepted for payment of food and lodgings incurred by registered guests. David and Harriette Lusty, Innkeepers.

Directions: From U.S. 1 or I-95, take Exit at York to Rte. 1A (the main street of York). Take Rte. 103 (a side street off Rte. 1A) and follow signs to Harris Island Rd.

I do not include lodging rates in the descriptions, for the very nature of an inn means that there are lodgings of various sizes, with and without baths, in and out of season, and with plain and fancy decoration. Travelers should call ahead and inquire about the availability and rates of the many different types of rooms.

Rates are comparable to those at hotels, motels, and resorts in the same geographic area. To me, this represents a travel bargain, for there is so much more offered at a country inn.

"European Plan" means that rates for rooms and meals are separate. "American Plan" means that meals are included in the cost of the room. "Modified American Plan" means that breakfast and dinner are included in the cost of the room. Some inns include a Continental breakfast with the lodging.

Important: *Many of the inns can be reached by public transportation, and arrangements can frequently be made to be picked up at bus and train stations, as well as airports.*

WHAT IS INNKEEPING REALLY LIKE?

I get dozens of letters annually from people who are considering a second career in country innkeeping. In this edition I am going to share some excerpts from letters I receive each year from CIBR innkeepers. A couple of them follow and the rest are dispersed throughout the book. I think they can answer the question far better than I.

". . . As usual life has been full and busy and we have many blessings to count. While it isn't an easy time to have an inn, what with rising costs of food and energy, we seem to be filling real needs in many people's lives, and for that reason seem to have gathered a great cheering section—so many guests and townsfolk take great delight in commenting on the prosperity of our inn. (It would be great if the innkeepers would prosper a bit more by hanging on to what comes in before it gets a chance to go out!)"

It gives us great joy to feel that we can have some small part in providing peace in a hectic world. I guess we're realistic enough to realize that we can't be all things to all people, but we're grateful for what our efforts do accomplish." —New Hampshire

"After eight years (can you believe that?) we are convinced that the difference between a country inn and a place to sleep is the total involvement of the innkeeper and the family. From seven a.m. until the last guest is retired, there is a doing in evidence seven days a week. The reaction is always the same: 'It's nice to know that someone cares' . . ." —Maine

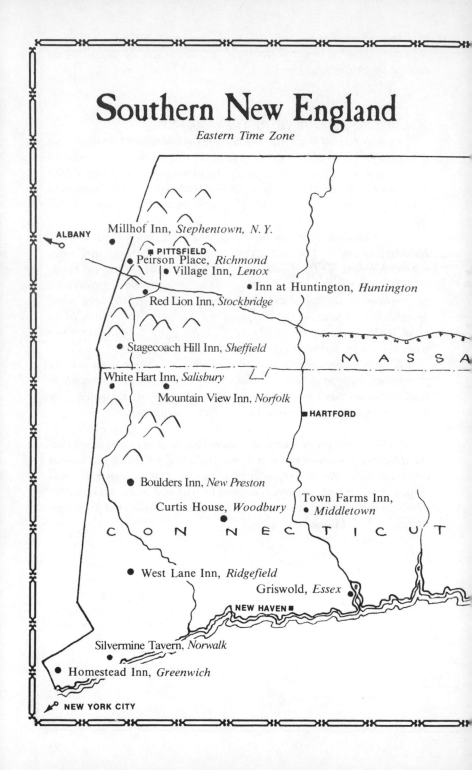

Southern New England

Eastern Time Zone

ALBANY →

Millhof Inn, *Stephentown, N. Y.*

■ PITTSFIELD
Peirson Place, *Richmond*
Village Inn, *Lenox*
Inn at Huntington, *Huntington*
Red Lion Inn, *Stockbridge*

M A S S A C H U S E T T S
M A S S A

Stagecoach Hill Inn, *Sheffield*

White Hart Inn, *Salisbury*
Mountain View Inn, *Norfolk*

■ HARTFORD

Boulders Inn, *New Preston*
Town Farms Inn,
Curtis House, *Woodbury*   *Middletown*

C O N N E C T I C U T

West Lane Inn, *Ridgefield*
Griswold, *Essex*

NEW HAVEN ■

Silvermine Tavern, *Norwalk*

Homestead Inn, *Greenwich*

NEW YORK CITY

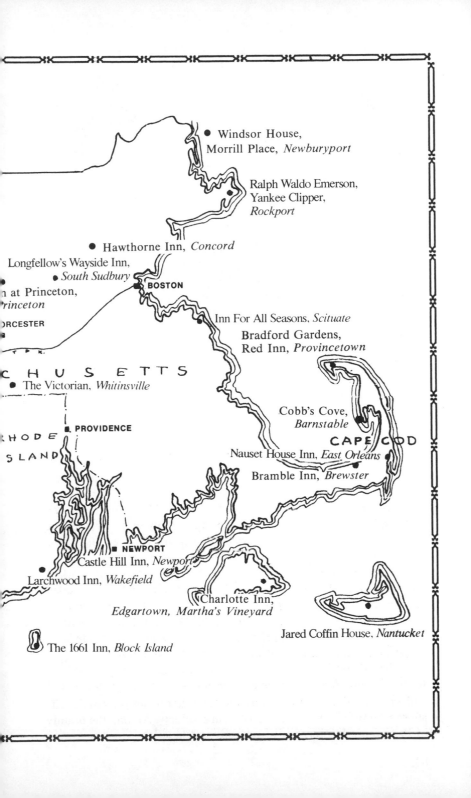

Windsor House,
Morrill Place, *Newburyport*

Ralph Waldo Emerson,
Yankee Clipper,
Rockport

● Hawthorne Inn, *Concord*

Longfellow's Wayside Inn,
● *South Sudbury*

BOSTON

ı at Princeton,
rinceton

Inn For All Seasons, *Scituate*

Bradford Gardens,
Red Inn, *Provincetown*

ORCESTER

C H U S E T T S

● The Victorian, *Whitinsville*

Cobb's Cove,
Barnstable

■ **PROVIDENCE**

RHODE

ISLAND

CAPE COD

Nauset House Inn, *East Orleans*

Bramble Inn, *Brewster*

■ **NEWPORT**

Castle Hill Inn, *Newport*

Larchwood Inn, *Wakefield*

Charlotte Inn,
Edgartown, Martha's Vineyard

Jared Coffin House, *Nantucket*

The 1661 Inn, *Block Island*

Rhode Island

LARCHWOOD INN
Wakefield, Rhode Island

Frank Browning looked up from the open grill on the patio with a twinkle in his eye. "This is yours," he said, indicating with a long-pronged fork one of the steaks on the charcoal fire.

The lady standing next to me asked, "Which one is mine?" Frank said, "The one up in the corner is yours. You said you wanted medium, didn't you?"

I was at the Larchwood Inn during Memorial Day weekend, and the spring flowers and flowering fruit trees were in their most delightful profusion. The red maples and pine trees were shimmering in the afternoon sun. There were both steaks and lobsters being done on the grill, and although there was no hint of rain in the air, the blue and white striped cover overhead would certainly protect us in case of a shower.

While we were watching Francis being happy in his work, I discovered that this lady was part of a family of four who had sailed up the Connecticut and Rhode Island coast from Greenwich, Connecticut, and were now enjoying the treat of a dinner ashore. "We just love this section of Rhode Island. The countryside is so pretty and there is a great deal of history to poke into."

The Larchwood itself reflects these engaging features of southern Rhode Island. Actually, it is a large mansion dating back to 1831 with conservative lodging rooms and food that benefits from the off-shore fishing as well as the hearty farm products. Among the bounty of the sea are lobster, native scallops and bluefish.

The interior has many Scottish touches, including quotations from Robert Burns and Sir Walter Scott, and photographs and prints of Scottish historical and literary figures. One of the dining rooms has wall paintings showing farms and seascapes of Southern Rhode Island.

Rhode Island is a state of stone walls. They come in various heights, thicknesses, and conditions of repair. The back roads, which are most numerous for a state that is reputedly small, often offer some interesting historical sites as well as beautiful homes. There is much to see and do, I discovered, within a short distance of the Larchwood. The nearby south shore beaches are often favorably compared with others elsewhere in New England.

The inn building has a fascinating history that has its roots in Indian raids in Nebraska, the discovery of gold in California, and the continuing saga of a restless New England family. It became an inn in 1926. I first visited it in 1968, and it's been a regular stop ever since.

The Scottish touches at the Larchwood Inn are never more evident than on "Bobby Burns Night" which takes place in January every year. Around the Larchwood Inn, this is more popular than New Year's Eve.

The evening features the presence of John Alder, a Scottish expatriate who "piped in" the Queen of England at Newport. He shares the spotlight with laymen in kilts who also bring their pipes. The event of the evening is the piping in of the haggis. I shared a similar experience to this at the King James Hotel in Edinburgh recently. Haggis is a pudding which is traditionally made of the heart, liver, and lungs of a sheep or a calf and minced with onions, oatmeal, and seasonings. After the procession, the pipers bring in the haggis, and a chosen guest recites Burns's *Ode to a Haggis*. Francis explained, "There are many other traditional Scottish dishes being offered on the menu for that evening."

Bobby Burns Night comes only once a year at the Larchwood and is usually booked three months in advance. It is, indeed, a "lee-lang" of an evening.

The Larchwood Inn has been in *CIBR* since 1969.

LARCHWOOD INN, 176 Main St., Wakefield, R.I. 02879; 401-783-5454. An 11-room village inn just 3 mi. from the famous southern R.I. beaches. Some rooms with shared bath. European plan. Breakfast, lunch, dinner served every day of the year. Swimming, boating, surfing, fishing, xc skiing, and bicycles nearby. Francis Browning, Innkeeper.

Directions: From Rte. 1, take Pond St. Exit and proceed ½ mi. directly to inn.

1661 INN
Block Island, Rhode Island

In an old photograph album, I have a faded print showing a smiling young man wearing a long coat, holding a horse, and in the background is a Victorian building. The young man was my father and the Victorian building was one of the all-but-completely-disappearing summer hotels on Block Island. For all I know, it may have been the Manisses.

My father often talked about his "summers on Block Island." Isn't it odd that these many years later I should feel a very strong connection with the Abrams family, innkeepers for the 1661 Inn and the old Manisses Hotel.

When my father visited there, before World War I, Block Island was one of the fashionable "watering places" of the times. Entire families would take the ferry from New London and spend the whole summer. As we all know, times have changed considerably, but Joan Abrams tells me that more and more people are spending more time at the 1661 Inn, rather than just coming over for a couple of days. "For one thing," she says, "it's not really necessary to have a car here because we meet all of our guests at the ferries, and once here, the marvelous bicycles at the inn are perfect for exploring. The roads are newly repaired. Of course, one of the best exercises is walking on the beach."

The 1661 Inn is a white house partially hidden from the road by thick hedges. There are 25 lodging rooms (11 with private baths). These rooms are all decorated with attractive wallpapers, braided rugs, and "countrified" furniture. It's a medium-sized building with a porch across the side facing the sea, and I'm sure that it was probably used as a "boarding-house" at the time my father was on Block Island.

Today, guests assemble late in the afternoon for a daily wine and cheese party when Rita Draper, Joan and Justin's newly married daughter, is usually on hand, along with her mother, to make certain that all of the inn guests are introduced. Rita makes a special spiced tomato jam which is served everyday at breakfast and it's also available in take-home jars.

Any account of what goes on in the 1661 Inn has to include an update on the continuing rehabilitation by the Abrams family of the Manisses Hotel, which is down the road from the inn. The Abramses decided to bring it back to its early Victorian splendor, and have been converting it, first into an intriguing restaurant with an outdoor terrace and now, bit by bit, into another accommodation complete with parlors and lodging rooms. It will not be fully operational until 1981.

Rita and her husband Steven will be hosts at the inn's Guest House which is now going to be open year-round, providing guests with the opportunity to experience Block Island in the winter months. For complete information, telephone the inn at any time; the ferries run all winter.

Although things are abuzz at the 1661 Inn, I'm sure that my father, who spoke often of the several hundred miles of stone walls, the impressive views of the ocean, and the marvelous lighting effects created by the skies, sun, clouds, and moon, would find the enduring things on the island completely unchanged.

The 1661 Inn has been included in *CIBR* since 1975.

THE 1661 INN, Box 367, Block Island, R.I. 02807; 401-466-2421 or 2063. A 25-room island inn off the coast of R.I. and Conn. in Block Island Sound. 11 private baths. Mod. American and European plans. Open from Memorial Day thru Columbus Day weekend. Breakfast and dinner served to travelers daily. (Guest House open year-round; Continental breakfast included in off-season rates; dinner upon request.) Lawn games on grounds. Tennis, bicycling, ocean swimming, sailing, snorkeling, diving, salt and fresh water fishing nearby. Block Island is known as one of the best bird observation areas on the Atlantic flyway. The Abrams Family, Innkeepers.

Directions: By ferry from Providence, Pt. Judith, and Newport, R.I. and New London, Ct. Car reservations must be made in advance for ferry. By air from Newport, Westerly, and Providence, R.I., New London and Waterford, Ct., or by chartered plane. Contact inn for schedules.

THE INN AT CASTLE HILL
Newport, Rhode Island

The October-November issue of *Historic Preservation,* published by the National Trust for Historic Preservation, has a most interesting article which deals with new uses for large estates. Among the ways that these beautiful homes and mansions of the past are being preserved is to convert them into resort-inns.

The article cites the Inn at Castle Hill as a prime example of a meaningful contribution to the preservation of Newport's architectural heritage and its open spaces along the ocean.

The estate at Castle Hill was built in 1874 by Professor Alexander Agassiz of Cambridge, Massachusetts. He established a laboratory there and studied with twelve Harvard students for twenty-five years, until the marine biological laboratory at Woods Hole, Massachusetts, was built. He donated part of his land to the government because it was the most obvious spot for a needed lighthouse, which was built in 1890. Today, it is a painted white granite tower, forty feet above the sea, and is visible for ten miles on Narragansett Bay.

I first visited the Inn at Castle Hill a number of years ago at the request of the owner, Mrs. Eileen O'Connell. It had been purchased by her father, Mr. J.D. O'Connell, a prominent Newport merchant a few years earlier, and she was seeking ways to make it into a viable year-round resort-inn.

Fortunately, a short time later another old innkeeping friend of mine, Paul McEnroe, was engaged by Mrs. O'Connell as the innkeeper and it is under his watchful eye that the Inn at Castle Hill has returned to its former effulgence. Paul was for many years the innkeeper at De la Vergne Farms Inn in Amenia, New York, which unhappily was burned to the ground in the early 1970s. However, he brought a wealth of innkeeping experience with him to Castle Hill. The Inn at Castle Hill is literally on the edge of a peninsula where the Atlantic Ocean funnels into Narragansett Bay. It's just a few paces from the lawn to the water's edge. From the porches and all of the bedrooms, guests have an uncontested view of both the pleasure craft and commercial ships that ply this beautiful historic waterway. It is a most advantageous point from which to view the finish of the yacht races which are held in Newport every summer.

Accommodations at the inn vary from the mansion-like rooms (some with enormous bathrooms) to housekeeping cottages which are rented by the week during the summer and fall. Reservations for summer and fall must be booked six to nine months in advance.

The menu is definitely Continental, and the service with the headwaiter and assistant waiters all moving about very smartly is reminiscent of several fine European restaurants. Reservations are almost always necessary, especially for weekends. Jackets are required for dinner, and no jeans (even designer style) are allowed in the dining rooms.

The article in *Historic Preservation* mentions that while the kitchen and bathrooms are new, the interior and exterior features of the house remain unchanged. It praises the oak wall and ceiling paneling, the fireplace of hand-inlaid wood, and the fact that Agassiz's furnishings preserve its original homelike atmosphere.

Sundays are gay times at Castle Hill. Brunch is served from 12 to 5 p.m. on the outside deck overlooking the bay, and there is Dixieland jazz and entertainment in the lounge with Walt Moelte on the piano for a sing-along.

INN AT CASTLE HILL, Ocean Drive, Newport, R.I. 02840; 401-849-3800. A 20-room mansion-inn on the edge of Narragansett Bay. Near the Newport mansions, Touro Synagogue, the Newport Casino, and National Lawn Tennis Hall of Fame, the Old Stone Mill, the Newport Historical Society House. European plan. Continental breakfast served to houseguests only. Lunch and dinner served daily to travelers. Guest rooms open all winter. Lounge open winter weekends. No pets. Swimming, sailing, scuba diving, walking on grounds. Bicycles and guided tours of Newport nearby. Paul Goldblatt, Manager. Paul McEnroe, Innkeeper.

Directions: After leaving Newport Bridge follow Bellevue Ave. which becomes Ocean Dr. Look for inn sign on left.

THE HOMESTEAD INN
Greenwich, Connecticut

I took the train from New York's Grand Central, and pulled into the Greenwich station exactly on time. It takes about forty-five minutes on the express. I joined the other commuters who were pouring into the station, and grabbed a handy taxi. It would be a two-minute ride to The Homestead Inn.

Almost immediately, I was in the residential area of this fashionable New York suburb, where beautiful homes were set back from the road. The taxi turned into the parklike grounds of the inn, with its gently floodlit trees. It was quite a transformation from the hustle and bustle of the city such a short time ago!

My hostesses were the co-innkeepers, Lessie Davison and Nancy Smith, two attractive, enthusiastic women who, a couple of years ago, saw the possibilities of restoring the property, and then spent a year returning it to its nineteenth-century effulgence.

"It's hard to realize," explained Lessie, "that the original building was built in 1799, because in 1859 it was completely remodeled in the 'carpenter Gothic' architecture which was so popular during the Victorian era. However, there are sections of the house that have some beautiful old exposed beams and posts, and chimneys which are part of the original building."

Both Lessie and Nancy were quick to credit noted interior designer John Saladino for the coordinated rehabilitation of the inn. "He and his wife Virginia were just wonderful to work with," exclaimed Nancy. "He saw the possibilities immediately and started coordinating the rich old woodwork with exciting wallpapers, draperies, bedspreads, and linens."

Between the two of them, Lessie and Nancy made certain that I saw every single one of the thirteen attractive guest rooms in the inn. Each one is quite different and has a very distinctive name which usually has some connection with the décor of the room. For instance, the Butterfly Room has the butterfly wallpaper pattern; the Bride's Room has a canopied bed; and the Sleigh Bedroom has beautiful sleigh beds. There's a Quail Room, a Mary Jane Room, and even a Tassel Room. All are splendidly furnished, including many antiques, and such comforts and appurtenances as clock radios, electric blankets, two pillows for every head, lots of books and magazines, and very modern bathrooms which contain the only make-up mirrors I've ever seen at a country inn. A Continental breakfast, included in the room charge, is served to overnight guests.

The restaurant at the Homestead is called "La Grange," and the French cuisine is the creation of Jacques Theibeult from Paris, whom I met briefly on a tour of the kitchen. I enjoyed a sumptuous dinner featuring a first course of billi-bi, a bisque of mussel which is served either hot or chilled. For the main course, I chose quenelles of salmon served with champagne—delicious. The dessert was triple chocolate cake, although I wavered between the dark and the white chocolate mousses. The restaurant has a timbered ceiling, and the tables looked most attractive with fine linens and fresh flowers.

With dinner over, we sat for a moment in the Backgammon Room, which is a drawing room with green felt walls and wooden shutters. "We have quite a few honeymooners who stay with us," said Lessie, "and also people who enjoy roaming in the many antique shops in the area."

I'm delighted to welcome Nancy and Lessie and the Homestead Inn to *CIBR*. It's an elegant, sophisticated inn in a country setting.

THE HOMESTEAD INN, 420 Field Point Rd., Greenwich, Conn. 06830. 203-869-7500. A 13-room inn located in the residential area of a suburb, 45 mins. from New York City. Lunch and dinner served daily except Christmas, New Year's, Good Friday, and perhaps others. Located a short distance from Connecticut countryside and shore scenes. Accessible by train from New York City. No amusements for children under twelve. No pets. Lessie B. Davison, Nancy K. Smith, Innkeepers.

Directions: The inn is 3 min. from Rte. I-95 via Exit 3. Turn left at traffic light, immediately before the railroad underpass. Go two blocks to end of street (stop sign). Turn left, proceed ¼ mi. to inn on right.

WEST LANE INN
Ridgefield, Connecticut

Our conversation first started in the bright, cheerful breakfast room at the West Lane Inn, and continued as we carried our cups of coffee out to the broad porch to enjoy the morning sunshine. "I guess I'm what is known as a commercial traveler!" he remarked. "That's a sort of old-fashioned term." We settled down into the handsome white wicker chairs and he continued, "Actually, I'm from Yorkshire. In England, business travelers like myself stay at places similar to this . . . converted great houses, mansions, or country houses."

He gestured with his free hand toward the broad lawn with its azaleas, tulips, roses, and maple and oak trees. "This is what I like about the place," he continued enthusiastically. "The simple garden and the quiet. The bedrooms are certainly much larger than my bedroom at home, and some have working fireplaces. I've stayed here a number of times, because I find it convenient to leave New York about four o'clock in the afternoon, avoiding the rush-hour traffic. I'm here in plenty of time to take a stroll around the village or a walk in the woods. It's up early next morning and on my way, either to Hartford or Boston, and I've had a good night's rest. Fortunately, there are telephones right in the room so I can make some business appointments or even call home.

"They have a very hospitable arrangement here with snacks in the pantry until ten p.m., in case I arrive a little late," he asserted. "And breakfast can either be Continental, which is included with the price of the room, or can be larger, more like my British breakfast. They have sliced bananas or fresh berries, poached eggs on toast, and things like that.

"Oddly enough," he said, "Ridgefield was the scene of a serious battle between the British and the Americans during the Revolutionary War. One of the British cannonballs went through Keeler's Tavern and so surprised the few occupants that they ran for the woods. Another cannonball hit one of the sturdy oak cornerposts of the Tavern and is still embedded there."

While we were talking, I noticed that the guests at the West Lane on this particular morning were about equally divided between businessmen, like my newfound acquaintance, and couples or families traveling with children. The latter group must have found the oversized bedrooms very convenient. The youngsters can watch the color TV.

By North American standards, Ridgefield with large, graceful trees, is a very old village, founded in 1708 by a small group of citizens from Norwalk. These early settlers laid out the town with great care, which can still be seen today. Many of the houses date from the early nineteenth century.

The building which later became the West Lane Inn was constructed in the early 1800s. The underlying colonial or Federalist architecture has been overshadowed by a number of Victorian features including, thankfully, the aforementioned broad porch. The main hall and reception area, with dark wood paneling, an impressive staircase, and wing chairs, creates a very quiet and relaxing mood.

Breakfast is the only regular meal served, although the staff is very happy to advise guests on the restaurants in the area.

Before we parted, I presented my Yorkshire friend with a copy of *CIBR* assuring him that if he enjoyed the accommodations and *esprit* at the West Lane Inn, he would find the other inns equally pleasant.

WEST LANE INN, 22 West Lane, Ridgefield, Conn. 06877; 203-438-7323. A 14-room inn in a quiet residential village in southwest Connecticut. Approx. 1 hour from N.Y.C. Open every day in the year. Breakfast and light snacks available until 10:30 p.m. Convenient to many museums and antique shops. Golf, tennis, swimming and xc skiing and other outdoor recreation available nearby. No pets. Maureen Mayer, Innkeeper.

Directions: From New York: follow I-684 to Exit 6, turn right on Rte. 35. 12 mi. to Ridgefield. Inn is on left. From Hartford: Exit I-84 on Rte. 7 south and follow Rte. 35 to Ridgefield.

BOULDERS INN
Lake Waramaug, New Preston, Connecticut

In the early spring of 1979, the Boulders Inn (which had been run by the Lowe family long before my first visit in 1969) was sold to another family, Jim and Carolyn Woollen, thereby ending one chapter in the history of this resort inn and beginning another.

The first thing that impressed me was their handsome new brochure. It is a model of information, design, truth, and not exaggerated in the slightest.

Let me share with you a portion of a letter I have from Jim and Carolyn which sums up their first full summer and fall at the Boulders, and at the same time gives us all an insight into some of the joys and vicissitudes of country innkeeping.

"We've had the busiest six months of our lives; the transition to innkeeping has involved many adjustments for all of us, but there is no question that the fulfillments and satisfactions are real.

"Although the younger children were reluctant participants to the life change, they are now involved (voluntarily!) in inn operations and making a place for themselves in their new high school. Peter (16) helps out as a bus boy in the dining room on occasion, washes dishes, and has proved very handy with inn repairs. He's on his high school varsity soccer team and a member of a choral group. Mary (18) assists in waitressing on weekends and is enjoying herself behind the scenes in the kitchen. She's the captain of the girls' cross-country team. Byron (20), finished his freshman year at Indiana University before our move and has been working full-time in the inn and will remain with us before he leaves for a stint in Europe. In the fall he'll return to college.

"Our objectives focus on one end: to provide a small, intimate retreat where care, attention, and the homelike atmosphere blend with a physical facility and setting which are outstanding. At the time when we first visited the Boulders we were impressed with the fact that this quiet, unspoiled area of northwestern Connecticut exists within an easy two-hour drive from Manhattan. This fall we brightened and freshened the atmosphere of the Boulders with wallpaper, paint, curtains, bedspreads, and new carpeting.

"For winter, we'll have cross-country skiing, ice skating on the lake, sledding on the "bunny hill," a bright fire in the two downstairs fireplaces, and tea from the samovar. We cleared our cross-country ski trails and are providing rental equipment; we installed fireplaces in six of our cottages, and are maintaining an open dining room Tuesday through Saturday for the winter months. Sundays, we feature brunch for inn guests as well as travelers."

Thank you, Jim and Carolyn. In summary let me say that the

Boulders has for years been a very warm, comfortable resort-inn on a lake with all kinds of water sports, tennis, acres of woods and trails for walking or skiing. Accommodations are in the main house, plus a series of small chalet-type buildings nearby.

Dick and Jane Lowe would certainly be a tough act to follow, but I believe that the Woollen family has an outstanding *dramatispersonae,* and will have an equally long and successful run.

BOULDERS INN, Lake Waramaug, New Preston, Ct. 06777; 203-868-7918. A 15-room year-round resort-inn, 20 mi. north of Danbury, 40 mi. west of Hartford. From Memorial Day to Labor Day, three meals a day served to transients as well as guests. Monday dinner an informal meal for houseguests only. Lodging during this period either on American or mod. American plan. From September through May, breakfast is served every day; dinner, Tuesday through Saturday. Open on Thanksgiving, closed Christmas Eve and Christmas Day. Tennis, swimming, boating, sailing, fishing, antiquing, hiking on mountain trails, bicycling, xc skiing, sledding. Golf, horseback riding, and downhill skiing nearby. 20 min. from chamber music concert series July through August. The Woollen Family, Innkeepers.

Directions: From I-84, take Exit 7 and follow Rte. 7 north to Rte. 202 (formerly 25) through New Milford. Proceed 8 mi. to New Preston then 1½ mi. to inn on Rte. 45.

CURTIS HOUSE
Woodbury, Connecticut

The Curtis House opened in 1754 and is reputed to be the oldest inn in Connecticut. There have been quite a few changes and alterations over the years, and many different owners. However, since four of them, all unrelated, were named "Curtis," I believe this is an appropriate name. The present owner is redhaired Gary Hardisty, himself a lifelong resident of Woodbury and a member of a family that has operated the Curtis House since early 1950.

I visited it on a chilly Saturday afternoon in February after a pleasant snowfall the night before. Everything combined to make it idyllically New England. The countryside was at its best in a white mantle, and the towns and villages in northwest Connecticut, with 18th-century homes and churches, gleamed in the bright sunshine.

The drive from the Massachusetts Berkshires (Woodbury is in the Connecticut Berkshires) took about 90 minutes and I was eagerly anticipating lunch. As I opened the old front door, the heavenly odors of hearty New England cooking wafted toward me.

I walked through a narrow hallway, past the stairway to the lodging rooms on two floors above, and entered the low-ceilinged, heavily-beamed dining room. Waitresses were bustling about carrying trays laden with plates of beef pot pie, Yankee pot roast, roast beef hash, scallops, and blueberry pancakes. The room was filled with happy people including quite a few families of students at the local prep school. I was given a quiet table in the corner, and my visit to the Curtis House began in earnest.

My luncheon included a delicious fresh fruit and sherbet cup, hot muffins, and a beef pie. From the desserts, I chose an apple crisp which was served with vanilla ice cream. I noticed that the dinner menu offered these things and much more, including sweetbreads, roast beef, and quite a few fish dishes such as broiled bluefish.

I was delighted to discover that there were 18 lodging rooms in this old inn, many of them with canopied twin or double beds. Twelve of the rooms have private baths. There are four more modern rooms in the nearby Carriage House.

Later, I chatted with Gary Hardisty in the living room with the fireplace and wide floor boards. He explained that the large inn signs outside were the work of Wallace Nutting who included many of the Woodbury buildings in his book, *Connecticut the Beautiful*. Gary explained that Woodbury was one of the antiquing centers of New England and there were many, many antique shops on Routes 6 and 47. The Glebe House, which was the birthplace of the American Episcopal church, is only a ten-minute walk from the inn.

Gary explained that as a rule dinner reservations are not accepted with the exception of New Year's Eve, Mother's Day, Easter, and Thanksgiving.

I learned that almost everything on the extensive menu is prepared from scratch and the inn does all of its own baking. Those warm muffins at lunch really hit the spot.

After spending the remaining part of the afternoon browsing through the village, I left Woodbury and the Curtis House as the setting sun created great red and orange streaks over the snowy hills and the lights of the inn were already casting their warm beckoning glow. This was the way it's been for well over 200 years.

CURTIS HOUSE, Route 6 (Main St.), Woodbury, Conn., 06798; 203-263-2101. An 18-room village inn, 12 mi. from Waterbury. Open year-round. European plan. Lodgings include Continental breakfast. Lunch and dinner served daily except Christmas. No pets. Antiquing, skiing, tennis, platform tennis, horseback riding nearby. The Hardisty Family, Innkeepers.

Directions: From N.Y. take Sawmill River Pkwy. to I-84. Take Exit 15 from I-84 in Southbury. Follow Rte. 6 north to Woodbury. From Hartford take I-84 to Exit 17, follow Rte. 64 to Woodbury.

GRISWOLD INN
Essex, Connecticut

The Griswold Inn is proof of the old saying: "Nothing succeeds like success." When I mentioned this to innkeeper Bill Winterer, he laughed modestly and said, "I'm not so sure we're successful, but I know we're working very hard at what we're doing and we love it."

Bill first visited Essex and saw the inn when he was an officer candidate at nearby New London Coast Guard Academy. After a few years in the world of high finance, he and his wife Vicky decided to start life anew here as innkeepers.

"Can you imagine," he said, "Only five families have owned this building since 1776. It was the first three-story structure in Connecticut and except for a couple of small changes, it remains the same. The Tap Room was built in 1738 and was the first schoolhouse in Essex. It was rolled on logs down the main street to its present location by a team of oxen."

"Our revolutionary activities began here in Essex in 1776 when the *Oliver Cromwell,* a ship of war commissioned by the Continental Congress, was built in the Essex shipyards." said Bill. "However, the

greatest excitement came during the War of 1812 when the entire Essex fleet was destroyed in the harbor by British ships. The British officers occupied the Griswold Inn, and I understand the commanding officer spoke of it as being 'long on charm but short on plumbing.' I think we have the plumbing under control today."

Today, the Griswold Inn has within its many dining rooms and parlors a remarkable collection of marine paintings, prints, ship models, firearms, binnacles, ship's clocks, a potbellied stove, humorous posters and prints, a genuine popcorn machine, and heaven-knows-what-all.

"We have four major collections of considerable importance," Bill remarked. "There are the steamboat prints by Currier and Ives; the Antonio Jacobsen collection of marine oils; at least fifty-five ancient firearms which trace the development of the handgun and rifle since the fifteenth century; and a considerable collection of artifacts from the riverboat era. These are integrated throughout the dining rooms and public rooms of the inn. They contribute to the total inn experience. They have been assembled by previous innkeepers for over two centuries."

One of the dining rooms was constructed from an abandoned New Hampshire Bridge, and in still another, the walls rock back and forth creating the impression of being on board ship. Fresh flowers, warm woods, open fires, and candles abound, and for the guests' edification, there are different kinds of entertainment almost every evening.

Most of the twenty-two guest rooms at the "Gris" have private baths and are furnished in early Essex. A lovely home next door to the inn is being converted into two suites. On the street floor of this building, a comfortable living room with a woodburning fireplace and a game room will provide houseguests with space for conviviality and relaxation.

The menu is basically American with a wide selection of fresh and salt-water fish, also beef and lamb dishes, which have been popular in this country since its very beginning. A Hunt Breakfast is served every Sunday which includes great, long tables of fried chicken, herring, lamb, kidneys, eggs, grits, creamed chipped beef, and the inn's own special brand of 1776 sausage.

Besides being a waterfront town bustling with yachts, sailboats, cruisers, and shipyards, Essex also has many attractive shops. Some of these are located just across the street from the inn in Griswold Square, which is a group of restored late Colonial and early Federal buildings.

GRISWOLD INN, Main St., Essex, Conn. 06426; 203-767-0991. A 22-room inn in a waterside town, steps away from the Connecticut River, and located near the Eugene O'Neill Theatre, Goodspeed Opera House, Ivoryton Playhouse, Gillette Castle, Mystic Village, Valley Railroad and Hammonasset State Beach. Most rooms with private baths. European plan. Complimentary Continental breakfast served daily to inn guests. Lunch and dinner served daily to travelers. Hunt breakfast served Sundays. Closed Christmas Eve and Christmas Day. Day sailing on inn's 44-foot ketch by appointment. Bicycles, tennis, and boating nearby. Victoria and William G. Winterer, Innkeepers.

Directions: From I-95 take Exit 69 and travel north on Rte. 9 to Exit 3, Essex. Turn right at stop light and follow West Ave. to center of town. Turn right onto Main St. and proceed down to water and inn.

TOWN FARMS INN
Middletown, Connecticut

Almost a year had passed since my last visit to the Town Farms Inn. Once again, following Bill Winterer's directions, I turned off Route 9 at Silver Street in Middletown, and followed the road through the Connecticut Valley Hospital complex. Cresting the hill, I looked down into the valley next to the Connecticut River, and there was the mellowed-red-brick building with which, by this time, I was quite familiar.

I walked into the parlor with its burning fireplace already sending forth a cheery glow against the chill of a mid-December afternoon. In one corner was a striking Christmas tree with small glistening white lights, red bows, and gold garlands and ornaments. I settled down into a deep sofa and immediately ordered a cup of tea — it seemed most appropriate in this elegant atmosphere that reminded me of an English country house-hotel.

This time it was Vicky Winterer who was able to join me for a few moments before we both went over to nearby Essex, Connecticut, to share the excitement of the tree-lighting ceremonies at the Griswold Inn.

"Bill and I have had such a wonderful experience here during the past year. The decorating is complete and we're pleased with the appearance of the grounds." "Of course," she said, as she set her teacup down on the mahogany table, "we still have more plans."

We strolled into the American Indian room which has very low ceilings and beautifully mellowed exposed posts and beams. The ladder-back chairs add a harmonious note. Twin fireplaces were decorated with Christmas garlands and white lights, and all of the candelabras were entwined with garlands of holly. There were red roses in vases on each table.

It was a most interesting contrast to walk into the River Room which is almost two stories high with magnificent chandeliers, a Palladian window, and a full view of the river and shore beyond. Vicky, referring to the terrace said, "We serve lunches out there during the summer, and everyone applauds when a train goes by." The inner wall has a new mural which depicts a scene on the river around 1865. The light blue walls are enhanced with beautiful green garlands, and in a little balcony at one end, a stringed trio was beginning to tune up for the evening's entertainment. "We find chamber music most appropriate, but we also have other types as well," she remarked.

Although the Town Farms Inn is at present a restaurant only, Vicky commented on the plans for twelve lodging rooms on the second and third floor. "I'm just not sure when we'll be able to undertake this major project," she said, "but Bill and I are both very excited at the prospect."

Besides the ambience of the Town Farms Inn, its popularity is quite obviously based on the menu. There are a lot of New England dishes, such as Boston scrod, bluefish, lemon sole and Cape Cod scallops. I also noted roast Canadian quail, hare cooked in wine and fresh mushrooms, chicken Cordon Bleu, and beef Stroganoff. There's a handy children's menu, too.

We returned to the parlor once again, and I noticed a rack of newspapers including the *Wall Street Journal,* the *New York Times*, the *Hartford Courant,* the *Wesleyan Argus,* the *Christian Science Monitor,* and the *National Review.* "It sort of reminds me of a club," I remarked.

"Funny you should mention that," she said, "many people who come here say that it has a 'club' feeling. Part of the reason may be that we have quite a few Wesleyan University faculty here both for lunch and dinner, and we do host small dinner parties for the college faculty and staff."

TOWN FARMS INN, Silver St., Middletown, Conn. 06457; 203-347-7438. A riverside restaurant just a few minutes from the center of Middletown. Lunch and dinner served daily except Christmas Eve and Christmas Day. Wesleyan Univ. nearby. Long Island Sound about 40 min. away. Bill and Vicky Winterer, Innkeepers.

Directions: From I-91 follow Rte. 9 south to Middletown and take Exit 12. Follow signs to Town Farms Inn.

MOUNTAIN VIEW INN
Norfolk, Connecticut

In a place of honor on the pantry shelf of my Berkshire farmhouse there sits a jar of some delicious-looking (and tasting) honey that would delight even the gods! The label reads: "The Aviary, Mountain View Inn." Over the years that I have been visiting Karl Jokinen, I have returned home with beautiful loaves of freshly baked bread, jars of pickles and preserves, and extra pieces of apple pie, *ad infinitum.* The honey is just another example of Karl's wide range of interest.

"I use a great deal of honey in my cooking" he said. "It is far superior to sugar in most respects. We've also been doing a lot of canning since we have been blessed with so many vegetables, fruits, pumpkins, and the like. I like to keep busy, and believe me, I've been busy all fall."

Beekeeping is just one of Karl's many talents. For one thing, he is a collector and repairer of old clocks, and the walls of the Mountain View Inn are enhanced by many of his prized timepieces — I've mentioned several times the one that runs backwards.

He built the small tables in the parlors from old sewing machines. They have all been refinished, the iron work has been repainted, and they make excellent *tête-à-tête* tables. All of this is aside from his considerable talent as a chef, which is expressed in the extensive menu of the inn. Karl's cuisine includes many original dishes, and I'm crazy about his roast duckling.

On the most recent visit, I drove down from Stockbridge through the Berkshire and Litchfield hills across Route 44 from Canaan to Norfolk. The houses with their Christmas trees and gaily colored lights, and all the Christmas decorations were spreading the holiday spirit. Even as in other years when I stepped to the front door, there was now-grown-up Jennifer Jokinen decorating the mantelpiece with Christmas cards. The tree was trimmed and some of the family presents were under it. The stockings were hung on the mantel and there were old-fashioned Christmas ornaments, with little arrangements of choir boys, reindeer, and Santa Clauses decorating the room.

This time it was another happy reunion, enhanced by meeting Linda and Gary Roth from Baldwin, Long Island, enthusiastic followers of *CIBR.* We had a long talk about their visit to Blueberry Hill with Martha and Tony Clark. I understand that the Roths also spent New Year's Eve at the Overlook Inn in Canadensis, Pennsylvania.

The Mountain View Inn is a rambling white house sitting at the top of a hill, just up the road from the Yale Summer School of Music in Norfolk. It has broad lawns and many trees and flowers. Norfolk is on the Hartford Road which links southern Connecticut and the Berkshires. It's quite ideal for a country holiday.

The lodging rooms, which have been redecorated and refurnished recently, are larger than usual and, because of the convenient distance from New York, are much in demand.

While we were all talking, laughing, and eating that evening, Jennifer Jokinen seemed to be everywhere at once, supplying fresh cups of coffee and more cookies. Joan confided to me that she is really a "born" innkeeper. "She has done just about everything there is to do here, including helping Karl in the kitchen. She wants to be a chef."

Although they were all saddened by the passing of Joan's mother Helen in 1979, the years have dealt well with the Jokinen family and their little inn in northwest Connecticut. Joan's father continues to be very much a part of inn activities.

Mountain View has been included in *CIBR* since 1969.

MOUNTAIN VIEW INN, Norfolk, Conn. 06058; 203-542-5595. A 7-room village inn, 40 mi. west of Hartford in the picturesque Litchfield Hills. European plan. Breakfast and dinner served daily to travelers except Mondays and Christmas Day. Open year-round. Golf, tennis, hiking, swimming, mountain climbing, bicycles, ice fishing, Alpine and xc skiing nearby. Karl and Joan Jokinen, Innkeepers.

Directions: Norfolk is on U.S. 44 which runs east-west. North-south roads which intersect 44 include U.S. 7, I-91, and U.S. 22. Inn is located off Rte. 44, ¼ mi. on 272 South.

SILVERMINE TAVERN
Norwalk, Connecticut

I wish that everyone could visit the Silvermine Tavern on such a day as I had on my last visit. It was mid-August, but a high pressure system from Canada had cooled our hot, humid air to a more bearable temperature. The sunshine was brilliant, and the sky was a clear blue as I drove down a tree-lined street through the residential section of Norwalk to the country crossroads where the Silvermine Tavern and Country Store are located. The Silvermine can be difficult to find and the first-time traveler has to follow the directions very carefully.

It was late afternoon, still a bit early for dinner. I walked through the lobby and found my way to the outer deck for dining which overlooks the mill pond and waterfall. I watched the ducks circle and play in the vicinity of a single white swan who floated serenely, apparently unaware of the majestic picture he was presenting. The sun shone through the trees as they towered over the deck, creating a dappled pattern on the tables and gleaming silverware.

The deck was built around the trees with holes cut in the floor to allow the trees to continue to grow comfortably. There were even rubber cushions lining the holes to prevent injury to the trees as they swayed in the wind. What a pleasant place to relax in the warm afternoon sun.

During the chilly months guests can enjoy the cozy atmosphere of the several different dining areas all of which are decorated with antique oil paintings, prints, wooden farm implements, and other artifacts of our agrarian heritage. There are fireplaces and many old tables and booths conducive to quiet conversation.

The lodging rooms at this inn are typical of many country inn rooms I have seen. They are from medium to small in size, furnished with antique country furniture, and have neither television nor telephones. Lodgings are scattered through the various buildings of the Tavern complex.

At dinner that evening Frank Whitman pointed out some of the offerings on the menu: "There are quite a few New England dishes," he said, "including Indian pudding, bread pudding, honey buns, native schrod, lobsters, scallops, and oysters. Thursday night, we have a buffet that includes roast beef, corned beef, and fried chicken. On Wednesday and Friday night during the summer, there's a barbeque, and our Sunday brunch buffet has as many as twenty-five different offerings on the big tables over there."

(A word about desserts: save room for cream pies, homemade fruit pies, and cakes!)

"By the way," he continued, "we find more and more people seeking our country inn atmosphere for weddings. Some come from as far as New York to be married here."

Silvermine Tavern has been in *CIBR* since 1975.

SILVERMINE TAVERN, Perry Ave., Norwalk, Ct. 06850; 203-847-4558. A 10-room country inn in the residential section of Norwalk. Long Island Sound and beaches 6 mi. away. European plan includes Continental breakfast. Lunch and dinner served to travelers daily. Open year-round. Closed Christmas Day and Tuesdays during winter. Golf, tennis, and fishing nearby. Francis C. Whitman, Innkeeper.

Directions: From New York or New Haven via I-95, take Exit 15. Pick up the new Rte. 7 going north. At the end of Rte. 7 (approx. 1 mi.) turn right, go to first stoplight, turn right. At next stoplight by firehouse turn right onto Silvermine Ave. Proceed down Silvermine Ave. about 2 mi. to Tavern. From I-84 and Danbury take old Rte. 7 south to Norwalk. Watch for Kelly Greens ½ mi. south of Merritt Pkwy. on the left, turn right on Perry Ave. opposite Kelly Greens. Follow Perry Ave. 2 mi. to Tavern. From Merritt Pkwy. take Exit 39 south on old Rte. 7 and follow directions above.

WHITE HART INN
Salisbury, Connecticut

"Northwestern Connecticut has names like Litchfield, Kent, Cornwall Bridge, Sharon, and Salisbury. There are winding roads, picket fences, old Colonials, horses, high hedges, and an appreciation for fine leathers and imported tweeds. The village of Salisbury sums it all up very nicely, and plump in the middle of it is the White Hart Inn, and the adjoining Country Store.

"There was a memorable day about six months ago when I held a five-minute conversation with the wooden Indian at the entrance of this Country Store, thinking it was Innkeeper John Harney (there is a resemblance).

"John says of the White Hart Inn: 'We're as New England as Mom's apple pie.' He ought to know. Unlike Ethan Allen, the hero of Fort Ticonderoga, who went from Salisbury to Vermont, John went the other way—from Vermont to Salisbury.

"The White Hart is a rambling old place with many fireplaces and chimney corners. The guest rooms are big and comfortable, and the food is plentiful. Sunday night buffets bring out many of the interesting people who have migrated to both the Litchfield Hills and the Berkshires from the metropolitan area. A lot of them have had their first taste of real New England as a result of staying at the White Hart on an earlier weekend visit.

"The Country Store is a replica of a similar emporium of 75 years ago, and sells all of the gimcracks, candles, soaps, spices, penny candy, etc., that we have come to associate with the late 1890s. However, I noted that there are quite a few new gadgets that may well be considered gimcracks in another hundred years. I have always found it very difficult just to browse and not to buy."

The above paragraphs are what I wrote in 1968 on one of my very first visits to the White Hart Inn. Everything I wrote then is true today, the only difference being that the White Hart has since celebrated its 100th birthday, and John Harney insists that he has been there at least 110 years!

Over the past few years I have described John beating me at checkers (I'm sure he's honest but why does he win every time?), John beating me at darts (I know he practices on the side), and John giving me history lessons about the lost community called Dudleytown. I have described the gingerbread village which is on display at the inn during every Christmas season, and also John's successes and failures in the world of politics.

I should make a mention of the fact that John is true to his last by offering not only traditional New England country fare on the menu, but also an extensive oriental menu as well including Peking duck, sweet and sour pork, hot spicy, tangy chicken ball and Buddhist delight vegetables. As John says, "They are all hot, spicy dishes, but you can order without the hot." For some years now, John has also been the chief blender and distributor of Sarum tea which is imported from many of the exotic countries of the world.

Just as John Harney and the White Hart are a tradition in northwest Connecticut, I guess one might say they are also a tradition in *Country Inns and Back Roads,* since they were both in the first edition in 1966!

WHITE HART INN, Salisbury, Conn. 06068; 203-435-2511. A 25-room village inn, 55 mi. west of Hartford. European plan. Breakfast, lunch, dinner served to travelers daily. Alpine and xc skiing, ski-jumping, golf, swimming nearby. John Harney, Innkeeper.

Directions: Exit the Taconic Pkwy. at Millbrook, N.Y. Proceed east on U.S. 44 to Salisbury. Inn is located at Jct. of U.S. 44 and 41.

Massachusetts

NEWBURYPORT, MASSACHUSETTS

"Newburyport is known as a Yankee city." I could hardly fault such a description. I saw it on a cool and windy January weekend when a bright sun provided direct lighting for its handsome homes and mansions, and reflected the whitecaps stirred up on the Merrimack River where the gulls swooped and scolded, and the wind caused all of us to huddle closer to the warm, red brick Federalist buildings on Waterfront Park and State Street.

When America was young and Yankee skippers were winning an international reputation for clever bargaining, Newburyport was one of our country's leading towns. Profits from fishing, ship-building, foreign commerce, and the coastal trade swelled the local coffers, and successful citizens vied with each other in building costly mansions filled with treasures from around the world.

Today, many of the early Newburyport homes with their matching fences and widow's walks, classic doorways and delicately carved woodwork still survive. The three-mile trip along High Street is, in many ways, a journey into the past. Along this route, it is said, there can be found in their original locations more buildings from the seventeenth, eighteenth, and early nineteenth centuries than along any similar street in the country. Like sections of Providence, Alexandria, Charleston, Concord, Natchez, Woodstock (Vt.), and Deerfield, careful and painstaking preservation and restoration in Newburyport help to keep some of the past vibrantly alive.

In addition to the delights of strolling around the town, Newburyport offers the natural attractions of the Parker River National Wildlife Refuge which is located on nearby Plum Island. It is a home for thousands of birds, a variety of mammals, reptiles, amphibians, fish, and plants. Because of the wildlife, the beautiful beaches, salt marshes, sand dunes and thickets, the island also appeals to several hundred thousand visitors each year who fish, birdwatch, hike, bicycle, sightsee, snowshoe, cross-country ski, hunt, pick cranberries and beach plums, clam, beachcomb, and photograph and study wildlife in its natural habitat.

Visiting hours are from dawn to dusk year-round but, as a result of some unusually intelligent planning, the number of vehicles allowed to enter the Refuge is determined by the available parking spaces. Motorists may be turned away after 9:00 a.m. during pleasant weather.

For further information about Newburyport and its environs contact the Newburyport Chamber of Commerce, (01950) which provides potential visitors with excellent brochures.

One further word . . . John P. Marquand, writing about New-buryport as his favorite town, advises his readers that Newburyport is not a museum town, but a vital, tolerant place and still able to keep up with the times "if you get to know it." He suggests walking along High Street to enjoy the great three-storied houses; passing the frog pond; and visiting the burying ground. He further suggests a slow walk down State Street to Market Square past the fire station to the old waterfront and the river. He observes that almost everyone in Newburyport walks slowly: "You can't help liking Newburyport if you take time enough to see it."

MORRILL PLACE
Newburyport, Massachusetts

Monroe was purring contentedly. I was purring contentedly. Small wonder, because we were both lounging on the couch in front of a wonderfully roaring fire, in the library of the Morrill Place listening to Rose Ann Hunter's account of Christmas in Newburyport. Monroe, I might add, was looking deep into my eyes from an advantageous position on my chest about four inches from my nose.

"Christmas is fantastic here," Rose Ann said, as her husband Paul put another log on the fire. "Santa arrives on November 25 by boat, and there's a parade and tree lighting on Market Square. The festivities continue throughout the month. All the historical houses are decorated for the holidays and the street lamps are festooned with garlands and bright bows. The Cushing House which is the headquarters of the Newburyport Historical Society is open for a number of afternoons and has been decorated by the many garden clubs. There are house tours, concerts, a piñata party, and hymn-sings throughout the month. On Christmas Eve, everyone goes to church in the New England tradition."

I was seeing Newburyport through the eyes of this very enthusiastic young woman who, with her husband Paul and her daughter Kristin, moved here a few years ago. In addition to showing me through the graceful Newburyport mansion which has been turned into a warm and receptive guest house, she was kind enough to take me on a comprehensive tour of the town and the Parker River National Wildlife Refuge on Plum Island.

113

"This mansion was built in 1806," Rose Ann said, "by Kathyrn and William Hoyt. The owners include three Newburyport sea captains; that's why there's a widow's walk. We have ten guest rooms and four-and-a-half bathrooms, and we are always open, even through the holidays."

We were joined for a moment by an ebullient Irish setter who answered to the name of Kerrie. He was immediately hugged around the neck by Kristin, who is an energetic five-year-old.

Earlier in the afternoon, my house tour started at the front of the house in the formal living room which is adorned with oriental *objets d'art.* I marveled at the double-hung staircase with the six-inch risers. "This was built at the time when women wore hoop skirts," Rose Ann explained. "Double-hung staircases are rare, even in Newburyport."

Many of the bedrooms have fireplaces and were being redecorated with distinctive period wallpapers. I saw my first "Indian shutters" which, when closed, left a narrow horizontal open slit. "In the 18th century, the real danger was from marauding pirates," she explained.

My room was named after Daniel Webster who was a frequent visitor to the house. There was a remarkably preserved print of Mr. Webster over the fireplace, and the furnishings were typical of other bedrooms, including an antique deacons' bench, two twin beds, each embellished with a pineapple motif, a lovely old chest of drawers, and a Boston rocker.

An unobtrusive, but welcome, contemporary touch will be the modest swimming pool to be constructed in the garden area immediately adjacent to the sheltered porch in the rear.

Our tour, as so many do, ended up in the kitchen where we had a refreshing cup of tea and I learned that Paul and Rose Ann were originally from Youngstown, Ohio. Paul is a horse-trainer by profession. Rose Anne explained that the breakfasts include juice, coffee or tea, cereal, fresh baked rolls and English muffins, topped off by "mother's strawberry jam."

Sue Caroll from the Mainstay Inn in Cape May, New Jersey, was the first to recommend the Morrill Place to me. "Tom and I liked it very much and we know you will too!"

How could I help but like the Morrill Place with a cat named Monroe?

MORRILL PLACE, 209 High St., Newburyport, Ma. 01950; 617-462-2808. A 10-room guest house on one of Newburyport's beautiful, residential avenues. All rooms share bath with one other room. Lodgings include Continental breakfast, only meal offered.

Open every day in year. Within a very convenient distance of all of the Newburyport historical and cultural attractions, and Plum Island Wildlife Refuge. Swimming pool to be constructed. Other recreational facilities nearby. Rose Ann Hunter, Innkeeper.

Directions: From Boston follow I-95 north and take Historic Newburyport exit and follow Rte. 113. This becomes High St. Follow it for about 2 miles. Inn is on right hand side at corner of Johnson and High St. From Maine: exit I-95 for Historic New-buryport and follow above directions.

WINDSOR HOUSE
Newburyport, Massachusetts

"How," asked the full-bearded Fritz, a skillet in one hand and reaching for the egg bowl with the other, "would you like your eggs this morning?"

"Scrambled, by all means," I replied.

Meanwhile, his wife Judith set out two more places on the great oval table in the sunken kitchen of the Windsor House, as other guests began to join us. Fritz continued our conversation even as he applied the whisk to the golden contents of the pan.

"The Windsor House was built in 1796 as both a residence and a ships' chandlery. The kitchen here was the original shipping and receiving room as you can see from those big outside doors." He pointed to the ceiling saying, "There is a series of trapdoors up there

115

which go to the fourth story of the house, where there is the original hoist wheel.

"The brick wall with the fireplace is part of a fire wall that also goes to the top story and separates the warehouse section from the living section. The posts and beams throughout the entire house were built by ships' carpenters, the same men who built the clipper ships."

The kitchen is really the pulse of the Windsor House. Not only do all the guests gather around in the morning to enjoy Fritz's prandial skill, but as Judith says, "It's the place where we all gather at any time during the day and tell tall tales and get acquainted. It's part of what we're all about—getting acquainted."

In this process of "getting acquainted," I discovered that Fritz, Judith, and I have one very strong interest in common: the theatre. In fact, Fritz and Judith met under most romantic circumstances when she was a director and he was an actor. They spoke warmly of The Playhouse, located in nearby Amesbury, which is open for almost the entire year, even on winter weekends. It's just one of dozens of things to do in Newburyport in all seasons.

On a tour of this impressive old building, we were accompanied by a silver toy poodle named Lillabet Silver Jubilee (named for Queen Elizabeth), and two cats: Sir Thomas Moore, and Erasmus of Rotterdam, who tagged along for the fun.

There were interesting contrasts between the rooms on the warehouse side of the firewall and the residential section. For example, one of the original storerooms, now converted to a bedroom, has a board wall on which some rough inventory figures written in chalk dating from the 1800s have been preserved. The other two walls are the beautiful original brick. It has attractive furnishings. Rooms on the residential side tend to have wooden paneling and other graceful features that would befit a residence.

There are six guest rooms, of which two have their own private bathrooms. The other four share one bathroom. I saw terry cloth bathrobes here for guests who have to use the bath "down the hall."

After going to the very top floor where I could look out of the bedroom windows and see the houses that survived the Newburyport fire of 1811, we returned to the kitchen where Fritz described the arrangement for dinners at the Windsor House.

"We can serve one dinner party a night, from two to six people. We require a three-day advance reservation. I work with the host and hostess to design the menu for the occasion. For instance, tonight we are doing a dinner party for two. It will be served in our formal dining room and we will use the sterling, crystal, and china which were our grandparents' wedding present to us, which in turn were wedding presents to them."

The door opened and two guests who had been doing the walking tour of Newburyport with the Clipper Trail folder, returned for a warming cup of coffee and a little conversation. "We decided to stay for two more days, there's just too much to see."

We all readily agreed.

WINDSOR HOUSE, 38 Federal St., Newburyport, Ma. 01950; 617-462-3778. A 6-room guest house located in the historic port section of Newburyport. Open every day during the year. Breakfast served to all guests; dinner by special 3-day advance reservation. A few steps from the Merrimack River Valley and a short distance from the Atlantic Ocean, Plum Island, and Parker River Wildlife Refuge. Within walking distance of all the historic buildings of Newburyport. Other available recreation includes deep sea fishing, swimming, art galleries, and year-round theatre. Some trundle beds available for children, no cribs or playpens. Parents must provide for infant care. Small housebroken dogs permitted. Fritz and Judith Crumb, Innkeepers.

Directions: From Boston and Maine: From I-95 use Exit to Rte. 113, turn right onto High St. (Rte. 1A) and proceed three miles to Federal St., turn left. Inn on left across from Old South Church (Rte. 1A is scenic drive from either Boston or New Hampshire).

RALPH WALDO EMERSON
Rockport, Massachusetts

"When it comes to rocks, ocean, and sky, I think we have more than our share," said Gary Wemyss. Gary pointed out to the breakwater about three miles in front of the "Emerson," as it is known to most of its guests, "In 1946 it was about three times the length it is now, but the storms and heavy seas have beaten it down until now in places it is barely visible. The far left end originally formed a harbor of refuge for sailing ships, but the builders ran out of money and gave up the construction.

"There is a reef out there beyond the breakwater known as Dry Salvages which was an inspiration for the T.S. Eliot poem. The town is trying to get the federal government to rebuild the breakwater because it protects us in winter's heavier storms."

Preoccupation with reefs, the ocean, and the swooping gulls is one of the big attractions at this country inn in Pigeon Cove. It is run by Gary Wemyss, the son of the innkeepers at the Yankee Clipper, which is about a mile away. The two inns make an interesting contrast, because the Emerson is built along somewhat conventional lines and has many rooms overlooking the water, whereas the Clipper is tucked away among the rocks overlooking the water and is much smaller.

Gary pointed to two lighthouses which, he explained, were located on Thatchers Island. "They are the only twin lighthouses on the eastern seaboard. However, only one of them has a working light. People like to sit out here in the evening and watch the stars over the ocean and the circling beam from the lighthouse.

"Besides the swimming pool, sauna, and whirlpool baths, one of the favorite activities of our guests is to join me in our little cabin sailboat. I'm always looking for any excuse to take it out, and it certainly provides a different view of Pigeon Cove and Rockport. I believe I took our friend Jim Mellow out in it a few years ago."

Gary explained that the guests include people of all interests and ages. "I think they mix well here," he said. "We find that the easiest thing is to not make any distinction in any way. Everyone seems to enjoy the things that are here — the village, the shore, and of course, the proximity to the sea. There is a real feeling of being relaxed and away from urban pressures, and I think that draws a lot of people together. It is such a relief just to have a few days' holiday."

Well, any kind of a holiday usually includes an emphasis on food, and at the Emerson the emphasis is on food from the nearby ocean waters, especially lobster. "People come to this part of New England for lobster, so we try to serve it as frequently as possible," Gary explained. "Sometimes our guests go up to the Clipper for dinner or people staying there come down here. It is part of the advantage of having two inns run by the same family."

Ocean, rocks, sky, reefs, lighthouses, bobbing lobster pots, plenty of homecooked food — all close to Rockport, Massachusetts, one of the most picturesque towns on the New England coast — that's what the Ralph Waldo Emerson is all about. It has provided vacationers with diversion and relaxation for many years. It has been included in *CIBR* since 1973.

RALPH WALDO EMERSON, 1 Cathedral Ave., Rockport, Mass. 01966; 617-546-6321. A 36-room oceanside inn, 40 mi. from Boston. Modified American and European plans. Breakfast and dinner served to travelers daily. Snack bar luncheon in season. Season: July 1 through Labor Day. Open Memorial Day through Nov. 1. No pets. Pool, sauna, and whirlpool bath on grounds. Tennis, golf nearby. Courtesy car Gary Wemyss, Innkeeper.

Directions: Take I-95 to Rte. 128 to 127 (Gloucester). Proceed 6 mi. on Rte. 127 to Rockport and continue to Pigeon Cove.

ROCKPORT, MASSACHUSETTS

Rockport has been an artist colony for over forty years. Once it was a sleepy fishing village, but then it was "discovered" by artists during the Depression of the thirties. Some of the most important people in painting have either visited or lived in Rockport. Now it attracts all kinds of creative people, including photographers, writers, and craftsmen, as well as artists.

The Rockport Art Association's annual exhibitions are always a big event. Rockport has been referred to as one of America's most paintable locations with its open ocean, snug harbors, picturesque fishing boats, and great, gorgeous rocks.

The town is filled with fetching little houses with beguiling roof lines, inviting gardens, and winding, elm-shaded streets. Furthermore, I am sure there must be at least a hundred different fascinating shops in this little seaside community.

How fortunate it is that the railroad from Boston has several trains each day.

YANKEE CLIPPER
Rockport, Massachusetts

The granite boulders loomed around me as I gingerly negotiated the rocky path, grateful that I had worn my rubber-soled deck shoes. With the aid of some strategically placed rope railings, and following Fred Wemyss's directions, I picked my way down to the water's edge.

On this warm September morning it was like a totally different world. There were small tidal pools in which I could see bright green moss and several species of marine life. Overhead a few gulls dipped and swooped, bright spots of white against the clear blue sky. I sat with my back against a warm granite boulder, enjoying the sun and salty sea air.

At dinner the previous evening I had heard the whole story of the inn. In 1946, Fred and Lydia Wemyss were here on vacation, when the idea of turning a private estate into an inn occurred to them. They have been here ever since.

"These have been wonderful years for us," Fred told me. "Our son, Gary, and our daughter, Barbara, have both grown up here. Gary stayed in the innkeeping business with us and is the manager of the Ralph Waldo Emerson in Pigeon Cove. The most satisfactory part of innkeeping has been the hundreds of people who have become good friends." Because Fred and Lydia are so warm and outgoing, many of the guests have been returning year after year.

The inn complex consists of three buildings. The first is the original building overlooking the water where the dining area is located, and where there are many large rooms with a sea view. A few paces away, there is the Quarter Deck which has an unobstructed view of the ocean and gardens. The third is called the Bullfinch House and is noted particularly for its architectural beauty. It is of Colonial Greek design named for its designer who also created the Boston State House.

My reverie was broken by a sailboat's passing not fifty yards from where I sat sunning myself. I decided to return to the inn and went back up the path to the grassy lawn with its carefully tended flower beds, the beautiful terrace, and the grape arbor. Lunch was being served under the shade of the old New England apple trees.

As I strolled past the pool, whom should I meet but Debbie Tallet, whose family runs the Millhof Inn in Stephentown, New York. She was a member of the Yankee Clipper staff and was having a wonderful time. "I just love it here," she said.

Fred, who is a seasoned amateur limerick composer, presented all of us at the innkeepers' meeting at Pleasant Hill with this bit of meaningful doggerel:

> "A seasoned old traveler named Flynn
> Said, 'of all of the places I've been
> To wine in, to dine in,
> To have a good time in,
> You can't beat an old country inn.'"

The Yankee Clipper has been included in *CIBR* since 1973.

YANKEE CLIPPER, Rockport, Mass. 01966; 617-546-3407. An intimate 26-room inn on the sea, 40 mi. from Boston. European plan available year-round. Modified American plan from May 15 to July 1 and Sept. 5 to Nov. 1. Breakfast and dinner served daily. Lunch served during July and August. Meals served to travelers by reservation only. No pets. Ocean view, shoreline walks, many antique shops and other stores nearby. Fred and Lydia Wemyss, Innkeepers.

Directions: Take I-95 to Rte. 128 to 127 (Gloucester). Proceed 6 mi. on Rte. 127 to Rockport and continue to Pigeon Cove.

CONCORD, MASSACHUSETTS IN BRIEF

The town of Concord is unique in all of America, because it has three famous periods in its history, any one of which would be a sufficient claim to distinction. The first began more than three hundred years ago in the days when the early Puritans made it the first Massachusetts settlement away from the tidewater. Next, Concord was the scene of the first battle of the War of the Revolution and, finally, during the nineteenth century, it was the home of Emerson, Alcott, Thoreau, and Hawthorne, the great authors of the period known as the "Flowering of New England."

It is not just a museum, but a beautiful elm-shaded town of homes, schools, farms, and businesses. An intellectually curious traveler could spend three days in Concord, wandering through its streets, admiring the lovely old New England houses, and literally bathing in its history.

Along the Lexington Road, originally called "The Bay Way," stone walls dividing the first grants may still be seen, and a dozen or more of the present-day houses contain within their walls the hand-hewn timbers of the early one-room houses. It is also the home of the famous Concord grape. Developed here from native seedlings, the Concord grape has become the foundation of farming prosperity in parts of western New York and California, although they are no longer grown commercially.

A great sense of antiquity is felt very strongly in the Hill Burying Ground where the epitaphs recite at length the qualities which were then considered virtues.

THE HAWTHORNE INN
Concord, Massachusetts

Let me quote from a letter I received early in 1979 from a reader who had been touring New England: "In Concord, we spent the night at the Hawthorne Inn. It is located down the road from the Alcott House on the route south to Lexington. The owner, Gregory Burch, came from Detroit about two or three years ago, bought this lovely old colonial home, and restored it to its original style.

"It was absolutely spotless with charming décor and off-beat paintings. The inn does not serve meals, but does offer a Continental breakfast which is included in the price. Gregory told us that a baker friend of his came in during the evening to bake the rolls which we enjoyed for our breakfast. They were served with heaps of fresh fruit, juices, plenty of butter and jams, and delicious coffee. We sat around a table in a lovely room with a fireplace and a lighted, built-in cabinet with some of Gregory's collection of primitive African and South American sculpture.

"Off the central hall was a Victorian sitting room with all the comforts of home available to those guests who wished to congregate there. There are five very attractive guest rooms. We found this experience delightful, and hope that you will be able to visit this spot sometime soon."

Well, visit, I did, and I was as delighted as that most considerate reader. I found that Gregory Burch was, indeed, a renaissance man, equally at home in front of the easel, with sculptor's clay, at an archeological dig, or entertaining his guests at the morning breakfast table. At present, he is also probably the youngest innkeeper in *CIBR.*

In Gregory's words: "This house was originally a private residence, probably built around 1870 and I'm quite sure this was Hawthorne's property. When I bought it, it had been empty for a while, but had been used for a number of years as a nursing home. I had to remove some bad carpentry work and refinished, repainted, and restored the house, room by room. I've decorated it with a great many of my own paintings and pieces which I think sort of fit into the ever-changing moods of Concord itself."

The Hawthorne Inn has very good-sized bedrooms, beds with pleasant patchwork quilts, and braided treads on the staircase; many rooms have hidden features, such as outside balconies.

Can it be that Gregory Burch, in his little bed-and-breakfast inn, is carrying on the literary and artistic thrust of nineteenth-century Concord? I can't help but feel that those great men who lived, worked, and left their stamp forever on the world and Concord, would nod in approbation of this young man. He says of Concord, "It's a good atmosphere. You are, indeed, recognized for doing your own thing and respected for it, but within certain confines, because everyone has his own little hedges. I live and work here in perfect composure. Keeping a country inn is exactly what I need. It is the best thing that ever happened to me."

Gregory Burch, you and the Hawthorne Inn belong in Concord.

THE HAWTHORNE INN, 462 Lexington Road, Concord, Ma. 01742; 617-369-5610. A 5-room bed-and-breakfast village inn approximately 19 mi. from Boston. Breakfast to houseguests is the only meal served. Open every day in the year. Within walking distance of all of the historic and literary points of interest in Concord. No pets. No credit cards. Limited facilities for young children, but ideal for young people who have an appreciation for history and literature. Gregory Burch, artist-in-residence, and Innkeeper.

Directions: From Rte. 128 (the beltway around Boston) use exit 2A (Lexington Rd.). Travel west 4½ mi. Hawthorne Inn is on the south side (left) across from the Hawthorne House. Available by public transportation from Boston.

LONGFELLOW'S WAYSIDE INN
South Sudbury, Massachusetts

Along with the Beekman Arms in Rhinebeck, New York, and the White Hart Inn in Salisbury, Connecticut, Longfellow's Wayside Inn has been in *Country Inns and Back Roads* since 1967. In many ways, it has helped me understand more fully the important role that history plays in the American country inn.

On an early spring evening, I was back at the inn having dinner with innkeeper Frank Koppeis and it seemed quite natural in such a historical setting for our thoughts to be turned backward in time. After all, the Wayside was one of the focal points of the events of the stirring days at the start of the American Revolution.

Frank was saying: "I'll bet Zeke Howe really had those Sudbury militiamen worked into a lather before they took off for Old North Bridge in Concord. He was the Colonel, you know, and I'll bet there was a lot of pounding on these old tables and shaking of fists in the direction of Boston. As they were nearing Concord, I believe it was the Colonel who is quoted as saying, 'If any blood has been shed, not one of the rascals shall escape.'"

"Gosh," I thought, "things like that happened here and the inn was already nearly seventy-five years old at that time!"

Today, the Wayside Inn, which became Longfellow's Wayside Inn as a result of the poet's famous "Tales From A Wayside Inn," is remarkably restored and preserved. It shares with the Beekman Arms the distinction of being one of the oldest continually operating inns in America.

The inn is set back from the road in a quiet countryside amidst the trees and meadows. Many's the morning I have heard pheasants in the nearby woods. It's hard to believe Copley Square is only 35 minutes away.

Among the famous rooms which are a part of the inn today are the old Bar Room, the Longfellow Parlor with much memorabilia of the famous poem, the Longfellow bedchamber with a pencil-post bed and canopy, the Early Kitchen, the Old Ballroom, and the Old Kitchen. Most of these rooms are still in public use.

Dinner that evening was Massachusetts duckling in orange sauce, some baked Cape Cod scallops, and baked Indian pudding with ice cream. The muffins were from meal, stone ground at the Old Grist Mill just down the road. I felt that if I were going Early American, I might as well go all the way!

Rooms at the Wayside Inn are furnished with antiques, but I'm happy to report that the beds are most comfortable and the conveniences have considerably improved since Ezekiel Howe's day. My favorite room is reached by a creaky staircase in the old part of the inn where the ceilings are quite low. I laid out my clothes very carefully on the chair in case Col. Howe should call *me* to arms, as well!

LONGFELLOW'S WAYSIDE INN, Wayside Inn Rd., off Rte. 20, South Sudbury, Mass. 01776; 617-443-8846. A 10-room historic landmark inn, midway between Boston and Worcester. Within a short distance of Concord, Lexington, and other famous Revolutionary War landmarks. European plan. Lunch and dinner served daily except Christmas. Breakfast served to overnight guests. Francis Koppeis, Innkeeper.

Directions: From the west, take Exit 11A from Mass. Tpke. and proceed north on 495 to Rte. 20. Follow Rte. 20 east to inn. From the east, take Exit 49 from Rte. 128. Follow Rte. 20 west to inn.

THE INN FOR ALL SEASONS
Scituate Harbor, Massachusetts

What do innkeepers do on their day off? On this particular day, a considerable group of innkeepers all came together at the Inn for All Seasons to renew old acquaintances and to enjoy one of Elaine Wondolowski's marvelous dinners. This particular meeting was something special, because a similar meeting planned the preceding year had to be canceled as a result of the great blizzard that had inundated all of the Massachusetts coast.

"I'm delighted that we have such a wonderful day, today," said Elaine. "I'm not at all superstitious; but I don't believe I could endure another ordeal like last year." We were all gathered in the parlor of the inn which is decorated in a mixture of turn-of-the-

century and Art Nouveau. The wallpaper is black with gold stripes and flocking; the corner cabinets have little china pieces; and there is a chest of drawers with a marble top. A ceramic zebra stands on the piano, and there are elegant beaded curtains at the window.

Elaine explained some of her philosophy: "Everything has to be pleasing. We try to have the colors and the mood of the season reflected in both the atmosphere and in the menu. It changes four times a year. We serve heartier meals in the fall and winter, and light, more delicate foods in the spring and summer. I think that we could call our cuisine 'Continental,' because it allows our chef Tom Jablonski, a graduate of the Culinary Institute, the opportunity to express his imagination with Spanish, French, Italian, and other European dishes."

Elaine warmed to her subject: "Tonight we're having crab crown pompadour which is one of our specialties; we originated this dish in our kitchen. We have it on the menu year-round. It's prepared in a casserole lined with buttered croutons and filled with an egg custard, seasoned with chives, and then filled with selected crabmeat. It is then inverted and looks like a crown, bejeweled with a pompadour sauce and chopped truffle. Another thing we do is to offer our guests the option of having salad *before* or *after* dinner. It is always served with a chilled fork and plate. We change the house dressing four times a year as well.

"We've originated a lot things in our kitchen, including chocolate cheesecake, and I guarantee you we make the best pecan pie anywhere. We've had requests from *Gourmet* magazine for the recipe many times. We always share our recipes. That includes the people who come to our dining seminars, which are held at various times during the year and enable our guests to talk directly to chef

Tom, who explains the dinner and discusses the preparation and presentation. Our manager, Bert Patterson is frequently the host."

Dinner was a rousing success—something that I know pleased both Tom and Elaine very much, because who could be more discriminating than keepers of other country inns? All of us spoke glowingly of the beautiful white dining room and the gleaming silverware and graceful stemware. There were so many little touches that make the room extremely attractive, both in the evening and for breakfast in the morning.

Elaine, of course, responded generously to the request for some of her recipes but when it came to the secret of the dessert, which was a trifle, she laughed and said, "Oh, trifles are simply a matter of inspiration."

Inspiration—there was certainly a generous amount of this highly desirable ingredient at the Inn for All Seasons.

The Inn for All Seasons has been included in *CIBR* since 1976.

INN FOR ALL SEASONS, 32 Barker Rd., Scituate Harbor, Mass. 02060; 617-545-6699. An 8-room inn in a picturesque south shore sea town, 32 mi. from Boston. Shared baths. European plan. Continental breakfast, lunch, and dinner served to travelers daily except Mondays. Reservations for all meals advised. Open year-round. Children over 12 years old and attended pets allowed. Bicycles, fishing, golf, swimming, tennis, antiquing, and deep-sea fishing nearby. Elaine Wondolowski, Innkeeper.

Directions: From Boston, take Southeast Expressway south to Rte. 3. Continue south on Rte. 3 to Exit 31. Turn left at bottom of ramp and take right on Rte. 123 at traffic light. Go approximately 8 mi. to traffic lights intersecting Rte. 3A. Come across Rte. 3A, and follow signs for Scituate Harbor. At end of town take a right turn at set of traffic lights on to Jericho Rd. Take second left after Pier 44 on to Barker Rd. The inn is two blocks up on the right.

CAPE COD

Cape Cod is one of the premier travel attractions of New England. It's a peninsula extending out into the Atlantic Ocean, which is shaped exactly like an arm in the position of flexing the biceps. The Cape was formed by glacial deposits, and a great deal of it is in sand dunes which are protected by the National Park Service. The inner Cape consists of the communities of Buzzard's Bay, Bourne, Falmouth, and Woods Hole. The middle Cape has Hyannis, Dennis, Brewster, Harwich, Harwich Port, and other similar towns. The outer Cape is Wellfleet, Truro, and Provincetown.

It takes about an hour to drive from Buzzard's Bay on the mainland to Provincetown on the Mid-Cape Highway, and much longer on the various attenuations of route 6A. The Cape is extremely popular during the two high summer months of July and August, and it is frequently very difficult to find overnight accommodations. The restaurants are quite apt to be totally reserved, especially on the weekends. The Cape particularly appeals to me in September and October, because the sun is still very high and the water is still warm enough for swimming. The Cape weather at this time is usually ideal. I can do my backroading, bicycling, and strolling in comparative solitude.

THE BRAMBLE INN
Brewster, Cape Cod, Massachusetts

"I believe, beyond a shadow of a doubt, that they are the ultimate 'inn T-shirts,'" I announced. Innkeepers Karen Etsell and Elaine Brennan were wearing said T-shirts as I lunched with them at The Bramble Inn. No ordinary T-shirts, these, with "The Bramble Inn" printed in green, rampant on a pink background—exactly matching, curiously enough, the pink and green décor of this inn. The tables are set with green placemats, and pink napkins are held in place by very attractive flowered rosebud napkin rings. These colors make an interesting contrast to the walls and woodwork which are sparkling white and the floorboards of differing widths which have been refinished to a warm brown patina. Further green accents are found in the plants hanging from the ceiling.

"Well, as far as we're concerned, it means that the inn has really 'arrived.'" Karen's eyes twinkled as she continued, "We also have inn letterheads in the same colors."

The full name for this inn is The Bramble Inn Gallery and Café. It's very obvious that Karen and Elaine have a great interest in art of various media, as can be seen in their collection of watercolors, oil paintings, lithographs, pastels, and wood lathe art which decorate the walls of the dining rooms. Elaine is an excellent photographer and not only do her photographs receive excellent reviews from local critics, but she has been the best-selling artist to be displayed at The Bramble Inn! On the other hand, Karen did the pen-and-ink drawing of the inn which is used on their stationery, and is an artist in her own right.

The waitress arrived with our main dish, and from the first bite I exclaimed with enthusiasm.

"I'm so glad you like it," said Elaine. "It's baked stuffed fillets of sole with a Mornay sauce. We've stuffed the sole with shrimp and chopped almond. It happens that baked stuffed fillets of sole is my favorite dish and I frequently order it when I'm dining out. This year we've added it to the menu, and we spent a wonderful winter perfecting it in our kitchen."

Other main dishes on the menu include chicken crêpes, crêpes St. Jacques, various and sundry cheese plates, Cape Cod clam chowder, and gourmet soup. These are all served with freshly baked bread right from the oven.

"Did you notice on the menu that Cape Cod Bramble is now a registered trademark?" Karen pointed to the green (naturally) menu which described the inn's Bramble as "an old-fashioned delicacy of chopped raisins and cranberries, gently sweetened and wrapped in tender pastry topped with vanilla ice cream." "And our quiche was written up in a local magazine as the 'Best quiche on Cape Cod,'" she asserted. "Some of our customers say it's the best quiche in the world."

There are two lodging rooms at The Bramble Inn. Both have flowered wallpaper and country furniture, and one has a double bed while the other has twin beds. Both of them share a bath. A Continental breakfast is served.

There have been a lot of very nice things happening at The Bramble Inn since my first visit in the fall of 1976. These attractive, alert women have combined their talents and hard work to create additional careers for themselves as successful innkeepers. Each year there has been something excitingly innovative. They're doing a marvelous job. I'm proud to include The Bramble Inn in *Country Inns and Back Roads.*

And now the real sign that they've arrived: Bramble Inn T-shirts!

THE BRAMBLE INN GALLERY AND CAFE, Route 6A, Main St., Brewster, Cape Cod, Ma. 02631; 617-896-7644. A village inn and art gallery in the heart of one of Cape Cod's northshore villages.

Lodgings include Continental breakfast. Lunch and dinner served daily except Mondays. Open May through October. Small, intimate inn does not meet the needs of most children. No pets. Swimming, sailing, water sports, golf, recreational, and natural attractions within a short drive. Adjacent to tennis club. No credit cards. Elaine Brennan and Karen Etsell, Innkeepers.

Directions: Take Exit 10 from Rte. 6. Follow the intersection of Rte. 6A (4 mi.). Turn right, one-tenth mile to inn.

COBB'S COVE
Barnstable Village, Cape Cod, Massachusetts

"That's the beach and harbor area out there, it's just a short and pleasant walk." Evelyn Chester and I had arrived at the top floor of Cobb's Cove, which is a very small, quiet inn in Barnstable Village on the north shore of Cape Cod. This particular room had a studio-type window which swept from the eaves almost to the top of the cathedral ceiling. Many of its features were also to be found in the other five lodging rooms, including massive exposed beams and posts, and natural wood walls and ceilings. Each has a full bath including a whirlpool tub, a dressing room, and private telephone lines which are available for extended stays. The bedroom furniture, draperies, and adornments harmonize beautifully with the colors and textures of the handsome wood. There are big fluffy towels reminiscent of those supplied by the paradors in Spain.

"At night it's fun to turn off the lights and look at the Cape Cod sky lit by the stars and moon, and to see the twinkling lights of towns in the distance," she remarked, as we returned to the first floor and the Keeping Room.

We were ushered through the dining room by an impressive cat named Fordham and a West Highland terrier, who answered to the name of Annie Laurie. There was a long trestle table where Evelyn and Henri-Jean, who was at that moment in the kitchen preparing dinner, serve their house guests. Floor-to-ceiling bookshelves displayed works on many subjects, sharing space with a wide variety of shell, mineral, and fossil collections. In one corner was a baby grand piano, and the strains of a Handel symphony wafted from a hi-fi system.

Henri-Jean, radiating good humor and the savory aromas of bluefish provencale, came out of the kitchen, and we all sat down in front of one of the most unusual fireplaces I've ever seen. "It's a Count Rumford fireplace," explained Henri-Jean. "You'll notice that it's quite shallow, but it was designed hundreds of years ago by a gentleman whose personal history would make a good book or movie. The design is such that it keeps the entire room bathed in generous heat. We have a book about the fireplace and its originator."

That was the beginning of a long and most enjoyable conversation which continued throughout the remainder of the beautiful sun-bathed December afternoon on Cape Cod. I heard all about how Henri-Jean, who is a civil engineer, designed, cut out, assembled, and physically built this beautiful colonial salt-box manor on its 1643 historical site. "Actually, Evelyn and I worked side by side in every phase of its design and construction," he said, sending a most loving look in her direction. "We've been open since 1976, but have maintained a restrained profile, acquiring our guests by personal referral. What we have here is a basic enjoyment of life and people, because everyone who visits us has something to share."

There is much to share, both at Cobb's Cove itself and in that particular section of Cape Cod. "We are on the low-key side of the Cape," asserted Evelyn with a smile. "Because it's more people-oriented rather than a resort section, most of the small craft shops like the weavers and the pottery and the Bird Barn are open year-round. We have many guests who come in the so-called off-season, and in many ways that's the best time. The beaches are even more beautiful because there's hardly anyone on them, except the seagulls. There are lots of opportunities for walking and bicycling."

I'm looking forward to many visits and evenings of sitting around the Keeping Room fireplace after a good dinner at Cobb's Cove. It would be a good place to write a book.

COBB'S COVE, Barnstable Village, Rte. 6A, Cape Cod, Ma. 02630; 617-362-9356. A 6-room secluded inn on Cape Cod's north shore. Lodgings include a full breakfast. Houseguests can arrange for dinner. Open every day in the year. Within a short distance of Cape Cod Bay and the Atlantic Ocean, the U.S. National Seashore, and Sandy Neck Conservatory, as well as many museums, art galleries, craft shops, and other attractions of the Cape. Active sports nearby. No facilities to amuse children at the inn. No pets. Credit cards not accepted. Evelyn Chester, Innkeeper.

Directions: From Rte. 6 (Mid-Cape Hwy.), turn left at Exit 6 on Rte. 132 to Barnstable. Turn right on Rte. 6A, approximately 3 mi. through Barnstable Village, past the only traffic light and turn left just past the Barnstable Unitarian Church. After approximately 300 yds., look for small wooden sign on left at a gravel driveway saying: "Evelyn Chester."

NAUSET HOUSE
East Orleans, Cape Cod, Massachusetts

"The conservatory," said Lucille Schwarz, "is completed and we had a wedding in it on December 1, which was the reason we stayed open so late in 1979. According to everyone who came, it was a huge success." The conservatory about which she was speaking is a middle-sized greenhouse originally built in 1908 as a conservatory on an estate in Greenwich, Connecticut. It was dismantled; each part was carefully labeled; and then it was sent to East Orleans by truck. Sounds easy, but I happen to know that it took much longer than expected to get it all reassembled. The Schwarzes will use it as a covered garden, and guests will enjoy breakfast or afternoon tea and refreshments in it.

The Nauset House Inn is really a combination of antique shop and bed-and-breakfast inn. There are actually more antiques in the inn than in the shop. Lucille and Jack Schwarz have been avid and knowledgeable collectors for some time, and I'm always fascinated to see the new pieces that have been added since my previous visit. There are beds made from sleighs, chairs that once were horse buggies, butter churns, spinning wheels, wonderful marine pieces, and many, many more.

Lodging rooms are in the main house and in the barn where one of the guest rooms has a canopy bed.

Breakfast is the only meal served and all sorts of New England and Cape Cod things are offered, including real maple syrup from the Schwarz's farm in Vermont. Lucille has a very winning way with scrambled eggs. For lunch and dinner they're happy to recommend restaurants on the Cape from Chatham to Provincetown. "Many of our guests go to the Bramble Inn, which is just across the Cape," said Jack, "and quite a few go out to the Red Inn in Provincetown and Cobbs Cove in Barnstable."

Guests at the Nauset House Inn have the entire Cape with its many natural attractions at their disposal. It's particularly enjoyable from late May through early June, and again after Labor Day. It's also fun walking on nearby Nauset Beach, and finding it almost deserted.

In my yearly visits to see Jack and Lucille, I found that there have been people from all over the world gathered around the breakfast table and seated under the orchard trees. One of them, T.R. Milligan, a professor of language and linguistics at Manhattan College in Riverdale, New York, who delights in writing poetry, sent a rather lengthy poem about his stay. The last two stanzas I think sum up his feelings about country inns:

The magic of this Inn is not performed
With mirrors. Breakfast helps: French toast itself
Deserving of a toast, and quiche beyond
The reach of stock superlatives. And those
Clocks that grace the wall: like guests, each one
A private face, with independent chime;
And some, perhaps believing time's too short,
Simply never make a sound at all.

Now if a blazing hearth defines a home,
Then the Nauset House has earned the definition.
To meet here is to be well met: good talk
Is made before a fire, and memories forged
Beyond a mere recycled recollection . . .

And so we say: salud, santé, and prost
To the hostess and the host! And to all
Who pass this way, let the good word be:
See you at the Home—and wait for me!

Nauset House Inn has been in *CIBR* since 1975.

NAUSET HOUSE INN, P.O. Box 446, Nauset Beach Rd., East Orleans, Cape Cod, Mass. 02643; 617-255-2195. A 12-room country inn 90 mi. from Boston, 27 mi. from Hyannis. Breakfast served to inn guests only. No other meals served. Some rooms with shared bath. Open daily from April 1 to Nov. 15. No children under 12 yrs. No pets. Within walking distance of Nauset Beach. Riding and bicycles nearby. Jack and Lucy Schwarz, Innkeepers.

Directions: From the Mid-Cape Hwy. (Rte. 6), take Exit 12. Bear right to first traffic light. Follow signs for Nauset Beach. Inn is located ¼ mi. before beach on Nauset Beach Rd.

BRADFORD GARDENS INN
Provincetown, Massachusetts

The light from the fireplace, so welcome at any time, flickered over the low ceiling of the bedroom and glanced off the polished headboard of the bed and bureau. I pulled the counterpane up under my chin and luxuriated in the delicious comfort of actually having a fire in my bedroom in the morning. Most of the rooms at Bradford Gardens have their own fireplaces, and one has a Franklin stove.

The front window of my room overlooked a corner of Provincetown Harbor and the shapes of the old houses, shops, and churches became more visible in the early morning light. The side window overlooked a beautiful rose garden with over 300 plants, and several flowering fruit trees, and many chairs and chaise lounges scattered about. An outdoor fireplace is also located in this area, and is used by some of the guests for their own cooking should the spirit move them. Breakfast is the only meal served at the Bradford Gardens, but Jim Logan, the innkeeper, is happy to describe the specialties of the various Provincetown restaurants, including, of course, the Red Inn.

I remained in bed until the very last minute and then hustled downstairs to meet Jim and the other guests at breakfast. On this particular morning we had eggs Franciscan. However, there are several different dishes offered on successive mornings. During the summer, lighter breakfasts are served in the Rose Garden.

It's very tempting to stay on and on at the Bradford Gardens Inn because there is so much to do in the immediate vicinity. The inn is located away from downtown Provincetown, but well within walking distance of all of the quaint shops and wharfs, the Pilgrim's Monument, the museums, and the dozens of other things to be enjoyed. The great Cape Cod National Seashore is only minutes away. It's fun to rent bicycles and use the many special bicycle paths that have been laid out among the sand dunes.

The Bradford Gardens Inn is rather small and quite informal. Guests become acquainted readily because Jim sees to it that everyone enjoys himself.

Each of the lodging rooms has its own character and descriptive name such as the Honeymoon Suite, which has a bedroom and sitting room with a garden view and a Franklin stove; the Jenny Lind Salon which has a beautiful spool bed; the Yesteryear Room with its astonishing brass bed; the Cherry Tree Room which is particularly lovely the last two weeks in June when the famous tree shows off; and the Sun Gallery Room which has its own private entrance, a fireplace, a garden view, and an excellent harbor view. Behind the inn, there is the Loft Lodge, which accommodates six people in two loft bedrooms. It has a deck, patio, fireplace, and includes a full kitchen with a washer and dryer.

I have been visiting the Bradford Gardens Inn since 1973, and it has been great fun to watch its growth during the years. Letters from readers praise the breakfast, the comfortable rooms, many with fireplaces, the growing art collection, and the feeling that there is somebody around who actually cares.

BRADFORD GARDENS INN, 178 Bradford St., Provincetown, Mass. 02657; 617-487-1616. A small 11-room village inn with working fireplaces overlooking Provincetown Bay. European plan includes complimentary breakfast. No other meals served. Open year-round. Within walking distance of Provincetown Harbor and shops. Bicycles, swimming, riding, tennis, golf, and dune buggies nearby. Jim Logan, Innkeeper.

Directions: Follow Rte. 6 to Provincetown, turn left at 2nd P'town exit, and left on Bradford St.

THE RED INN
Provincetown, Massachusetts

On the map, Cape Cod looks like an arm flexed at the elbow with the fingers curling in. The Red Inn in Provincetown is located right at the tip of those curling fingers.

For ten years this restaurant has been owned and operated by Ted and Marce Barker with assorted sons, daughters, brothers, uncles, aunts, and now a growing list of newer members by marriage.

Some of these people have become so adept and knowledgeable in their jobs that they are part of what Ted calls "The Southern garrison," which is the Sea Hut Marina Restaurant at Snead Island, Palmetto, Florida. In the Florida section of this book, I have a complete report.

What I'd like to share with everyone this time is an account of some of the activities at Thanksgiving and Christmas at this year-round inn. They illustrate the tender care and wholehearted concern that everyone at the Red Inn feels for their guests.

As Ted writes, "At Thanksgiving, the preparation begins many days ahead of time with the relishes, sauces (cranberries everywhere), breads (oh, the breads!)—banana-nut, date-nut, and cranberry bread, too. The Hubbard squash has to be cooked at least a day ahead—a squash worth its salt has to be at least a day old in order to have achieved good full flavor. Marce's Aunt Honey traditionally makes the pumpkin, mince, and apple pies for our Thanksgiving 'groaning board.'

"Leading up to Christmas, it's a day-by-day process of decoration. There's a lot of advance planning. It all takes on a 'homemade' approach. Many years before they could be purchased in stores, Mother Barker made all of our calico wreaths, yarn dolls, and countless ornaments, including yarn tassels, antique bowls, pitchers, jugs, cream cans, milk cans, and baskets of all sizes and shapes. All of these, as if by some magic husbandry, begin to grow evergreen branches mixed with bittersweet and wild cranberries. There are bows of red, calico, and even plaid.

"As for Christmas trees, we now have three. There's a little tree at the front door festooned with our handmade yarn tassels. The next tree is full and bushy and very traditional, and stands in the corner of the Tavern Lounge by the fireplace. This is also our family tree under which Santa places all the presents. The third tree stands tallest in the greenhouse dining area, perhaps ten or twelve feet high.

"We are blessed with a large 'combined' family, as you know, but as we have grown in Provincetown, and now in Palmetto, we have added to our 'family,' people who have grown with us and shared the spirit necessary to operate a good country inn.

"Incidentally, last winter we moved some of the dining room tables into the Tavern Lounge room, up next to the fireplace, and served late lunch, early supper, and dinner there. It's a restaurant within a restaurant. Picture, if you will, the view of Provincetown Harbor, calm or stormy, dinner by candlelight, and a warm wood fire in the huge hearth! Shall I make a reservation?"

Yes indeed, Ted, you should certainly make a reservation, and I'm sure many people will visit Provincetown again in the winter and enjoy the fullness of the spirit of service at the Red Inn.

The Red Inn has been included in *CIBR* since 1974.

THE RED INN, 15 Commercial St., Provincetown, Mass. 02657; 617-487-0050. A waterside country restaurant with a striking view of Provincetown Harbor. No lodgings. Open for lunch and dinner every day of the year. Within walking distance of all Provincetown lodging accommodations and recreational activities and attractions. Ted and Marcie Barker, Innkeepers.

Directions: Follow Rte. 6 to end of Cape Cod.

JARED COFFIN HOUSE
Nantucket Island, Massachusetts

Arriving in Nantucket on the ferry, there's the game of picking out the landmarks as the boat makes its way into the breakwater and the dock. The high-spired churches, the waterfront buildings and towers gradually take form. Then, there is the fun of actually going across the gangplank and putting your foot right down smack on Nantucket Island, the same Nantucket where ship-owner Jared Coffin built his house.

The Jared Coffin House is truly extraordinary. It was built in 1845 by one of the island's most successful ship owners. A number of years ago the buildings were restored to their original style both in architecture and furnishings. Today, the JC helps recapture the spirit and feeling of the glorious days of Nantucket's reign as queen of the world's whaling ports.

It's difficult to believe that this sturdily built, Federally dimensioned house is an inn. Only the discreet murmur of voices and muffled clinking of silver from a tree-shaded patio gives its identity away. It seems just like the other handsome houses of Nantucket whaling captains.

Nantucket was seriously damaged by the Great Fire of 1846 and the discovery of gold in California, and the subsequent discovery of oil in Pennsylvania (see Wells Inn, Sistersville, West Virginia), caused the depletion of the great whaling oil industry on Nantucket. These combined to isolate the island for many years.

Although Nantucket was known for years primarily as a summer resort, it has become more and more popular as an out-of-season resort as well. A visit early in the year will bring unusual glimpses of an early New England spring, while the fall months offer some of the most beautiful days, warm and clear, with vivid colorings of the moors which are unforgettable. And Christmas at the Jared Coffin is really special!

I enjoy just strolling about the winding streets, happily coping with the cobblestones, and bicycling out to look at the Scotch heather, wood lilies, and wild roses on the moors. These also provide a haven for rare birds such as the Swedish nightingale and the yellow-bellied bulbul.

It hardly seems possible that it's been twelve years since my first visit to the Jared Coffin House. At that time, Peggy and Phil Read were innkeepers. They have now become the sole proprietors of this classic inn and, in 1978, a beautiful 1821 Federal house on Summer Street was purchased and has been converted into additional lodgings with six lovely rooms decorated and furnished in keeping with the Federal style.

One of the most accommodating developments in recent years has been the "hospitality hostess," who has a special phone and desk in the front lobby and is there to help all of the guests with questions and suggestions about where to go and what to see on this fascinating island.

A visit to Nantucket is really an adventure in history. Many guests like to take their small children and, with this in mind, Phil Read has provided a children's menu and allows portion-sharing and special requests to make children feel welcome and their parents comfortable. A box of toys and books for small children are provided and there are puzzles and board games for those a little older. "Children old enough to appreciate historical and natural things are happy here," said Phil. "We try to make them feel comfortable."

Incidentally, it is not necessary to have a car on Nantucket and it's possible to reach Woods Hole, Massachusetts, by bus and then to take the ferry over—a two-and-a-half-hour ride. Check with the Steamship Authority (617-540-2022) for advance auto reservations and current schedules, but cars are not recommended for short stays.

Jared Coffin House has been in *CIBR* since 1969.

JARED COFFIN HOUSE, Nantucket Island, Mass. 02554; 617-228-2400. A 46-room village inn 30 mi. at sea. European plan. Breakfast, lunch, dinner served daily. Strongly advise verifying accommodations before planning a trip to Nantucket in any season. Swimming, fishing, boating, golf, tennis, riding, and bicycles nearby. Philip and Margaret Read, Innkeepers.

Directions: Accessible by air from Boston, New York, and Hyannis, or by ferry from Woods Hole and Hyannis, Mass. Automobile reservations are usually needed in advance: 617-540-2022. Seasonal air service from New York and ferry service from Hyannis are available May thru October: 617-426-1855. Inn is located 300 yards from ferry dock.

CHARLOTTE INN
Edgartown, Martha's Vineyard, Massachusetts

"I guess you'd call us a combination inn, art gallery, and French restaurant," said Gery Conover. "We have five gallery rooms plus a gift shop on the first floor, and the lodging rooms are located on the second floor."

Gery and I were having lunch at the Chez Pierre, which is a French restaurant operated in conjunction with the Charlotte Inn. It had a kind of indoors-outdoors atmosphere with many, many plants arranged around the brick garden and with trees arching overhead. A discreet gate on South Summer Street separated us from the passers-by, who were doing what so many people do in Edgartown—strolling and looking at the beautiful Federalist and Greek Revival houses.

Chez Pierre is noted as one of the top French restaurants on the island, to which visitors come from all over the Cape to dine. It's run by a young couple who take great pride in their cooking.

Gery's two sons, Gery, Jr., 17, and Timmy, 10, stopped off on their way to go sailing in the Edgartown Harbor. "Many of the inn guests find the harbor a very pleasant diversion," he remarked, "and they can rent different types of sailboats and power boats from the boat livery."

"We are open year-round. Good sailing days start early in the spring and extend through the fall. It's interesting, though, how many people come out to visit us during the so-called off-season. Edgartown is delightful when it is more quiet and has fewer visitors. Our guests enjoy shopping in town, walking along the beaches, and biking down to Chilmark which is at the other end of the island. You can really work up a good appetite. It's beautiful here during the Christmas and New Year's holidays. All of the Islanders are very proud of their home decorations."

Like many other Edgartown houses, the Charlotte Inn is a classic, three-story white clapboard with a widow's walk on top. It was the former home of a Martha's Vineyard sea captain. There have been some changes, but basically, the building is the same as it was during the days of Edgartown's whaling heyday.

Lodging rooms at this inn are individually furnished and great care has been exercised in their decoration. All the rooms are very quiet and have their own private baths. A warm feeling of hospitality and a romantic atmosphere greets each guest. My large room had a working fireplace for guests to use in the winter, and was furnished with antiques, including a four-poster queen-sized bed. It had a pleasant view of the garden and courtyard.

As in all the other rooms, there were fresh flowers, lots of books and magazines, good reading lamps, and candlewyck bedspreads.

Guests may enjoy a Continental breakfast served in their rooms.

Later that afternoon Gery, Jr., and Timmy returned in time to lend a hand with the inn chores. "They are both very helpful," said Gery, "and I'm happy to say that Gery, Jr., is really taking to innkeeping with great enthusiasm. He knows the island history and enjoys advising our guests about the best beaches, and the best fishing and sailing."

1980 update: Just before press time, Gery informed me that arrangements have been made to lease an adjoining property, an old whaling home, which will give the inn several more rooms. "They will be redone in keeping with our standards in the main inn," he said, "and also, in the character of an old whaling home in Edgartown."

CHARLOTTE INN, So. Summer St., Edgartown, Martha's Vineyard Island, Ma. 02539; 617-627-4751. A 10-room combination inn-art gallery and restaurant located on one of the side streets in the village of Edgartown, just a few short steps from the harbor. European plan. Rooms available every day of the year. Continental breakfast served to inn guests. Chez Pierre restaurant open for lunch and dinner from mid-March through New Year's Day. Other island restaurants open year-round. Boating, swimming, beaches, fishing, tennis, riding, golf, sailing, and biking nearby. No pets. Gery Conover, Innkeeper.

Directions: Martha's Vineyard Island is located off the southwestern coast of Cape Cod. The Woods Hole-Vineyard Haven Ferry runs year-round and automobiles may be left in the parking lot at Woods Hole. Taxis may be obtained from Vineyard Haven to Edgartown (8 mi.). Check with inn for ferry schedules for all seasons of the year. Accessible by air from Boston and New York.

WESTERN MASSACHUSETTS

THE INN AT PRINCETON
Princeton, Massachusetts

This time I journeyed to Princeton on a different route, coming west on Route 2 on a trip from Maine. I turned off on Route 31 south, and drove through the Leominster State Forest on a very pleasant back road that continued on for some time alongside a large pond. I was tempted while passing a busy bathing beach on this very warm afternoon to stop and take a dip, and I could imagine the guests at the Inn at Princeton occasionally using this beach.

I continued south, joining Route 140, and then branched off on 31 alone for another three miles to Princeton; continuing past the post office, I turned right and then up the hill past the beautiful Italianate clock tower and white clapboard Congregational church.

The Inn at Princeton is really a jewel. It was once a mansion, with a lower story of beautiful fieldstone and an upper story of traditional weathered New England shingles. It is set slightly apart from the town in its own spacious gardens and lawns. Like so many other country inns, it represents a wish fulfillment—in this case, for two attractive women who discovered a few years ago that they each wanted to leave the teaching profession and open a country inn.

"It has been tons of fun and tons of work," said Suzanne Reed who, with Liz Sjogren, is joint-owner of the inn, "but the moment we saw the house, we knew it had to be ours—it was exactly what we wanted."

From the Sun Room, one of the two dining rooms on the first floor, there is a lovely view of lawn, trees, and a country road through the ten handsome bay windows. The other dining room overlooks the great sweeping valley with rolling fields, and in the evening, the lights of Boston in the distance.

Guests entering through the front door are greeted by a fireplace on the right, and by an expansive living room on the left with a collection of very colorful and cleverly-lit oil paintings and water-colors. An old trunk holds firewood for the living room fireplace. There is an air of style and grace about these rooms with their highly polished parquet floors.

Decorated in attractive period furnishings and bright cheery wallpaper, the bedrooms have many special touches, such as the cradle I found in one, and cleverly framed old photographs.

A breakfast tray is thoughtfully delivered to each room every morning with juice, coffee and sweet rolls or muffins.

It was now early evening and we were all out on the terrace of this quiet, rather sequestered inn, when Suzanne said, "I think it has grown dark enough now to see the lights of Boston."

"Really? But Boston is at least fifty miles away," I exclaimed.

"Well, come and see for yourself," she said, and we walked to the end of the terrace which is the highest point on the inn property. Sure enough, there, twinkling in the distance, I could see some of the lights of the Boston skyline.

"Yes, and when it gets pitch dark a little later on they look like little diamonds in the blackness," said Liz.

For dinner that night I had sweetbreads Divan which were served on a bed of broccoli with a most unusual sauce. I was especially fond of the squash which was wonderfully spiced. Among the other items of Continental cuisine are paupiettes du veau, lamb chops en croute, and scallops Provencale. Dessert was a fresh Straw-berry Torte—delicious.

After dinner I decided to take another short constitutional with Elite and Easter, two friendly dogs from the inn. We visited with a beautiful registered Welsh pony named Molasses, who has an A-frame stall adjacent to the barn. She will undoubtedly be driven in her own Governor's cart during 1980. Liz and Suzanne have also

143

completely restored a 1929 model A Ford town sedan in beautiful browns and beiges, with velour appointments. As her name, Belle, implies, not only is she a thing of beauty, but she provides transportation, too.

Sure enough, now that the night was inky black, the distant lights of Boston seemed ever so much closer.

THE INN AT PRINCETON, Mountain Rd., Princeton, Ma. 01541; 617-464-2030. A 5-room village inn 60 mi. from Boston and 14 mi. from Worcester near Mt. Wachusett State Reservation. European plan. Dinner served to travelers Wednesday thru Sunday, from 5-9 p.m. Open year-round. Closed Christmas, January through March. No pets. Not oriented for younger children. Tennis, swimming, skiing, hiking nearby. Suzanne W. Reed and Elizabeth A. Sjogren, Innkeepers.

Directions: From Boston: Rte. 2 west to Intersections of Rte. 2 and 31. From Conn. and Mass.: Mass. Tpke. to Rte. 122A to Holden Center, right at Rte. 31. From Vt.: I-91 to Rte. 2 to Rte. 31.

THE VICTORIAN
Whitinsville, Massachusetts

Although I am especially partial to book-lined dining rooms (offhand I remember those at the Redcoat's Return, the Pump House, and the Griswold Inn), and the Victorian's is particularly pleasant, but this time I was having lunch at the Victorian on the sun porch, which has been beautifully decorated and furnished in a kind of Sadi Thompson-cum-Art Nouveau motif. We sat in the fabulous white wicker South Sea Island chairs amidst a collection of hanging plants which Martha Flint identified as Swedish ivy, wandering Jew, and Boston fern. "Everybody wants to sit out here," she said. "It's so wonderfully bright, especially with windows on three sides."

The cover of the luncheon menu, like the dinner and dessert menus, was adapted from designs of the 1920s showing very modish men and women looking as if they had all stepped out of a page of a French fashion magazine of the time. Orin Flint pointed out to me that, indeed, they were reproductions of prints from the French journal, *Falbalas and Fanfreluches*.

It was the *inside,* however, that interested me most, and the choice today included several types of omelets, including crabmeat and cream cheese, spinach and sour cream; a variety of salads, crêpes, coquilles St. Jacques, and eggs Victorian.

While I was at it, I also took a peek at the dinner menu featuring "Medallions of the Huntress," which the menu described as two small filets of beef with a classic brown sauce. There were also prime ribs of beef, scallops gratinée, duckling served with sweet and sour sauce and garnished with a peach mousse, veal Oscar, filet of sole, and shrimp scampi.

"Our first course, which is included with each dinner, is described by the waiter or waitress. We prefer to serve salads after dinner in the Continental manner," Orin explained.

The dessert menu included crêpes, cheesecake, apricot sherbet, brandy Alexander pie, chocolate mousse, and lime Bavarian pie. An additional menu described the various kinds of coffees and after-dinner specialties, such as Irish coffee, café Amaretto di amore, café chocolat anisette, and café Caribbean; all of these had short descriptions to help the relatively uninitiated, such as myself.

After lunch we walked back through the library, and once again I couldn't help pulling out a couple of volumes at random. This time, I found a copy of George Bernard Shaw's, *Captain Brassbound's "Conversion."*

The Victorian is an imposing mansion that sits regally above the road on a grassy slope. There is rich wood paneling everywhere and appropriate, somewhat massive Victorian furniture. Unusual touches include hand-tooled leather wainscoting in a charming third-floor room with lovely arched windows, and intricately tiled floors in the bathrooms.

Some of the seven bedrooms have walk-in closets, and one has a dressing room with full-length mirrors mounted on the mahogany doors. Little "extras" at the Victorian include apples in the guests' rooms, turn-down service, hot mulled wine, and a Continental breakfast for houseguests. The exterior has been graced with real awnings and new flower beds.

I'm certain that the Whitin family, who built this beautiful mansion during the 19th century and for whom the town is named, would thoroughly approve of the warm spirit of hospitality that pervades it today.

THE VICTORIAN, 583 Linwood Ave., Whitinsville, Mass. 01588; 617-234-2500. A 7-room Victorian mansion in a quiet town 15 mi. from Worcester, Ma. and 40 mi. from Narragansett Bay in R.I. European plan. Dinner served to travelers daily except Mondays. Lunch served to travelers daily except Mondays and Saturdays. Overnight guests receive Continental breakfast. Very small pets only. Lawn games, ice skating, fishing on grounds. Golf and tennis nearby. Orin and Martha Flint, Innkeepers.

Directions: From Providence, follow Rte. 146 north and take the Uxbridge exit. From the traffic light in Uxbridge, proceed north on Rte. 122 approximately 1½ mi. to Linwood Ave. (there will be a sign on the corner saying "Whitinsville — Left"). Bear left here. The inn is a few hundred yards around the corner. From Worcester, follow Rte. 146 south to the Whitinsville-Purgatory Chasm exit. Proceed into Whitinsville and keep right at the set of traffic lights onto Linwood Ave. The inn is on the left at the other end of Linwood Ave. — about 1½ mi.

THE INN AT HUNTINGTON
Huntington, Massachusetts

Murray Schuman is an academic chef, a man who is equally at home in his own studio kitchen at The Inn at Huntington and in the classroom. Furthermore, he speaks with great clarity and depth when he is discussing food and its preparation.

"Cuisine," he says, "is *la raison d'etre* of our inn. To release and reveal the essential flavors of fresh wholesome food and combine and complement them with herb sauces and simple garnishes is our goal. The freshest of produce available in local markets is fashioned into meals deliciously reminiscent of the European countryside."

Murray, among other things, studied cooking and classic table service at the Ecole Hoteliere in Lausanne, Switzerland and was also Dean of Instruction at the Culinary Institute in Hyde Park, New York. He and his wife Barbara met in Hyde Park where she was developing the library. Out of their mutual dream of a certain kind of "special country inn" has grown their concept of total integration of decor, service, and menu.

Barbara has gained considerable reputation in her own right with the formation of the *Cookery Bookery,* a unique catalogue which combines her love of books with the knowledge gained in the specialized field of cooking and gastronomy. The catalogue, available by mail, lists many rare and valuable out-of-print cookbooks.

Imported music, mostly baroque, is played throughout the dinner period at the inn. Live performances of chamber and choral music have been a feature of the Christmas Feast, held during the past three years. The Schumans, further indicating their backgrounds, have instituted a series of Beaux Arts Concerts — musical recitals held at the inn during fall and early winter. They feature accomplished musicians and chamber groups from the Pioneer Valley and surrounding area.

Furthermore, in the fall of 1979, a series of cooking workshops and demonstrations was inaugurated at the inn and will be an ongoing occurrence. These include classes in basic culinary techniques, a pasta fiesta, and a class in holiday *haute cuisine.*

The menu at The Inn at Huntington changes frequently, reflecting Murray's ideas and inspirations, among which are duckling *aux framboises* or with a ginger or walnut sauce, poached fresh salmon, filet of beef, lobster pocket, sautéed fresh fish with shallots, and highly original desserts prepared in the kitchen.

Huntington is in one of the relatively "undiscovered" portions of western Massachusetts on Route 20, which parallels the Massachusetts Turnpike, but avoids the heavy traffic.

Yes, The Inn at Huntington where Barbara and Murray and their two young junior innkeepers, Hans and Aaron, hold forth, is a very exciting place.

THE INN AT HUNTINGTON, Worthington Rd., Huntington, Ma. 01050; 413-667-8868. A restaurant featuring European countryside cuisine on Rte. 112 (Worthington Rd.) 1 mi. from downtown

Huntington. No lodgings. Dinner served nightly except Monday, June-Oct. 15; Wed.-Sun., Oct. 15-May. Reservations strongly suggested. Open February 1st to December 31st. Dinner Concert Schedule—Sundays at 2 p.m., fall and spring; call for info. Closed Thanksgiving, Christmas Eve, Christmas Day. No credit cards. Murray and Barbara Schuman, Innkeepers.

Directions: Huntington is on Rte. 112, off U.S. Rte. 20, halfway between the Westfield and Lee exits of the Mass. Tpke. From Northampton use Rte. 66 to Rte. 112 to Huntington.

PEIRSON PLACE
Richmond, Massachusetts

Margaret Kingman and I were seated by the pond at the Peirson Place, and so placid was the surface that it mirrored a willow tree by the waterfall. It was early fall, and already the sugar maples, oaks, ash, hickory, birch, and walnut trees on the grounds of this delightful, historic hideaway were beginning to feel the faint touch of autumn's brush.

"I've spent years researching the history of this property," she said. "It's a Historical Landmark in Berkshire County. We have two houses here, plus a great many outbuildings—this beautiful big barn behind us, and 150 acres of wooded hillside."

Margaret warmed to the subject, "The smaller of the houses is called Cogswell and was built in 1762 by Joseph Cogswell. He had to buy it twice, once from the Indians and once from the Colonial Government Proprietors of Berkshire County. A few years later Nathan Peirson built a tannery on this land, thereby starting a connection through a later marriage between the two families. Joseph Cogswell and his four sons were minute-men serving at

Bennington, Bunker Hill, and Valley Forge. Nathan Peirson was a lieutenant in the Revolutionary Army for which he supplied boots and saddle leather, and which enabled him to build a new tannery here in 1784.

"The main house was built in 1788 on the site of the first tannery, and the Cogswells and the Peirsons were united when Nathan's oldest daughter married a grandson of Joseph Cogswell.

"I think that the Peirson Place has probably changed very little outwardly from the steel engraving in the *History of Berkshire County*, published in 1875. Our front hall still has the original French wallpaper of 1789. Ells have been added to both houses and we have modern bathrooms, instead of 'curtained washrooms.'"

The Peirson Place is really very unusual. Within this circumference of history and natural beauty, Margaret has created an intimate bed-and-breakfast inn that is markedly different from other accommodations in the Berkshires. She has many guests who have been returning year after year because they enjoy the shaded quiet of the Victorian gazebo and the tranquility of the woods. Many follow the birdwatcher's path or the unusual trail for the blind, perhaps the only one I've ever heard of which allows sightless people to enjoy the woods and fields by "smell and tell." During my short visit, I saw many guests riding bicycles, and some were swimming in the pond and enjoying the use of the sauna.

Breakfasts or afternoon teas are great fun here because guests have been to Tanglewood, Jacob's Pillow, or the Berkshire Playhouse, or perhaps visited Williamstown, or the nearby Hancock Shaker Village, so the conversation is quite lively. The fresh croissants and crumpets disappear just about as quickly as the attractive young girls in their red-checked cobbler's aprons can bring them in.

Accommodations are in a wide variety of environments, including the main house which has very sumptuous rooms, and the barn. There are more frugal but most interesting quarters-hosteling facilities. "We make refrigerator space available for guests who wish to picnic by the pond, and there are dozens of good restaurants here in the Berkshires."

PEIRSON PLACE, Richmond, Mass. 01254; 413-698-2750. A 10-room country house, 6 miles from Pittsfield on Rte. 41 near all of the scenic attractions of the Berkshire hills: Tanglewood, Hancock Shaker Village, marvelous backroading in western Massachusetts, eastern New York, and southern Vermont. Various accommodations: 4 rooms with private baths, 6 rooms share 3 baths. Lodgings include morning coffee and pastry, afternoon tea, and all of the facilities in the woods and the nearby fields. Pond, sauna, badminton, darts, boating, hiking on grounds. Tennis, golf, horseback riding, etc. nearby. No pets. No facilities to amuse children under 12. Open every day from Memorial Day through Columbus Day. One-day rentals not accepted on weekends during Tanglewood season. Margaret Mace Kingman, Innkeeper.

Directions: From Boston: Take Massachusetts Turnpike to Exit 1. Follow Rte. 41 north through Richmond. Peirson Place on left-hand side. From New York: Leave Taconic State Parkway at Rte. 295 and continue east to Rte. 41. Turn left.

STAGECOACH HILL
Sheffield, Massachusetts

I like to arrive at Stagecoach Hill just at dusk as the carefully tended stone walls along Route 41 become vague shapes, and occasionally my headlights reveal some deer out in the meadow. This route is aptly named Undermountain Road, for along this stretch I feel as if I am driving directly underneath the imposing, protective influence of Mount Race.

Entry is through ponderous Victorian doors and up a short flight of stairs to a lounge area, dimly-lit by candles flickering in red jars. Except in the warm summer months, additional light is provided by fires on two raised hearths.

More candles grace the dining rooms, which are most inviting with their red tablecloths, white napkins and gleaming silverware. The walls have sporting and hunting prints and a generous sprinkling of photographs and prints of the English royal family, including Queen Victoria, Queen Mary, and King George.

The innkeepers are John and Ann Pedretti who have lived in the Berkshires for a number of years. Oddly enough, they moved to England for two years in the early 1970s, and since Ann is from Lancashire, England, they're both very pleased to have found such an English inn in such a beautiful setting. In some ways, it reminds me of a traditional English inn in Ann's own Lancashire country called, "Hark to Bounty."

In addition to doing all of the cooking, Ann also does the extremely neat lettering on the blackboard menu which on my last visit showed such interesting main courses as baked scallops, duckling Bigarade, steak and kidney pie, and roast prime rib of beef served with Yorkshire pudding. "I learned to cook several different veal dishes because John is from northern Italy and he loves them. I also do a New England oyster pie," she said.

In looking at the menu, I realized that it was a choice of either an

à la carte or table d'hote, or a mixture of each. Certain appetizers are offered at no additional charge, as well as certain desserts.

The "Coach" as it's known locally, is an ideal distance from either Boston or New York. Its situation in the Berkshires makes it ideal for a visit in any season, because there are several ski areas within a very short drive, and also good cross-country skiing. In summer, all of the Berkshire recreational and cultural advantages are most accessible.

In the 1979 edition, I reported that John and Ann were planning to create additional lodgings by converting some of the second-floor rooms in the old brick building. This was accomplished, but it was soon discovered that the location of these rooms over the two busy dining rooms of the inn made them impractical for the use of guests. There are a few other overnight accommodations available, particularly in an old red barn and in a small outbuilding on the property. "Some of these are not country inn rooms," says John. "We try to make that fully understood when people telephone for reservations. They are, however, clean and cozy, and many of our overnight guests have been returning for years. We're just a short distance from two Berkshire ski areas, and in the summertime, Tanglewood is only a few miles farther."

Stagecoach Hill has been included in *CIBR* since 1966.

STAGECOACH HILL INN, Undermountain Road, Sheffield, Mass. 01257; 413-229-8585. Inn with British overtones on Rte. 41 midway between Salisbury, Conn. and Great Barrington, Mass. European plan. Dinner served nightly except Wednesday. Closed Christmas Day. Near South Berkshire ski areas, Tanglewood,

Jacob's Pillow, and all summertime attractions. John and Ann Pedretti, Innkeepers.

Directions: From Mass. Tpke., take Exit 2 and follow Rte. 102 west to Stockbridge. Take Rte. 7 south to Great Barrington, then follow Rte. 41 south to inn.

THE RED LION INN
Stockbridge, Massachusetts

It was Washington's Birthday in Stockbridge. A mid-February thaw, enhanced by warm sunshine that gives New Englanders new hope for spring, had created wet corn snow and little pools of water around the sidewalks on Main Street. Dozens of cars with out-of-state license plates were circling the town, much as they do in summer, looking for a place to park.

On the porch of The Red Lion Inn, a number of people who were in Stockbridge for the day or the weekend were sitting on the rails, pointing out Norman Rockwell's home nearby or some of the tiny shops along Main Street.

There has been an inn on this spot since 1773. Back then it served as a stop for stagecoaches on the Albany-Hartford-Boston route. A year later it was the site of a Boston Tea Party-like convention when delegates from various Berkshire County towns protested the use of articles imported from England.

On this February day, The Red Lion was functioning as it has for 200 years, supplying excellent food and lodgings for travelers and townfolk alike. When I entered the low-ceilinged lobby I found almost every chair and sofa occupied. A soft fire was hissing in the fireplace and in the center of the room was a bright flower arrangement of blooms in advance of the season—forsythia, daffodils, and even a few daisies. The Red Lion has received recognition for its wonderful summer flower plantings.

State Senator Jack Fitzpatrick and his wife Jane, the owners of the inn, walked through the lobby, stopping frequently to greet old friends. Jack, by the way, plays Santa Claus during the Christmas season. He walks up and down Main Street dressed in a red suit and a white beard. His familiar "ho, ho, ho" is a welcome sight and sound. In one corner of the lobby there was a display of beautiful colored photographs showing the inn in the midst of summer. One of the most striking of these was a picture of the inn courtyard where I have enjoyed many a luncheon and dinner under the trees during the warm weather.

Stockbridge is a very pleasant town with a wide main street with many trees. There is much to do at the height of the summer, winter, and fall seasons with Tanglewood, the Berkshire Theatre Festival, Jacob's Pillow Dance Festival, and other musical and theatrical offerings nearby. In winter there is downhill and cross-country skiing, and walking the streets of the village which is especially beautiful when the snow falls.

In the "off season" it is a quiet, pleasant experience and there are always quite a few guests at the inn 'tween seasons who enjoy a quiet respite from a world that gets rather hectic at times. Incidentally, the Norman Rockwell Museum, just down the Main Street from the inn, is open year-round.

I was briefly joined by Betsy Holtzinger, the radiant blonde innkeeper: "Come on, let's have a cup of tea!"

How could I refuse?

The Red Lion Inn has been in *CIBR* since 1966.

RED LION INN, Stockbridge, Mass. 01262; 413-298-5545. A 95-room historic village inn dating back to 1773 in the Berkshire Mountains. Adjacent to Tanglewood, Norman Rockwell's Old Corner House Museum, The Berkshire Playhouse, Jacob's Pillow, Chesterwood Gallery, Mission House, and major ski areas. European plan. Breakfast, lunch, and dinner. Open year-round. (From Nov. 1 to May 1, only 30 rooms open.) Outdoor heated pool. Tennis, golf, boating, fishing, hiking, mountain climbing, and xc skiing nearby. Betsy Holtzinger, Innkeeper; Jack and Jane Fitzpatrick, Owners.

Directions: From the Taconic State Pkwy, take Exit 23 (N.Y. Rte. 23) to Mass. Rte. 7. Proceed north to Stockbridge. From the Mass. Tpke. Exit #2 Lee, follow Rte. 102 to Stockbridge.

THE VILLAGE INN
Lenox, Massachusetts

It was one of those delightfully warm days in late April when I drove the few miles from Stockbridge to Lenox, taking the winding road up Prospect Hill past Lake Mahkeenac, entering Lenox through the woods from the south.

As many times as I have driven this road it has always given me a real lift to see the lake, hills, and open marshes where so many birds reside in all seasons. It is a reflection of the many moods of New England from the gentler one of this day to the rugged wind-whistling days of January—that same unpredictable weather that delighted Melville, but distressed Hawthorne. Both lived in the Berkshires and in fact, tradition says, met in a nearby cave on a rainy day.

The crocuses and daffodils were in luxuriant profusion in Lenox, and there were signs of early May flowers on the lawns of the Village Inn, where I was looking forward to meeting friends for a pleasant lunch.

The village of Lenox, with its tree-lined streets, has an interesting history dating from Colonial days and continuing through the eighteenth and nineteenth centuries. In many ways, the Village Inn reflects quite a few of those historical events. The building itself dates back to the American Revolution and has been operated for over a hundred and fifty years as an inn.

It is a two-and-a-half-story yellow clapboard building with a basic Federal design that has been adapted to meet various needs over many years. The two rear wings were well-constructed barns moved from another part of Lenox and joined to the inn about one hundred years ago. They form an L-shaped sheltered terrace with a lawn on which there are a number of beautiful maples, a small fountain, and an American flag. Plantings of iris, daffodils, petunias, peonies, roses, and tulips brighten the picture throughout the warmer weather.

The inn is open every day of the year serving "all-morning breakfast" from eight a.m. until eleven-thirty. Brunch-lunch goes from noon to two-thirty. Because there is no evening meal served, a great deal of emphasis is placed on lunch, which is Marie Judd's particular interest. "We have all kinds of quiches such as mushroom and quiche Lorraine, also a wide variety of crêpes." There are other hearty luncheon dishes, including asparagus spears served with cheese sauce and bacon. I am very fond of the particularly good homemade soups which are served in bucket-shaped bowls. Larger appetites favor the luncheon steak which is served with garlic bread and salad.

Guests at the Village Inn are delighted with the bulletin board which lists literally dozens of suggestions for activities in all seasons of the year. One of these is cross-country skiing, and there is an excellent group of marked trails nearby at the Pleasant Valley Sanctuary. I have skied there myself several times, and also walked the same paths which become nature trails in summer.

Other nearby attractions for year-round entertainment are the Clark Art Museum in Williamstown, the Norman Rockwell museum in Stockbridge, and the Berkshire Museum in Pittsfield. In the summertime, the Boston Symphony performs at Tanglewood, and the Berkshire Playhouse gives performances in nearby Stockbridge. Jacob's Pillow is just a short distance away in Lee.

The spotlessly clean lodging rooms are models for a country inn. The Village Inn is just a short walk from the bus stop and many of the inn guests from New York and Boston, and even points farther distant, find this an ideal way to travel to Lenox.

THE VILLAGE INN, Church St., Lenox, Mass. 01240; 413-637-0020. A 25-room inn in a bustling Berkshire town 4 mi. from Stockbridge, 8 mi. from Pittsfield, and 1 mi. from Tanglewood. Lenox is located in the heart of the Berkshires with many historical, cultural, and recreational features. Breakfast and luncheon served daily to travelers. Open every day of the year. No pets. Swimming pool privileges across the street from inn. All seasonal sports including xc skiing and downhill skiing available nearby. No credit cards. Personal checks accepted. Richard and Marie Judd, Innkeepers.

Directions: After approaching Lenox on Rte. 7, one of the principal north-south routes in New England, exit onto Rte. 7A to reach the Village Center and Church Street. When approaching from the Mass. Tpke. (Exit 2) use Rte. 20N about 4 mi. and turn left onto Rte. 183 to center of town.

Mid Atlantic

Eastern Time Zone

LAKE HURON

ONTARIO

Grandview Farm, *Huntsville*

The Briars, *Jackson's Pt.*

TORONTO

LAKE ONTARIO

Oban Inn,
Niagara-On-The-Lake

Clarkson House,
Lewiston

Asa Ransom House,
Clarence

STRATFORD

Holloway House
East Bloomfield

Glen Iris Inn, *Castile*

LAKE ERIE

NEW

PENNSYLV

Eagles Mere Inn, *Eagles Me*

WILLIAMSPOR

INTERSTATE 80

Tavern, *New Wilmington*

PITTSBURGH

PENNSYLVANIA

Century Inn, *Scenery Hill*

Hickory Bridge Farm, *Orrtanna*

Fairfield Inn, *Fairfield*

TPK

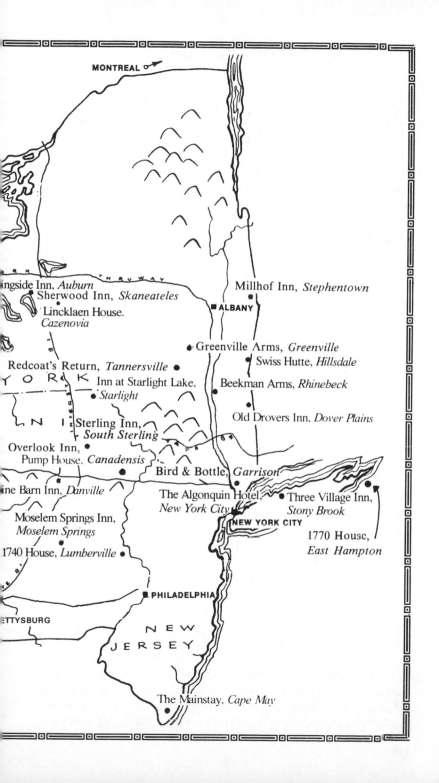

MONTREAL

ngside Inn, *Auburn*
Sherwood Inn, *Skaneateles*
Lincklaen House.
Cazenovia

Millhof Inn, *Stephentown*

■ ALBANY

Greenville Arms, *Greenville*
Swiss Hutte, *Hillsdale*

Redcoat's Return, *Tannersville* ●

Y O R K   Inn at Starlight Lake,
● *Starlight*

Beekman Arms, *Rhinebeck*

Sterling Inn,
South Sterling

Old Drovers Inn, *Dover Plains*

Overlook Inn, ●
Pump House. *Canadensis*

Bird & Bottle, *Garrison*

ine Barn Inn, *Danville*

The Algonquin Hotel,
New York City

Three Village Inn,
Stony Brook

■ NEW YORK CITY

Moselem Springs Inn,
Moselem Springs

1740 House, *Lumberville* ●

1770 House,
East Hampton

■ PHILADELPHIA

ETTYSBURG

N E W
J E R S E Y

The Mainstay, *Cape May*

New Jersey

MAINSTAY INN
Cape May, New Jersey

There they were, as big as life and twice as handsome, on the front cover of the July/August 1979 edition of *Americana!* There were Tom and Sue Carroll standing in front of the Mainstay, with Tom in a straw boater leaning on an 1887 high-wheeled bicycle known as an "ordinary." The caption said, "Seaside holiday at a Victorian Inn."

Beginning on Page 30, there were *six* pages of very entertaining information and handsome photographs of Tom, Sue, and the Mainstay. The writer David Trainer and photographer Bill Ray did an exhaustive and excellent job on the attractions of the inn and the virtues of the innkeepers. Four of Sue's tasty breakfast recipes were also featured. It certainly made me very proud of what Tom and Sue have accomplished.

In the 1976 edition of *CIBR,* I told about visiting Tom and Sue when they had another Cape May home which they had converted into a guest house. I had been immediately impressed with their enthusiastic involvement with their guests.

Tom and Sue bought the present Mainstay, an Italianate villa, in 1977 from a retired Baptist minister who ran it as a guest house for nearly thirty years. Many of the furnishings are original pieces custom-built for the house. A pair of matching love seats and two brass chandeliers are identical to those found in a plantation in Natchez, Mississippi. The copper bathtub enclosed in a wood frame is like the one in Washington Irving's house. At one time it had been a gambling club, and one of the early operators employed a lady to sit in a rocking chair on the front porch to watch for the police. If she rocked violently, the gamblers inside would quickly stash their evidence and when the police arrived they would be attending a harmless musicale.

In addition to the ten-foot mirror, ornately carved headboards, and marble-topped dressers, there are other unusual Victorian features. Under the beds are chamberpots which roll out on wooden trays. The original mosquito nets are attached to small pulleys in the ceilings.

Most of the guest rooms are very elegant and spacious with twelve-foot ceilings, while others in the maids' wing are small and cozy.

Among the handsome photographs in the *Americana* article, there's one showing Sue straightening the candelabra on the beautiful long dining room table where there is a place setting for breakfast with the pistol-handled flatware and some of her quiche and fresh breakfast cake. Another photo shows the great mirror which runs from floor to ceiling in the main hallway, and also the other handsome pieces of Victorian furniture. Guests are shown in still another picture seated on the side porch enjoying afternoon tea.

In addition to all of this, Mr. Trainer makes mention of the fact that a Cape May planning report seventeen years ago argued that only the development of big new motels would stimulate Cape May's then-sagging economy, stating that travelers would not stay in the old-fashioned Cape May houses! How wrong those planners proved to be!

Incidentally, *Americana* is published by the American Heritage Publishing Company at 381 West Center Street in Marion, Ohio, 43302.

THE MAINSTAY INN, 635 Columbia Avenue, Cape May, N.J. 08204; 609-884-8690. A 9 room inn in a well-preserved Victorian village just one block from the ocean. Modified American plan. Breakfast served to houseguests. Open every day of the year from April to October; weekends in March and November. No pets. Boating, swimming, fishing, bicycles, riding, golf, tennis, and hiking nearby. Not suitable for small children. No credit cards; personal checks accepted. Tom and Sue Carroll, Innkeepers.

Directions: From Philadelphia take the Walt Whitman Bridge to the Atlantic City Expy. Follow the Atlantic City Expy. to exit for Garden State Pkwy., south. Go south on the Pkwy. which ends in Cape May. The Pkwy. becomes Lafayetts St.; turn left at first light onto Madison. Proceed 3 blocks and turn right onto Columbia. Proceed 3 blocks to inn on right side.

GARNET HILL LODGE
North River, New York

The time was 7:30 a.m. and there was a bit of haze on 13th Lake and its surrounding mountains. The mid-July half-moon was gradually fading from sight as the sun became the dominant force of the day.

I was on the broad front porch which runs the entire length of the Log House at Garnet Hill Lodge. The scenery reminded me a great deal of looking out over the Smoky Mountains at Hemlock Lodge in western North Carolina. In front of me a permanent croquet game was awaiting the next contest; I also noticed a volleyball court, a big ash tree with a tire hanging from its branches, and the most inviting-looking hammock I have ever seen.

Meantime, the tantalizing aromas of Mary Heim's breakfast were wafting across the terrace and mixing in with the natural sweet smell of grasses and trees.

"Doesn't it look wonderful!" George Heim, who had probably been up for hours taking care of the many chores of the inn, dropped into one of the rustic chairs beside me. "It's the ever-changing aspect of the seasons that never ceases to thrill me. You must come up, of course, in the autumn when this foliage is absolutely spectacular. The end of September is an excellent time. It's wonderful for hiking to the abandoned garnet mine, or to one of the distant ponds. In wintertime, it is breathtaking. We have miles and miles of cross-country ski trails and everything is literally buried in snow."

I was already impressed, because the night before George and Mary had shown me some slides of Garnet Hill Lodge in all seasons and one of them showed snow up to the roof of the porch, so that it was possible to walk in through the second-floor window. The slides showed guests cross-country skiing, snowshoeing, and hiking, and the summer scenes included sailboating, canoeing, and fishing.

"Fishing is a big thing here," said George. "We have landlocked salmon and brook trout in 13th Lake, and the nearby lakes and streams have lake trout, rainbow, brownies, bass, walleyes, and pickerel. Another thing that impresses our guests is the unusual number of wild animals. In a morning walk down to the beaver pond, they can see beavers, deer, hares, loons, blue herons, foxes, weasels, and raccoons. The owls, hawks, and ravens are very popular with bird watchers. Many bring their tape recorders." I asked about black bear and he replied, "Oh yes, we have them, but they don't bother anybody."

Garnet Hill Lodge is a rustic resort-inn centered in the Log House, which was built in 1936 high in the Adirondack Mountains, with its own beach on 13th Lake.

A few years ago, after a twenty-year hitch in the United States Navy, George, Mary, and their six children came to the Adirondacks looking for "just the kind of a place that Garnet Hill Lodge turned out to be." Besides the Heim family, some of whom are still at home, there are also a handsome malamute, a beagle, and several other pet animals . . . including an extraordinary cat who is a mixture of tabby and "raccoon."

Lodgings are in individual bedrooms, very clean and neat; about half have private bathrooms. The *chef de cuisine* is Mary Heim and the specialties include generous portions of pot roast, chicken, baked fish, and other hearty offerings.

The kids like it because pizza is served on the weekend.

George stood up and suggested that after breakfast we might go down and look for beaver. He pointed to the mountains, and said, "I'm certainly glad we found our way up here."

I am too.

GARNET HILL LODGE, 13th Lake Road, North River, N.Y. 12856; 518-251-2821. A 15-room rustic resort-inn high in the Adirondacks, 32 mi. from Warrensburg. Open year-round with the exception of two weeks in April. Mod. American and European plans available. Breakfast, lunch, and dinner served to transients. Swimming, boating, hiking, fishing, and xc skiing on grounds. Downhill skiing, long distance hikes, and beautiful Adirondack drives nearby. The area has many museums, art and craft centers, and historical points. No pets. No credit cards. Taxi service provided to bus stop 30 mi. away. George and Mary Heim, Innkeepers.

Directions: From the Northway (I-87) take Exit 23 and follow Rtes. 9 and 28 north 4 mi. Take left fork (Rte. 28) 22 mi. to North River. Take second left (13th Lake Road) 5 mi. to Lodge. For more explicit directions, write for brochure.

CLARKSON HOUSE
Lewiston, New York

A light snow was falling on an early December evening when I first visited the Clarkson House in Lewiston, New York, a number of years ago. The Christmas tree lights were already blinking out their happy message, and there was a small group of sculptured figures depicting the Holy Family across from the inn. I ventured down the street to see the appealing miniature Christmas tree lights draped around each of the trees in the business district. It all made a very happy holiday effect.

This was my first visit to this corner of New York State dominated by the presence of Niagara Falls. I learned about the Clarkson House from my good friend, Robert Lenz, now the innkeeper of the Asa Ransom House in Clarence, New York. Bob said that it was very special, and he proved to be right.

I found the Clarkson House to be an excellent restaurant — something I knew the moment I smelled a most delicious aroma which I discovered came from the charcoal grill right in the middle of the dining area, where the filets and lamb chops were sizzling away merrily. Around it, there is an unusual arrangement of booths and tables, and on the walls a collection of tools and gadgets used more than 100 years ago. "They haven't discovered the use for some of them!" said Marilyn Clarkson. There are old-fashioned kerosene lamps on the tables, and the walls have several good paintings interspersed with wall lamps.

On that first trip I discovered that Bob Clarkson is a great believer in having things under control. For example, there are 22 tables, all carefully spaced out on the wooden floor which is scrubbed

every day. This means that reservations are most advisable as only a limited number of diners can be accommodated.

Secondly, the menu has been judiciously pared down to a few entrees which are very carefully prepared and most tastefully arranged on the plates. There is an emphasis on beef, including sirloin, filet and prime rib. There are also delicious French-cut lamb chops. A combination of beef filet and lobster tail, or half of a Maine lobster (flown in fresh) are also offered. That, plus four desserts, including cherries jubilee and baked Alaska, is the menu. I mustn't forget to mention that there was a little sign on one of those delicious-looking baked potatoes that said, "Eat all you like, I've been scrubbed and tubbed."

The newest thing at the Clarkson House is a lobster tank which holds up to two hundred lobsters in artificial sea water. "We've always served lobsters," explained Bob, "and now we can serve lobsters fresh from the sea!"

I have revisited the Clarkson House several times since that December evening a number of years ago, and have noted with great satisfaction the continued growth of the Niagara Falls area, including the Art Park. They have a wide variety of programs ranging from Broadway plays to popular dance, ballet, opera, and jazz, featuring some of the leading artists from the United States and Canada. Niagara-on-the-Lake with the Shaw Festival is just a short, pleasant drive into Canada.

The Clarkson House has been in *CIBR* since 1973.

THE CLARKSON HOUSE, 810 Center St., Lewiston, N.Y. 14092; 716-754-4544. A country restaurant, 7 mi. from Niagara Falls and Olde Fort Niagara. No lodgings. Dinner served daily except Mondays. Closed Christmas. Bob and Marilyn Clarkson, Innkeepers.

Directions: From I-190 exit at Lewiston and follow Rte. 104E for 1½ mi. Turn right on Rte. 18F and travel 2 blocks west to restaurant.

ASA RANSOM HOUSE
Clarence, New York

Sparkly-eyed Judy Lenz and I were standing in the Clarence Hollow dining room of the Asa Ransom House. "We're changing the inn all of the time," she said. "We subtract and add different ideas. For example, when we set aside the Ransom Room for non-smokers a few years ago, it was quite innovative. Furthermore, we've kept the atmosphere in the two rooms quite different."

Yes, indeed, they are. The Clarence Hollow Room has blue table mats and ladder-back chairs. There are framed maps of Western

New York State, a plate rail with plates and tea pots interspersed with a lantern or two that Bob and Judy have collected over the years. The curtains are blue and there's a big fireplace at one end. The Ransom Room has green tablecloths, ball-fringed curtains, many growing flowers, and two matching antique lamps hanging from the ceiling.

"When it came to decorating the guest rooms, Bob and I had a wonderful time. First, we decided that instead of numbers, they should have names to fit their personalities. For example, the Red Room is proud of the 1825 Cannonball double bed. The Blue Room is a soft, lovely bedroom with a canopied bed and is very popular with honeymooning couples. The larger Gold Room is outfitted with twin iron-and-brass beds with a table between them. We have finally completed the new room, and I must say I'm so pleased with the hours of stenciling that I did on the walls. It has an American Eagle theme with each individual color and individual shading of pineapple below the ceiling. One wall is of natural brick which is a marvelous contrast. We always have lots of books and flowers in the rooms and whenever possible, bowls of fruit. Of course, each room has its own bath, and I'm happy to say they're so popular that most of the time they're booked in advance."

The Asa Ransom House reflects Bob and Judy's innovative flair. For example, their religious convictions prohibit serving pork and shellfish. As a pork substitute, "One of our favorite dishes" asserted Bob, "is smoked cornbeef with apple raisin sauce." There are also "country pies," including salmon pond, which is a house specialty, chicken pot pie, and steak and kidney pie. In the kitchen of the inn, they whip their own cream, use honey, and natural raw-milk cheese from a local cheese factory; and never any MSG. Three types of butter are served.

Breakfast to houseguests consists of fresh fruit, muffins, and a beverage, as well as Judy's special breakfast egg pie. Lunch is served one day a week only: Wednesdays. Two tables are set up on the front porch for both lunch and dinner when the weather permits. Bicycles are now available for houseguests.

Jennifer, the Lenz's nine-year-old daughter, likes to stop in after school to help clear the dishes on Wednesdays. Judy said she hopes that this continues into Jennifer's late teens! Incidentally, there is a park and playground, along with a duck pond, just down the street for those guests who do bring their children. Bob says, "Children enjoy that and we supply the bread for the ducks."

There are many more delightful original ideas at the Asa Ransom House, including Sunshine Square, a most interesting gift shop which is made in the form of a village of gifts. The herb garden has now reached such a proportion that Bob and Judy had to provide a diagram showing the many varieties. These, of course, are used in the kitchen.

The Asa Ransom House is closed on Fridays and Saturdays because Bob and Judy are members of the Worldwide Church of God. However, Sunday evening, the inn is filled again with happy diners.

ASA RANSOM HOUSE, Rte. 5, Clarence, N.Y. 14031; 716-759-2315. A 4-room village inn approximately 15 mi. from Buffalo near the Albright Knox Art Gallery, The Studio Arena Theatre, the Art Park, and Niagara Falls. European plan. Dinner served Monday through Thursdays 4:30 to 9 p.m.; Sundays, 12:30 to 8 p.m. Lunch is available on Wednesday only. Closed Friday and Saturday. No pets. No credit cards. Tennis, golf, fishing, swimming nearby. Limited amusement for children under 12. Bob and Judy Lenz, Innkeepers.

Directions: From the New York Thruway traveling west, use exit 48A-Pembrook. Turn right to Rte. 5 and proceed 11 mi. to Clarence. Traveling east on the N.Y. Thruway, use Exit 49; turn left on Rte. 78, go 1 mi. to Rte. 5 and continue 5¼ mi. Coming from the east via Rte. 20, just east of Lancaster, N.Y., turn right on Ransom Rd., go to end and turn left.

GLEN IRIS INN
Castile, New York

I was standing on the pillared porch of this beautiful inn with the morning sun streaming across the circular bed of radiant iris. The sun, through the evergreens, maples, and oaks of the forest created a dappled pattern at the edge of the broad lawn. It was a clear morning in mid-June and I had just finished one of Peter Pizzutelli's hearty

breakfasts, and would be off in a few moments for a tour of Letchworth State Park.

Wherever I walked on the grounds, I could hear the sounds of the falls. In fact, the previous evening some people coming out of the dining room had thought that it was raining. The roar of the falls does, indeed, sound like a heavy downpour, which they are, actually. These are the Middle Falls of the Genesee River which cuts through this section of New York State, creating a series of S-turns and cutbacks between the banks that very much resemble the conformation of the Grand Canyon in Arizona, except, of course, they are not as deep.

The Glen Iris, originally a two-story frame house, was the former home of William Prior Letchworth, a nineteenth-century philanthropist.

The most recent addition is a new expanded terrace off the main dining room which provides more comfortable seating arrangements for more people. The many large windows seem to bring the outdoors right inside. The original Letchworth dining room, which was a gift shop for many years, has now been returned to its former status of a small, pleasant dining room. It has very appropriate furniture to go with the beige and brown wallpaper.

The bedrooms are reached by a twisting, turning staircase of dark chestnut wood and, instead of having numbers, they have names of trees found in the park. All are comfortably furnished in nineteenth-century style. A motel unit is located in a nearby grove for additional overnight guests.

The unusual combination of a beautiful country inn next to a spectacular waterfall in a totally protected state park located in a historical section of western New York State attracts large numbers of visitors to the area; I cannot emphasize too strongly the advisability of having reservations for any of the meals or lodgings.

Guests visiting the Glen Iris for an overnight stay or a meal, are reminded to give the waitress the $1.50 park toll ticket, which is deducted from whatever is spent at the inn.

The bill of fare at the Glen Iris offers many tempting choices. One of the selections is called chicken Virginia—boneless whole breast of chicken, sautéed to a golden brown, topped with a creamy wine sauce with mushrooms and then served over sliced ham. The roast beef choices include a hefty cut for a full appetite and a lighter cut for the not-so-hungry diner. They're served with fresh-baked popovers. It was at the Glen Iris that I made my first acquaintance with non-alcoholic pina-colada made from fresh coconut and pineapple juice—it has changed my life.

Cora Pizzutelli joined me on the front terrace. "Oh, I wish you could be here in October. Last year the foliage was especially gorgeous. There were record numbers of people coming to view it and also to have lunch. We have an amazing number of repeat dinner and overnight guests who have become like family members. Our guests are very special to us. Each fall at closing time, when the trees are stripped bare and the park begins to show signs of winter approaching, many guests make a special visit to say 'good-bye' for another season and to wish us well. It's very touching."

GLEN IRIS INN, Castile, N.Y. 14427; 716-493-2622. A 20-room country inn located at the Middle Falls of the Genesee River in Letchworth State Park. European plan. Breakfast, lunch, and dinner served to travelers daily. Open from Easter Sunday through first Sunday in November. Footpaths, swimming, and bicycles nearby. Historical sites in Park and spectacular views within walking distance. Peter and Cora Pizzutelli, Innkeepers.

Directions: Inn is located off Rtes. 436, 19A and 39 in Letchworth State Park, 55 mi. from Buffalo and Rochester.

THE HOLLOWAY HOUSE
East Bloomfield, New York

I was headed west on Route 20 toward Buffalo and Niagara Falls. I had just visited the Sonnenberg Gardens in Canandaigua where there are over 5000 rosebushes set against a background of evergreens and a gleaming white Grecian temple—quite unusual for central New York State. Passing through the little town of East Bloomfield, I was attracted to a beautiful white clapboard house set back among large old maple trees. The sign told me that it was "The Holloway *Houfe,*" a country restaurant.

I pulled into the parking space, walked up the stone steps into the front hallway, and found myself in what resembled a most gracious home. There were several fireplaces and lots of comfortable furniture. Lunch was still being served, so I decided to remain and asked for a table by the window.

An attractive woman came over and introduced herself. That's how I met Doreen Wayne. She and Fred are the keepers of the Holloway House, and both of them were kind enough to give me a tour after lunch and explain how all of this came about.

"Peter Holloway, the village blacksmith, built this house in 1808 and operated it as a tavern," explained Doreen. "You can still see the many hand-hewn beams and square nails.

"In those days cooking was done in the cellar and as a kind of reminder, this large open fireplace with a Dutch oven was built. In reconstructing our country dining room, old homemade bricks were used, and we have tried to preserve the early 19th-century feeling."

I found that the Waynes have been at the Holloway for 19 years and have a marvelous reputation for serving delicious and interesting food. Among the items on the menu is Killarney Kress, a sweet pickle sauerkraut which is green in color. They also serve homemade Sally Lunn bread every day. "The original recipe came from Bath, England," Doreen explained. "It's cooked with a great many eggs and has a cakelike texture. It's made daily by our baker who has been with us for fourteen years." The menu has unusual depth. It includes fried chicken and biscuits, baked ham, and turkey. Fred said that turkey is the most popular item on the menu. There is also a choice of beef and seafood dishes as well. "Lots of people come on Sundays because that's when we serve black-bottom pie and creamed mushrooms."

The kitchen at Holloway House is absolutely immaculate, roomy, and cool, and anyone is welcome to look in on it at any time. The kitchen floor and varnished tables are shining clean. I would feel at home dining there myself.

Innkeeping runs in the family at this inn in East Bloomfield. Son Steve, who is a Cornell Hotel School graduate, runs the grill and also serves as host. David, eighteen years old, is now at Cornell in the Hotel School. He and I had a brief reunion when I visited Cornell in the fall of 1978. The third member of the family, Linda, is also a Cornell graduate. "In another field," as Doreen says.

The Holloway House has been in *CIBR* since 1976.

THE HOLLOWAY HOUSE, Rtes. 5 & 20, East Bloomfield, N.Y. 14443; 716-657-7120. A country restaurant 8 miles west of Canandaigua, N.Y. No lodgings. Lunch and dinner served daily except Mondays. Open April 1-Dec. 1. Sonnenberg Gardens, golf courses, and Finger Lake Racetrack nearby. Fred, Doreen and Mildred Wayne, Innkeepers.

Directions: From N.Y. State Thruway take Exit 45, follow Rte. 96E 3 mi. to Victor N.Y. Go south on Victor-Holcomb Rd. 5 mi. Turn right at light in Holcomb then second left to Rte. 5 & 20.

SPRINGSIDE INN
Auburn, New York

Barbara Dove and I were standing in front of the long list of "things to do" in the Finger Lakes District, all within a reasonable drive of the Springside Inn.

"Oh, our guests seem to just love this," exclaimed Barb, "and everyone is grateful for the assistance." The list was on a wall-mounted scroll about four feet long and included places to go antiquing, to rent boats, to birdwatch, to rent bicycles; where to find churches, golf courses, museums, and glass factories; how to reach the nearby Indian village, and ten colleges in the area; where to play tennis; and a list of shops with unusual gifts and crafts.

It also listed trips to nearby wineries and many interesting activities for any season of the year.

We walked up the red-carpeted stairway to the second floor to look at several of the rooms which had been redecorated since my last visit. "Here's one that we finished last summer," she said, "and it has been occupied 'most every night. Would you believe we hung pictures and mirrors ten minutes before the first occupants arrived? It was sheer madness, but we made it."

Each of the lodging rooms is decorated to give a different feeling. One is in shades of pink with a pink bedspread and matching curtains. A friendly rocking chair is in front of the window overlooking the lake.

Another room has twin beds, Victorian furniture, and lamps with red bows. By way of contrast, a room on the top floor is done in shades of beige and yellow with formal valances on the window, a Tiffany-type lamp, hooked rugs, and twin beds.

We paused for a moment where the open staircase is L-shaped, and once again talked about how many weddings are held at the Springside and how many bridal bouquets have been tossed from this particular point on the stairs.

Barbara explained that about 85% of their overnight guests were traveling with *Country Inns and Back Roads*. "They seem to enjoy the food, our summer dinner theatre, and, of course, our ducks," she said. "We've had comments about the comfortable mattresses, and quite a few guests have left notes praising our 'breakfast-in-a-basket.'

"We enjoy meeting so many people from all over the United States and Canada. Many of them came from Toronto and Montreal. They seem especially pleased to get a jar of our homemade salad dressing to take home."

The Springside Inn, on the northern end of Owasco Lake, is one of the most beautiful spots imaginable in autumn. It is particularly enjoyable to drive along the lakeside roads where there are many farm stands offering apples, pumpkins, pears and other Finger Lakes fruits and vegetables.

"There aren't nearly as many people in the region at that time either," explained Barbara. "We like it because we have more of a chance to spend some time with our guests and take some day trips ourselves."

Springside Inn has been in *CIBR* since 1971.

SPRINGSIDE INN, 41 West Lake Rd., Auburn, N.Y. 13021; 315-252-7247. A 7-room country inn, 1 mi. south of Auburn with a view of Owasco Lake. In the heart of the historical Finger Lakes. Lodgings include Continental breakfast. Some rooms with shared baths. Open Tuesday through Sunday, May 1 to Sep. 30. Open Wed. through Sunday, Oct. 1 to April 30. Closed Memorial Day, July 4th, Labor Day, Christmas, and New Year's Day. Boating, swimming, bicycles on grounds. Golf, riding, Alpine and xc skiing nearby. Bill and Barbara Dove, Innkeepers.

Directions: From N.Y. Thruway, take Exit 40 and follow Rte. 34 south through downtown Auburn to Rte. 38. Follow Rte. 38 south to traffic circle at Lake and take 2nd exit right at West Shore of Owasco Lake, Drive ¼ mi. to inn.

THE SHERWOOD INN
Skaneateles, New York

Joy Eberhardt was reminiscing about the first few years after she and her husband Bill had acquired the Sherwood Inn. This venerable building which has a beautiful view of Lake Skaneateles has an interesting history which dates back to the early nineteenth century.

"At first the two of us had to be prepared to do everything, including make the beds, cook the dinners, show people to their tables, and run the dishwasher. Fortunately, even as young as we were, both of us had some experience, particularly in the kitchen. When I think back on those days, it really makes me smile, and then I look around and see what wonderful progress was made. Almost from the first day we met which, by the way, was when we both worked in another restaurant, we knew that we wanted to own a country inn. We looked at a number of them, and then found The Sherwood and knew it was right for us."

We were having lunch in the same lively dining room where I had taken dinner the night before. The day was beautifully snowy in the Finger Lakes area in early February. I had traversed Route 20 from Cazenovia, thoroughly enjoying the roller coaster feature of the road as it dips into the valleys formed by ancient lakes, now departed.

The central New York State farms, their staunch buildings and barns and silos filled with produce and silage, all looked prosperous. The orchards, which are laden with blossoms in the spring and rich fruit in the fall, now stood mute in the blowing snow.

I stepped into the cherry warmth of the inn lobby to find a small group of people gathered in front of the fireplace. Next to the piano there was an exhibition of art which I subsequently learned had just replaced the gingerbread Christmas village which was already a tradition at the Sherwood Inn.

Joy Eberhardt was there to greet me, apologizing for Bill's absence. She suggested that there was still time enough before lunch to see some of the newly decorated lodging rooms on the floors above. "We're really very happy about them," she said.

The beautifully finished floorboards of different widths caught my eye immediately as we reached the second floor. The original pristine character of the pine shines through. "There must have been eight coats of paint on them," she asserted. The selection of wallpapers, furniture, and decorations was most appealing.

There are eleven lodging rooms and three large apartments. Joy showed me the honeymoon suite which is done in shades of blue, and the pattern of the quilt on the four-poster canopied bed matches both the drapes and the wallpaper. There is a beautiful view of the lake. All but three of the rooms have a lake view.

Now we were in the dining room enjoying a really delicious quiche which she told me was prepared by Pinky Lipe who had also created the gingerbread village during the holiday season, and who does all the desserts.

"As you can see, our menu is pretty much oriented to central New York State. We have roast duckling, London broil, roast beef, turkey, and lamb dishes. We serve a traditional Sunday dinner here and also a full Sunday brunch. On Fridays and Saturdays we have sing-alongs and everybody joins in."

Today, the Sherwood Inn which started its life as a stagecoach tavern is probably in the best possible hands. These young inn-keepers have already established themselves as part of the community, and like so many other inns, it is the center of much village activity. The good people of Skaneateles take a more than proprietary interest in it.

THE SHERWOOD INN, 26 West Genesee St., Skaneateles, N.Y. 13152; 315-685-3405. A 12-room village inn on the shores of Lake Skaneateles in the Finger Lakes district of New York State. Continental breakfast included in room tariff. Lunch and dinner served daily to travelers. Open every day except Christmas. Tennis, swimming, golf, and indoor winter ice skating available nearby. Near Everson Museum, Barrow Art Gallery, and William Seward House. William and Joy Eberhardt, Innkeepers.

Directions: From New York State Thruway use Weedsport exit and follow Rte. 34 south to Auburn (6 mi.). Turn east on Rte. 20, 7 mi. to Skaneateles. Inn is located in center of village.

LINCKLAEN HOUSE
Cazenovia, New York

I was back at the Lincklaen House. The hour was 11:15 p.m. I had arrived at approximately 10 o'clock and found the ubiquitous Helen Tobin still at the inn. We sat in front of the parlor fireplace for a nice hour-long chat. One of the things she mentioned was that people using Exit 34 on the New York State Thruway had the advantage of coming up Route 13 past Chittenango Falls, which is just a few minutes away from Cazenovia.

"They are actually higher than Niagara," she said, "and it is such a beautiful spot. During the wintertime the ice formations are spectacular."

Guests staying at the Lincklaen House and meeting Helen for the first time frequently say, "Oh, I feel as if I have known you for a long time." This is because Helen has genuine warmth and con-sideration, and the Lincklaen House reflects this feeling. It's this feeling, also, that keeps the paneled walls and ceilings as gleaming as the white tablecloths. She also insists on fresh flowers, crisp vegetables, hot popovers, hearty portions, lots of bath towels and, above all, a feeling of rapport with her guests.

"I try to talk with everyone while they're here," she said. "Many become good friends and I hear from them at Christmas." Speaking

of Christmas, Helen has framed many of the Christmas cards from the Golden Lamb Inn in Lebanon, Ohio, and they hang in the lobby.

"Nineteen-eighty is going to be a very exciting year," she said. "My son Edward whom you met for the first time in 1967, will receive two Master degrees: one in engineering and the other in business administration. My daughter Ann, who graduated from the Cornell Hotel School, entered The Wharton School in January. My daughter Barbara, who was here for many years and was married a couple of years ago, continues to live in California and she and her husband John are very happy."

Cazenovia is one of the attractive towns along Route 20 in central New York State, and its situation on a beautiful lake is an added attraction for Lincklaen House guests. The inn has been called the best example of early 19th-century architecture. Fortunately the classic Greek Revival lines have been well-preserved.

The area has recreation for outdoor-minded guests in both summer and winter, and there is especially good downhill and cross-country skiing nearby.

"Being an innkeeper is so much fun," Helen said, as we walked through the dining room which was faintly lighted by the last glow of the fireplace. "It's taken quite a while to have things right, but returning guests make it all worthwhile. Some say they were here the day the deer came through the side door; others remember the day that Ann was accepted at Cornell. It's just great."

"Cazenovia is getting to be a very special event-minded community," Helen remarked. "We have the Winter Festival every

February; the Lorenzo needlework exhibit the whole month of June; arts and crafts on our village green, plus a parade and fireworks over the Fourth of July; the Lorenzo driving competition, which takes place on July 19th; the Franklin car reunion each year in August; and our own events here at the Lincklaen House at Christmastime.

"We serve afternoon tea here every day and it's the one time of the day that I make every effort to be back here to meet my guests and to introduce them to each other. It's one of the nicest times of the day at the Lincklaen House when we are all sitting around the fire or in the courtyard."

Lincklaen House has been included in *CIBR* since 1968.

LINCKLAEN HOUSE, Cazenovia, N.Y. 13035; 315-655-3461. A 27-room village inn, 20 mi. east of Syracuse. Near several state parks, the Erie Canal Museum and the Canal Trail. European plan. Modified American plan upon request. Breakfast, lunch, and dinner served to travelers daily. Open year-round. Tennis, golf, bicycles, Alpine and xc skiing nearby. Helen Tobin, Innkeeper.

Directions: From west on N.Y. Thruway, take Exit 34A, follow Rte. 481 south, take Exit 3E and follow Rte. 92 east to Cazenovia. From east on N.Y. Thruway, take Exit 34 and follow Rte. 13 south to Cazenovia. From Rte. 81, take Exit 15 (LaFayette) and follow Rte. 20 East, 18 mi. to inn.

MILLHOF INN
Stephentown, New York

"Oh, we just love people from *Country Inns and Back Roads!*" Ronnie Tallet was in a gay mood as we all sat around the fireplace of this small inn, located in the Berkshires on the border of Massachusetts and New York. "They come from all over the country and even from Europe. We know that when *CIBR* travelers call us, they are looking for a *real* inn. Many times they have stayed at the Redcoat's Return in the Catskills, the Springside in Auburn, or the Lincklaen House in Cazenovia."

The Millhof is similar to many European country inns I have visited. Particularly, in Germany's Black Forest. Most of the bedrooms have balconies overlooking the brook on one side and the forest on the other. The railings and window shutters have been hand-carved and colorfully decorated.

The word "Millhof" really means millhouse, and this building was actually used as a sawmill for many years. Frank and Ronnie have made numerous alterations and additions, but the basic structure remains the same. A few years ago they saw great

175

possibilities in it, and since Frank is from a French background and Ronnie was born in Yugoslavia, a lot of the furnishings and decorations are from the old country. Ronnie is quite an accomplished artist and has done quite a few of the paintings which are displayed in the inn.

There was much for us to talk about over dinner. Young Gregory Tallet, who had shown me about the grounds and taken me up to see the new swimming pool on a earlier visit, was a year older and was missing two front teeth. "He's still our official guide and is very helpful to many of our guests," said Ronnie.

Debbie, who is now quite grown-up at seventeen and will graduate from high school in June of 1980, had spent most of the summer on the staff at another of the *CIBR* inns: the Yankee Clipper in Rockport, Massachusetts.

Ronnie does the cooking and, among other things, her blanquette de veal and chicken alba are among the most admired dishes. A hearty breakfast features stone-ground wheat cakes and maple syrup, and also a wide variety of omelets.

The European Alpine theme extends throughout the inn and particularly to the lodging rooms, each of which is individually decorated and all have plants, books, and magazines. Frank has done almost all the decorating and redesigning, which continues to be a tribute to his skill and ingenuity.

"Our new deck which I built last spring has really been very popular," he said. "It overlooks the brook and has a nice view of the hills. We serve breakfast out there whenever possible."

Gregory was finally packed off to bed, and Debbie excused herself to study for a Spanish test. Frank went to find some more popcorn for the skiing guests, and Ronnie said she was so glad that they had put in the swimming pool. "It's not very big," she said, "but our adult guests really find it a very nice place to relax and chat.

Many people who come during the summer to go to Tanglewood, stay over Monday, Tuesday, and Wednesday, as well." Winter or summer, it's fun to visit the Millhof Inn.

MILLHOF INN, Route 43, Stephentown, N.Y. 12168; 518-733-5606. A 10-room central-European-style country inn. 14 mi. from Pittsfield and 12 mi. from Williamstown. A pleasant drive from both Tanglewood in the summer, and Jiminy Peak and Brodie Mountain in the winter. European plan. In wintertime, breakfast is served every morning, and dinner is served on the weekends and during holiday weeks by reservation; breakfast and lunch are served daily during the summer. Open every day from May 26 through March 31. Swimming pool on grounds,. Hiking, skiing, backroading, and all of the famous Berkshire recreational and cultural attractions nearby. No pets. Frank and Ronnie Tallet, Innkeepers.

Directions: From New York: exit the Taconic Parkway at Rte. 295. Travel east to Rte. 22 north. Turn east at Stephentown on Rte. 43. The inn is one mile on the left. From Boston: exit Mass. Turnpike at New Lebanon. North on Rte. 22 to Rte. 43, etc.

BEEKMAN ARMS
Rhinebeck, New York

For many years I have been sharing with our readers some of the historical significance of the Beekman Arms which is according to the beautiful new sign on the front lawn, "The Oldest Inn in America." It is in the historic town of Rhinebeck, located in the center of the lovely Hudson River Valley. I'm sure everyone knows about this beautiful section of the country because as innkeeper Chuck LaForge says, "Washington Irving was our first press agent."

The inn's origins go back to the early 1700s, and by 1769 it had increased to two full stories with a roomy attic which later became a ballroom. When trouble arose between the Indians and the white men, the entire community would take refuge within its walls.

During the Revolution, George Washington and his staff enjoyed the inn's fare, and the window from which the Commander-in-Chief watched for his couriers is still there. Those were anxious days, and Lafayette, Schuyler, Hamilton, and Arnold also spent many hours at the inn. In fact, over the years, hundreds of men who helped fashion the destiny of our nation partook of the inn's hospitality.

There have been courtships, weddings, political rallies, quarrels, assignations, plots, counterplots, concerts, balls, and parties galore. In short, it's now rounding out its third century of being the center of community activities.

I was made even more aware of this during a Christmas visit. It was one of those days when leaden skies and sullen winds were harbingers of a real snowstorm.

Inside, Earl Bebo put another log on the fire for a group of very excited ladies who were here for a Christmas holiday lunch. He also lit the little candle sconces, and the true cheeriness of the inn began to pervade the atmosphere. I commented on the attractiveness of the American primitive furniture, with which all the dining rooms and parlors of the inn are now outfitted, and Earl replied that the Water Wheel Wood Works in nearby Pine Plains is also making specially designed furniture for the inn's lodging rooms. "We have completed transforming four rooms into two with private baths," he said. "This means that we will have sixteen rooms with private baths."

A beaming Chuck LaForge, my friend of many years, greeted me exuberantly, and we continued our stroll about the inn as he proudly pointed out many things that had taken place since my last visit.

In the Tap Room with its beautiful paneled walls, there's a blackboard which told everybody that the luncheon that day started with Bavarian lentil soup, followed by pepper steak or braised short ribs of beef, or sardines on toast points served with raw onions, plus cole slaw and/or potato salad.

More and more of the village businessmen and curious and expectant travelers were filling the inn at lunchtime, and there was a wonderful air of pre-Christmas hustle and bustle as the attractive waitresses chatted with the guests and made note of their luncheon orders.

The village of Rhinebeck grew up around the original crossroads tavern. It is within an easy driving distance of a great many of the restored and preserved homes of the Hudson Valley. One of the delightful diversions for visitors is to walk around the corner to the Firehouse Gift Shop which, along with other shops, is housed in what used to be the old Rhinebeck Firehouse.

Today, the Beekman Arms is much more than a historic inn which thousands of people visit because of its fascinating authentic colonial decor. Like many other country and village inns, it is very much the center of all community activity. Decisions, great and small, have been made within its walls for almost three hundred years.

It's a living link to America's past.

The Beekman Arms has been included in *CIBR* since 1967.

BEEKMAN ARMS, Rhinebeck, N. Y. 12572; 914-876-7077. A 13-room village inn with an adjacent 4-room guest house, 1 mi. from Amtrak Station at Rhinecliff. Short drive to F.D.R. Library and Home in Hyde Park. European plan. Lunch and dinner served to travelers daily. Closed Christmas. Open year-round. Golf, tennis, swimming nearby. No amusements for young children. Charles LaForge, Innkeeper.

Directions: From N. Y. Thruway, take Exit 19, cross Rhinecliff Bridge and pick up Rte. 199 south to Rte. 9. Proceed south on Rte. 9 to middle of village. From Taconic Pkwy. exit at Rhinebeck and follow Rte. 199 west 11 mi. to Rte. 308 into village.

GREENVILLE ARMS
Greenville, New York

I was swinging on one of the swings at the Greenville Arms, going higher and higher almost as if on the backward swoop I would swing right into the swimming pool. I could look down on the beautiful lawn to the volleyball court, and then on across the fence to the field where there were horses grazing, and a farm beyond. I pumped again, straining to go higher. Now, I could look into the uppermost branches of the twenty-six-year-old blue spruces, but not nearly as high as the fir trees that were planted fifty years ago. I could see the balustrade on the top of the Greenville Arms, and to my left, the converted barn with the connecting porch, that was once part of the hayloft.

There were the gentle sounds of a summer Sunday — birds flitting about among the tall trees on the village streets with their pleasant white clapboard homes, and the hollow sounds created by a stroller's footsteps on the slate sidewalks. The sky was blue with white clouds, and a gentle Catskill Mountain breeze relieved what would otherwise have been an uncomfortably warm day.

It was at the height of the summer, just a few days after the Fourth of July. All of the flowers carefully planted and nurtured by Ruth Stevens were in full bloom. The geraniums, impatiens, clematis, peonies, and roses sent forth their colorful message. There were other guests seated around the poolside tables and children using the wading pool. Some had been visiting the Catskill Game Farm nearby, and another family had spent part of the day at Howe Caverns in Cobleskill.

The Greenville Arms is a Victorian country mansion with several interesting porches, cupolas, gables, and corners. It's well-shaded with tall trees and beautifully landscaped with bushes and shrubs. Lodging rooms are in the main house and also in the converted barn to the rear. Throughout, the atmosphere could best be described as "homey and inviting." There is even an old-fashioned water cooler on the front porch.

I left my high-flying swing to join Ruth Stevens over a lemonade, and she told me about her menu: "There's a set meal on Saturdays, Sundays, Tuesdays, and Thursdays. On the other days, our guests have choices. A typical Sunday meal would be fruit cup, roast turkey, dressing, mashed potatoes, squash, peas, relishes, celery, cottage cheese, breads, and a choice of sundaes.

"There were five sisters in my family, and four out of five of us became innkeepers. We all learned cooking from my mother. We all grew up here in the Catskills. I guess my cooking is kind of old-fashioned, but our guests tell me they've enjoyed it for the last twenty-six years."

Holding to this tradition, the Greenville Arms has weekly rates which include two meals a day as well as the use of all the sports and recreational equipment on the premises. "The difference in rates is based on the type of accommodations. It's most necessary to call ahead for reservations, not only for rooms, but for meals as well." Winter guests enjoy skiing at Windham Mountain and in spring there's trout fishing and hiking. There are many historical houses and places nearby. In the summer and fall, guests can go horseback riding, play golf, or spend the day in the mountains. The bus from New York stops right in Greenville.

As we were strolling about the grounds around the swimming pool, I found a penny. "Pick it up and you will have good luck all day," said Ruth. The date on it was 1976, the first year that I visited the Greenville Arms.

That was one of my luckier days.

GREENVILLE ARMS, Greenville, N.Y. 12083; 518-966-5219. A 20-room country inn with many resort features 20 miles from Catskill, N.Y., on Route 32. Modified American or European plans. Breakfast and dinner served to travelers by reservation only. Open every day; no meals served Thanksgiving and Christmas. Children most welcome; cribs, cots, and highchairs available. Pets accommodated in nearby kennels. Pool and lawn sports on grounds. Riding, golf, skiing, hiking, backroading, antiquing nearby. No credit cards. Personal checks accepted. Ruth Stevens, Innkeeper.

Directions: Exit N.Y. Thrwy. at 21B. (Coxsackie-New Baltimore). Turn left on 9W South 2 mi. to traffic light. Turn right on Rte. 81W 13 mi. to Greenville. Turn left at traffic light. Inn is second house on right. Via Taconic Pkwy., exit at Ancram on Rte. 82W over Rip Van Winkle Bridge and follow Rte. 23 to Cairo. Turn right on 32N, 9 mi. to Greenville.

THE REDCOAT'S RETURN
Tannersville, New York

"If there's one thing that I think innkeepers should have in great abundance," asserted Tom Wright, "it is a sense of humor!"

That the Redcoat's Return abounds with a wonderful sense of humor is almost immediately obvious to even the first-time visitor. The name alone gets it off the mark. Peggy Wright explains it this way. "Tom is British, but he's been in this country a long time, and he and I thought this would be a great name for an inn kept by a Briton in the Catskills. A lot of people comment on it. We've even carried it through to the new inn sign which has a painting of Tom on one side and of me on the opposite side."

181

This wonderful sense of humor also includes the new brochure for the inn which carries on the cover the legend: "England is ten minutes from Tannersville." The brochure has a complete history of the beautiful old house which starts with its days as a "summer boarding house" in 1910. There's a marvelous description of what life in the Catskills was like for the summer visitors.

When Tom and Peggy Wright, who call themselves refugees from Manhattan, took over in the fall of 1972, the first project was to winterize the hotel completely and to convert it into an English country inn. For the past few years, Tom has been not only the chef, turning out prime ribs with Yorkshire pudding, poached filet of sole, roast duck in orange sauce, steak and kidney pie, as well as English-style fish and chips, but also the carpenter enlarging rooms, and adding bathrooms. "I would stop hammering and sawing," he said, "and run downstairs and check the sauce and test the roast. I'm happy to say that a great deal of the remodeling is done, and I can spend more time in my beloved kitchen."

The Redcoat's Return is in the center of the Catskill Game Reserve and there is a wealth of recreational activities available to the guests in every season of the year. Hiking trails actually lead from the inn into the mountains where there are magnificent views of the Hudson Valley. There's a lot of golf, swimming, tennis, and horseback riding nearby. During the winter season, there's downhill skiing at Cortina Valley, Hunter Mountain Ski Bowl, and Windham Mountain. There's also plenty of cross-country skiing throughout the area. The British ski team stayed at the inn while training at Hunter Mountain for the Winter Olympics.

Lunch is not served at any time at the Redcoat's Return. It will close for one week in early November, and anyone planning to visit at that time should call ahead for details.

Peggy Wright and her daughter Christine have gotten involved in pottery-making and have a cozy studio in the basement with all of the necessary paraphernalia. A small gift shop is anticipated and will also carry handcrafted items from other artists in the area, as well as their own pottery.

Although I have visited in the summer, my favorite time to drive over is in mid-December, when the inn is already decorated for Christmas. It's especially cozy on a chilly night when there's snow on the ground, and the wind whistles through the trees. On the last visit I found the red setter contentedly sharing the couch with the cat, and some good "Fats" Waller records being played lightly in the background.

Yes, the Redcoat's Return has all the ingredients of an ideal country inn, including generous dollops of humor.

THE REDCOAT'S RETURN, Dale Lane, Elka Park, N.Y. 12427; 518-589-6379. A 12-room English inn approx. 4 mi. from Tannersville, N.Y., in the heart of the Catskill Mts. Within a short drive of several ski areas and state hiking trails. European Plan. Lodgings include breakfast. Dinner served daily except Thursdays; no lunches served. Open from Memorial Day to Easter. Closed 1 week in early Nov. Please call for details. No pets. Hiking, nature walks, trout fishing, croquet, skiing, swimming, ice skating, riding, tennis nearby. Tom and Peggy Wright, Innkeepers.

Directions: Exit 20 or 21 from N.Y. Thrwy. Follow 23A to Tannersville; turn left at traffic light onto County Road 16. Follow signs to Police Center 4½ mi. Turn right on Dale Lane.

SWISS HUTTE
Hillsdale, New York

It was a very bright, very cold, blowy Saturday afternoon in January. I was at the Swiss Hutte for a spot of lunch and a chat with Tom and Linda Breen.

I sat in a warm, sunny corner with the panorama of the Catamount Ski Area spread out before me. It was a little too cold to ski, and quite a few people had come in for lunch. There was a great deal of kidding about going back on the slopes in the afternoon.

This same scene is quite different in the middle of the summer with the rushing brook gurgling its way down the mountain, and both the artificial and natural swimming pools out in front of the inn surrounded with people sunning themselves.

183

Catamount ski area

Oddly enough, the people who were here today were almost as tan and ruddy as the summer guests.

The Swiss Hutte is a Continental-type inn in a hidden Berkshire valley right on the New York-Massachusetts line. It is actually in Hillsdale, New York, but I can't help thinking of it as being a Massachusetts inn.

There are two types of accommodations available. One is in the main inn where there are country inn-type rooms. The other 15 rooms are in chalet-type motel units, each with its own balcony and excellent view of the mountains. In the summer, everything feels sequestered among the trees.

Coming up the Taconic Parkway from New York, it is an ideal distance for leaving late in the afternoon and arriving in time for dinner. Even today there was a variety of license plates in the parking lot, including one from California and one from West Virginia.

In spite of all the natural beauty, perhaps the Swiss Hutte is best-known for its food. Both lunch and dinner are leisurely affairs with individually prepared dishes. That particular day, I ordered French pancakes filled with chicken. The cool, fresh salad was delicately bathed in a perfect combination of oil and vinegar and condiments. The fresh French bread was hot to the touch. Among the other entrées are sweetbreads in Bernaise sauce, weinerschnitzel, sauerbraten, and veal chops Normande.

Desserts which are included in the price of the main dish, include creme carmel, French apple torte cheesecake, and a super delicious raspberry cream pie.

At the Swiss Hutte guests can enjoy tennis, swimming, hiking, skiing, cross-country skiing, and many other seasonal attractions. In summer, Tanglewood, Jacob's Pillow, and the Berkshire Playhouse are just a few miles away. Berkshire backroading is famous; you can start right at the front door using dirt roads that lead through the forest.

That's the Swiss Hutte. A little bit of the Alps in the Berkshires. Its been included in *CIBR* since 1970.

SWISS HUTTE, Hillsdale, N.Y. 12529; 518-325-3333. A 21-room Alpine country inn overlooking Catamount ski area, 6 mi. from Gt. Barrington, Mass. Modified American plan omits lunch. Breakfast, lunch, and dinner served to travelers daily. Closed month of April and from Nov. 15 to Dec. 15. Pool, tennis, putting green, Alpine and xc skiing on grounds. Tom and Linda Breen, Innkeepers.

Directions: From Boston, travel on Mass. Tpke. and take Exit 2. Follow Rte. 102 to Rte. 7. Proceed on Rte. 7 to Rte. 23. From New York City, follow Taconic Pkwy. and Rte. 23. From Albany, follow N.Y. Thruway and Taconic Pkwy. Inn is 10 mi. east of Pkwy. on Rte. 23.

OLD DROVERS INN
Dover Plains, New York

Menus are some of my favorite reading, particularly menus from country inns. This time I was reading the portable menu at the Old Drovers Inn. It was hanging on one of the low beams next to the fireplace, but innkeeper Trav Harris is prepared to move it to any corner of the dining room so that everyone may contemplate the culinary marvels awaiting his choice. There are the famous Old Drovers cheddar cheese or cold lemon soups, also onion or Russian cabbage soup.

A second course could be, among others, a paté of duck livers, Portuguese sardines, or a shrimp cocktail. Choosing an entreé involves deciding between dishes like roast duckling, curry of turkey or lamb with chutney, sautéed calves liver, beefsteak and kidney pie, shrimps rarebit, rainbow trout, or julienne of veal served Zurich style (that's veal sautéed in butter and white wine with mushrooms, shallots, and sour cream served over rice).

The desserts that evening included one of the inn's famous sweets: fresh key lime pie. There was also strawberry meringue glacé, peach Melba, and pecan pie.

I've gone into some detail about this menu because luncheon and dinner are the main reasons why most people visit Old Drovers Inn. The atmosphere in the dining room is romantic, to say the least,

with red leather benches, low wood ceilings, and an attractive combination of rough beams and stone walls. Lining the walls, just below the ceiling, is a collection of glass, copperware, and brass. An old musket hangs over the fireplace. Oversized glass hurricane lamps protect the candles on the tables, and it is great to come in on a chilly day to this beautiful room with a cheery fire crackling in the fireplace. The atmosphere reminds me very much of English country house hotels I've visited.

The three somewhat sumptuous lodgings on the floors above are reached by a box-like staircase hung with marine prints. A most comfortable sitting room on the second floor has a fireplace, deep-cushioned chairs, and plenty of books and magazines. The Federal Room, where breakfast is served, is decorated with some interesting Hudson Valley murals.

There is a handsome, double-sized sleigh bed in the corner bedroom which also has its own fireplace and is wood-paneled. Another bedroom has twin beds with beautiful quilts, more handsome paneling, a tall chest of drawers, and a fireplace. The curved ceiling in one room indicates that before its conversion into a spacious bedroom, it must have been part of the ballroom. These rooms, by the way, are usually booked considerably ahead and are available only to guests who also plan to have dinner.

Dining at the Old Drovers Inn is an elegant, luxurious experience, and the prices reflect the skillful preparation of top-quality food and drinks, fine tableware, and expert service. Inn-keeper Harris says, "Guests spending the night and taking dinner and a full breakfast should plan on sixty to seventy dollars each."

A dining experience like this must be savored in the most leisurely and unhurried fashion. But imagine, with all of this, I can still order browned turkey hash served with mustard sauce and delicious, crispy, crunchy-on-the-outside-and-soft-on-the-inside popovers!

OLD DROVERS INN, Dover Plains, New York 12522; 914-832-9311. A 3-room authentic 18th-century luxury country inn midway between New York City and the Berkshires just off New York Rte. 22. European plan. A full breakfast available to house guests at à la carte prices. Closed on Tuesdays and Wednesdays and for 3 weeks prior to Dec. 30 each year. Luncheon served weekdays from noon to 3 p.m. Dinner served weekdays from 6-9 p.m., Saturdays and holidays from noon to 9:30 p.m., Sundays from 1-9 p.m. No credit cards. No amusements for children under 12. Travis Harris, Innkeeper.

Directions: From New York follow Saw Mill River on Hutchinson River Pkwy. to I-684 which leads into Rte. 22 at Brewster. Go north to Dover Plains.

BIRD AND BOTTLE INN
Garrison, New York

"This place hasn't always been an inn," explained Nancy Noonan. "It was built in 1761 and called Warren's Tavern. It was the place where the Albany stages stopped to change horses. During the American Revolution, a group of Connecticut soldiers encamped here for some time, and I imagine that the old place saw a lot of activity then."

Nancy and I were standing on the bridge which spans the brook immediately behind the Bird and Bottle Inn. It afforded me an excellent view of the original building and the wings that had been added at each end. It was mid-April and the spring flowers were just beginning to show off their fresh colors. The forsythia was almost gone, but the tulips and daffodils which Nancy and Tom had planted around the old wooden fence were starting to bloom.

"We're right across the river from West Point," she continued. "It is not hard to imagine all of the secret meetings and discussions that probably took place here leading up to Benedict Arnold's defection. That didn't come until later on in the war, but I am sure that Mr. Warren, the landlord, must have had an interesting time keeping the Tories and the Patriots separated. This area had decidedly divided loyalties.

"Warren sold the tavern in 1832 to a man named Justice Nelson, and it became a farm for three generations. It was re-established as an inn in 1940 and has been one ever since."

The lodging rooms at the Bird and Bottle have been beautifully furnished for comfort and eye appeal. All of them are furnished in early American antiques and have either a canopied or four-poster bed. All have private baths and woodburning fireplaces. There are two double rooms, and a suite which includes a cosy sitting room. There is a further lodging in a small cottage on the grounds which also has a fireplace and some very interesting pieces that Tom and Nancy have found on their travels. These include an old-style briefcase, which is really a portable writing desk with secret drawers. Continental breakfast is served to all houseguests.

We all enjoyed dinner in the candlelit dining room with the snowy linen, gleaming silver, and sparkling glasses. The beautiful lavender flowers provided an interesting contrast. The main dish was rack of lamb which was carved at our table and served with delicious gravy and broiled seasoned tomatoes. The appetizer was troutlets served on squares of toast soaked in a delightfully flavored sauce.

The choice of desserts included chocolate rum cake, apple tart with apricot glaze, cheesecake, and almond cake.

For the most part, the food appeals to the more sophisticated palate. I always allow extra time for the meals since each dish is prepared individually.

In searching for the right combination of words to describe the Bird and Bottle, it occurs to me that "country chic" fits. The buildings are very old with low ceilings and wide floor boards, and the country antique furniture just belongs.

The Bird and Bottle Inn has been included in *CIBR* since 1972.

BIRD AND BOTTLE INN, Garrison, N.Y. 10524; 914-424-3000. A 4-bedroom country inn, rich in antiquity located on Rte. 9, a few miles north of Peekskill, N.Y. A short distance from Boscobel Restoration, U.S. Military Academy at West Point, and Sleepy Hollow Restorations. Dinner served Monday through Saturday, and all day Sunday. Closed Mondays and Tuesdays from Nov. to Memorial Day. Thomas and Nancy Noonan, Innkeepers.

Directions: From NYC: cross George Washington Bridge and follow Palisades Pkwy. north to Bear Mtn. Bridge. Cross bridge and travel on Rte. 9D north 4½ mi. to Rte. 403. Proceed on Rte. 403 to Rte. 9, then north 4 mi. to inn. From I-84, take Exit 13 and follow Rte. 9 south for 8 mi.

HOTEL ALGONQUIN
New York City, New York

A country inn in the city! I first became intrigued with this idea when Andy Anspach, the manager of the Hotel Algonquin, wrote me a letter back in 1970. At that time he had visited several of the inns included in this book and suggested that the Algonquin had the same qualities of warm, personal hospitality. I decided to spend a few days at the Algonquin and found it such a refreshing experience that I've been staying there ever since.

Among the very nice things that have happened as a result of including it in *Country Inns and Back Roads,* is that a number of people, despairing of ever finding a good small hotel in New York, have written us letters of thanks. (I think this is one of the most rewarding aspects of writing this book every year.)

One lady wrote: "One of the reasons that I enjoy staying at the Algonquin is that the garage is located right across the street. Parking in New York is a problem and it's a great feeling just to drive into that garage and not worry about the car until I am ready to leave."

Another letter said: "One of the Algonquin's joys is the late evening supper buffet. What a pleasure to know that after the theatre or the pro basketball or hockey game, we'll be able to swing into that warm friendly lobby and have a choice of so many different dishes. One of my favorites is Welsh rarebit. With the special salads, fluffy cakes, apple pie, ice cream, lobster Newburg, and similar goodies spread out on large tables, it's like being invited to your own birthday party."

This small hotel was made famous fifty years ago when the Algonquin Wits, Benchley, Parker, Mencken, and others of their ilk, met there to enjoy the food and shred literary and artistic reputations.

One of my greatest disappointments in recent years was the fact that I was in Italy visiting villas and country houses at the time that the Algonquin Hotel was given a seventy-fifth birthday by their neighbors, the *New Yorker* magazine. This was most appropriate, because legend has it that the *New Yorker* was actually brought to life in a room in the Algonquin during the 1920s.

It's particularly significant that all of the Algonquin's house-guests are presented with a copy of the *New Yorker*. It's a guide to what's going on in New York, among other things.

Today, guests are liable to see the most interesting people in the elevator—and hear the most interesting conversations. Recently, standing in front of an Algonquin elevator, a fragment of a conversation floated over to me. A voice of some depth and quality was saying, "And I told them I would not sign a two-picture contract."

I'm still trying to place that voice.

Hotel Algonquin has been included in *CIBR* since 1971.

ALGONQUIN HOTEL, 59 W. 44th St., New York, N.Y. 10036; 212-687-4400. A quiet, conservative 200-room country inn in the heart of Manhattan. Convenient to business, theatres, and shopping. European plan. Breakfast, lunch, dinner, and late supper buffet served to travelers daily except Sunday dinner. Open year-round. No pets. Very near bus, rail and air transportation. Garage directly opposite entrance, with complimentary parking for weekend visitors arriving after 5 p.m. Fri. or Sat. for minimum 2-night visit. Andrew Anspach, Innkeeper.

Directions: 44th St., is one-way from west to east; 43rd St., from east to west. Garage is accessible from either street.

THREE VILLAGE INN
Stony Brook, Long Island, New York

On a fresh August morning, I was sitting in one of the beach chairs under a tree on the terrace in front of my cottage at the Three Village Inn. Seagulls circled over the scene which included the broad lawn leading down to the marina, with its many sailboats and cruisers, to the marshes beyond and the low cliffs on the northern shore of Long Island in the distance. A friendly robin lighted on the rustic fence and began poking his way through the entangled rambler roses.

The previous afternoon, I had taken the ferry from Bridgeport, Connecticut to Port Jefferson, Long Island, a trip that took an hour and thirty minutes, and then followed Route 25A through one or two villages, arriving at Stony Brook just about six-thirty in the evening. Once again it was Whitney Roberts, who has literally grown up in this inn, who greeted me with the news that his mother and father, Monda and Nelson, along with his brother Larry, would be joining me for dinner a little later on.

The Three Village Inn is, at all odds, a Long Island institution and tradition. The Roberts family has a background of innkeeping which began with Whitney's grandfather who came from Rockland, Maine and opened a restaurant called "The Maine Maid" in nearby Jericho, Long Island.

Originally, accommodations were found only in the main house of the inn, but since 1971, the year of my first visit, several cottages have been refurbished or built to accommodate guests. These are furnished with colonial reproductions. Monda Roberts says that they are quite a favorite with honeymooners, and with people who like to escape from New York City for a weekend. Some of them have fireplaces.

The redesign of the entire east wing of the inn was completed in 1979. It now consists of the Jonas Smith Room, which has a fireplace and is available for banquets and parties. It has been decorated with wood paneling and brass chandeliers. In addition, there are two more lodging rooms on this side of the inn, each with its own outside entrance. One of these rooms has a ramp entrance and facilities are designed to accommodate the handicapped.

A ramp has been added to the front entrance of the inn, and also to the side entrance to the Inn n' Out restaurant. The entire dining room is now accessible by wheelchair.

In addition to walking along the sandy beach behind the inn and watching the boats from the marina, there are many things to do on the north shore of Long Island, which is rich in colonial history. There's quite a gathering at twelve o'clock noon each day at the Stony Brook post office where an enormous carved wooden eagle with a twenty-foot wingspread slowly flaps its wings.

From the very beginning, Nelson and Monda Roberts have placed a great deal of emphasis on food. They are very particular about not using foil for the baked potatoes, baking them in rotation for the evening and using fresh vegetables whenever they are available. The menu is one of the largest I have ever seen. It includes lots of fresh seafood as well as generous helpings of beef, pork, veal, and lamb. The extra touch of serving fruit sherbet with the main meal is something I have always enjoyed.

The Inn n' Out dining room, which was really the inspiration of Larry Roberts, has been very popular. Now there is an outdoor grill to add to the excitement. Imagine watching the cook prepare luncheon while sitting on a lawn with a view of the marina! The interior of the restaurant features oil paintings and prints of four-masted schooners, and there is a boat model in a glass case that has tiny little lights running up and down the rigging.

The Three Village Inn has been a way of life for the Roberts family for almost thirty years and by the looks of things, they've had fun doing it.

Three Village Inn has been included in *CIBR* since 1972.

THREE VILLAGE INN, Dock Rd., Stony Brook, L.I., N.Y. 11790; 516-751-0555. A 9-room village inn with 19 adjacent cottage/motel

*accommodations, 5 mi. from Port Jefferson, N.Y., on Long Island's
historic north shore. Near the museums of Stony Brook. European
plan. Lunch and dinner served to travelers daily. Closed Christmas.
No pets. Golf, swimming, and boating nearby. Special attention
given to handicapped persons. Nelson and Monda Roberts, Innkeepers.*

*Directions: From L.I. Expressway, take Exit 62 and travel north on
Nichols Rd. to Rte. 25A. Turn left on Rte. 25A and proceed to next
light. Turn right onto Main St. and travel straight ahead to inn.
Available from New England via L.I. ferries from Bridgeport during
the summer. Ferry reservations advisable.*

1770 HOUSE
East Hampton, Long Island, New York

I became acquainted with Sid and Miriam and all of the
members of the Perle family while sitting in the library and reception
area of the 1770 House with its beautiful wood paneling, exposed
beams, and lovely old fireplace. "It was originally the residence of the
Dayton family," explained Miriam, "but over the years it has been a
dining hall for the boys from Clinton Academy, next door (which
was the first accredited high school in New York state), a general
store, a private home, and a public inn."

Miriam, who is the chef at the inn, explained that she formerly
conducted a cooking school for twelve years in Great Neck, Long
Island, and had studied earlier at the Cordon Bleu in Paris.

"Actually, acquiring the 1770 House was part of a long-time
dream for all of us," asserted Sid." We have been very busy searching
for and restoring antiques for our six guest rooms. It's really a family
affair because my daughter Wendy and her husband Burton Van
Deusen are very much involved, as is our son Adam. He is an
entertainer, singer, and songwriter. Both Burton and Adam tend
bar."

Miriam explained that dinner which changes weekly at the 1770
House was, with the exception of dessert, a complete meal. "I'm very
fussy about every aspect of the menu," she said. "For example, our
appetizers include unusual things such as cold asparagus tarragon;
leek and mushroom tart; fettucini al pesto; and a French fish
chowder. We also serve country lentil soup and a crabmeat and
tomato tart. The salads are different every week, as are the salad
dressings. For instance, tonight we are having romaine salad with
guacamole dressing. Last week, we had an endive and beet salad with
caesar dressing.

"Because we're here on the outer end of Long Island where lots
of fresh fish is available, we always have a choice of two, and

sometimes three, fish dishes. Tonight, there's a lemon herb weakfish and a fresh soft-shell crab amandine. We also have steamed sole Chinois; swordfish al pesto, and other Long Island fish specialties."

"Taken over all," said Sid, "I'd say we have an eclectic menu with American, French, Oriental, and Italian dishes predominating. We're having roast duck with lemon ginger glaze this evening, as well as lamb brochettes served with chutney mint butter."

"Personally, I like Miriam's desserts," chimed in Burton. "She makes the most delicious holiday cheesecake and banana chestnut mousse."

While we were chatting, two of the guests at the inn returned after an afternoon of touring the many antique shops. "The one you told us about really turned out to be a jewel," exclaimed the man. "They had the mirror we were looking for, and the proprietor even recommended one or two other shops for us, as well. This is certainly a wonderful place to go antiquing." I gathered that antiquers must have a wonderful time, because the Perles themselves have been very successful in finding four-poster beds, lovely old chests of drawers and wardrobes, and a rather impressive collection of coaching lamps.

Downstairs in the Tap Room there is a beautiful beehive fireplace, and many old trivets and other artifacts on the wall. The atmosphere is quite similar to an English pub.

"Your readers might be interested in the fact that on Thanksgiving we have hors d'oeuvres and soup in the Tap Room, then everyone goes upstairs to the main dining room for dinner, and dessert is offered in the library — but not until we have all had a walk in the village!"

1770 HOUSE, 143 Main St., East Hampton, Long Island, N.Y. 11937; 516-324-1770. An elegant 6-room village inn near the eastern end of Long Island. Open all year. Dinner served Wed. thru Sun. in season; Fri. and Sat. off-season. Not comfortable for children under 14. No pets. Convenient to many cultural and recreational diversions, including antiquing and back roading. Available by public transportation; consult innkeepers. The Perle family, Innkeepers.

Directions: From New York City: take the Long Island Expressway to Exit 70, and then turn south to Rte. 27 East, which is the main street of East Hampton. The inn is located diagonally across the street from Guild Hall.

Pennsylvania

THE CENTURY INN
Scenery Hill, Pennsylvania

"My husband and I cannot say enough about the Century Inn," said the letter. "In fact, I'm sure our friends are getting tired of hearing about it. One of the most important things was that we felt so welcome. The innkeepers were so pleasant and willing to talk about the inn. We are antique buffs, so we truly enjoy that marvelous collection."

Another letter said, "Our first stay was at the Century Inn, and what a beautiful old place this is. We had a lovely bedroom furnished with delightful antiques and enjoyed a huge, delicious home-cooked dinner. The cole slaw has got to be the best ever. Our breakfast was equally good and we ate it in the fascinating 'Keeping Room.' We left the Century Inn with regret, saying that we would return again."

The Century Inn was built before 1794 and is the oldest continuously operating tavern on the National Pike, most of which is today's U.S. 40. Consequently, the inn has played an important role in the history of southwest Pennsylvania. General Lafayette stopped here on May 26, 1825, and Andrew Jackson was a guest twice, once on his way to his inauguration as President of the United States.

As the letters imply, the interior of this handsome old inn is filled with rare antiques, and there is a story behind almost every piece. Typical of the collection is a Chippendale highboy which was brought from Carlisle, Pennsylvania, probably by Conestoga wagon, in the late 18th century. It is in marvelous condition, and, oddly, the carved shell at the top is upside down. All the antique treasures are in a perfect setting created by the original exposed stone walls, wood

paneling, low ceilings, and numerous fireplaces (in some cases, two to a room!).

Among delicious temptations on the menu are turkey which comes from a farm just down the road, and baked stuffed pork chops. There's also Virginia ham, chicken croquettes, ham and asparagus roll, and a mouth-watering hot turkey sandwich.

Desserts include fresh strawberry shortcake, pecan balls with butter sauce, and a wide variety of homemade pies.

Today, the innkeepers are Gordon Harrington, Jr., and his wife, Megin, who are continuing in the tradition of his mother and father, Gordon and Mary Harrington, who restored this inn and generously supplied it with not only their own antiques, but the gifts of many friends.

One of the most impressive antiques at this inn is the original flag flown during the Whiskey Rebellion, which took place in western Pennsylvania in 1794. The flag is framed and hangs on the wall of the front parlor.

The Century Inn will be looking forward to its own bicentennial soon.

The Century Inn has been in *CIBR* since 1971.

THE CENTURY INN, Scenery Hill, Pa. 15360; 412-945-6600 or 5180. A 10-room village inn on Rte. 40, 12 mi. east of Washington, Pa., 35 mi. south of Pittsburgh. European plan. Breakfast served to house guests only. Lunch and dinner served to travelers daily. Closed approximately Dec. 21 until March 1. Contact inn for exact opening and closing dates. No pets. No credit cards. Personal checks welcome. Megin and Gordon Harrington, Jr., Innkeepers.

Directions: From the east, exit the Pa. Tpke. at New Stanton. Take I-70W to Rte. 917S (Bentleyville exit) to Rte. 40E and go 1 mi. east to inn. From the north, take Rte. 19S to Rte. 519S to Rte. 40E and go 5 mi. east to inn or take I-79S to Rte. 40E and go 9 mi. east to inn. From the west, take I-70E to I-79S to Rte. 40E and go 9 mi. east to inn.

THE TAVERN
New Wilmington, Pennsylvania

The year was 1973. For years I had been fascinated with the "plain people" who live in eastern Pennsylvania. These include the Amish, Dunkards, Moravians, and Schwenkfelders. I had always enjoyed the back roads of Lancaster and Berks counties and admired the picturebook farms and industrious people.

Now at the western end of Pennsylvania, I was once again in "Dutch Country." I had heard there was a sizable community of Amish here, but I was surprised at the scope.

The purpose of my visit was to meet Mrs. Ernst Durrast and visit The Tavern in New Wilmington. When I drove through the town, I saw the familiar black buggies and plain dress of these pious folk who originally fled from Europe in the 18th century to obtain religious freedom.

"Oh, yes," Mrs. Durrast explained over a cup of tea, "this is Amish country, and they are a people who are quite proud of their ancestry. I hope that while you're here you'll drive out to the countryside to see those neat farms and spotless buildings." We talked about New Wilmington and Westminster College and some of the joys of living in western Pennsylvania. "Well, I've had this inn for forty-five years," she said, "and I just can't imagine living anywhere else. This is a lovely little town. I like it especially because there's a constant flow of young people from the college."

The talk then shifted to the startling number of entrées on the luncheon menu. Just for fun, I counted twenty-seven, plus an appetizer, vegetables, fritters, salad, rolls, dessert, and a beverage. It was real country fare including gourmet beef balls, creamed chicken on a biscuit, cabbage rolls, grilled smoked pork chops, ham steaks, cheese and cheese soufflé with creamed chicken. Two warm honey buns with whipped butter are always served.

As I could see, lunch was a substantial meal. Mrs. D. explained to me that a great many of her noontime patrons are older people and prefer to eat their meal at midday.

Dinners include a great many of the luncheon offerings plus

about twelve other main dishes. There's usually a most unusual combination of white meat of chicken and lobster tail served in a special sherry sauce. How does that sound?

There's a small lodge across the village street with a few sleeping rooms available. One of these is frequently occupied by my dear friends Claire and Lucy Dee Dee of Grand Rapids, Michigan. They first recommended Mrs. Durrast's splendid establishment to me back in 1972.

New Wilmington is just a few minutes from I-80, the east-west highway that traverses northern Pennsylvania. It's about two hundred and forty miles from the Poconos where there are at least three country inns that I have found most comfortable.

"It wonders me," said Mrs. Durrast, borrowing a quaint Amish saying, "why it has taken you so long to find us."

THE TAVERN, Box 153, New Wilmington, Pa. 16142; 412-946-2020. A bustling country restaurant on the town square with 5 sleeping rooms in a lodge directly across the street. European plan. Lunch and dinner served daily except Tuesdays. Reservations required. Closed Thanksgiving and Christmas. Sports and cultural events at Westminister College nearby. No credit cards. No diversions for small children. Mrs. Ernst Durrast, Innkeeper.

Directions: From I-80, take Exit 1-S, and follow Rte. 18 south to Rte. 208. Proceed east on 208 to town square. From I-79, follow Rte. 208 west for 14 mi. to New Wilmington.

EAGLES MERE INN
Eagles Mere, Pennsylvania

Kathleen Oliver and I were on a combination walking/driving tour of Eagles Mere Lake, which is one of the many attractive features of this two thousand-foot-high resort area. "The lake was formed by the receding glacier," she explained. "It is actually located on the top of a mountain. The Indians first hunted and camped here. The great eagles nested in the trees and later the French influence gave the place its name."

We walked down to the edge of the sandy beach, and I noted the unusual number of canoes and sailboats available for hire. A motor launch left from one of the docks transporting passengers to the other end of the lake.

"Everyone uses the lake," she said. "We swim, canoe, sail, skate, and fish on it. It means so much to many people."

As we continued our journey, she explained that the community is made up of people who have been coming to Eagles Mere for many years. "The entire community supports things such as our Athletic Association which maintains a summer program for young people in which our inn guests can also participate. There are riding stables nearby and the riding paths convert into at least 65 miles of cross-country skiing in the winter. Guests of the inn also have the privilege of playing on the lovely 18-hole golf course of the Eagles Mere Country Club.

"Speaking of winter, this is when Eagles Mere is really at its most unusual, because we have a toboggan slide operated by the volunteer fire department on the weekends which provides at least a 1200-foot ride on specially constructed toboggans down the hill to the lake surface. The speeds get up to 65 miles an hour. Our inn guests love this too."

Kathleen and I continued our stroll on the footpath which completely encircles the lake. I learned that this lovely Irish colleen met her husband Bob, who is a rather hearty outdoor type, when they were both students at St. Lawrence University.

Even if Eagles Mere were not a small community, I have a feeling that people would naturally gravitate towards the inn anyway, because it has a homey feeling which was very obvious to me as soon as I stepped in the front door. The sitting rooms and parlors on the main floor were all most comfortably furnished and, much to my surprise, I found a Baldwin piano tuned to concert pitch. "Once I had aspirations to become a concert pianist," explained Kathleen, "however when we came to Eagles Mere, I decided to set that aside for a while."

Meals at the inn are prepared by a lady from the village who has quite a way with things like roast pork, beef Bourguignon, and stuffed flounder. They are served in the new air conditioned dining room, although the air conditioning is seldom needed. Bob told me that they were anticipating canning lots of chili sauce, blueberry jam, peach rum jam, and other goodies in the fall.

In 1980, a new community fine arts building will be built just a block from the inn, where more summer recitals, plays, and musicals may be enjoyed.

All the Olivers at the Eagles Mere Inn—Bob; Kathleen; Maureen who is eighteen; Eileen, fifteen; Karen, thirteen; and Kevin, six; create a wonderful and natural relaxed family atmosphere at this warm-hearted inn.

Eagles Mere, itself, may be one of the last unspoiled vacation places in the East.

EAGLES MERE INN, Mary and Sullivan Aves., Eagles Mere, Pa. 17731; 717-525-3273. A 9-room, all with private baths, small village inn high in the Allegheny Mountain range about an hour's drive north of Williamsport. 16 mi. from Dushore and Hughesville. Near Eagles Mere Lake, World's End State Park, Sullivan County Historical Museum, and the LaPorte Little Theater. Modified American plan in season; European plan (room and breakfast) out of season. Breakfast and dinner served to travelers. Open every day from May 15 to Oct. 15; open from Friday dinners through Sunday breakfast, October 16 to March 16, except closed December 24-27. All summer and winter sports nearby. No pets; no credit cards. Robert and Kathleen Oliver, Innkeepers.

Directions: Exit 34 (Buckhorn) from I-80. Follow Rte. 42 north 32 mi. to Eagles Mere. Turn right on Mary Avenue to inn.

THE PINE BARN INN
Danville, Pennsylvania

Marty Walzer, innkeeper of The Pine Barn Inn, was waxing historical: "The fact is that I have been doing a little research," he stated. "Myles Standish's soldiers, early Dutch traders, and Governor Bradford's Plantation officials needed places to stay as they traveled through the early American colonies. That's why the first inns started in this country. Early innkeepers were charged by the courts 'to be well-provided with the necessities for the entertainment of Strangers and their horses in respect to good diet and bedding.' "

Barbara Walzer came tripping into the lounge where Marty and I were enjoying a happy reunion. "What are you two up to?" she asked. "Well, right at the moment," I retorted, "Marty is giving me a short review of colonial America."

"Oh, he's always into something like that," she replied, "I think he secretly yearns to write a book about country inns!"

We moved into the dining room and by mutual consent the subject turned more specifically to The Pine Barn Inn. "Barbara has really done a marvelous job redecorating all of our oldest guest rooms," asserted Marty. "Oh yes," Barbara chimed in, "We've tried to make them as 'countrified' as possible, even though they are constructed in a motel style. I think this lovely old barn with the dining room and the gift shop are what makes us more like a country inn, and we have wonderful crafts from central Pennsylvania in the gift shop."

The main building of this inn was a large nineteenth-century Pennsylvania barn which was restored in 1967. A considerable amount of the original heavy stone walls have been preserved and the beams and pillars have been exposed. The dining room is furnished with handsome reproductions of Pennsylvania Windsor chairs, with candles on each table. A scattering of old country furniture adds to the atmosphere.

"We have a new chef now working alongside Roger and Larry," Marty informed me. "His name is Ralph Richardson and he graduated from the Culinary Institute. Some of his specialties are coquille St. Jacques; fresh fillet of Boston schrod which he makes with shrimp; crabmeat with sherried cheese sauce; veal Francaise; roast duckling; and French tarragon chicken."

"What is really happening is that Marty's age and waistline are racing each other to reach forty," said Barbara merrily.

"I could take umbrage at that remark," said Marty, a la Groucho Marx, "but I noticed that umbrage is not on the menu tonight."

There were certainly a lot of other things on the menu that evening, including a generous number of seafood offerings such as

haddock, flounder, scallops, and sole. These are all delivered fresh, not frozen, to The Pine Barn several times a week from Atlantic waters.

"Our desserts aren't helping my waistline any, either," said Marty. "My problem is I just can't resist those homemade pies, cobblers, muffins, jams, jellies, and homemade bread. I think my real downfall will be the chocolate mousse pie, that's good for three inches."

The talk turned to Marty's father, "Dad seems to be pretty content to play golf every day in Orlando. I suppose I will have to take over his job here as outside gardener. He has done such a wonderful job over the past few years with our flowers and plants that we are a virtual blanket of color."

PINE BARN INN, Danville, Pa. 17821; 717-275-2071. A picturesque country restaurant with 45 attractive motel rooms in central Pennsylvania. European plan. Breakfast, lunch, and dinner served daily except Christmas, July 4th, and Memorial Day. Pets allowed in some rooms. Near several colleges and historic sites. Golf, tennis, water skiing, sailing, and canoeing nearby. Martin and Barbara Walzer, Innkeepers.

Directions: From Exit 33 of I-80, go south 3 mi. to Danville. Take a left at the first traffic light. Proceed 10 blocks and follow signs to Geisinger Medical Center. Pine Barn adjoins the Center.

OVERLOOK INN
Canadensis, Pennsylvania

For those readers who have been following the steady progress of Bob and Lolly Tupper and the Overlook Inn, which is located in the pine-scented forests of the Pocono Mountains of eastern

Pennsylvania, here are excerpts from the most recent letter from Lolly, which I believe mirrors the inn and its qualities very well. "It's been a good year! We completed all of our projects and now have private baths for almost all of our rooms and have enlarged a number of them as well. (They all have books and plants, adding to the 'home away from home' feeling.)

"We converted the right side of the front porch into a new dining area and in the summer, when the cool breezes waft through large screen windows, we will be serving breakfast and lunch there.

"Our chef, Joe Vibercik has added quiches, clams casino, veal, and Overlook chicken to our menu and we serve only fresh homemade soup and always all fresh vegetables; many of these are from our garden.

"It's really been fun to be open for all the holidays. At Thanksgiving, we had a buffet with turkeys and hams carved by Joe in the dining room, and everybody feels like 'family' about five minutes after they arrive.

"Christmas is a mixture of young and old and in-betweens. The inn is festooned with handmade and old-fashioned ornaments and treasures from the past. Three trees are adorned with lights, pop corn and cranberry strings. The tables are set with Joe's handmade Christmas tree candles and the door of each room has its own pine cone spray or wreath. Each guest also receives a 'gift of love' from the Overlook — peach preserves made during the past summer at the inn.

"New Year's is wonderful, too. Although it's low key, we all have the *best time.* There's a midnight spread of goodies, a fire, and lots of singing around the piano.

"When the snow comes we have our own cross-country skiing and good ice skating on local ponds. There's even indoor tennis, nearby. In the summer our own pool and woods provide lots of diversions for our guests and we have tennis, golf, fishing, and riding just over the hill and through the woods.

Lolly's reference to Chef Vibercik brought back a conversation I had with him about what he liked to cook the most. He reeled off everything from duckling with French orange sauce to marinated chicken. He also has a considerable assortment of desserts, including homemade cheesecakes and fresh fruit pies. He has, wonder of wonders, a delicious rice pudding which is very hard to find these days.

I did mention in a recent edition that the inn always receives several telephone calls and letters in the late fall from people who are looking for a place to spend the Christmas holidays. Apparently, the holiday guests at the Overlook were delighted with a wonderful snowstorm on one Christmas Eve.

An inn with much love, the Overlook Inn.

OVERLOOK INN, Dutch Hill Rd., Canadensis, Pa. 18325; 717-595-7519. A 23-room resort-inn in the heart of the Poconos, 15 mi. from Stroudsburg, Pa. Mod. American plan. Dinners served to travelers. Open every day of the year. No pets. Pool, archery, shuffleboard, bocci, hiking on grounds; golf, tennis, Alpine slide, ice skating, downhill and xc skiing, indoor tennis, antiquing, backroading, summer theatre nearby. No amenities for small children. Bob and Lolly Tupper, Innkeepers.

Directions: From the north (New England, New York State and Canada) use I-84 and take Rte. 390 south through "Promised Land" about 12 mi. to traffic light in Canadensis. Make right hand turn on Rte. 447 north—go 1/3 mi. to first right hand turn (Dutch Hill Road). Inn is 1½ mi. up hill. Look for new sign on right. From New York City, take George Washington Bridge to I-80 west. Turn off at Pennsylvania Exit 52. Follow Rte. 447 north straight through Canadensis traffic light. Turn left and right on Dutch Hill Road as above.

STERLING INN
South Sterling, Pennsylvania

I could not resist it any longer—I had been listening to the gurgling waters of the Wallenpaupack Creek for about twenty minutes on a warm, lazy afternoon. I was sitting on a lawn chair about fifty paces from the back of the Sterling Inn, just two feet from the bank of the creek. The smell of the freshly-cut lawn mingled with the scent of the forest on the other side of the water. What a place, I thought, to propose to some pretty girl.

I kicked off my shoes, rolled up my pants, and waded out to stand on the flat, smooth shelf of rock in the middle of the creek. The water was clean and cool. There was a little pool about twenty-five feet away, deep enough for me to sit in and have the water come up to my chest. A flash of red and another of blue signaled a cardinal and a bluejay darting into the woods, deep in the Pocono Mountains of Pennsylvania.

I climbed back on the bank and was drying my feet when one of the other guests came and plunked down on a nearby chair. "I think this is one of the best-kept, neatest places that I have ever visited," she said. "It's as American as apple pie and fresh vegetables. The rooms are so comfortable, and I'm very glad I came. Don't you just love it here?"

Even if her enthusiasm hadn't been catching, I would have had to agree.

This was the friendly and unpretentious atmosphere that Alice Julian had in mind over forty years ago when she acquired the Sterling Inn. This is the way that her daughter and son-in-law, Carmen and Henry Arneberg, are keeping it today.

The Sterling Inn is on a back road in the Poconos. There are enticing hiking and walking trails on the inn property and nearby. One of them, Henry told me, leads to a waterfall on the ridge behind the inn. There is a very pleasant nine-hole putting green, a swimming area with a sandy beach, and a little pond with willow trees and a few ducks.

Lodgings are to be found in several very attractive buildings in this parklike atmosphere. The Wayside, Lodge, Meadowlark, Hilltop, and Spring Run are all beautifully situated with extremely attractive rooms that have been colorfully decorated. There are sixty-seven accommodations which are well-dispersed and give no feeling of being crowded together.

The menu includes such entrées as roast lamb, pot roast, and standing rib roast, because, as Carmen Arneberg says, "This is the kind of food that some people serve only when they are having guests for dinner." All of the baking is done in the warm, friendly kitchen.

In many ways this Pocono Mountain inn personifies the things I find most delightful in country inns. For example, fresh flowers are on the dining room tables at all times, and there are books and magazines everywhere, not only in the guest rooms, but in the many parlors and sitting rooms. When guests advise either Carmen or Henry of their arrival time, the inn automobile will meet buses and airplanes. A still further example of their care and consideration is

the fact that guests who are on a special diet are served foods they are allowed to have.

Although the Sterling has been here for more than forty-five years and has many old friends who return almost yearly, there are a great many honeymooners who find the quiet atmosphere much to their liking. It's a very good place for children because, even on rainy days, there's lots for them to do. In addition to the dozens of outside amusements and diversions for children, there are also shuffleboard and a game room. "We've always been very much of a family-oriented place," says Carmen.

To tell the truth, I discovered the Sterling Inn one day when I took a wrong turn and got lost in the Poconos. I returned the next year to see if it was all true.

Believe me, it was.

Sterling Inn has been included in *CIBR* since 1974.

STERLING INN, Rte 191, South Sterling, Pa. 18460; 717-676-3311. A 67-room secluded resort-inn in the Pocono Mountains, 8 mi. from I-84 and 12 mi. from I-380. American plan. Reservation and check-in office closes at 10 p.m. Breakfast, lunch, and dinner served to travelers daily. Breakfast served 8-9 a.m.; lunch served 12:30-1:30 p.m.; dinner served 6-7:15 p.m. Jackets required for dinner. No liquor served. Open weekends only, beginning May 4 (Friday to Monday a.m.) until May 24; open every day thereafter until October 22 closing date. No pets. Swimming, putting greens, shuffleboard, all-weather tennis court, and woodland walks on grounds. Golf courses and horseback riding nearby. No credit cards. Henry and Carmen Arneberg, Innkeepers.

Directions: From I-80, follow I-380 to Rte. 940 to Mount Pocono.
At light, cross Rte. 611 and proceed on Rte. 196 north to Rte. 423.
Drive north on Rte. 423 to Rte. 191 and travel ½ mile north to inn.
From I-84, follow Rte. 507 south through Greentown and New-
foundland. In Newfoundland, pick up Rte. 191 and travel 4 mi. south
to inn.

PUMP HOUSE INN
Canadensis, Pennsylvania

When I think of the Pump House Inn and Todd Drucquer, high up in the Poconos in northeastern Pennsylvania, two of the words that come immediately to my mind are: "innovative" and "enthusiastic." Todd was bubbling over in both departments when I was last with him.

"The new Penthouse Suite—three restaurants all within the present confines of the inn—wow!"

I asked him to explain his three-restaurant concept while Mark Kaplan, the chef, brought us a sample of his most recent creation, a chocolate velvet cake.

"In your large city hotels," he expounded, "travelers and guests have had the advantage of choosing the type of cuisine and décor they might fancy, on any given evening, by selecting one of the restaurants within the hotel. Well, we're doing the same thing, we want to give our guests this same advantage."

He went on, "Our main dining room will continue to offer all the great cuisine and service that has established the inn's national reputation: rack of lamb Persille, Chateaubriand, and duckling Normande.

"The English Grill Room will be under the direction of our resident manager, John Keeney, and will have its own menu featuring cuisine typical of many of the great grills I have visited abroad. It will offer thick soups, Dover sole, broiled calves' liver, and roast beef with Yorkshire pudding.

"Meanwhile, downstairs, we have the *hors d'oeuvriere*. This, in my opinion, will be a great success because it's a dining room that is small, informal, and intimate, and guests will be able to choose any number of hot or cold hors d'oeuvres, and make a big meal or a small one, depending on what and how many they choose. Desserts and espresso will also be available."

As Todd went on filling me in on more details, I began to get the picture more clearly. Here were three different choices of evening meals, both in terms of the menu, the atmosphere, and the price. The fascinating part of it is that they are all located in this country inn, which I first visited in 1971.

Although the emphasis at the Pump House is on the menu, there are five very pleasant country inn bedrooms on the second floor, some of which are suites. All have private baths.

"Enthusiastic and innovative." Yes, the Pump House is always awash in both of those qualities.

The Pump House has been included in *CIBR* since 1972.

THE PUMP HOUSE INN, Canadensis, Pa. 18325; 717-595-7501. A 5-room country inn high in the Poconos, 1½ mi. north of Canadensis village and 16 mi. northeast of Stroudsburg. European plan. Sophisticated country dining. Dinner served to travelers daily. Closed Mondays in summer and Mondays and Tuesdays in winter. Closed Christmas and New Year's Day: Month of Jan. Bicycles and golf nearby. The Drucquer Family, Owners. H. Todd Drucquer, Innkeeper.

Directions: From the north, follow I-84 to Rte. 390 south. Inn is located 13 mi. south on Rte. 390. From the south, follow I-80 to Rte. 191. Travel north on Rte. 191 to Rte. 390 north. Follow signs to Canadensis. Inn is 1½ mi. north from light in Canadensis.

INN AT STARLIGHT LAKE
Starlight, Pennsylvania

The Inn at Starlight Lake is situated on a back road in the rolling hills of Northeastern Pennsylvania. It has been in operation since 1909 and originally was intended to be a summer refuge for people living in New York or New Jersey. In May 1974, Jack and Judy McMahon bought it and resolved to preserve the character of the early period when if flourished.

The inn is a rambling, old-fashioned, comfortable place with the accumulated furniture of years. The lobby is a big room with a fireplace in one corner and a piano and guitar in another corner. It looks like a good place for children. There's an indoor game room and four McMahons for company.

Along with the usual sports offered at resort-inns—swimming, boating, canoeing, sailing, tennis, and hiking—there is another family-type activity that I was glad to see. The inn has extensive cross-country ski trails that run two, five, and six miles into the natural forests of the area.

"We also have one of the largest wild deer herds in the area," said Judy. "We often see deer from our front porch and from the dock in front of the lake. Many of our guests love the idea that the wild creatures are so close."

The food is most interesting. There are a number of German specialties including a Jagerschnitzel and weïnerschnitzel. Some other dishes I sampled were cream of cauliflower soup, Hungarian goulash, sauerbraten, buckwheat cakes, and blueberry pie. "We like holidays here," said Judy, "when families gather for Thanksgiving and Christmas. We're open and everyone's welcome."

For children under 12, there is a TV room and a game room in the main house, and plenty of outside activities, depending upon the season, ranging from swimming to bicycling, skiing, and skating. There's a very pleasant lakeside play area. Small children can have their meals at separate sittings, if desired. Also, there's a nearby farm where they can watch the milking. Lucky, too, the small guest who has a birthday during a visit, because "Happy Birthday" will be sung by everybody.

It's now possible to enjoy the cottage buildings all year. One of them has a fireplace, some have two rooms with connecting baths which are very good for small children. The annex is popular for large family reunions or for several couples who might desire some privacy together.

In May of 1980, a new book, *Country Inns and Back Roads, Britain and Ireland,* will, among other things, tell the story of my visits with Michael and Maureen Turner, who have a lovely inn in the Scottish Highlands. Michael and Maureen and one of their children visited with many of the other innkeepers in *CIBR* at a three-day annual symposium which was held this year at Pleasantville, Kentucky. In this process, they met Jack and Judy McMahon who were at the meeting with two of their four children, Cecilia and Will. The result is that Cecilia may be working with the Turners at their inn in Scotland this summer and perhaps, in time, the Turners will be sending one of their sons to the Inn at Starlight Lake!

So, Cecilia may not be at the inn in the summer of 1980, but there's a good possiblility that a young Scottish lad might be very much in evidence. It ought to be a great deal of fun for everybody concerned. But fun is what the Inn at Starlight Lake is all about.

THE INN AT STARLIGHT LAKE, Starlight, Pa. 18461; 717-798-2519. A 30-room resort-inn located 5 mi. from Hancock, N.Y. Modified American plan. Breakfast, lunch, dinner served daily between May 15 and April 1. Closed Easter if it falls within above dates. Swimming, boating, canoeing, sailing, fishing, hunting, tennis, hiking, bicycling, xc skiing, and lawn sports on grounds. Canoeing, hunting, fishing, golfing nearby. No pets. Judy and Jack McMahon, Innkeepers.

Directions: From N.Y. Rte. 17, exit at Hancock, N.Y. Take Rte. 191S over Delaware River to Rte. 370. Turn right, proceed 3½ mi. turn right, 1 mi. to inn. From I-81, take exit 62 and go east on Rte. 107. Turn left on Rte. 247 to Forest City. Turn left on Rte. 171, go 10 mi. to Rte. 370. Turn right, proceed 12 mi. Turn left, 1 mi. to inn.

1740 HOUSE
Lumberville, Pennsylvania

"Many people have a preconceived idea of what a country inn should be," says Harry Nessler, the innkeeper of the 1740 House, "and we do our best to live up to it. We do as many of the important little things as we possibly can." Harry believes it's the "little things" that make an inn special—like turning down the beds at night, and never rushing his guests through dinner, providing attentive, quiet, and deft service at meals.

The inn has an interesting history. Harry Nessler decided many years ago that he would like to get away from New York, and dreamed of owning a country inn. He searched and eventually found an 18th-century farm on the banks of the Delaware River, a few miles north of New Hope, Pennsylvania. This was the beginning. It took time and patience to create the unique atmosphere that is now the 1740 House. There is a remarkable blend of old and new, in a setting of great serenity and comfort. Everything is furnished with exceptional care and taste, with attention to interesting fabrics and textures, and even to such details as appropriate Allen Saalburg prints on the walls. Every room has a balcony or terrace overlooking the river and canal.

Harry explains his painstaking attention to detail quite simply. "This is my home," he says. "It is an extension of everything I hold dear . . . good taste, good food, and good manners. We welcome everyone who shares these enthusiasms."

Speaking of good food, the inn has it in abundance. An ample and varied buffet breakfast is included in the room rate (the British idea of "bed and breakfast"). It is served in the cheery, airy, many-windowed dining room overlooking the river. Dinner is served by candlelight on pink tablecloths. I've enjoyed the chateaubriand with sauce Bearnaise and the duck a l'orange many times, and Harry's chef does interesting things with fresh vegetables. The homemade desserts are scrumptious.

Bucks County and the surrounding area are rich in Revolutionary lore. Lumberville is just a few miles from the site of Washington's famous crossing of the Delaware on Christmas night, 1776. Soldiers of both armies crisscrossed this land many times. What is perhaps most remarkable is that some of the clapboard and stone buildings dating back to Colonial times are so well preserved.

Evening is one of the most enjoyable times at the 1740 House. After dinner, some guests gather in the paneled living room with its large fireplace to get acquainted and share the day's adventures. Others settle in the card room for bridge or Scrabble, or choose a book from the shelves to take to their rooms later.

For me, it is a joy to awaken early and take a quiet walk along the old canal towpath or paddle a canoe on the canal. Thickets along the river are a never-ending source of bird life and small game. While walking, I have flushed out many a pheasant. It's a beautiful opportunity to regain a sense of privacy.

The 1740 House has been in *CIBR* since 1973.

1740 HOUSE, River Rd., Lumberville, Pa. 18933; 215-297-5661. A 24-room riverside inn, 6½ mi. north of New Hope, in the heart of historic Bucks County. Lodgings include breakfast which is served to houseguests daily; dinner served daily except Sundays and Mondays, by reservation only. Open year-round. Pool and boating on grounds. Golf and tennis nearby. Harry Nessler, Innkeeper.

Directions: From N.Y.C., travel south on N.J. Tpke., and take Exit 10. Follow Rte. 287 north to another Exit 10. Proceed west on Rte. 22 to Flemington, then Rte. 202 south over Delaware Toll Bridge. After an immediate right U-turn onto Rte. 32N, drive 5 mi. to inn. From Pa. Tpke., exit at Willow Grove and proceed north on Rte. 611 to Rte. 202. Follow Rte. 202 north to Rte. 32 and turn north to inn. From Phila., take I-95 to Yardley-New Hope exit, follow 32N through New Hope and 7 miles to inn.

FAIRFIELD INN
Fairfield, Pennsylvania

If I quote from quite a few letters in this book, it's because I feel that oftentimes they are the best way to obtain a deeper insight into the true nature of an inn. A case in point is this letter from David Thomas, the young, enthusiastic innkeeper at the Fairfield Inn.

"The past two years have been busy and fruitful here in Fairfield. We restored the oldest room in the inn—the 1757 Room. Actually, the room was originally a separate building from the mansion house. The room probably was the first tavern on the property, and was a one-and-one-half-story structure. It was quite fascinating and surprising to find the remains of what was a baking oven in the fireplace. A large number of oyster shells, some old coins, and china fragments were found when the floor boards were lifted and the old hand-hewn support logs were exposed. The town 'locals' performed much of the work done in the room. We spent many hours consulting

with neighbors and friends as to the best procedure to follow in the restoration work.

"In 1979, we added a carriage house to the rear of the building, and presently are remodeling a nearby guest house. If all goes well we hope to have it restored, furnished, and open by April. The building, which so far I have traced back to 1857, had been sitting empty and idle and, as a result, the wide floorboards, carved mantel, raised-panel doors and other features are intact.

"We started what I hope will become a tradition at the inn in 1978. On the first Sunday in December, we celebrate the Feast of Christmas. There are strolling carolers throughout the building, the yule log is brought in, and all the guests are seated for a candlelight dinner. The foods served are items that one doesn't normally find on our menu. Last year's feast was a gratifying success. Many of the guests are what we term 'regular,' even though many are from Washington, Richmond, Philadelphia, and surrounding areas. What could be more fun, or a nicer way to begin the Yuletide season?"

There were just two lodging rooms at the Fairfield Inn, as of January 1, 1980, so the main reason people stop is the food. Three meals are served each day, except Sundays when the inn is closed.

Everything served is made from scratch, including chicken and biscuits, country ham steak (the salty kind), a "fizzled city ham," and family-style meals which include everything from appetizers to desserts. Desserts always include deep dish apple pie served with a

213

pitcher of cream or a wedge of cheese, and other seasonal treats.

The inn building has a long and fascinating history. It was built by the Miller family who settled in Fairfield in 1755. It was once a stagecoach stop on the Great Road from York to Hagerstown. During the Civil War, Jebb Stuart lingered long enough to steal seven hundred horses from the valley.

The Confederates occupied the town for ten days in 1864 during the Battle of Gettysburg. General Lee and his men retreated to Fairfield after the battle was over. The women of the town made huge kettles of bean soup and fed the starving troops as they retreated south. By the way, ham and bean soup is one of the specialties of the inn today.

I'm sure with a young, ambitious innkeeper like David, many things will develop at the Fairfield Inn in the future.

FAIRFIELD INN, Main St., Fairfield, Pa. 17320; 717-642-5410. A country restaurant near Gettysburg with 2 lodging rooms available. Breakfast, lunch, and dinner served daily. Closed on major holidays, Sundays, and last week in August. Dinner reservations advised. No pets. Nearby region is rich in history, including Gettysburg Battlefield. David W. Thomas, Innkeeper.

Directions: Fairfield is 8 mi. west of Gettysburg on Rte. 116.

HICKORY BRIDGE FARM
Orrtanna, Pennsylvania

I first met Nancy Jean Hammett and her husband "Dr. Jim" in the summer of 1975 when they were the innkeepers at the Fairfield Inn. Since then there have been a number of interesting changes in their lives, which included selling the Fairfield Inn to David Thomas and purchasing the land and buildings that comprise Hickory Bridge Farm.

From the very beginning, I was captivated by Nancy Jean's great enthusiasm for all the challenges of life and equally impressed with the way she and Jim have shared so many things together. I'm sure there has never been a time in their married life when they haven't had several projects in progress, even while they were also involved in raising a most impressive family.

Hickory Bridge Farm is their new project, and even since the 1979 edition of *CIBR,* there have been some major changes. "For the first two years here we served dinners, but now we have decided to send all of our guests over to David at the Fairfield Inn, and we are concentrating on our tranquil farmhouse here in the foothills, and enjoy having our guests for breakfast around our big table. We have restored three bedrooms in the main farmhouse, and the two little cottages next to the creek up in the woods nearby have four more rooms. We still serve large dinner parties and functions in our red barn which is always set up for meals, but breakfasts are the only meals served here at the farm."

If Nancy Jean and "Dr. Jim's" many friends think that this is a diminution of their many interests and activities, I can assure them that nothing could be farther from the truth. "For one thing," Nancy Jean said, "it was necessary to make a lot of improvements and changes in all the farm buildings and adjacent woods and meadows. We'll have an excellent pond with some fishing available on a small scale in the very near future. Jim has built a deck out in the back of the house over the creek where we will all enjoy breakfast on warm, happy days. Jim says I make wonderful pancakes.

"We have our two festivals every year; one on the first weekend of May, and the second in October. The first one is in apple blossom time and the second is during the harvest. Many local craftsmen, musicians, and farmers participate, and last year we had over 2,000 people. We have country music, square dancing, and hayrides. There's also a country store museum in one of our outbuildings.

"Luther Lightner, our good friend and neighbor, has a wonderful hobby of putting back into working order some of the old-time farm machinery that we've collected, and all our guests enjoy talking to Luther and marveling at some of these lovely old machines.

"I know you have been traveling in Britain," she said, "so I know you are quite aware of the fact that our British cousins all enjoy walking, and we have maps for wonderful walks and hikes, starting

right here at our own front porch which lead through the woods and up into the hills."

"Yes," chimed in Dr. Jim, "and there is good trout and bass fishing. We also have small game hunting."

"It's really wonderful keeping a smaller inn," said Nancy Jean, "because we have a much better chance to get acquainted with all of our guests. Be sure to tell all of your 'travellers' to make reservations, even in the winter months."

HICKORY BRIDGE FARM INN, Orrtanna, Pa. 17353; 717-642-5261. A country inn on a former farm 3 mi. from Fairfield and 8 mi. from Gettysburg. Near Gettysburg Battlefield National Park, Totem Pole Playhouse. Open year-round. 7 lodging rooms available in 2 cottages and the farmhouse. Breakfast available to guests. Hiking, biking, hayrides, square dancing, fishing, hunting on grounds. Golf, swimming available nearby. The Hammett Family, Innkeepers.

Directions: From Gettysburg take Rte. 116 west to Fairfield and follow signs 3 mi. north to Orrtanna.

Important: *Many of the inns can be reached by public transportation, and arrangements can frequently be made to be picked up at bus and train stations, as well as airports.*

I do not include lodging rates in the descriptions, for the very nature of an inn means that there are lodgings of various sizes, with and without baths, in and out of season, and with plain and fancy decoration. Travelers should call ahead and inquire about the availability and rates of the many different types of rooms.

Rates are comparable to those at hotels, motels, and resorts in the same geographic area. To me, this represents a travel bargain, for there is so much more offered at a country inn.

"European Plan" means that rates for rooms and meals are separate. "American Plan" means that meals are included in the cost of the room. "Modified American Plan" means that breakfast and dinner are included in the cost of the room. Some inns include a Continental breakfast with the lodging.

WHAT IS INNKEEPING REALLY LIKE? (con't)

"We have completed our third year of operation and with some nice surprises and some disappointments. The bad news is that we, too, perhaps especially, have been affected by the gas crisis. We have managed to 'hold our own,' but have experienced no growth at a period when we had hoped for a surge. On the other hand, we have experienced a growth in our reputation for excellence which is extremely satisfying . . ." —Massachusetts

". . . Here are some things we think are important: warm, fresh-baked breads; flowers in rooms of newlyweds; wood fires in cool weather in the antique wood stove in the lobby and in the fireplace in the dining room; apples; the Monday night clambake; and crackers and cheese in the lounge each evening . . ." —Massachusetts

"We're so glad that after spending eleven seasons as innkeepers, we still love it. The past season was the best yet. Our staff was so cooperative and desired to serve. We're convinced that in order to be successful innkeepers, we must enjoy people and care enough to serve. The guests come from all phases of American living: doctors, attorneys, heads of government and state departments, shopkeepers, college presidents and professors, railroad executives, school-teachers, oil men, probation officers, and on and on. They all share their lifestyle in our wonderful U.S.A. One becomes aware of God's beautiful earth and personal blessings as he gazes at the rising fog on the mountains in full view, giving the Smokies their rightful name—or the thrill of watching our eastern bluebirds building nests in the early spring . . ." —North Carolina

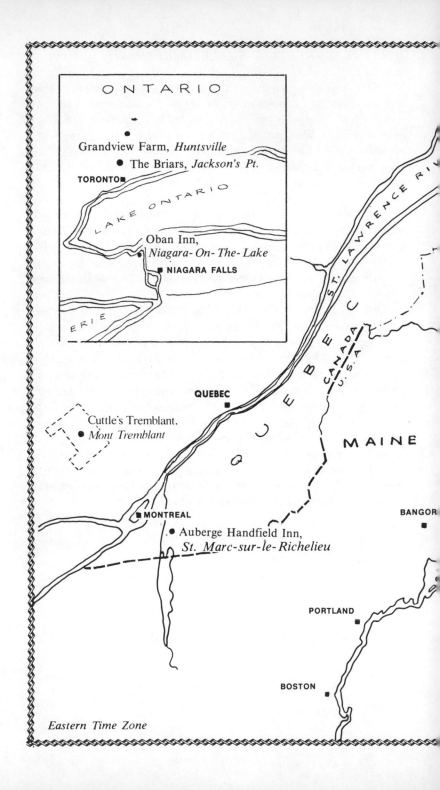

ONTARIO

Grandview Farm, *Huntsville*
● The Briars, *Jackson's Pt.*
TORONTO■

LAKE ONTARIO

Oban Inn,
Niagara-On-The-Lake
■ NIAGARA FALLS

ERIE

ST. LAWRENCE RIVER

QUEBEC

CANADA
U.S.A.

QUEBEC ■

Cuttle's Tremblant,
● *Mont Tremblant*

MAINE

■ MONTREAL
● Auberge Handfield Inn,
St. Marc-sur-le-Richelieu

BANGOR
■

PORTLAND
■

BOSTON
■

Eastern Time Zone

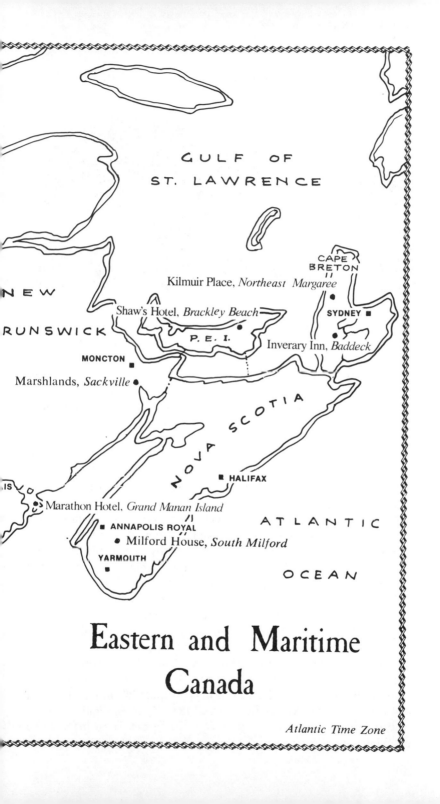

GULF OF
ST. LAWRENCE

CAPE
BRETON

Kilmuir Place, *Northeast Margaree*

SYDNEY ■

Shaw's Hotel, *Brackley Beach*

P. E. I.

Inverary Inn, *Baddeck*

N E W

R U N S W I C K

MONCTON ■

Marshlands, *Sackville* ●

N O V A   S C O T I A

■ HALIFAX

IS

●● Marathon Hotel, *Grand Manan Island*

A T L A N T I C

■ ANNAPOLIS ROYAL

● Milford House, *South Milford*

YARMOUTH
■

O C E A N

Eastern and Maritime Canada

Atlantic Time Zone

Ontario

THE BRIARS
Jackson's Point, Ontario

I'm sure that many readers share my enthusiasm for the famous *Jalna* books written by the Canadian author, Mazo de la Roche. That's why it was such a thrill for me to be standing in front of the cottage called "Birdie" at The Briars, where she was a guest during the last five summers of her life. "As a young woman, she spent vacations at Lake Simcoe," explained John Sibbald. "She also wrote extensively about the area in her autobiography."

John and I were enjoying a purposeful walk through just a few of the 200 acres of The Briars' grounds on a chilly December afternoon when the air was filled with shimmering snowflakes. John and his wife Barbara are the innkeepers of this resort-inn 45 miles north of Toronto. The land has belonged to the Sibbald family for more than a century, and as we walked through the woods to Golfer's Lane, John explained that there are actually two sections:

"There is Sibbald House," he said, "which has many guest rooms, and the Country Club, which has been a seasonal resort since 1942. There are several private cottages next to the 18-hole golf course, and also by the lake. We opened the original homestead in 1977, and we are now a year-round holiday and conference center."

We flushed a few birds out of the undergrowth as we cut through a portion of the woods, and John pointed out the five acres of garden which provide a great many of the table vegetables at the inn. Our walk continued around the ice skating rink and the tennis courts, and we tramped across the snow-covered lawns into Sibbald House to the drawing room where a cup of tea was in order. Here, in front of a crackling fire, I learned about Susan Sibbald, John's great-great-

great-grandmother who came to this part of Ontario in 1835. "I'm sure she provided some inspiration for Mazo de la Roche," said John, as he passed the cream.

"She would be very happy with what's happened here a hundred years later. There's always been an emphasis on family holidays, and children in particular have a good time because we have an entertaining program for young people throughout the week, and this allows grownups freedom to do their own thing if they desire. We have two heated outdoor swimming pools, tennis courts, a sauna, and bathing in the lake, besides shuffleboard and badminton. The children even have their own playground.

"In the wintertime we have great cross-country skiing, snow-shoeing, ice-fishing, and lots of opportunities just to curl up quietly in a corner with a good book."

Accommodations at The Briars are in the Sibbald House (where the cosily furnished bedrooms have such names as the Four-Poster Room, the Petit Point Room, and the Canopy Room), as well as in seventeen additional guest cottages which are scattered about next to the golf course and along the lake. They are named after golfing expressions.

"One of the most important members of our staff is the reservations manager," said John. "We try to match up our guests with the many types of accommodations available, and I believe we have something for everyone in every season of the year." The dining room menu has hearty offerings which satisfy holiday-inspired appetites, and it changes every day.

John, who might himself be a model for one of the *Whiteoaks* characters, arose from the divan and said, "Come, let's take a drive down by the lake to St. George's church and see some more of the Country Club on the way. I'll show you where the trains used to come in next to the lakeshore."

THE BRIARS, Jackson's Point, Ontario, LOE 1LO Canada, 416-722-3271. A resort-inn on the shores of Lake Simcoe, approximately 45 miles north of Toronto. Open every day. Breakfast, lunch, and dinner served to non-residents. Summer activities include 18-hole golf course, two outdoor swimming pools, lakeshore swimming, two all-winter tennis courts, and many lawn sports. Winter sports include xc skiing, skating, tobogganing, snowmobiling, ice-fishing, and curling. There is an excellent children's program during the summer and Christmas holidays. Excellent for families in all seasons. John and Barbara Sibbald, Innkeepers.

Directions: Jackson's Point is located near Sutton, Ontario, and can be reached by Highway #48 from Toronto.

GRANDVIEW FARM
Huntsville, Ontario

Bruce Craik throttled down the speed of the motor boat so that we were barely moving through the canal between Fairy Lake and Penn Lake. "There is a blue heron that lives here," he said, "and perhaps we can catch sight of him. These lakes, St. Mary's, Fairy, and Penn, are all connected by this canal which was built many years ago as part of a transportation system from Toronto that included passage on a lake steamer and another short journey on a narrow-gauge railway. This has always been a popular resort area."

The water was very still at twilight, and he nudged me to point out a beaver who was busily engaged on a half-submerged log. It was about as close as I have ever been to a beaver in its natural habitat.

We were in the twilight of a near-perfect summer day. I had made the pleasant trip from Niagara Falls, New York, and arrived at Grandview Farm just in time to see Bruce and part of a working crew load the last of the bales on the farm cart. There were horses in the meadow, and as I drove past the barn, once again the two goats, Homer and Jethro, poked their heads out of the window and eyed me with some justifiable suspicion. A few of the farm dogs barked their greetings.

I had time for a quick swim and then joined Bruce and Judy under the beautiful yellow canopy that covers the terrace in the summertime. In addition to being a resort-inn, with many activities during summer and winter, Grandview Farm Inn is also a restaurant serving three meals a day. Specialties include roast beef with

Yorkshire pudding, which is served on Wednesday and Saturday nights. Other nights there are three different entrées such as chicken done in many different ways, fish, duck, stuffed roast pork, and veal.

For dinner the waitresses wear very attractive costumes with long skirts, which are replaced by entirely different costumes at breakfast and lunch.

Lodgings are in the main house and in six other attractive cottages set among some fine old trees either on or near the lakeshore.

All the rooms are very comfortable, from the corner room in the inn with the four-poster, to the fireplace rooms in the "Tree Tops," and those in the little waterside cottage called "Puffin Hill."

While I was browsing in the Rafters, the small gift shop at the inn, I picked up the Grandview Farm brochure. It was extremely handsome with full color photographs of all of the activities, the lake views, and the lodging rooms. I found it very helpful when writing this account.

Back on our odyssey through the lake, Bruce put his finger on his lips and pointed ahead. I saw a stately, graceful blue heron standing in the bulrushes along the side of the lake. "When he is frightened," Bruce whispered, "he stands up as straight as possible and that long neck blends into the background of the shore." Suddenly our friend flapped his large wings and took flight, skirting the shore. Bruce speeded up the boat to stay as close as possible, saying, "He likes to play like this and continues for quite a few minutes. I think he understands that we really mean no harm."

Addenda: Just before press time, Bruce told me that the new barn has been built to house the workshop and provide the living quarters for the livestock, including my friends, the two goats Homer and Jethro. A play area has been created with a swing, sandbox, seesaw, and so forth, for young children. The big barn is being renovated to expand meeting facilities as well.

Most of those six children whom I met the first time I visited in 1976, have now gone out into the world on their own. Peter is an enthusiastic sailor and was on the southern ocean-racing circuit this past winter. Ian has completed his second year in the Royal Navy and when last I heard was sailing aboard the *H.M.S. Bulwark.* Ginny is a graduate nurse; Sandy, the third son, is at McMaster University in Hamilton; Tim is in Lakefield College; Heather is also in college, as well as working at the inn (I thought many of the friends of the Craik family would be interested in an update).

GRANDVIEW FARM, Huntsville, Ontario, Canada POA 1KO; 705-789-7462. A 29-room resort-inn on Fairy Lake, 142 mi.

(227km) north of Toronto in a beautiful lake and mountain resort area. American and Modified American plans. Breakfast, lunch, and dinner served to travelers daily. Open mid-May to mid-October; December 26th to March 31st. Closed Christmas Eve and Christmas Day. No pets. Tennis, swimming, sailing, windsurfing, waterskiing, canoeing, xc ski trails (10km), alpine skiing close by. The Craik Family, Innkeepers.

Directions: From Niagara Falls, N.Y. (I-95): take Rainbow Bridge, Rte. 420 to Queen Elizabeth Way, north to Toronto, Rte. 427 north to Rte. 401 east to Rte. 400 north to Barrie, then Rte. 11 north to Rte. 60 (just north of Huntsville), then right for 4½ mi. (7km.) Grandview Farm is on your right. Hwy. 60 is the main route to Ottawa from this part of Ontario.

THE OBAN INN
Niagara-on-the-Lake, Ontario

Innkeeper Gary Burroughs and I were seated for a moment in "Shaw's Corner" in the Victorian pub at the Oban Inn in front of the lovely warm fireplace. It was decorated with many photographs of actors and actresses who have appeared at the nearby Shaw Festival. In the center of the buffet bar was the star of the midday repast: a turkey pie with a big, beautiful crust. There was also a large salad bowl, cold cauliflower, mixed peas and lima beans, cold sliced meats, sliced eggs, and generous helpings of tomatoes, beets, and pickles. It was, indeed, quite British.

"To really understand Niagara-on-the-Lake," said Gary, "I think that it's well to know its past, because in many respects, the past, the present, and the future are existing here, side by side. This village has been known as Loyal Village, Buttlersville, West Niagara, Newark, Niagara, as well as its present name."

Gary was warming to his subject: "We have many 'firsts' here. This was where the first Canadian Parliament was held in 1792 when the town was known as Newark. I daresay that most Americans do not realize that this was the scene of battles during the War of 1812. Fort George was built in 1797 and then damaged by American fire and largely demolished during the War of 1812. It was restored by the Niagara Parks Commission, and a great many visitors enjoy walking around the replica. You see, the United States is just across the river.

"Our building has an interesting history. It was once the home of Captain Duncan Malloy, a laker captain whose home was in Oban, Scotland, a beautiful seaport town. It was built about 1824, and later turned into an inn. In 1914, there were additions made and the Oban Inn became a Canadian Officers' Mess."

The Oban is essentially a Canadian inn. However, because of its evident English heritage, it recalled English inns that I have visited such as the Crown in Chiddingfold, which has the same cozy village air, and the Mermaid Tavern in Rye, where the atmosphere is also drenched in history.

The dinner menu also indicates that the Oban really is a mix of the old world and the new. For example, among the appetizers was a homemade paté which is a tradition in England and the Continent, and the main menu items have the ring of the English countryside: roast prime ribs of beef with Yorkshire pudding, and calves' sweetbreads with bacon served on toast.

There was a mixture of patrons during the noon hour, including businessmen from the town, as well as a few Canadian and American visitors. I noted a piano in one corner, and Gary said that in the evening there were formal jolly sing-alongs, as well as quiet entertainment. With the fire crackling away on a rather chilly day, it was all very heartwarming and hospitable.

This hospitality at the Oban Inn extends to some very homelike lodging rooms. Some have a view of Lake Ontario and all are quite neat, typical of country inns, with individual color schemes and furniture. Many have plants and bookshelves.

In recent years, one of the principal reasons for visiting Niagara-on-the-Lake is to enjoy the Shaw Festival Theater, since 1962 one of the outstanding summer and fall theaters in North America. There is also the Canadian Mime Theater, Canada's first professional mime-in-residence group, which offers full-scale productions of the silent art from mid-May through August, every day except Monday.

While I am devoted to the theater, I personally prefer Niagara-on-the-Lake during the quiet off-season. Then it's possible to enjoy the town, the museums, and the beautiful homes in a more leisurely fashion.

THE OBAN INN, 160 Front St., Box 94, Niagara-on-the-Lake, Ontario LOS IJO; 416-468-2165. A 23-room village inn on a quiet street in one of Canada's historic villages approx. 12 mi. from Niagara Falls, N.Y., on the shores of Lake Ontario. Near Ft. George and Ft. Niagara, the Shaw Festival, and Mime Theater. All plans available. Breakfast, lunch, dinner served daily to travelers. Open every day of the year. Owner-controlled pets welcome. Golf, xc skiing, sailing, fishing, tennis nearby. Gary Burroughs, Innkeeper.

Directions: Exit Hwy. 55 at St. Catherines from the Queen Elizabeth Hwy. Follow signs to Niagara-on-the-Lake.

Quebec

CUTTLE'S TREMBLANT CLUB
Mont Tremblant, Quebec

I trained the telescope along the forest of masts and ballooning sails that seemed to fill the lake in front of Cuttle's on this perfect sailing afternoon in July. For me there is nothing in the world that has the same appeal as a group of sailboats crossing the starting line.

I turned the 'scope slightly to watch four people on the tennis court enjoying a final game of doubles before dinner, and then I swept the slopes of Mont Tremblant immediately across the lake. It was easy to follow the many interesting ski trails and lifts that are so busy during the wintertime here in this Canadian Laurentians resort.

"I wish you could have been here last week when we had our annual windsurfing regatta." Betty Cuttle had joined me; she and her husband Jim are the innkeepers. "Windsurfing has really been taking off here. It combines sailing, surfing, and skiing.

"It seems hard to realize that there will be six to eight feet of snow up here, doesn't it? Incidentally, we have a very active ski program with our own instructors and we use video equipment to help our students improve their techniques. Skiing brought Jim and me to the Laurentians originally; it doesn't seem possible that we've been here for well over twenty years."

Winter is a magic time here at Cuttle's. In addition to the downhill skiing at the famous ski area across the lake, there is snowshoeing and excellent cross-country skiing, and many of these trails begin at Cuttle's front door. Mont Tremblant Park offers fifty miles of marked and groomed trails for Nordic skiers of all abilities. "We put up a box lunch for them here," said Betty, "and we have a waxing room and repair bench, as well. You know we've had quite a few movie companies here this year," she went on. "The actors and directors stayed with us, and it was interesting for the other guests."

In the beautiful late afternoon, surrounded by poppies, marigolds, and tulips, with swallows flitting among the maples and birches, a few of the tanned vacationers were already gathering for dinner. Before excusing herself to take care of some last-minute details, Betty paused along enough to tell me about an unusual dining plan: "Guests on our Modified American Plan may dine out at one of the three other hotels in the area at no extra charge. This allows our guests to see what some of the other hotels are like, and their guests in turn can have an evening out at Cuttle's."

I found the dinners at Cuttle's to be most interesting with the emphasis on French cuisine, including onion soup, cold seafood plate featuring fish from the Gaspé Peninsula, roast leg of veal, braised calves' sweetbreads, and boned chicken Bayonnaise. The menus are bilingual so everyone can practice his French or English, as the case may be.

Although the word "club" is used in the name of this somewhat sophisticated resort-inn, it is, nonetheless, open to the public. Guests come in all seasons and stay for one night or three weeks. There are lots of Americans, because the Canadian exchange rate is favorable.

I happened to mention that I hadn't seen Charlie, the collie, and Meg, the Irish setter, as yet. "Well, Meg ran afoul of a porcupine the day before yesterday, and I think she's still nursing her wounds. Charlie's here somewhere. He'll be glad to see you."

Yes, it's good to be back at Cuttle's again.

CUTTLE'S TREMBLANT CLUB, Mont Tremblant, Quebec, Canada JOT 1ZO; 819-425-2731. A 32-room resort inn on Lac Tremblant facing Mont Tremblant, the highest peak in the Laurentians. Modified American plan omits lunch. Breakfast, lunch, and dinner served daily to travelers. Open year-round. No pets. Tennis, swimming, sailing, windsurfing, boating, fishing, and xc skiing on grounds. Golf, riding, trap shooting, Alpine skiing nearby. Jim and Betty Cuttle, Innkeepers.

Directions: From Montreal, 85 mi. northwest via Laurentian Autoroute 15 to St. Jovite. Turn right on Rte. 327 north 7 mi. to Lac Tremblant. Cuttle's is on the west shore facing the mountain.

HANDFIELD INN, (AUBERGE HANDFIELD)
St. Marc-sur-le-Richelieu, Quebec

In 1978 I visited the Handfield Inn twice. The first time was in late March when Tom Noonan of the Bird and Bottle Inn in Garrison, New York, flew me in his airplane to Montreal. The two of us went to a "sugaring off party" which was being held by innkeeper Conrad Handfield at his own maple sugar grove a few miles from the inn. The spell of winter was still on the land with much snow and many cross-country skiers.

Tom and I were bundled into a car and taken to the "sugar shack," a low-ceilinged rough building where there was a great fire roaring with great iron cauldrons of maple syrup boiling down. There were at least 80 French Canadian innkeepers and their wives all enjoying a great feast of pancakes and sliced maple-cured ham and eggs all served with the maple syrup. There was a fiddler in one corner and an accordion player in the other, and everyone was singing at the top of their lungs.

Innkeeper Handfield explained that these sugaring parties start at the beginning of March and run to the end of April and are very popular with the inn guests. "They are part of the fun of visiting Auberge Handfield at this time of year," he said.

He also persuaded me that I should return to see the inn at the height of the Quebec summer, and on the spot I fixed the date.

The second time, the Richelieu River (part of the waterway which carries boats down to the St. Lawrence and to the tip of Florida) was blue and sparkling in the summer sun. The Marina in front of the inn had several visiting boats, and there were people sitting around the swimming pool enjoying animated conversations in both French and English. The fields were bursting with ripening

grain and I could see a number of farm animals, including sheep, goats, ducks, and geese.

I was greeted upon my arrival by Madame Huguette Handfield who enthusiastically explained all the things there were to do, both on the inn grounds and in the immediate area. She also explained that theatrical performances were given on the converted ferry boat, *l'Escale,* which is moored on the river a few hundred yards from the inn. (These performances are in French, but I had no difficulty in catching the drift.)

With her help in translating the menu, I found that among the main courses that evening were a homemade paté (quite traditional among the European restaurants), salmon from the Gaspé, duck, chicken in wine, filet mignon, and steak au Poivre.

Accommodations were in rustic rooms decorated and furnished in the old Quebec style, but with touches of modern comfort including tile bathrooms and controlled heating. My room had rough wooden walls and casement windows overlooking broad fields. Madame Handfield explained to me later that most of the inn is decorated either with antiques or furniture made by local craftsmen.

The village of St. Marc was wonderfully French and I had animated communication with the village baker, he in French, I in English, while the aroma of his bread and rolls sent my gastronomic senses reeling. The little supermarket reminded me of similar stores I had visited in France. St. Marc stretches along the Richelieu River, and has a twin village on the opposite side called St. Charles, which is reached by ferry.

The Handfield Inn is a great many things: it is a venerable mansion that has seen a century and a half of history; it is an enjoyable French restaurant; a four-season resort; and perhaps best of all, it is an opportunity to visit a French Canadian village which has remained relatively free from the invasion of developers with its ancient stone houses remaining untouched and its farms, where good stock and poultry are still being raised.

HANDFIELD INN (Auberge Handfield), St. Marc-sur-le-Richelieu (Saint Marc on the Richelieu River), Quebec, JOL-2EO, Canada; 514-584-2226. A 45-room French-Canadian country inn about 25 miles from Montreal. Different lodging plans available. Please consult with the inn in advance. Some rooms have shared baths. Breakfast, lunch and dinner served daily to travelers. Ladies are expected to wear a skirt or dress and gentlemen a coat at dinner. Open every day all year. No pets. All summer and winter active sports easily available. Many handcrafts, antique, and historical tours in the area. M. and Mme. Conrad Handfield, Innkeepers.

Directions: From Champlain, Victoria, or the Jacques Cartier bridges, take Hwy. 3 to Sorel, turn right at Hwy. 20. From the east end of Montreal go through the Hyppolite LaFontaine Tunnel. Rte. 20 passes through St. Julie, St. Bruno, and Beloeil. Leave Hwy. 20 at Exit 112 turning left on Rte. 223 north. Handfield is 7 miles distant.

New Brunswick

MARATHON INN
Grand Manan Island, New Brunswick

As the ferry from Black's Harbour approached the wharf at North Head on Grand Manan Island, I could readily see that this was a place where men made their living from the sea. There were fishing boats, seining weirs, and weathered docks on tall stilts; a necessity because of the very high tides in the Bay of Fundy.

Once again, I could see the Marathon Inn at the top of the hill — a gleaming three-story building with a mansard roof.

It is a quiet, unspoiled island of great natural beauty, fifteen miles long and about four miles wide — a paradise for naturalists, bird watchers, photographers, artists, divers, bicyclists, and rock hounds. One of the best ways to experience its great natural unspoiled beauty is by walking.

The owner-innkeepers of the Marathon are Jim and Judy Leslie, and Jim's mother, Fern. The Leslies are all Canadians. Fern is from Saskatchewan, and both Judy and Jim were brought up in Toronto. They first met when they were youthful figure skaters together, and later went to the same high school.

There's no doubt that the Marathon Inn is a real family undertaking. "It's really the only way we can do it," said Jim, who is an enthusiastic individual. "Fern, my mother, is in charge of the kitchen. I try to keep all of the new projects moving both inside and out, and Judy is very busy with the housekeeping details, checking people in and out and, of course, being a mother, as well."

I visited the Marathon, which is a bilingual destination-inn, during early October and found the weather and the feeling absolutely ideal for a vacation. I felt no misgivings about leaving my car at Black's Harbor and came over on the ferry as a foot passenger. Jim has some mopeds and bikes available for tours around the island.

In the conversation with one of the year-round "Grand Mananers" in the very clean passengers' cabin on the ship, I learned that October was the best month for sighting whales, and we were not disappointed.

The first thing I did on arrival was to take a plunge in the new heated swimming pool and arrange for a game of tennis on the new courts. Jim joined me about an hour before dinner on the front porch overlooking the harbor.

"Our guests often like to take advantage of the chance to go deep sea fishing for herring, pollock, and haddock with the island fishermen. There are also boating trips to Gannet Rock, Machias Seal Island, and Tent Island. Children seem to have such a wonderful time here, and that is very gratifying. I think one of the reasons that Judy, Fern, and I moved out to the island to begin with was that we thought it would be a wonderful place to raise children. By the way, we now have a resident naturalist at the inn."

I had a long talk with Fern regarding the inn menus. "We always have a choice of fresh fish or another meat at every evening meal," she said. "We offer our seafood chowder and another soup, and there's a choice of desserts. We've received many compliments for our raisin and walnut pie, and also our rum pie. I make homemade buns every day and all of the desserts."

Later, after a very pleasant stroll down to the docks to look at the fishing boats which had been tied up for the evening, I returned to join all of the Leslies around the kitchen table for a piece of raspberry pie. "Yes, things are going well here, but there are still a lot of challenges," said Fern. "More and more people are discovering us, but we think that Grand Manan will remain basically unspoiled. By the way, remind your readers, when they cross into Canada at Calais, to remember to set their clocks ahead one hour." She looked at me with a big grin because I had forgotten to change my watch and I missed the ferry!

MARATHON INN, North Head at Grand Manan, New Brunswick, Canada EOG 2MO; 506-662-8144. A 38-room resort-inn on Grand Manan Island in the Bay of Fundy, 40 mi. from St. John in New Brunswick. Modified American and European plans. Open all year. Breakfast and dinner served to travelers daily. Pets allowed on ground floor annex. Heated swimming pool, tennis courts on grounds. Beachcombing, bird watching, swimming, fishing, hiking, diving, bicycles, golf nearby. Jim, Judy, and Fern Leslie, Innkeepers.

Directions: Gran Manan Island is reached by ferry from Black's Harbour which is just off Rte. 1, midway between Calais, Maine, and St. John, New Brunswick. Check inn for schedule.

MARSHLANDS INN
Sackville, New Brunswick

Every year I hear from a great many people who drive across Maine into New Brunswick to reach Nova Scotia, Prince Edward Island, and Newfoundland the long way—by land.

Almost all of these letters make some reference to the Marshlands Inn, which is located just a few miles from the Nova Scotia

border and the P.E.I. ferry. This is what one couple reported: "Our first stop was the Marshlands Inn. We had planned a three-week camping trip with an occasional overnight stop to get a bedroom and an adjoining bathroom, the pleasures you miss even in the best Provincial parks. Our itinerary brought us to the Marshlands Inn for a late lunch. We must admit the setting, decor, and food exceeded our expectations." (I have many letters from people who stop at the Marshlands and mention the fact that they never expected to find such a sophisticated inn so far north.)

"While paying our bill we found a copy of *Country Inns and Back Roads*, perused the table of contents, and noticed your entry regarding the Marshlands. We found that we were in complete agreement with your comments and enjoyed your personal observations. Believe it or not we never expected that such a purchase would determine the roads that we would eventually take." Incidentally, that couple also visited the Inverary Inn and the Milford House in Nova Scotia, both a single day's drive from Sackville.

My personal dilemma when visiting the Marshlands is to make a choice of entrées at dinner. The Atlantic and Miramichi salmon are very tempting, but the curried lamb with Marshlands chutney is most enjoyable, too. There are also lobsters, scallops, beefsteak and kidney pie, the famous fiddlehead greens, and many curry dishes. All the rolls, breads, ice cream and sherbets are homemade.

I am happy to say that Innkeepers Herb and Alice Read continue to pursue the Marshlands tradition of leaving a thermos pitcher of hot chocolate in the front parlor for guests who like a late snack. That welcoming pitcher was there on my first visit in 1974.

Although the Marshlands seems like it is just a few miles from the North Pole to those of us who live below the Canadian border, it would be unusual in any setting. The dinnerware is sterling, the china is Spode, and all the waitresses wear dark blue uniforms with white collars and aprons.

The breakfast offerings include freshly squeezed (honest) orange juice, baked apples, fresh homemade apple sauce, stewed foxberries, (*fox*berries?), slow-cooked oatmeal, cracked wheat porridge, creamed salt cod, buckwheat pancakes with maple syrup . . . should I continue? . . . should I continue?

The Marshlands is not only a place where East meets West, but also a place where North meets South—then all sit down to eat!

Marshlands Inn has been included in *CIBR* since 1974.

MARSHLANDS INN, Box 1440, Sackville, N.B., Canada EOA 3CO; 506-536-0170. A 16-room village inn near Tantramar Marshes and Fundy Tides. European plan. Eight rooms with private baths. Breakfast, lunch, and dinner served to travelers daily. Closed during the Christmas season. Golf, xc skiing, curling, hiking, and swimming nearby. Herb and Alice Read, Innkeepers.

Directions: Follow Trans-Canada Highway to Sackville, then Rte. 6, 1 mi. to center of town.

Prince Edward Island

Prince Edward Island is one of the great surprises of North America. For one thing, ocean water temperatures along the wide P.E.I. beaches average 68 to 70 degrees in summer and the sun is excellent for tanning. It has one of Canada's finest national parks stretching 25 miles along the Gulf of St. Lawrence. There are wild seascapes, breathtaking views and an atmosphere of hospitality because this has been a resort area for more than a century.

During the summer months there is an excellent theatre at the Confederation Centre of the Arts in Charlottetown offering a choice of musicals which play to capacity houses most every night. Cavendish Beach is the locale of Lucy Maude Montgomery's stories of Ann of Green Gables. A small, gabled, green cottage has been built with some reminders of Ann stories.

Prince Edward Island is very popular in July and August, so reserve well in advance and be sure to obtain ferry information.

SHAW'S HOTEL
Brackley Beach, Prince Edward Island

"We open around June 15th and close around September 15th," said Gordon Shaw, "and I think that the first two weeks and the last two weeks are two of the best times of the season." We were sitting on the side porch of Shaw's Hotel watching all of the fun as a large group of children played with two big sheep dogs.

"It's very warm and pleasant here in June," he continued. "You know that because you were here yourself in June. September is always excellent and, since most of the young people have gone back to school, it becomes our 'quiet season.' We have 30 or 40 children at the height of the season."

Shaw's Hotel was a great discovery for me a few years ago. I went over to P.E.I. on the ferry from Caribou, Nova Scotia, to Wood Islands and shared the trip with a group of young French students who lived on one of the islands in St. Lawrence Bay. As I recall, they sang during the entire trip.

I found my way to the Brackley Beach area and visited several pleasant guest houses and resorts. However, as soon as I walked through the front gates at Shaw's and saw old barns and the house with its red mansard roof, I knew that this was something special.

"It all started in 1860," said Gordon, "and it has been in the family ever since. We have about 75 acres of the original Shaw pioneer farm, a property which was settled in the 18th century. We've added quite a few accommodations including cottages, and some of these have two, three, and four bedrooms because we have a lot of the families every summer. Five of the cottages have fireplaces.

"We still keep a lot of farm animals here because it's a wonderful opportunity for city people to become familiar with them. It's only a short distance through the forest to the beach. That's one of the principal attractions for all of our guests."

All of this summertime outdoor activity, including swimming, sailing on the bay which adjoins the hotel property, deep-see tuna fishing, golf, tennis, bicycling, walking, and horseback riding contribute to very big appetites. Consequently, the cooks at Shaw's are busy from morning to night preparing all kinds of dishes including salmon, lobster, mackerel, cod, and halibut. Naturally, the fish is fresh. Dinners are fun because everyone is eager for a hearty meal and the atmosphere is full of enthusiasm about the day's activities.

"I guess we are the oldest family-operated summer resort in Eastern Canada," exclaimed Gordon as he settled back into his chair. "I grew up here. It has been my home and always will be. What I enjoy most is sharing it with families like these every summer."

Shaw's Hotel has been in *CIBR* since 1975.

SHAW'S HOTEL and Cottages, Brackley Point Road, Brackley Beach. Prince Edward Island, Canada C0A 2H0; 902-672-2022. A 24-room country hotel within walking distance of Brackley Beach, 15 mi. from Charlottetown. American plan. Some rooms with shared baths. 10 guest cottages. Breakfast, lunch, dinner served to travelers daily. Open from June 15 to Sept. 15. Pets allowed in cottages only. Tennis, golf, bicycles, riding, sailing, beach, and summer theatre nearby. No credit cards. Personal checks accepted. Gordon Shaw, Innkeeper.

Directions: Prince Edward Island is reached either by ferry from Cape Tormentine, New Brunswick (near Moncton), or Caribou, Nova Scotia. In both cases, after arriving on P.E.I. follow Rte. 1 to Charlottetown, then Rte. 15 to Brackley Beach. P.E.I. is also reached by Eastern Provincial Airways, Canadian National Railways, and Air Canada.

Nova Scotia

INVERARY INN
Baddeck, Nova Scotia

Baddeck, Nova Scotia, is a small Scottish village on the shores of Loch Bras d'Or. By air, its about 2½ hours away from Boston via Halifax and Sydney, Nova Scotia. In terms of more ethereal measurements, it might as well be the moon.

And yet I probably have received more mail from people visiting the Inverary Inn than any other country inn in this book! Here's an example from a recent letter.

"Dear Berkshire Traveller, I have read your book, stayed at several of your country inns, and found myself on some back roads you may not have discovered, but these few days at the Inverary Inn have been a delight with excellent food and comfortable beds. We've enjoyed thoughtfulness and reading lamps, freshly-squeezed orange juice, a fire in the fireplace, and new friends—all made possible by the imagination and concern of Isobel MacAulay.

"When we mentioned *Country Inns and Back Roads,* the conversation continued well into the night over tea and lemon pie in the kitchen. This inn is a fine example of the spirit of the country inns. I'll certainly be returning to the Inverary as soon as I can." That was from a lady in New Jersey.

Here's an excerpt from some guests from Calgary: "We're coming back for the food! The salmon was heavenly and so fresh! For breakfast, we've never tasted anything like that Scottish oatmeal porridge and bannoch (a Scottish scone made with buttermilk and sour cream). And the oatcakes—oh, the oatcakes."

Another letter spoke of the warmth, graciousness, and hospitality at the Inverary and took me to task for omitting some of the historic events of Nova Scotia history. They were particularly complimentary toward the staff of the inn who, they said, seemed to be enjoying themselves as they went about their work.

Over the years, some very exciting things have happened at Inverary, including the fact that Isobel and Dan MacAulay's son, Scott, whom I have known since he was a wee bairn, is now the manager of the inn.

In 1979, the "Gathering of the Clans" was held at Inverary, and Isobel wrote me that it was really a wonderful time. The Duke of Argyll visited and was pleased to see the new addition to the inn called Argyll Lodge.

In 1980, the inn will have enlarged its gift shop considerably, carrying many authentic Cape Breton handcrafted gifts.

Literally dozens and dozens of people have found their way to the Inverary with copies of *Country Inns and Back Roads* in their hands and Isobel MacAulay has made them all feel as though their arrival was the most important day in her life. In 1975 I said that the Inverary might just be the most famous country inn in Nova Scotia and I think it is safe to say that it *is* the most famous country inn in Nova Scotia. However, such well-deserved fame does not go unnoticed, and so it is most necessary in all seasons of the year to have advance reservations.

Thank you Isobel for being so warm and generous to our "Travellers."

Inverary Inn has been in *CIBR* since 1972.

INVERARY INN, Box 190, Baddeck, Cape Breton, N.S. Canada 902-295-2674. A 40-room village inn on the Cabot Trail, 52 mi. from Sydney, N.S. On the shores of Lake Bras d'Or. European plan. Some rooms with shared bath. Breakfast and dinner served to travelers daily. Open from May 15 to Nov. 1. Bicycles and children's playground on grounds. Boating and small golf course nearby. Isobel MacAulay, Innkeeper.

Directions: Follow Trans-Canada Hwy. to Canso Causeway to Baddeck.

KILMUIR PLACE
Northeast Margaree, Cape Breton, Nova Scotia

"I've never used a mix in my life, and never will." Isabel Taylor stood with her hands on her hips, tossed her head back, and her eyes flashed. "After all, my mother and father started this place over 50 years ago and our guests love the old-fashioned ways. I can tell the difference when something is made from a mix, and I'm sure everybody else can, too."

"Indeed, they do. And I'm a guest who has been coming for 40 straight years."

This time the speaker was a lady from Philadelphia who walked into Isabel's and Ross's cozy kitchen as if on cue.

"In those days it took some persistence and motivation to come out to the Margaree," she said, settling down into one of the comfortable upholstered chairs in one corner of the kitchen. "Now you can get here from Sydney in about an hour and a half and from Halifax in about three and a half hours. In the old days the roads weren't paved and sometimes Ross had to get a team to pull us out of the mud.

"One thing that pleases me is that we have so many young people. A lot in their early 20s. They're so *interested* in everything!"

Ross asked her if she would like to have another piece of his chocolate cake, reminding her that he had been up at the crack of dawn that morning making it. She demurred, saying that she couldn't possibly eat another bite.

While we were chatting, Isabel deftly carved a generous slice of roast beef and poured pan gravy over a big helping of mashed potatoes on my plate. She topped it off with some cauliflower.

"Here you are," she said, "if you don't mind eating in the kitchen." Well, I've never eaten anywhere but in the kitchen at the Kilmuir Place. It's the one way to find out what Ross and Isabel have been doing over the past winter.

"One thing we do is feed birds all winter. They keep us company. All of the summer birds come back every year. Tell your friends to bring their binoculars and notebooks. This is really good bird country."

The Kilmuir Place became known for the fine salmon fishing on the Margaree. Ross knows all the good fishing holes in this most beautiful of rivers. Now, however, guests also come to the Kilmuir to tour the Cabot Trail and enjoy a few days of rest, reading, and conversation.

I must add that this is a very tiny inn. It has only three rooms with private baths and two of them without. Don't even think of coming without a reservation.

But when you do come, be prepared to wish fervently on the day you leave that you could stay several days longer.

Kilmuir Place has been in *CIBR* since 1972.

KILMUIR PLACE, Northeast Margaree, Cape Breton, N.S., Canada BOE 2HO; 902-248-2877. A 5-room country inn on Rte. 19, 28 mi. from Baddeck. Some rooms with shared baths. Modified American plan. Breakfast and dinner served to houseguests only. Open from June to mid-October. Salmon fishing in the Margaree

River, touring the Cabot Trail, and both fresh water and salt water swimming nearby. Not suitable for children under 12. Mr. and Mrs. Ross Taylor, Innkeepers.

Directions: After crossing Canso Causeway to Cape Breton, follow either Rte. 19 (coast road to Inverness) and turn right on Cabot Trail at Margaree Forks, or follow Rte. 105 and turn left on Cabot Trail at Nyanza.

MILFORD HOUSE
South Milford, Nova Scotia

Once again, Wendy Miller and I were seated on the swings next to the Milford House. We first sat here during the summer of 1973, when Wendy was twelve years old and even then, a very important part of all of the many activities at this Nova Scotian woodland country inn. Now, it was mid-June and the lady's-slippers, and other early summer flowers were blooming in profusion. A few of the many varieties of birds that frequent this part of Nova Scotia had already returned from winter quarters and were setting up housekeeping.

It was difficult for me to believe that this attractive young woman, who first showed me around all of the lakes and cabins, patiently explaining about the fireplaces, maid service, trout fishing, canoeing, and the walks along the woodland trails, might not be here in 1980, as she is pursuing a career in geology.

Every year we've had good chats like this one. Sometimes walking through the woods, others while canoeing, and sometimes at the dinner table. I think I've pictured the Milford House through Wendy's eyes and her great love of this wonderfully sequestered natural country where it's still possible to see deer, otter, wild duck, and beaver.

"Tell me about a typical day here for the guests," I asked.

"Well, they generally wander up to the main lodge for a breakfast of bacon, eggs, muffins, and coffee," she said. "Then there are just so many things to do like tennis, swimming, canoeing, volleyball, fishing, croquet, and maybe a picnic, or just lying in the sun. While they relax, the cabin is tidied, the beds are made, a load of logs is delivered to the fireplace, and another block of ice is delivered to the ice box."

The cottages are spread out along the shores of two lakes. Each of them has its own dock and a living room with a fireplace, electricity, and a bathroom with hot and cold running water and a shower or a tub.

"The only noises here are birds and frogs. We don't allow outboard motors on our lakes. But there is wonderful canoeing

among the several lakes. The whole area is a fisherman's delight. There is speckled trout, native and stocked, and the salmon rivers aren't very far away.

"After a day's activities or a day of doing nothing, people return to the lodge for dinner. We serve home-baked bread, pastry, vegetables from our garden, roasts, fresh fish, blueberries, and raspberries. After dinner there is nothing to compare with a quiet evening on the porch of the cottage, watching the sun go down, listening to the strange laughing call of a loon.

"Mother and Dad are really very excited about the fact that we have constructed some new housekeeping cabins for use in the early and late season, in addition to the summer. We're making reservations for some weekends and have bookings for Christmas as well. We have very good cross-country skiing here, because once the snow comes it stays in the woods and is just beautiful. We have lots of ski trails that are usually well-prepared by snowmobiles. We think that there is going to be an increased interest in the Milford House during the winter in coming years."

On my very first trip in 1973, Wendy explained to me that when guests leave, all the remaining guests stand on the porch and wave their napkins or handkerchiefs, and the departing guests wave back until they pass the oak tree on the corner of the property.

Once again, Wendy, along with her father and mother, innkeepers Margaret and Bud Miller, stood on the porch as I made another reluctant farewell. I always weep a little, but this year, perhaps, there was an extra tear or two of joy, because I realized that Wendy, now grown up and going out into the world, would always carry with her an abundance of the spirit of the Milford House.

MILFORD HOUSE, South Milford, R.R. #4, Annapolis Royal, N.S., Canada, BOS IOA; 902-532-2617. A rustic resort-inn with 24 cabins on 600 acres of woodlands and lakes, 90 mi. from Yarmouth, N.S., near Kejimkujik National Park. Modified American plan. Breakfast and dinner served daily with picnic lunches available. Open from June 18 to Sept. 15; fall and winter by special reservation. Tennis, fishing, croquet, canoeing, bird-watching, and swimming on grounds. Deep-sea fishing and golf nearby. Warren and Margaret Miller, Innkeepers.

Directions: From Yarmouth follow Rte. 1 to traffic lights in Annapolis Royal. Turn right and continue on to Rte. 8, 15 mi. to inn.

Important: *Many of the inns can be reached by public transportation, and arrangements can frequently be made to be picked up at bus and train stations, as well as airports.*

I do not include lodging rates in the descriptions, for the very nature of an inn means that there are lodgings of various sizes, with and without baths, in and out of season, and with plain and fancy decoration. Travelers should call ahead and inquire about the availability and rates of the many different types of rooms.

Rates are comparable to those at hotels, motels, and resorts in the same geographic area. To me, this represents a travel bargain, for there is so much more offered at a country inn.

"European Plan" means that rates for rooms and meals are separate. "American Plan" means that meals are included in the cost of the room. "Modified American Plan" means that breakfast and dinner are included in the cost of the room. Some inns include a Dontinental breakfast with the lodging.

"... *A great deal of work has been accomplished since your last visit. You may recall, there was a porch running along the east side of the inn which served as a fire exit. It was an ugly construction that broke the line of the building. A new interior fire escape was included as a part of the addition I raised on the south, and so I was finally able to pull off the exterior one. Two exterior doors leading to the old porch have been removed; one replaced with double windows, the other blacked out. All that remains to be done is the finishing coat of stucco, and the building is again looking clean and Colonial. In the spring, I shall replant the bushes and re-lay the walk to the entrance. In the cellar, I found an old brick well filled in and capped with concrete. I have broken the seal and am doing a bit of archaeological excavation. Thus far I have found fifteen cobalt blue bromo bottles, two whiskey bottles, two undetermined bottles, a milk bottle, several broken mantels from kerosene lamps, and many pieces of willowware ...*" —Massachusetts

"*Our troubles are different from those of people in other parts of the country. We are semi-isolated, connected by three ferry lines and a long drive around the peninsula, about three hours. This replaces the bridge over the Canal which dissapeared after the great wind of February. It will take a year to get even a temporary bridge across the Canal. Now, it takes four ferry rides for the trip, with much waiting for the boats, overcrowding, causing many to be left at the dock. In spite of all this, plus the gas shortage and inflation, after eighteen years, we still love it.*" —Washington State

"... *As I see it, the inn always was and is the center of the town's activities and I want very much for that feeling to stay with us, for what else can add more to the character and success of a country inn than the support and interest of her neighbors?*" —Pennsylvania

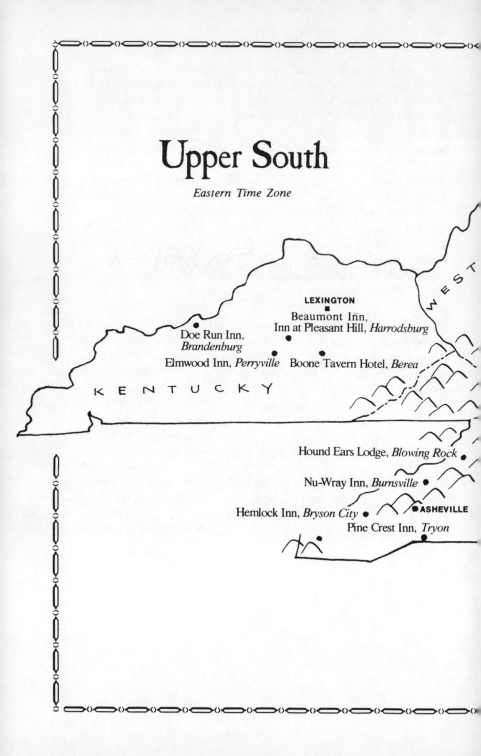

Upper South

Eastern Time Zone

LEXINGTON

Beaumont Inn,
Inn at Pleasant Hill, *Harrodsburg*

Doe Run Inn,
Brandenburg

Elmwood Inn, *Perryville*   Boone Tavern Hotel, *Berea*

K E N T U C K Y

WEST

Hound Ears Lodge, *Blowing Rock*

Nu-Wray Inn, *Burnsville*

Hemlock Inn, *Bryson City*   ASHEVILLE

Pine Crest Inn, *Tryon*

Wells Inn, *Sistersville*

Country Inn, *Berkeley Springs*

Red Fox Tavern, *Middleburg*
Wayside Inn, *Middletown*

WASHINGTON

Old Club Restaurant, *Alexandria*

Maryland Inn, *Annapolis*

Robert Morris Inn, *Oxford*

M A R Y L A N D

V I R G I N I A

Graves Mountain Lodge, *Syria*
Prospect Hill, *Trevelians*
■ CHARLOTTESVILLE
Hollymead Inn, *Charlottesville*

General Lewis Inn, *Lewisburg*

Alexander-Withrow House, *Lexington*

Gristmill Square, *Warm Springs*

iverside Inn, *nce Springs*

V I R G I N I A

■ RALEIGH

N O R T H

C A R O L I N A

North Carolina

HEMLOCK INN
Bryson City, North Carolina

Ella Jo Shell was explaining the way that she and John felt about owning the Hemlock Inn high up in the foothills of the Great Smokies. We were seated at the open end of the large room that serves as a combination dining room and sitting room and has a beautiful view of the mountains.

"John and I are from Marietta, Georgia, and ever since the first time we came up to these mountains all that we ever wanted to do was find a way to live here permanently. The previous owner, knowing that John was in the insurance and investment business, asked for help in finding a buyer."

At this point, John entered the room and continued the narrative. "The next day I called him and said, 'I think I found a buyer for your inn . . . me!'" We all laughed, and I felt as though I had known the Shells for a long time. That's the way they are—warm, outgoing, considerate, and highly involved with their guests.

This is best illustrated by the fact that breakfast and dinner, which are the two meals served at the Hemlock Inn, are served at large Lazy Susan tables which accommodate twelve or more. The food is served family style, and every effort is made to see that guests sit at a different table for every meal. This makes getting acquainted a very simple and very happy process. Incidentally, John says grace before each meal.

John summed it up by saying: "We don't have a swimming pool, television, or a golf course. But what we do have is a plain old mountain inn where folks can just be themselves and unwind. We find that when they arrive they are frequently very tired and grumpy, but after a couple of days of this mountain air and our good cooking, they are as happy as larks."

The Hemlock Inn, like so many country inns, is a family affair, with John and Ella Jo and their children, Jennifer and Laurel Ann, pitching in to do a little of everything. Three local ladies do the cooking. Guests are summoned to meals by a bell, and since the dinner is served at six, there is plenty of daylight left after the meal for shuffleboard or skittles or just sitting and rocking and looking at the mountains.

"How do we feel about owning a country inn?" Ella Jo replied with a smile, "It's like having company all the time."

In the most recent letter I had from Ella Jo, she said the Prime Minister of Monaco, his wife, and two of his lifelong friends came to Hemlock Inn in October because, "Several years ago while on a working trip to America, they read about the Hemlock Inn in a very interesting book: *Country Inns and Back Roads.*"

Hemlock Inn has been included in *CIBR* since 1973.

HEMLOCK INN, Bryson City, N.C. 28713; 704-488-9820. A 25-room Smoky Mountain inn 4 mi. from Bryson City and 60 mi. from Asheville. Near Fontana Village, Cherokee, and Pisgah National Forest. Modified American plan omits lunch. Breakfast and dinner served to travelers by reservation only. Sunday dinner served at noontime. Open from early May to early November. No pets. Shuffleboard, skittles, ping-pong, hiking trails on grounds. Tubing, rafting, and golf nearby. No credit cards. Ella Jo and John Shell, Innkeepers.

Directions: Located 1 mi. off Rte. 19 between Cherokee and Bryson City, N.C. Take paved road to top of mountain.

HOUND EARS LODGE and CLUB
Blowing Rock, North Carolina

The balcony of my room at Hound Ears seemed to rest almost in the top branches of an oak tree. By now the sun was directly overhead casting a dappled pattern on the floor of the porch. In the distance, Grandfather Mountain was shimmering and to my left, perched on various levels of the lower mountains, were the attractively designed homes of the Hound Ears community.

Below, in the foreground, were some young people walking to

the swimming pool, which I intended to visit shortly. However, dominating the valley floor, with many of the trees and greens visible from my vantage point, was the Hound Ears golf course.

Perhaps it was this picture of verdant greens and fairways punctuated by clear, white, menacing sand traps that momentarily made it difficult to realize that there had been eight or nine inches of snow here last Christmas and that the other face of Hound Ears, the winter visage, is one that includes spectacular skiing, roaring fireplaces, and the exhilaration of pure winter air.

After a cool night's sleep, I strolled across the flower-lined walk to the main lodge for breakfast, and was on the first leg of the Hound Ears tour.

As I moved from the accommodations in the main lodge to the chalets, and from the swimming pool to several of the private homes of native stone and wood, I found excellent taste everywhere.

The furnishings, appointments, interiors, and exteriors were carefully harmonized. For example, my room was done in complementary shades of brown with yellow sheets on my bed. All of the buildings were set among rhododendrons and evergreens, and in many places huge handsome boulders were allowed to remain where they rested. The road was built around them, curving and twisting and climbing.

Hound Ears is a luxurious American plan resort-inn, and the rates reflect the additional services and elegance.

The whole concept of Hound Ears which, by the way, is named for a rock formation on the mountain behind the lodge, is the inspiration of the Robbins brothers, all of whom were born and raised in this part of North Carolina. They saw the marvelous possibilities in making a resort-inn to which were added skiing and golf facilities.

Other resort-inns with extensive golf facilities include the Ojai Valley Inn and The Inn at Rancho Santa Fe.

Hound Ears Lodge has been included in *CIBR* since 1971.

HOUND EARS LODGE and CLUB, P.O. Box 188, Blowing Rock, N.C. 28605; 704-963-4321. A luxurious 25-room resort-inn on Rte. 105, 6 mi. from Boone. Near natural attractions. American plan. Meals served to houseguests only. Open year-round. 18-hole golf course, swimming, skiing, and tennis on grounds. Bill Jeffcoat, Innkeeper.

Directions: From Winston-Salem, follow Rte. 421 west to Boone, then travel south on Rte. 105 to inn. From Asheville, follow Rtes. 19 and 19 E to Pineola, then Rte. 181 to Linville and Rte. 105 north to inn. From Bristol, Va., and I-81, follow Rte. 421 east to Vilas (mountainous), then Rte. 321 east to Boone. In Boone, pick up Rte. 105 and turn on Shulls Mills Rd.

THE NU-WRAY INN
Burnsville, North Carolina

Innkeeper Rush Wray was telling me what he serves for dinner at the Nu-Wray Inn: "We always have fried chicken or country-baked ham and four or five vegetables, biscuits and honey, and salads. The desserts are homemade cobblers, including peach or cherry, or different custards, ice cream, or homemade cakes.

"One of our main features is our fried chicken, which we feel is a little different than most because we fry it in a large pan. It is cooked slowly and takes quite some time, which I think enhances the flavor. It is always done on the inside. Often your deep-fried chicken is done on the outside but not on the inside. We have our own hams which are baked and served cold in the evening. We rotate ham and chicken because they seem to be most in demand by our guests. We have special dishes like our own baked beans. These are not the same as your New England baked beans. We put a little more seasoning in ours, like tomato sauce. It could be more like Spanish beans, in a way, and of course we use a little larger bean, whereas in New England, beans are usually the pea beans. We bake our beans for quite some time just as you do in New England. People often enjoy them because they're a little different and we put in a little bit of onion, green pepper, seasoning, and strips of bacon."

We were enjoying breakfast at the Nu-Wray Inn which, like dinner, is served at long tables where everybody "passes" the plates and gets acquainted quickly. At eight o'clock I had been roused from my sleep by the famous Nu-Wray bell; at eight thirty, it had rung again, and we all made for the dining room from whence were

249

drifting tantalizing aromas of coffee, scrambled eggs, ham, pancakes, and delicious honey in the comb!

Now Rush continued, "For people who are staying longer than just a few days we vary the menu and work out different things. A lot of our guests stay on the American plan . . . some for two and three weeks. We've had some people for a month or two, and even three months. We had a couple who came back for fifteen years and stayed for three months at a time. There's a lady coming on Sunday who will be here for eight weeks. A lot of people like to come and 'stay put,' instead of moving around.

"On the other hand, there are a lot of young people traveling with *CIBR*. They're so excited and they feel they've just discovered something that no one else knows about. They say they'll never stay at another commerical highway inn. It's just a thrill to hear them talk about it. These people love to go from place to place, inn-hopping, and it's always good that I can recommend other inns. I had a wonderful letter yesterday from a young girl in California. She said that the Nu-Wray was the highlight of her whole trip."

Almost all the letters I get about the Nu-Wray say that it's different. I've been visiting there for some years. In past editions I've written about the great backroading in the beautiful mountains; I've described the flora and the fauna, and the beautiful antiques. This time I thought readers would enjoy hearing about the country food.

The inn is now closed January, February, March, and half of April. Otherwise it's open every day of the year.

The Nu-Wray has been included in *CIBR* since 1973.

THE NU-WRAY INN, Burnsville, N.C. 28714; 704-682-2329. A 35-room village inn on town square on Rte. 19E, 38 mi. north of Asheville. A few miles from Mt. Mitchell. Modified

*American plan omits lunch and Sunday night supper. Breakfast and
dinner served every weekday to travelers. Noon dinner served on
Sundays only. Open daily mid-April through Dec. Golf, swimming,
hiking, and skiing nearby. Rush T. Wray, Innkeeper. Mrs. Annie
Wray Bennett, Hostess.*

*Directions: From Asheville, go north on Rte. 19-23 for 18 miles,
then continue on 19. Five miles from Burnsville, 19 becomes 19E.
From the north via Bristol or Johnson City, Tenn., take Rte. 19-23 to
Unicoi. Turn left on 107 to N.C. State Line. Take 226 and turn right
on Rte. 197 at Red Hill to Burnsville.*

PINE CREST INN
Tryon, North Carolina

The Pine Crest Inn is in the foothills of the Blue Ridge
Mountains near Asheville, in the town of Tryon, which in itself is a
very interesting place. Many artists and writers have moved there
over the recent years, finding inspiration in these mountains where
nature has been so generous. Because of its advantageous location
and its healthful climate, Tryon is an ideal place to spend a vacation.
Many guests return to the Pine Crest year after year and make
arrangements to meet each other on the next trip. Many people who
travel to and from Florida stop off for days at a time at each
end of their trip, and it's particularly important to make advance
reservations.

The rooms in the individual cottages are furnished in Carolina
furniture which is handmade locally, and many of them have
splendid views of the mountains. One of them, by the way, is called
"Swayback," and was at one time occupied by F. Scott Fitzgerald.
All have distinctive names, and most have fireplaces.

The innkeepers at Pine Crest are Fran and Bob Hull who say of
themselves, "We left Fairfield County, Connecticut, and corporate
living many years ago, and have found a completely different way of
life here keeping a country inn."

"Fran," said Bob, "is in charge of the kitchen. It is something
that she really likes to do. She wouldn't feel right unless she knew
what was going on. Our guests seem to expect it. She can make
practically everything from scratch, including bread, rolls, desserts,
pies, and cakes."

In the dining room there is a big stone fireplace at one end and
beautiful oak tables which need no tablecloths to enhance them.
There are flowers and candles on the tables, and as everybody agrees,
the food is marvelous. Many of the waiters have been here for over
twenty years.

The inn, which is always a model of neatness, was repainted during 1979 and has been nominated for the National Historic Register.

Apparently this way of life agrees with Bob and Fran, and with their guests as well. "We like to do things in our own way," says Bob. "We like jackets and ties on gentlemen at dinner, although ties can be eliminated in warm weather. We now require a minimum visit of two nights, and reservations are required at all times. We think it's important to have the morning paper at the table at breakfast, and a delivery of ice to the room late in the afternoon."

I asked Bob about the famous Tryon "thermal belt."

"This is caused by a temperature inversion," he explained, "resulting in a temperate zone which escapes the frost of the valley and the deep freeze of the mountains. The foliage here is fresh and green compared with that above and below. Scientists have studied this unusual condition for years. We love it."

PINE CREST INN, P.O. Box 1030, Tryon, N.C. 28782; 704-859-9135. A 34-room resort-inn midway between Asheville, N.C. and Greenville/Spartanburg, S.C. Breakfast, lunch, and dinner served daily by reservation to travelers. Coats required for gentlemen at dinner. Closed Jan. 2 to Feb. 15. Closed Christmas. Attended, leashed pets allowed. Golf, tennis, and swimming at nearby country clubs. Reservations required at all times. Minimum visit 2 nights. Robert and Fran Hull, Innkeepers.

Directions: From Asheville, take I-26 to Tryon exit, then 108 to Tryon. Go through town. Do not cross railroad tracks but bear left to Pine Crest Lane. The inn is at the end of the lane. From

Spartanburg/Greenville take I-85 north to I-26. Exit at Columbus, N.C. Take Rte. 108 toward Tryon—go through town. Do not cross railroad tracks but bear left to Pine Crest Lane. The inn is at the end of the lane.

West Virginia

THE COUNTRY INN
Berkeley Springs, West Virginia

Fifteen years of searching for country inns has made me a firm believer that inns take on the character traits and personalities of their innkeepers. For that reason, in my search for inns, I am as keenly interested in the innkeepers themselves as I am in the food, accommodations, and atmosphere.

The warmhearted hospitality and good humor at The Country Inn (which was known as the Park View Inn when I first visited it in 1971) are extensions of the genuine interest and concern of innkeepers Jack and Adele Barker, and Bill North. I met the Barkers first in 1972 when my son Keith and I were inn-tripping through Maryland, West Virginia, and Pennsylvania.

When an arriving guest walks in the front door and Jack Barker comes forward with his firm handshake, saying, "Welcome to The Country Inn," there's no way to feel but good. He has a booming voice and a marvelous Tennessee accent that lets everyone within earshot know that he loves life and wants others to enjoy it with him. Adele, on the other hand, imparts a very gentle feeling of concern for her guests. She has a wonderful laugh.

I was sitting with Jack, Adele, and Bill in a corner of the newly completed outdoor dining area called the Country Garden and Cafe, which seats about seventy guests. About three quarters of the area is covered with a low-profile arrangement of massive beams and thick cedar shake shingles. It was tastefully decorated with fifty hanging baskets, filled with plants and gay flowers. In one corner, water softly splashed from a waterfall near the sunken garden surrounding a dance floor. "We have soft lights and sweet music," Bill said, smiling.

The exterior of the inn is red brick, with white columns extending two stories on both the front and sides. It is immediately adjacent to the village park and the bandstand, and is surrounded by sycamore and oak trees and flowering hedges. Even though it's in the middle of the town, a small brook must be crossed to reach the front door.

"We are trying to recreate the gracious colonial style of living," said Bill. "The name was changed to 'The Country Inn' a few years ago, because we felt it more closely expressed our real nature."

The menu is an extension of the homey atmosphere with such popular offerings as country ham, smothered chicken, salmon soup, duckling with orange sauce, and homemade hot breads.

There's much to see and do in the vicinity of Berkeley Springs, including an eighteen-hole Robert Trent Jones golf course and good cross-country skiing in the Cacapon State Park. There are a great many circle tours which conduct guests to some of the interesting towns and hamlets of West Virginia and southern Pennsylvania. The Springs and Bath House, maintained by the state, are just a few paces from the inn.

Jack and Adele Barker are just the kind of people who should be keeping a country inn. Now with Bill North, who is a Cornell Hotel School graduate, they all bring a genuine concern for guests' comfort, a wealth of experience, generous amounts of intellectual curiosity and practicality, and the good sense that it takes to run a very demanding business.

I have a feeling that if country inns hadn't been invented, the Barkers would have invented them.

The Country Inn has been in *CIBR* since 1973.

THE COUNTRY INN, Berkeley Springs, West Va. 25411; 304-258-2210. A 37-room resort inn on Rte. 522, 34 mi. from Winchester, Va. and 100 mi. from Washington, D.C., or Baltimore, Md. Berkeley Springs Spa adjoins inn. European plan. Most rooms with private baths. Breakfast, lunch, dinner served to travelers. Open every day of the year. Hunting, fishing, hiking, canoeing, antiquing, championship golf nearby. Jack and Adele Barker, Innkeepers.

Directions: Take I-70 to Hancock, Md. Inn is 6 mi. south on Rte. 522.

GENERAL LEWIS INN
Lewisburg, West Virginia

I had just returned from a walking tour of Lewisburg with its 19th-century residences and generous sprinkling of historic markers. I paused for just a moment at the bottom of the crescent-shaped drive that leads to the inn to read a marker which said, "Confederate troops under General Henry Heth on May 23, 1862, were repulsed by Colonel George Crook's Brigade."

As I settled into one of the rocking chairs on the long, shaded veranda, Mrs. Nell Burke, the manager, came out and joined me. "Well, what do you think of our little town?" I readily admitted that I was completely captivated.

"It was established in 1782 and is the third oldest town in the state," she said. "It was named for General Andrew Lewis, who defeated the Indians at the first battle in the American Revolution in 1774.

"The old part of the inn where the dining room is located was built in 1798 as a private dwelling. Later on, additions were made, and in 1929 it was opened by Mr. and Mrs. Randolph Hock as an inn. It took them many years to collect all of these antiques, including that four-poster canopy bed you are going to sleep in tonight."

The General Lewis Inn is like a permanent flashback to old West Virginia. It is furnished almost entirely in antiques. There is a sizable collection of old kitchen utensils, spinning wheels, churns, and other tools used many years ago, as well as an unusual collection of chinaware and old prints. The parlor has a friendly fireplace flanked by some of the many different types of rocking chairs that are scattered throughout the inn. The atmosphere is made even more cozy by the low-beamed ceilings.

The inn is surrounded by broad lawns, and in the rear there are

fragrant flower gardens, tall swaying trees, and even a small rock garden.

The menu has many things that I associate with country cooking—pork chops, apple butter, pan-fried chicken, and West Virginia ham, to name a few.

Dusk had fallen while we were talking, and the gaslights which illuminate the tree-lined streets began to dot the late twilight. Our talk turned to some of the famous golf courses here in the Greenbrier area, and we discussed some circle tours of the mountains that would include the fabulous scenery and a generous glimpse of rural West Virginia

Small wonder that some call it "almost heaven."

General Lewis Inn has been included in *CIBR* since 1973.

GENERAL LEWIS INN, Lewisburg, W. Va. 24901; 304-645-2600. An antique-laden 30-room village inn on Rte. 60, 90 mi. from Roanoke, Va. European plan. (Modified American plan only during W. Va. State Fair.) Breakfast and evening meal served daily with an additional meal on Sundays at noon. Dining room closed Christmas Day. Famous golf courses nearby. Mrs. Nell Burke, Manager.

Directions: Take Lewisburg exit from I-64. Follow Rte. 219 south to first traffic light. Turn left on Rte. 60, two blocks to inn.

THE RIVERSIDE INN
Pence Springs, West Virginia

"Screening-in this porch was one of the best ideas we have ever had!" This was Ashby Berkley, wearing a leather vest and knee britches and sporting a well-trimmed black beard. It was a summer afternoon, and the sun was filtering through the white cedars, birch, and sycamore trees which screened The Riverside Inn. This large log cabin on the banks of the Greenbrier River benefits from the abundant supply of air conditioning provided by the serenely-flowing waters.

"Our guests love watching spring burst into life here, and the magnificent foliage during the fall. We like to think of our little inn on its riverbank as a step back to times when life moved at a more leisurely pace.

"There are really a great many things to do here in southern West Virginia," he continued. "The river out there has excellent bass fishing and canoeing. There's white-water rafting on the National New River and Bluestone Lake, and Pipestem State Park has recreational facilities aplenty. The Sunday flea market held from April to October at the Pence Springs Water Company is often filled with antiques, local arts, and mountain crafts."

Kelley and Ashby Berkley have succeeded in recreating an atmosphere akin to early 17th-century Jamestown, Virginia, in this as yet unspoiled section of West Virginia. It has the intimacy of a colonial roadside tavern where travel-weary guests refreshed themselves with the table fare of their host. Both Kelley and Ashby dress in colonial costumes, as does the entire staff of the inn.

There is always a fire in the big fireplace of the low-ceilinged dining room with its candelabra of handcrafted tin. The heavy oaken tables are always set with pewter plates and pistol-handled knives.

The table fare includes many delicious offerings, some of which have become traditional. There is a six-course meal which starts with an appetizer such as hot cider, and continues with homemade soups and scalded English slaw. Entrées include roast goose on wild rice with glazed grapes; colonial meat pie; roast meats and steaks. The dessert tray has raisin bread pudding with fresh lemon sauce, rum pie, apple cobbler, and fresh fruit ice cream.

"Light eaters can order a single entrée," said Kelley, who had joined us on this late afternoon idyll. "Our menu centers around early American or English country dishes such as game pie, pheasant, and rabbit. The baking is done by Ashby's mom."

There are two dinner seatings one from 5 p.m. to 7 p.m., and another from 9 p.m. to 10 p.m. The restaurant is open from April 15 through October and is closed November and December, except for parties and banquets. In January, February, and March the inn is completely closed.

There are limited accommodations available in modest outbuildings from Memorial Day to Labor Day, but reservations are almost always necessary. Ashby cautions, "Be certain to remind your readers to bring sweaters or other warm clothing, because even in midsummer it gets chilly here in the evening."

Yes, time seems to be standing still on the banks of the Greenbrier River.

RIVERSIDE INN, Rte. 3, Pence Springs, W. Va. 24962; 304-445-7469. A country restaurant 12 mi. from Hinton, W. Va., located in the beautiful West Va. mountains on the Greenbrier River on Rte. 3 between Hinton and Alderson. 12 mi. from Lake Bluestone. Limited lodgings. Dinner served daily from April 15 thru Oct.; 2 seatings: 5-7 p.m.; 9-10 p.m. Closed Nov.-Dec., except for parties and banquets. Lunch served by special reservation only. Skiing, boating, hiking, swimming, spelunking, white water canoeing nearby. O. Ashby and Kelley Berkley, Innkeepers.

Directions: From the east, take Alta exit off I-64, follow Rte. 12S to Alderson then Rte. 3-W 8 mi. to Pence Springs. From the west, from W. Va. Tpke. follow Rte. 3 from Beckley through Hinton to Pence Springs. The inn is located in Pence Springs on Rte. 3 between Hinton and Alderson.

THE WELLS INN
Sistersville, West Virginia

The Wells Inn is a flashback to days of late 19th-century opulence, with its Victorian parlor, where there is a Tiffany lamp, striped wallpaper, mahogany wainscoting, marble-top tables, and handsome settees. On the wall is an oil-portrait of Ephraim Wells, the builder of the hotel and the grandson of the founder of Sistersville.

The main dining room has original gas chandeliers, now converted, hanging from an old-fashioned ceiling of molded metal. The walls are covered with rich, flocked paper in a red and gold pattern that presents a most interesting contrast to the green velvet upholstered dining room chairs.

My bedroom on my last visit had a brass bed, thick carpeting, and a kerosene-type lamp suspended gracefully on a draped chain from the ceiling.

"Here is your old friend, Victoria" said Martha McGinnis. "She hasn't spoken a word during your absence."

I must say Victoria, an alabaster statue in the lobby of the inn was very much in style. Her pristine whiteness showed up strikingly well against the gold velours of the walls, the rich, "gay nineties" carpeting, and the velvet cushions on the circular bench where we were seated.

The original Wells Hotel was built in 1894, but faded into obscurity about 1912. It was remodeled in 1929 and had a second grand opening. In 1965, Wells Kinkaid, a grandson of the original builder, bought the hotel at auction; by this time it had fallen into a

state of some disrepair. He and his son, Jack, made the happy decision to make it a turn-of-the-century hostelry. Period furniture was obtained, some of the 1894 furnishing were donated by townspeople, and major reconstruction took place with one thing in mind: providing modern conveniences in an authentic gay nineties style of decor. So, there was a third grand opening.

Jack is very proud of the fact that The Wells Inn has kept right in step with the rest of downtown Sistersville. Because of the unusually well-preserved Gothic, Greek Revival, and Romanesque buildings, Sistersville has been designated as a National Historic District. Anyone visiting should plan to spend at least a part of a day on a tour that would include St. Paul's Episcopal Church, the Henderson Hotel building, the Sistersville High School, and the bank buildings at the corner of Wells and Diamond Streets.

Because the town is on the North/South border, the menu offers excellent examples of each style of cooking, such as roast beef with mushrooms, French peas, turkey, chicken salad, and fresh fruit pie, all of which were served back in the early days, as well.

A recent development has been the addition of Thermacuzzi baths for twenty of the lodging rooms. The former "Black Gold Room" has been changed into an informal coffee shop called the "Back Porch," which is already quite popular with the townspeople of Sistersville.

However, I am sorry to say that none of this has had any effect on the obdurate immovability of Victoria. Again, she refused my invitation to dinner, and not even mentioning the rainbow trout amandine had any visible effect on her. However, there was one ray of hope: when I offered to drape my jacket around her Praxitelesian shoulders, I fancied I saw a faint twitch of her lips and a flicker of an alabaster eyelid!

The Wells Inn has been included in *CIBR* since 1971.

THE WELLS INN, 316 Charles St., Sistersville, W. Va. 26175; 304-652-3111; 1-800-631-1601. A restored Victorian 36-room village inn, 50 mi. south of Wheeling, 38 mi. north of Parkersburg. Sistersville is a former oil boom town of the 90s. European plan. Breakfast, lunch, dinner served daily. Open year-round. Skiing nearby. Martha McGinnis, Innkeeper; Jack Kinkaid, Owner.

Directions: From the south, leave I-77 at Parkersburg and proceed north on Rte. 2. From the north, leave I-70 at Wheeling and travel south on Rte. 2.

Virginia

THE ALEXANDER-WITHROW HOUSE
Lexington, Virginia

"Even though the Alexander-Withrow was not included in *Country Inns and Back Roads, 1979,* we still continue to get a great many guests from it." Beth Braford, the attractive innkeeper of the A-W House, and I were seated for a moment in the small courtyard next to the entrance to this Lexington, Virginia, village inn. For me, it was a very happy occasion because I was making plans to include it in the 1980 edition after a year's hiatus, which is my general policy when an inn changes hands. Now it was obvious that Beth, along with the new owners of the inn, Mr. and Mrs. Peter Meredith and sons, were finding innkeeping a very happy experience.

"Of course, Patty and Carlson Thomas had done a marvelous job restoring it and they furnished each room with such exquisite taste," said Beth. "We've made a few changes in the last two years, and the antique shop is now my bookstore. Basically, however, it's pretty much the same, except that we now have seven rooms or suites, and although we don't emphasize television, there are sets — usually kept in the closets — available to be plugged into our cable system."

The unusual design of the A-W House impressed me immediately when I first saw it in 1974. I was surprised that such a sophisticated building had been built in 1789, just two years after the original founding of Lexington. It has four corner chimneys, a most elaborate brickwork which is known as "diapering," and an Italianate roof.

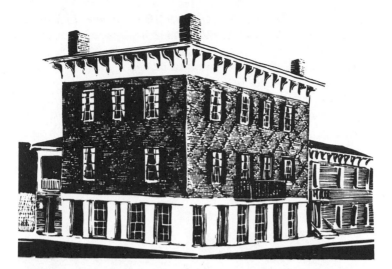

Today, this historic building, which is now included in the National Register for Historic Places, is an exquisite guest house. It is one of the few structures to survive a disastrous Lexington fire in 1796.

Each of the suites has its own sitting room, bedroom, and small refreshment area. The furnishings are beautiful antiques and reproductions. There are no meals served at the A-W House. However, everyone goes around the corner to the pastry shop, and breakfast can be enjoyed in the room or in the courtyard. Beth has suggestions for area restaurants for lunch and dinner, and sees to it that her guests are deluged with material about Lexington, including the famous walking tour.

Over the years I have found that many people who come to Lexington for one night, stay longer, because there's really so much to offer for the intellectually curious traveler. Among other things, it's the home of the Washington and Lee University and Virginia Military Institute.

Of course, I couldn't leave the A-W House without spending some happy moments browsing in the bookstore, which is one of the most attractive stores of its size that I have ever seen.

Yes, I'm happy to say the the A-W House, which sits in the foothills of the Blue Ridge Mountains in Virginia, is once again on the *CIBR* itinerary, and for the many friends of former innkeepers Patty and Carlson Thomas, let me add that they are well and happy and send kind regards to all of their friends. As Patty said in her letter to me, "I know that you're going to be very pleased with Beth Braford and the new owners."

THE ALEXANDER-WITHROW HOUSE, 3 West Washington St., Lexington, Va. 24450; 703-463-2044. An elegant restored 6-suite and 1-room guest house. Lodgings only. No meals served. Advance reservations recommended. Open year-round. No pets. Within walking distance of Virginia Military Institute, Washington and Lee University, and the George C. Marshall Research Library. Natural Bridge, Blue Ridge Parkway nearby. Golf, hiking, Appalachian Trail, canoeing also available. Mr. and Mrs. Peter Meredith and sons, Owners; Beth Braford, Innkeeper.

Directions: Take any Lexington Exit from I-64 or I-81. Follow signs into Lexington. The Alexander-Withrow House is on the corner of Main and Washington Streets.

GRAVES MOUNTAIN LODGE
Syria, Virginia

Graves Mountain Lodge nestles at the end of a road in Syria, Virginia, in the Blue Ridge Mountains. At one time the road ran to the other side of the mountains, but when the Shenandoah National Park was built during the 30s the road was closed. Now this valley is a secluded spot with a three-thousand-acre working farm and a country inn.

There is a wide variety of accommodations. The several different rustic lodgings located in what were at one time farm outbuildings are popular with the younger generation. These include farmhouses, cabins, and cottages, many with their own fireplaces. There are also lodgings available in two modern motel units located on the side of the mountain above the Main Lodge.

The Main Lodge, as is the case with all the buildings, is built out of lumber taken right out of the hills. It contains the big country dining rooms where food is served family-style on long tables, a large recreation room and gift shop, and the W.C. Bader Room, named for the man who does the beautiful wood inlays of all kinds of birds and outdoor scenes which adorn the walls. There is a welcome apple barrel in one corner of the room as well.

Graves Mountain Lodge is an easy two-hour drive from Washington, D.C., but is as far removed as possible from an urban environment. On this gorgeous spring day, the flowering trees and shrubs were in full bloom; the bees were buzzing and the birds were singing.

"Many people who come back again request the rooms with fireplaces," Rachel Graves explained, as she passed a plate of pancakes fresh from the kitchen. I helped myself to several of the pancakes and some scrambled eggs and crisp strips of bacon from another platter.

"I wish you could have been here during our Apple Festival," Rachel said, pouring another cup of coffee. "We had a big pot of Brunswick stew on the fire and people came from all over and picked their own apples. You know, some of the kids had never seen apple trees before. Later they went over to the farm to look at the pigs and the cattle. For many of them it was their first farm experience."

Excerpts from a letter I received in November 1979 may provide us with an insight into some of the trials and joys of operating a country inn in the mountains: "We lost the bridge in front of the Lodge during Hurricane David and a tornado tore down a cattle barn. On October 10, we had an absolutely devastating snowstorm and it took days to get things cleared and cleaned up. There was no electric current for 24 hours at the Lodge and one cabin was without it for three days. Also, a lot of trees were down on fences, across roads, and so forth. Fortunately, through all this, business continued and October was a great month and the apple harvest weekends were a great success. We are building our own cannery for apple butter making and cider pressing. We're going to open with our annual fish fry . . . the first Saturday in April. We'll have fireworks for the Fourth (if red tape doesn't prevent our obtaining them). The apple harvest is held on the second week of October and finally, our Thanksgiving buffet of ham, roast turkey, oysters and all the trimmings, means that things are perfectly wonderful at the Graves Mountain Lodge." Indeed they are . . .

Graves Mountain Lodge has been included in *CIBR* since 1972.

GRAVES MOUNTAIN LODGE, Syria, Va. 22743; 703-923-4231.
A 38-room secluded resort-inn on Rte. 670, off Rte. 231, 10 mi.

north of Madison, Va., 38 mi. N. W. of Charlottesville, Va. American plan. Rustic lodgings including 11 cottages and cabins and two modern motel units. Breakfast, lunch, dinner served to travelers by reservation only. Closed Dec. 1 to late March. Swimming, tennis, riding, fishing, basketball on grounds. Golf nearby. Jim and Rachel Graves, Innkeepers.

Directions: Coming south from Wash., D.C., take I-66 to Gainsville. Follow Rte. 29 south to Madison, turn right onto Rte. 231 West, go 7 mi. to Banco, turn left onto Rte. 670 and follow 670 for 4½ mi. to lodge.

GRISTMILL SQUARE
Warm Springs, Virginia

Kathy Hirsh was talking about the seasons in southwestern Virginia: "Spring is such a wonderful season, with its beautiful array of dogwood and mauve redbud trees. In June, we have laurel and rhododendron in the mountains, and in the woods we have trailing arbutus, which is really quite rare. Lady's-slippers, trillium, blood-root, dogtooth violets, and wild azaleas abound. In the little stream just in front of Gristmill Square, we often have tiny native trout. There are wild flowers throughout the summer. I remember that a young man from the *National Geographic* stood in midstream with his tripod and camera taking pictures. He later told me that he had taken pictures of thirteen varieties of wild flowers within four feet of where he was standing.

"Birdwatchers love us because we have so many varieties. I have identified over one hundred species in the last fourteen years just by looking out of my dining room windows."

Cathy and Philip Hirsh began the restoration of Gristmill Square in the Bath County seat in 1973. Decay and dilapidation in the center of this little town were replaced with a complete refurbishing of several buildings, including a mill which has been turned into a rustic and yet elegant restaurant. All around Gristmill Square are small shops and guest accommodations, including two-bedroom apartments, each with a bath, kitchen, living room, balcony or sundeck, and a woodburning fireplace. Other accom-modations include double rooms or small suites, also available with fireplaces. The furnishings are extremely tasteful, with a number of rooms done in authentic antiques. In addition to these accom-modations, last year the Hirshes added "Craig's Cottage," which is on their farm four miles west of Gristmill Square. During 1980, the Lodge at Meadow Lane Farm will be available with twelve more overnight accommodations. As Philip says, "It's like living on an

estate with lovely views and a wonderful set-apart feeling."

He continued, changing the subject, "Did you know that when we started renovating the old Victorian house which is in the center of Warm Springs, we discovered an old log cabin *inside* of it? Now, we're restoring the log cabin and that will give us still one more room for guest accommodations."

There's one important change at this attractive resort-inn with its three all-weather tennis courts and swimming pool: lunches will be served only on Sunday, when a party buffet lunch is served at the Waterwheel restaurant. Dinners, however, are served every night except Monday. The menus include fresh rainbow trout from nearby hatcheries, curried chicken, shepherd's pie, and absolutely super chili.

A Continental breakfast is served to all overnight guests of Gristmill Square. There's horseback riding, fishing, hunting and hiking. In the winter there's down hill and cross-country skiing. Of course, when it comes to golf, Hot Springs is just a few minutes away.

GRISTMILL SQUARE, Warm Springs, Va. 24484; 703-839-2231. An unusual restoration which includes a restaurant, accommodations, small shops, and many resort attractions, in a small country town approx. 19 mi. from Covington in the Allegheny Mts. European plan. Dinner served Tues. thru Sat. Lunch served Sundays only. Closed Mondays. Many different types of accommodations available. Suggest telephone for details. Children welcome. Pets allowed but not permitted loose on grounds. Tennis, swimming pool on grounds. Golf, skiing, skating, riding, hiking, fishing, hunting, antiquing, back roading nearby. Philip and Catherine Hirsh, Innkeepers.

Directions: From Staunton, Va., follow Rte. 254 to Buffalo Gap, Rte. 42 to Millboro Spring, Rte. 39 to Warm Springs. From Lexington, take Rte. 39 to Warm Springs. From Roanoke, take Rte. 220 to Warm Springs. From Lewisburg, W. Va. take I-64 to Covington, Rte. 220 north to Warm Springs. From northern W. Va. travel south to Rte. 39 east to Warm Springs.

HOLLYMEAD INN
Charlottesville, Virginia

"And here, sir, are your choice of desserts."

Right there on a gleaming silver tray just a few inches from my nose were three fantastic-looking confections that defied description.

"This is a chocolate mousse, and this is rum pie, and here's a chiffon cheesecake."

Hobson had an easier choice.

I had left Washington, D.C., a few hours earlier, after lunching at the Old Club in Alexandria. It was like old times for me to be on Route 29, driving through Warrenton and Culpeper, with its rolling country and the many impressive, typically Virginia, homes and markers from Civil War battlefields.

The directions said to watch for the sign for Hollymead on the east side of the road just six miles north of Charlottesville. And there it was.

Innkeepers Peg and Joe Bute were both at the door to wish me welcome, and the fun of visiting a country inn for the first time began. Each of them bubbled over with information. "The floors and beams are original," said Peg. "It was built by Hessian soldiers taken prisoner at Saratoga during the Revolutionary War. They were housed nearby, but when conditions became overcrowded they constructed the first part of the house, which we call the Hessian Room.

"The center part of the house was built around 1815 and used for a while as a private boys' school. The boys lived in two rooms on the third floor. They had their lessons in this room which we now keep as a private dining room."

There is a great deal more, including a radio program every week from the inn during which guests and well-known people visiting the nearby University of Virginia are interviewed. Peg explained that she used to be a cook at one of the fraternities and the boys from that fraternity are now waiters at Hollymead.

One of the unique features is a country butcher shop located in the basement, The Hook and Cleaver, where Virginia hams and beef are sold. There is also a sportswear and gift shop.

I was delighted with the atmosphere, cleanliness, and really crisp look of Hollymead; and the food was equally exciting.

Dinner started with a relish tray that had beets, beans, creamy cucumbers, apple butter, and cranberry sauce. These were served with homemade muffins and a very good garden salad. I ordered the baked chicken with Hollymead sauce served over rice. It was so delicious, I wish I had some right now.

Peg explained that besides the steaks, seafood, and the fresh batter-fried mushrooms which are available with every meal, there are daily specials which might be beef Wellington, trout stuffed with crabmeat, flounder stuffed with shrimp, ribeye steak, scallops in mushrooms and wine, or country stuffed pork chops.

While I was eating, a number of tweedy faculty-types from UVA popped in for dinner, as well as some blue-jeaned students. "Oh yes, everyone comes here," said Peg.

This brings me back to where we started. I was really going to fend off the desserts with regret, but the chocolate mousse was too much for me. And, like the man in the television ad, I can't believe I ate the whole thing!

It didn't hurt a bit.

HOLLYMEAD INN, Rte. 8, Box 367A, Charlottesville, Va. 22901; 804-973-8488. A country restaurant a few minutes north of Charlottesville on Rte. 29. Near Monticello, Ash Lawn, University of Virginia, and Skyline Drive in Blue Ridge Mts. No lodgings. Dinner served Tuesdays through Saturdays. Lunch served Tuesday through Friday. Open year-round. Closed Christmas Eve, Christmas Day, and New Year's Day. Mr. and Mrs. Joseph Bute, Innkeepers.

Directions: Proceed 6 mi. north of Charlottesville, Va., on Rte. 29 North.

OLD CLUB RESTAURANT
Alexandria, Virginia

For me the Old Club is a gateway to the South. I try to stop as often as possible to renew my taste for southern cooking. Take ham, for example: on my last visit, innkeeper Lee Palmer and I were discussing the subject. He explained his hams are "real country" hams from Culpeper, Virginia. "We soak it overnight, boil for about three hours, cool it and then put in the oven with vinegar, and let glaze for two hours.

"Country ham is best served thinly sliced and salty. Our guests like it warm over bread with black-eyed peas and candied sweet potatoes.

"I'm very proud of the fact that we have one cook who has been with us nearly thirty years," he said, "and another for thirteen, one for eight, and none under five years. Our dining room staff all has been here around ten years, as well."

The oldest part of this colonial mansion in Alexandria was built by George Washington and his friends as a private club, hence the name. The little brick building on the north was said to have been young Washington's office while he was surveying this area. There are dozens of stories connected with this sedate restaurant, including the fact that during the War of 1812, when the British were at the gates of Alexandria, all the handsome wooden furniture was buried in what is now the vegetable garden.

The Old Club has been included in *CIBR* since the late 1960s and, as on that first visit, I have always led off my meal with a cup of peanut soup, which is a feature of this historic restaurant. I find that a cup is sufficient, because there is still enough appetite left for the choices on the menu, which has changed very little during my tenure.

Besides the Virginia country ham served over cornbread, covered with maple syrup, there is Allegheny mountain trout, which is boned and stuffed with mushrooms and rice, and topped with tartar sauce. I have also enjoyed chicken Laura Lee, which is a chicken breast on hickory ham served with a mushroom sauce.

The Old Club is located in the historic section of Alexandria where there are many buildings dating back to colonial days. In recent years, Alexandria has had an excellent program of restoration and preservation, which includes at least twenty-seven historic sites and buildings that are really architectural jewels. There is an excellent walking tour available with an explanation of such landmarks as Christ Church, Captain's Row, Gadsby's Tavern, and Carlyle House. Mount Vernon is just a few miles away by car.

I had finished my helping of country ham on cornbread, and Lee suggested I top it off with some deep dish apple pie. "It is made with a little apple wine and a little ice cream. Our guests sing its praises all the time."

We finished dinner and walked out on the flagstone patio and Lee explained that the Old Club is becoming a popular place for rehearsal dinners and wedding receptions. "As a matter of fact," he said, "we have had six marriages at the Old Club this year."

We said good-bye and Lee said, "Come back real soon."

OLD CLUB RESTAURANT, 555 So. Washington St., Alexandria, Va. 22314; 703-549-4555. Just across the river from Washington, D.C. in one of the country's best preserved colonial cities. No lodgings. Lunch and dinner served daily except Mondays and Christmas. Convenient to Christ Church, Robert E. Lee House, Gadsby's Tavern, Old Apothecary Shop, and Potomac River. Mt. Vernon and Gunston Hall nearby. Lee Palmer, Innkeeper.

Directions: North and southbound traffic on 495 take Exit #1 North to Rte. 1. Turn right on Franklin St. and left on Washington St., 1 block to inn. (Mount Vernon Memorial Hwy. is Washington St. in the city.)

PROSPECT HILL
Trevilians, Virginia

Bill Sheehan and I were strolling through the grounds of this former Virginia wheat plantation when we came upon what he described as a "fairy ring"—a delicate group of mushrooms about six or eight inches high in a small semicircle about four feet across. "According to the Irish legend," said Bill, who is in a very good position to know, "this means that the leprechauns danced here, and we have a bit of good luck coming our way."

269

Prospect Hill is one of the oldest homes in this area of Virginia, and was part of a grant from King George III. There was a house and farm here in 1730, and in 1793 it was sold to one Richmond Terrill, the first slave owner who built the slave quarters which remain today. One of them, "Uncle Guy's House," has been converted by the Sheehans to two guests rooms with original fireplaces, brick walls, and wide-board floors.

As Bill tells it: "In 1840, the property was purchased by the Overtons who tripled the size of the house by adding two wings, and by 1850, it was a thriving wheat-growing plantation. The son of the family, William, was a student at Virginia Military Institute and fought under Stonewall Jackson during the Civil War. Barefoot, he walked back home from Lee's surrender at Appomattox Courthouse to find his fields unworked and overgrown. While he languished in despair, his wife Nancy took over the reins by sharecropping with the black families who had remained, by running a school, and by taking in guests, mostly relatives and city 'cousins.' This was the beginning of a 100-year history of innkeeping at Prospect Hill. The inn is now one of thirteen plantations designated a National Historic District, and is part of Historic Green Springs.

"My wife Mireille (who is from Menton, France) and I purchased Prospect Hill in 1977, and have been restoring the main house and the old slave quarters. We have also renovated the Overseer's House and two rooms in the main house for overnight guests. Four of our rooms have working fireplaces and all are air-conditioned.

"Mireille and I do all the cooking, and with our son Mike, sixteen, and daughter Nancy, fifteen, we are a small family operation. We offer no menus or choices at dinner, but make every effort to determine our guests' preferences when they make reservations. Because Mireille was raised in France, most of our meals have a French accent; for instance, medallions de fillet de boeuf, coq au vin, and escallops de veau. We serve breads freshly baked from our oven and all our desserts are homemade.

"We also offer our houseguests breakfast in bed, which is a full meal including juice and coffee and one of our special surprises, such as french toast using our own bread, or cheese soufflé pancakes."

We continued our walk through the park-like grounds, admiring the house with its fresh coat of yellow paint and green shutters, and strolling on into the traditional English arboretum begun over 100 years ago with fifty varieties of rare and unusual trees. "I know you saw this about fifteen months ago," said Bill, "and I'm sure you can see what a tremendous chore it has been to clear out the vines and undergrowth. My son Mike has done a wonderful job."

I'd say that the entire Sheehan family has done a wonderful job, and we're proud to include Prospect Hill in *Country Inns and Back Roads*.

PROSPECT HILL, Route 613, Trevilians, Va. 23070; 703-967-0844. A 5-room country inn on a historic plantation 15 mi. east of Charlottesville, Va.; 90 mi. southwest of Washington, D.C. European plan. Breakfast in bed for houseguests. Dinner served daily, Tuesday thru Saturday by reservation. Dining room closed Sunday and Monday. Accommodations in manor house and restored slave quarters. Children welcome. No pets. Beer and wine only served. Bill and Mireille Sheehan, Innkeepers.

Directions: From Washington, D.C. Beltway to I-66 west to Warrenton. Follow Rte. 29 south to Culpepper, and then Rte. 15 south to Gordonsville; Rte. 33 east 8 mi. to stop sign. Turn left, then right onto Rte. 613, 7 mi. to inn. From Charlottesville; Follow I-64 to Exit 27; Rte. 15 south to Zion Crossroads; Rte. 250 east 1 mi. to Rte. 613. Turn left, 3 mi. to inn on left.

TALLY-HO

The area around Middleburg, Virginia in Fauquier and adjoining Loudoun counties, has some of the best backroading I have ever experienced. Most of the roads are unpaved and there are honeysuckle-covered walls, and beautiful pastures and farmlands. It is this lush countryside that makes Middleburg a center for point-to-point and hunt race meets. The National Beagle trials are held here, and the nearby Upperville Horse Show is the oldest in the United States. There are also several steeplechase courses, one of them just a few moments from Middleburg. Incidentally, an excellent map for backroading is available at the front desk of the Red Fox Tavern.

RED FOX TAVERN
Middleburg, Virginia

There are not many country inns in North America that have remained in the same building more than 200 years. However, the Red Fox Tavern in Middleburg, Virginia, which started as a simple way station when the road to the west was known as "Ashby's Gap Turnpike," has passed the midway point of its third century, and is an integral part of American history.

Joseph Chinn was the first proprietor and it became known as Chinn's Ordinary. His first cousin was George Washington, who was engaged by Lord Fairfax to survey the area around the tavern, which in turn became known as Chinn's Crossroads.

It's probably true that soldiers from both the American and British lines stopped at this local tavern during the war for American Independence.

The Assembly of Virginia chose Chinn's Crossroads as a specific town and established Middleburg on 50 acres of land November 2, 1787. Mr. Leven Powell, then owner of the property, subdivided the land and named the streets after his Federalist friends, some of whose names still survive.

In 1812, Chinn's Ordinary became the Beveridge House and was enlarged to thirty-five rooms. It was the political, social, and economic focal point of Middleburg, which was already an important grain and farming area.

During the War Between the States, Confederate General J.E.B. Stuart needed lodgings for the night and chose the large rooms above the tavern. It was in these rooms that Colonel John Mosby and his Raiders had a celebrated meeting with Stuart, and it was downstairs in the tavern where many of the wounded received care.

The inn became known as the Middleburg Inn around 1877, and was changed to the Red Fox Tavern in 1937, no doubt to recognize one of the most famous four-footed residents in this part of the country, for Middleburg had already gained a reputation as one of the nation's foremost areas for thoroughbred horse breeding and fox hunting.

There are seven tastefully decorated lodging rooms; six are in the main building, some with sitting areas and 18th-century, documented wallpapers and paint colors. Each room is furnished

with period antiques and has canopied beds and working fireplaces. There is a two-bedroom suite in an ancient stone building a few doors away.

On the second floor of the tavern there is a very comfortable pine-paneled lounge with two fireplaces, deep leather couches and chairs, and a warm feeling that draws everyone close together.

The main entrance leads directly into one of the two low-ceilinged dining rooms where the thirty-inch-thick walls are appropriately decorated with fox-hunting regalia. Cheery fires are always lit during the chilly months. A secluded terrace to the rear of the inn underneath the trees has an intimate outdoor feeling and is very popular during the spring, summer, and fall months.

The menu includes fresh crab-cake platter; chicken l'orange, which is fresh boneless breast of chicken rolled with thinly sliced ham and served with a delicious orange sauce; and baked, sweet Virginia ham, which has been glazed with brown sugar, mustard, and cloves, served with raisin sauce.

It was at the Night Fox, a small bistro located behind the main building, that I discovered the skill of playing darts has reached a new dimension. Not only are there friendly games each evening, but frequent tournaments are held. The true devotee owns his own darts and carries them about in a mahogany or walnut box. There are as many dart rules as there are croquet rules, both English and American. The Night Fox has a little second-floor porch with white iron furniture and a very intimate and romantic air.

Of course, there have been some renovations and additions and modernization of Chinn's Tavern, but I'm sure that Joseph Chinn would thoroughly approve of everything; particularly the fact that travelers to Middleburg are still received with gracious Virginia hospitality at the Red Fox Tavern.

RED FOX TAVERN, Middleburg, Va. 22117; 703-687-6301. A 7-room historic village inn near the Blue Ridge Mountains, approximately 40 miles from Washington, D.C. Near Manassas Battlefield, Oatlands, and Oak Hill (President Monroe's White House). European plan. Breakfast, lunch, and dinner served to travelers. Open every day of the year. Spectator sports such as polo and steeplechasing available nearby. No activities available for small children. Consult innkeeper for policy on pets. The Reuter Family, Innkeepers.

Directions: Leave the Washington D.C. Beltway (495) at Rte. 66 West, to Rte. 50. Follow Rte. 50 West for 22 miles to Middleburg.

WAYSIDE INN
Middletown, Virginia

The flickering candlelight in the Slave Kitchen cast our shadows on the smoke-blackened beams overhead and was reflected in the pewter plates, pitchers, and old windows. The fireplace radiated a warm glow and two cast iron pots on the crane gurgled and boiled.

"This room was hidden," explained Leo Bernstein, owner of the Wayside Inn. "It was discovered by accident, and restoring it was a great deal of fun. Those are the original brick walls, and I see you've already noticed the adz marks on the beams. All of the tools are from the Colonial period."

The Wayside Inn dates from at least 1797. It is correctly referred to as a historic restoration. It was carefully restored to its present form after 1960 when Leo, a lawyer and banker from nearby Washington, happened to drive through the main street in Middletown and recognized the inn's tremendous possibilities. The inn is an antique lover's paradise. Its room are packed with a mind-boggling collection of tables, chests, paintings, and *objets d'art.*

Innkeeper Marjorie Alcarese was busy during the last winter preparing a booklet that would catalog every item of note in the inn. It will include a few words of description of the history, origin, and period of every piece, so that the inn becomes a "walking museum."

In earlier days the Wayside Inn served as a way station where fresh teams of horses waited to harness up to arriving stagecoaches traveling the Shenandoah Valley Turnpike. Soldiers from both the North and South frequented the inn, then known as Wilkinson's Tavern, seeking refuge, comfort, and friendship during the War Between the States.

The menu includes some very old country recipes, such as spoon bread and peanut soup, whole baked tomatoes, Virginia country ham with red-eye gravy, and both smothered and pan-fried chicken. Homemade bread and real whipped butter accompany every dinner.

Young people wearing the costume of the era serve these tempting dishes. One of the favorite desserts is German chocolate cake which is always brought to the table warm, as are the fruit pies and breads.

Guest rooms at the Wayside Inn are decorated in many different styles because of Leo's passion for collecting. He has an eye out for antiques of any kind, hence, each lodging room is quite apt to be a potpourri of anything from Byzantine to Victorian pieces.

Guests at the inn have always had a wealth of diversions at their disposal, including the Wayside Theater which has extended its season through December. Dinner is served starting at five p.m. on show nights, to provide guests enough time to walk the one-and-a-half blocks to the theater.

Guests are also invited to visit Wayside Wonderland, a two-hundred-and-fifty-acre recreational park with natural woodlands, offering swimming at Half Moon Beach, hiking, fishing, boating, and a tour of Crystal Caverns.

Today the Wayside Inn is many different things. It has history, regional offerings on the menu, an opportunity to spend an extended vacation enjoying all of the attractions in the Shenandoah Valley, and it is a haven for collectors of all kinds. It's been in *CIBR* since 1972.

WAYSIDE INN, Middletown, Va. 22645; 703-869-1797. A 21-room country inn in the Shenandoah Valley, about 1½ hrs. from Washington, D.C. European plan; breakfast, lunch, and dinner served Monday through Saturday. Sunday: breakfast and dinner. Open every day of the year. Professional Equity Theater, Belle Grove, Cedar Creek Battlefield, Blue Ridge Parkway, Crystal Caverns, Hotel Strasburg, Washington's Headquarters, and Wayside Antique Warehouse nearby. Convenient to Apple Blossom Festival. Marjorie Alcarese, Innkeeper.

Directions: Take Exit 77 from I-81 to Rte. 11. Follow signs to inn.

Kentucky

THE BEAUMONT INN
Harrodsburg, Kentucky

"And now Robert E. Lee's favorite dessert!" I looked into the faces of the Dedman family: Bud and Mary, and their son Chuck and his wife, Helen. I had reason to suspect they might be joshing me, because during the afternoon and evening when we had been touring the Beaumont Inn, there had been many jokes and lots of laughter. The Dedman family all have the great capacity to laugh.

A most delicious-looking confection appeared on the table. A four-layered, lemon-orange cake which was served with a small scoop of ice cream. "Yes, General Lee is reputed to have expressed great preference for this recipe," said Mary Dedman. "I believe it has been used at this inn for as long as anybody can remember."

"As long as anybody can remember" covers a lot of territory here at the Beaumont Inn. The truly handsome brick building with the six supporting Ionic columns was built in 1845 as a school for young ladies. Later, it became known as Daughters' College, and still later as Beaumont College. In 1916, it was purchased by Mr. and Mrs. Glave Goddard and converted into the Beaumont Inn. The ownership and management passed from Mrs. Goddard to her daughter, Mrs. Dedman, and then to Mrs. Dedman's two sons. Today, Bud Dedman is the owner-manager and his son, Chuck, is following tradition and becomes the fourth generation trained in the innkeeper's art.

The inn, as befits its previous academic history, is set in the campus-like atmosphere surrounded by maples, dogwood, walnut, and catalpa trees. One of the catalpa trees in the front has been used literally for generations by families and guests for appropriate photographs.

The decorations and furniture in all the parlors and lodging rooms reflect American history. The hallways on the main floor have several cabinets with beautiful old china and silverware. The sitting rooms have elegant fireplaces and wallpaper decorated with roses. The entrance hall is dedicated to Robert E. Lee and has many pictures of this noble gentleman, some of them dating back to his youth. There is also a framed copy of General Lee's farewell address to the army of northern Virginia.

One might expect that with so many venerable pieces in such an impressive old building there would be an attempt to preserve the inn as a kind of museum. "Not a bit of it," explained Chuck Dedman. "There were five children in our family and this was our home. Mother and dad taught us respect for old things, but we were expected to enjoy them. We want our guests to feel the same way."

"There's so much for everybody to enjoy nearby," chimed in his pretty wife Helen. "Old Fort Harrod, the Lincoln Marriage Temple, the Perryville Battlefield, and, of course, Shakertown is just a few miles away."

"And don't forget the Keeneland Racetrack and the Kentucky Horse Park," added Mary Dedman.

Children are quite happy at the Beaumont Inn. "We have a children's playground, swimming pool, and tennis courts," explained Mary. "There's lots of room and youngsters enjoy it."

Besides General Lee's favorite dessert, the Beaumont is famous for its food, including mock scalloped oysters, corn pudding, Kentucky fried chicken—which Bud Dedman assures me is "the real thing," and especially two-year-old Kentucky hams.

A very large number of innkeepers from *CIBR,* as well as a few innkeepers from Britain, gathered at the Inn at Pleasant Hill and the Beaumont Inn for three days in October, 1979. Some guests were lodged at Pleasant Hill and others at the Beaumont. The final "wind up" dinner was hosted by the Dedmans at the Beaumont Inn and it was a most memorable event. In addition to a delicious dinner and the opportunity for the innkeeper-guests to roam around the inn and visit the sumptuous gift shop which is now completely managed by Helen Dedman, arrangements also had been made for a very talented musician and folk singer to entertain us in the dining room.

It was a lovely scene with the candles on the tables, and all of us joined in singing some of the lovely old songs that everyone seems to know, even our guests from across the sea.

The atmosphere and friendliness of the Beaumont Inn drew us all together, as it's been doing with guests for many, many years.

BEAUMONT INN, Harrodsburg, Ky. 40330; 606-734-3381. A 27-room country inn in the heart of Kentucky's historic bluegrass country. All lodging plans available. Lunch and dinner served to travelers. All three meals to houseguests. Open every day from March 1 through November 30. Tennis, swimming pool, shuffleboard on grounds. Golf courses and a wide range of recreational and historic attractions nearby. No pets. Lodging rate includes Continental breakfast. The Dedman family, Innkeepers.

Directions: From Louisville: Exit 48 from east I-64. Go south on Ky. 151, to U.S. 127 south to Harrodsburg. From Lexington: U.S. 60 west, then west on Bluegrass Parkway to U.S. 127. From Nashville: Exit I-65 to Bluegrass Parkway near Elizabethtown, Ky., then east to U.S. 127. From Knoxville: Exit north I-75 at Mt. Vernon, Ky., then north on U.S. 150 to U.S. 127. Use bypass at Danville, Ky. Go north on U.S. 127 to Beaumont Inn entrance which is on east side of highway as you enter Harrodsburg.

BOONE TAVERN HOTEL
Berea, Kentucky

It may have been former innkeeper Dick Hougen who first remarked, "I'd classify our food as southern gourmet rather than southern fried." Well, whoever said it, it's a perfect description of the menu at the Boone Tavern. Fortunately, a great many of the recipes still in use are in three of Mr. Hougen's own cookbooks: Southern Peanut Soup, Plantation Ham, Boone Tavern Chicken Pie, Georgian Sweet Potato, Hollyberry Salad, Black Walnut Pie and Kentucky Blackberry Dumpling with Milk Dip, among others. And, of course, spoonbread. Spoonbread makes a southerner out of a "damn Yankee" in about thirty seconds.

I was astonished to learn that over 200,000 visitors stop at the inn each year for lodgings and meals. It is on Route I-75, south of Lexington and only 120 miles from Cincinnati.

At Berea, the college, the inn, and the town are all interlocked. It is impossible to speak of one without speaking of the other two. The college is a unique educational experience because the tuition is comparatively low. However, all students are expected to engage in a work program, and I'm happy to report that it actually works!

To the promising young men and women from Appalachia

Berea College Campus

(many of whom find here their only opportunity for college), Berea offers a liberal arts education of the highest academic standard.

On a student-conducted tour, I saw students working in woodcraft, making brooms, weaving, pottery, lapidary, and several other crafts.

Ninety percent of the inn staff are students, many of whom are majoring in hotel management. In fact, with the exception of the cooks and key personnel in the front office, the students run the whole show.

The inn is comfortable and inviting, and has, among other things, a skittles game and Chinese checkers set up in the lobby. These are both manufactured in one of the college craft shops and are sold commercially. The craft shop is also the source for the furniture in the inn, including tables, corner cupboards, beds, benches, and the like. Many of the designs were given to the college by the famous New England furniture designer, Wallace Nutting.

As I have mentioned elsewhere, a sizable group of innkeepers from *CIBR* spent three wonderful days in Kentucky last fall, and one of the highlights was our lunch at the Boone Tavern Hotel.

One of the visiting innkeepers from England was so impressed that she purchased all three copies of Mr. Hougen's cookbooks, and was determined to try out some of those lovely Kentucky recipes at her inn located in the lake country of northern England.

Boone Tavern has been included in *CIBR* since 1969.

BOONE TAVERN HOTEL, Berea, Ky. 40403; 606-986-9341. A 60-room village inn in a unique college community on I-75, 40 mi. south of Lexington, Ky. European plan. Breakfast, lunch, dinner served daily to travelers by sittings only. Dinner and Sunday noon coats required for men, dresses or pant suits for ladies. Open every day of the year. All campus activities open to guests; campus tours twice daily except Saturdays and Sundays. Tennis on grounds. Golf, pool, bicycles nearby. Berea is on Eastern Time. Curtis Reppert and Cecil M. Connor, Innkeepers.

Directions: Take Berea exit from I-75. One mi. north to hotel.

DOE RUN INN
Brandenburg, Kentucky

America has had many frontiers since the landings in Jamestown and on Cape Cod, but there is certainly no more colorful frontier than western Kentucky when it was fought over by Indians and settlers during Daniel Boone's time.

I was talking to innkeeper Curtis Brown about the considerable Daniel Boone tradition that is present at the Doe Run Inn. "Well, Daniel Boone was never here because it was built in 1816. However, his brother Squire Boone discovered the property in 1778 and was the original landowner. Patrick Henry, who was the Governor of Virginia at the time, signed the original deed. Incidentally, it was known as 'Little York, Virginia.'"

Pioneer America lives at the Doe Run Inn. I'm sure that it has changed very little in 165 years. The building with the huge, four-foot-thick limestone blocks on the outer walls was made to repel Indian attacks. The tremendous front door could withstand 'most any attempt to break in, and the huge fireplace still sends warmth radiating through the room.

Interestingly, the property has changed hands relatively few times and has remained virtually intact over the years. There has been no intrusion on the natural environment which takes in 1,000 acres. There are many walks and trails through the woods. An early innkeeper was "Wash Coleman," the great-grandfather of Lucille Brown, who is Mrs. Curtis Brown. The building was originally a woolen mill and then a gristmill. An old record shows a payment made to Abraham Lincoln's father who worked as a stonemason on the building. Lodging rooms are most unusual. Many have antique beds, tables, and chairs that would be in place in a museum. Just a few have private baths. The lodging rooms are much the same as they have been for the last fifty years, and there has been very little "modernization." As Curt says, "There's very little we can do with this old building. The folks that like us always have a good time, but sometimes they expect more than we have."

The food is real "Kentucky." Hot homemade biscuits, vegetables served southern style. Kentucky fried ham and fried chicken and gravy. The old-fashioned lemon pie tops the desserts.

Thanksgiving Day is always special with many foods that were offered at the first Thanksgiving, such as turkey, chicken, turnips, sweet potatoes, and fried pies!

The Doe Run Inn has been included in *CIBR* since 1972.

DOE RUN INN, Rte. 2, Brandenburg, Ky. 40108; 502-422-9982. A 17-room country inn reminiscent of the backwoods on Rte. 448, 4 mi. south of Brandenburg, 38 mi. south of Louisville. Near Fort Knox. European plan. 5 rooms with private bath; 12 rooms with shared baths. Breakfast, lunch, and dinner served to travelers daily. Closed Christmas Eve and Christmas Day. Hiking, fishing, and swimming nearby. Curtis and Lucille Brown, Innkeepers.

Directions: From Louisville take 64W through Indiana to 135 S. Cross the toll bridge to Kentucky and follow 1051 to the dead end. Turn right on 448 and follow signs to Doe Run Inn.

ELMWOOD INN
Perryville, Kentucky

The luncheon salad looked delicious. It had many varieties of fresh fruits arranged around a generous scoop of sherbet. There were also freshly made hot biscuits filled with Kentucky fried ham. Ham and hot biscuits—what a treat for a visitor from New England!

I could have ordered the southern fried chicken with cream gravy. "That's what Colonel Sanders always orders when he eats here," innkeeper Gladys Coyle explained. "He loves the chicken, hot biscuits, new small potatoes, a big salad, and a huge helping of peas. He's been here five times and says it's the best chicken he's ever eaten."

The Elmwood Inn could happen only in Kentucky. Surrounded by a grove of maple and sweetgum trees beside the Chaplin River in Perryville, the inn features traditional southern dishes in an atmosphere of Greek Revival elegance. The building was constructed in 1842 and became a field hospital following the Battle of Perryville during the Civil War.

The main entrance with its twin two-story columns faces the river. The lawns sloping down to the river are filled with sugar maples, black locust, hemlock, pine, ash, gingko, and willows. Next to the building there is a very large and colorful bed of tulips which must be breathtaking when in full bloom.

The inn has been carefully furnished in antiques and Kentucky and Civil War memorabilia. Each of the six serving rooms has been named for some worthy individual, well-known to the region or community. For example, there is the T.C. Poynter Room, named for the founder of a school which occupied the building for many years.

After lunch I took advantage of a few extra moments to visit some of the important sites in Perryville. One is the restoration of the old Perryville historic district. It was here that I learned that Perryville was originally known as Harberson's Station and was founded by some settlers from Pennsylvania. Many of the buildings are being restored, including the Karrick-Parks House which is directly across the river from the Elmwood Inn. A footbridge is planned to connect this historic section of Perryville with the inn.

I also visited the Perryville Battlefield which is just a few miles from the town and was the scene of one of the most desperate battles of the Civil War. It is very popular with tourists and history buffs.

At the end of a pleasant afternoon filled with Kentucky history, I was happy to return for the evening meal at the Elmwood. Confronted by myriad choices, including sweetbreads, fried shrimp, Florida pompano, and other tempting dishes, I decided to try the fried chicken with cream gravy.

I think I know why Colonel Sanders keeps coming back.

Addenda: In late October 1979, at least one hundred and ten innkeepers from *CIBR,* who had a lovely three-day holiday and meeting in central Kentucky, descended upon the Elmwood Inn for a delicious dinner and the opportunity to tour this gracious old place. Chef Charles Bradshaw received many compliments from our party, which included several innkeepers from Great Britain who were present as our guests. I did have an opportunity to talk with Charles in the kitchen on that trip and he reported that the inn, which is currently being leased and will eventually be bought, was doing very well, "with many guests from *CIBR*."

ELMWOOD INN, Perryville, Ky. 40468; 606-332-2271. A country restaurant in an historically important Kentucky town on Rtes. 150 and 68, 9 mi. from Harrodsburg and Danville. Near the Perryville Battlefield State Shrine. No lodgings. Lunch and dinner served daily except Mondays. Closed Christmas Eve and Christmas Day. Open year-round. Gladys Coyle, Innkeeper.

Directions: Exit Bluegrass Pkwy. at Bardstown and take Hwy. 150 into Perryville. From Harrodsburg take Rte. 68 to Perryville.

INN AT PLEASANT HILL
Shakertown, Kentucky

In late October, 1979, a large group of *CIBR* innkeepers, as well as several innkeeping guests from Great Britain and Europe, enjoyed a three-day meeting at the Inn at Pleasant Hill. It was an opportunity to get together with old friends, exchange solutions to innkeeping problems, and particularly to partake of the hospitality afforded to all visitors at this unusual country inn-cum-historic restoration.

One morning at breakfast, a group of us were sitting around a table with Ann Voris, the innkeeper, and someone asked about the life of the Shakers in this unusual community. She explained:

"The founders of Pleasant Hill belonged to a religious sect, the United Society of Believers in Christ's Second Appearing. They were actually an offshoot of the Quakers. Pleasant Hill was established in 1805, and by 1820 they had a prosperous colony of 500 persons. The Shakers lived in communal dedication to their religious beliefs of celibacy, public confession of sins (which culminated in the frenetic trembling dances which gave them the name of Shakers), renunciation of worldliness, and common ownership of property.

"There were five families at Pleasant Hill, each with its own house, shops, barns, farming lands, and orchards," Ann continued. "'Family' had a particular meaning since the Shakers did not believe in marriage. Men and women, they maintained, could live more happily as brothers and sisters, helping one another, but living personally apart.

"The Shakers also held some advanced social ideas. They were pacifists and believed in equality of sexes and races. They were hospitable to visitors and took in orphans and unwanted children.

"One of their most fundamental beliefs was in hard work and austere discipline that sought perfection. There were so many innovations made by Shakers, it always amazes me.

"The Civil War, plus nineteenth-century industrialism and worldliness seeped into the Pleasant Hill Shakers, and the celibacy rule prevented natural increase in their numbers. In 1910 they were dissolved."

The Trustees' House is one of 25 buildings clustered along the single country road, all furnished with Shaker pieces or reproductions. To construct buildings of enduring strength, some with walls three or four feet thick, the Shakers quarried limestone from the river bluffs and hauled granite slabs a mile uphill from the river. Most of the buildings are of deep red brick or limestone with a Federalist design.

There was ample opportunity during the time that we were all meeting at Pleasant Hill for us to see demonstrations of Shaker crafts going on right in the village. Several innkeepers returned home with some handsome reminders of our good time together. I have two marvelously simple glass chimneys which now shelter the candles on my dining room table.

The most frequent comments that we all exchanged were about the delicous food, most of it from Shaker recipes. One visitor from England extolled the Pleasant Hill chicken, and another enjoyed the combination of chicken and country ham. Quite a few of our innkeepers purchased the cookbooks authored by Elizabeth Kremer, who is the director of foods at Shaker Hill. Among the recipes are dove's breasts in creamed gravy, rabbit, sausage and egg casserole, turkey turnovers, oatmeal pie, and many special salad dressings.

A great many of us enjoyed early-evening strolls about the

village, and the sweet scent of honeysuckle, sage, and bluegrass caught us all up in the spirit.

This was our second meeting at Pleasant Hill, the first being in the spring of 1973, and several of the innkeepers had been present at that time as well.

We all agreed that our stay at Pleasant Hill was not only enjoyable, but also very meaningful.

Pleasant Hill has been in *CIBR* since 1971.

INN AT PLEASANT HILL, Shakertown, Ky., P.O. address: Rte. 4, Harrodsburg, Ky. 40330; 606-734-5411. A 63-room country inn in a restored Shaker village on Rte. 68, 7 mi. northeast of Harrodsburg, 25 mi. southwest of Lexington. European plan. Breakfast, lunch, dinner served daily to travelers. Open year-round. Suggest contacting Inn about winter schedule. Closed Christmas Eve and Christmas Day. Ann Voris, Innkeeper.

Directions: From Lexington take Rte. 68 south toward Harrodsburg. From Louisville, take I-64 to Lawrenceburg and Graeffenburg exit (not numbered). Follow Rte. 127 south to Harrodsburg and Rte. 68 northeast to Shakertown.

Maryland

MARYLAND INN
Annapolis, Maryland

In November of 1978, at least 170 people—innkeepers and their wives from North America and Europe—gathered together for an annual meeting of *CIBR* inns at the Maryland Inn. I'm sure that in the almost two-hundred-year history of the inn, it had never before played host at one time to such a large group of country inn aficionados.

285

Everyone agreed the food, accommodations, entertainment, and cooperation of the inn staff were superb. Personally, I can't think of a better recommendation.

We arrived to find that the ambitious program of restoration undertaken years ago by proprietor Paul Pearson had been completed. Paul took us outside to show us the work that's being done on the roof with the intricate copper cornice gutters completely replaced and the slate mansards entirely restored, partially with slate, he said, from the great dome of the nearby State House.

"The inn is in many ways a museum piece," he remarked. "The earliest part was built during the Revolution and then expanded about a hundred years ago. However, there are no 'do not touch' signs. Guests may feel and touch to their hearts' content."

There is much to feel and touch—original stone walls in the basement dining room, wood beams, and brick chimney arches in the 1784 King of France Tavern, where we all enjoyed the music of Charlie Byrd, the great jazz guitarist, who spends several weeks a year entertaining for his Maryland friends.

The fact is that jazz is a very important art form at the Maryland Inn, and particularly at the King of France Tavern, where not only Charlie Byrd holds forth, but there is an ongoing parade of such jazz musicians as Earl "Fatha" Hines, Teddy Wilson, and Ethel Ennis. This is the only inn of my acquaintance that has a policy of offering top jazz artists.

Ever mindful of the role that good food plays in their success, our innkeepers were glowing in their praise of the Maryland Inn Crab Imperial as well as the broiled rock fish, oysters Rockefeller, and the Duke of Gloucester, which is baked filet of flounder stuffed with a delicately seasoned crabmeat.

There were lots of opportunities for us to take walking tours of the city of Annapolis, which started as a Colonial seaport and has seventeen miles of waterfront within its boundaries.the inn is conveniently located in the midst of the great historic city of Annapolis, where there are tours of some of the finest Colonial townhouses in America, including the restored home and gardens of Governor Paca, one of the signers of the Declaration of Independence. Tours to the nearby Naval Academy can also be arranged.

The organized tours of the historic and cultural attractions of Annapolis are among the reasons why guests of all ages enjoy staying at the Maryland Inn. "We also have family matinées from time to time at the King of France Tavern," asserted Paul Pearson. "Charlie Byrd, along with other jazz entertainers, does special shows for children, so your readers should bring the kids, too."

During one of the quieter moments of our meeting, a group of us were standing on the porch of the inn with Paul Pearson, talking about the traditions of the city, and he pointed out some of the Maryland Inn's own traditions: "We commemorate such occasions as Bastille Day, with dancing in the street; Halloween, when we have sort of a zany, costumed 'freakers ball'; and Heritage Weekend with its big celebration à la Charles Dickens at Christmastime."

After breakfast on the third day, when most of us were packing our cars and getting ready to return to inns in all parts of North America and beyond, many of the innkeepers made a special point of saying how much they had enjoyed our time together, and wondering out loud how soon we would be returning to the Maryland Inn.

MARYLAND INN, Church Circle, Annapolis, Md. 21401; 301-263-2641. A 44-room 18th-century village inn in a history-laden town, 20 mi. from Baltimore and Washington, D.C. Near U.S. Naval Academy and Chesapeake Bay. European plan. Breakfast, lunch, and dinner served to travelers daily. Sunday brunch served year-round. Jazz Club, music nightly except Mondays in the King of France Tavern. Tours arranged to historic and scenic points of interest. Tennis and sailing school available. Paul Pearson, Proprietor; Peg Bednarsky, Innkeeper.

Directions: From Baltimore, take Rte. 2 south to first directional turnoff "Washington/Annapolis." From Washington, take Rte. 50 east to exit "Annapolis Naval Academy, Rowe Blvd."

ROBERT MORRIS INN
Oxford, Maryland

Every autumn I receive a wonderful long letter from Wendy Gibson of the Robert Morris Inn. It's usually about three pages on both sides of a yellow legal pad. She brings me up to date on the progress of her husband Ken, their sons Ben, six, and Kent, eight. There is also news of other members of the family, as well as Mr. Miller, the maitre d', and Morris, the basset hound.

The Robert Morris Inn is on the banks of the Tred Avon River in Oxford on Maryland's eastern shore. This is some of the most beautiful country on the eastern coast, and the town of Oxford has remained surprisingly sedate, unchanged, and serene for more than two hundred and fifty years. The inn was built about 1710 and has been enlarged several times. The staircase which leads to the guest rooms is the enclosed type of the Elizabethan period. There is original flooring of Georgia white pine in the upstairs hall. Four of the guest rooms have handmade wall-paneling, and the fireplaces were built of brick made in England and used as ballasts in the early sailing days.

In addition to lodging rooms in the main building, guests are accommodated in the Lodge, which is located just a few paces away on a point of land overlooking the bay. The old carriage house has been turned into two attractive waterfront lodgings, complete with bay windows, wood paneling, and waterfowl wallpaper.

The inn's location in the Chesapeake Bay area means that there is considerable emphasis on seafood at lunch and dinner. Breakfast, oddly enough, includes scrapple, as well as homefries, omelettes, and blueberry pancakes.

Now let's hit a few of the high spots of Wendy's letter: "I'm not only involved in the inn, but also school committees and looking after a few friends in the nursing home. We are finding we can use the inn as a vehicle to help people who are 'shut in,' by taking them a much-appreciated meal now and then. It's nice to be able to share what you have." (Wendy has had early training as a nurse.)

"I am presently waiting for all of my chrysanthemums to bloom after nursing them for seven years. We have quite a colorful display in the fall. The flower garden in front of the inn is strictly of the 'old time' flowers. All are perennials which happily come back every year. We have something blooming almost every month.

"Ken's brother, Jay, is still with us and doing his usual best in food buying. Mr. Miller continues to oversee the waiters and waitresses, and occasionally puts on one of his gourmet performances at the 'Inn Table.' He prepares and serves a six-course dinner that is just exquisite.

"Morris, the bassett hound, grows longer and lower. My mom is still very much a part of the inn. She helps decorate the rooms, and I really wish I had her talent.

"Ken's forte is with the guests; he makes everyone feel special and is never too busy to answer questions or to give a smile. Even if he is my husband, I think he is wonderful!"

I've saved some of the newspaper clippings she has sent me over the years. There is the account in 1975 of their acquiring ownership of the inn, and there is a photograph of the two of them in front of the inn on the occasion of receiving the *Holiday-Travel* magazine's 1978 "dining distinction" award.

Ken and Wendy, I'm just bursting with pride for your whole family and The Robert Morris.

Robert Morris Inn has been included in *CIBR* since 1970.

ROBERT MORRIS INN, Oxford, Md. 21654; 301-226-5111. A 35-room village inn in a secluded colonial community on the Tred Avon, 10 mi. from Easton, Md. European plan. 15 rooms with private baths; 20 rooms with shared baths. 4 rooms with private porches overlooking the Tred Avon. Breakfast, lunch, and dinner served to travelers daily. Open year-round except Christmas Day. No pets. Tennis, golf, sailing, swimming, and bicycles nearby. Kenneth and Wendy Gibson, Innkeepers.

Directions: From Delaware Memorial Bridge, follow Rte. 13 south to Rte. 301 and proceed south to Rte. 50, then east on Rte. 50 to Easton. From Chesapeake Bay Bridge, follow Rte. 50-301 to Rte. 50 and proceed east to Easton. From Chesapeake Bay Bridge Tunnel, follow Rte. 13 north to Rte. 50 and proceed west to Easton. From Easton, follow Rte. 322 to Rte. 333 to Oxford and inn.

". . . Gery and Timmy (sons) continue to be a fantastic help to us and it makes it so much fun and more meaningful when it's a family business . . ." — Massachusetts

". . . Our biggest occasion was the wedding of our daughter Tina in the beautiful month of May. A large Episcopal church wedding, then the reception by the lily pool at the inn, and a sit-down dinner for three hundred. All candlelight and perfectly gorgeous . . ."
—Florida

"We just made a major investment of two 82-gallon hot water heaters. This was necessitated because of severe drops in water pressure in the old water system when several baths were running simultaneously . . . In redecorating each guest room, we started with thick carpets, which are luxurious to walk on and help to reduce noise. Big thick towels is another one of our 'musts.' We hate those typical skimpy hotel towels. We feel the most critical area of any inn is the beds and mattresses. Since the one thing we're selling is sleep, we want to go first-class." — Maine

"This has been a year of new beginnings for the entire family. We have had the busiest six months of our lives; transition to innkeeping has involved many adjustments for all of us, but there's no question that the fulfillments and satisfactions are real. Although the younger children were reluctant participants in the life change, they are now involved (voluntarily!) in inn operations and making a place for themselves in their new high school . . . We have busied ourselves this summer and fall in 'learning the business' as well as beginning to place our statement on what was already an established and attractive facility. Our objectives focus on one end: to provide a small intimate retreat, where care, attention, and a homelike atmosphere blend with a physical facility and setting which are outstanding." —Connecticut

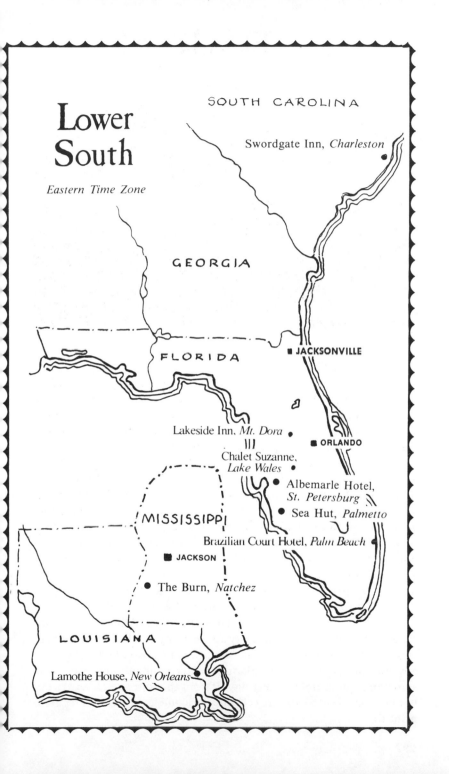

Lower
South

Eastern Time Zone

SOUTH CAROLINA

Swordgate Inn, *Charleston*

GEORGIA

FLORIDA

■ JACKSONVILLE

Lakeside Inn, *Mt. Dora*

Chalet Suzanne,
Lake Wales

● ORLANDO

● Albemarle Hotel,
St. Petersburg

● Sea Hut, *Palmetto*

MISSISSIPPI

Brazilian Court Hotel, *Palm Beach*

■ JACKSON

● The Burn, *Natchez*

LOUISIANA

Lamothe House, *New Orleans*

Florida

ALBEMARLE HOTEL
St. Petersburg, Florida

"I've been vacationing in Florida for the last ten years, and I'm here to tell you that there's no place like the Albemarle!" It was March in St. Petersburg, and I was seated in the long, graceful lobby of the Albemarle Hotel having a conversation with a well-tanned gentleman. We were looking at a calendar of the month's activities at the hotel. "I'm one of those individuals who took an early retirement, and have never worked so hard in my life," he said. "About the middle of March I like to get away from our home in southwest Virginia and come down here to St. Pete because that's where the action is. Just look at what is going on here in the hotel this month: there are travel movies, a craft and hobby show, English taxi rides, a cruise on Tampa Bay, a trip to Cypress Gardens, a book review by Jeanne Tucker, several party nights, and a St. Patrick's Day wine-and-cheese party. When I come here I want to *do* things . . . I just don't want to sit around and vegetate and watch TV!"

That statement, I believe, is the essence of the Albemarle and St. Petersburg—it's the opportunity to *do* things. When I mentioned this to manager Bill Tucker, he said, "That's absolutely right! The key to the Albemarle is planned entertainment and we have something going almost every day. It's not that our guests *have* to do it, but if they want to, they're certainly welcome . . . and they seem to want to.

"They enjoy going to Disney World, Busch Gardens, and we have dinner music, organ concerts, bingo twice a week, and something for everyone. They can walk to the beach or the Pier where there's usually an appearance by a show-business personality. They can play shuffleboard, or go lawn bowling, take a sail, or a speedboat ride, watch the major league baseball teams in training, and dozens of other things. Let's just say that no one can be bored at the Albemarle!"

This attractive in-town hotel has exactly the kind of atmosphere for which I was searching in Florida. In the first place, it has been owned by the same family, all of whom have been very active in management and staffing. This includes Mrs. Grace Tucker, who raised her sons Bill and Tom right here in the hotel. "Yes, we've done everything there is to do at the Albemarle," said Bill.

The average tenure of staff members is fifteen years, but Sylvester Norton, the hall porter, has been here for thirty-five years! The lodging rooms are bright and comfortable and there's an elevator, a swimming pool, a shuffleboard court, and sunbathing area.

The menu, like that of the Sterling Inn in the Pennsylvania Pocono Mountains, features dishes like Yankee pot roast, roast loin of pork, and lamb shanks—"The kind of dishes that people don't often serve themselves at home," added Tom.

My newfound friend suggested that I might care to join him on a walk on Beach Drive (naturally), which is St. Petersburg's shopping area. It faces the beautiful harbor and is lined with stately palms. "My wife and her friends love it," he said. "We can take a peek at the Museum of Fine Arts on the way. Yes, sir, your readers are going to love St. Petersburg and the Albemarle."

I believe he's right.

THE ALBEMARLE HOTEL, 145 Third Ave. N.E., St. Petersburg, 33731; 813-822-4097. A 140-room hotel in a quiet section of St. Petersburg just a short walk from Tampa Bay, the sand beach, the Shuffleboard Center, the replica of the HMS Bounty, *and many of the city's cultural and recreational activities. Mod. American and European plan. Open Nov. 1 to April 15. Breakfast, lunch, dinner served to non-residents. Swimming pool, shuffleboard on grounds. Golf, fishing, tennis, sailing nearby. A planned entertainment program for all guests. William Tucker, Manager.*

Directions: Leave I-275 at North Bay Dr. Exit and follow Fourth Ave. north to Beach Dr. N.E. Turn right 1 block to Third Ave. N.E., and right ½ block to hotel.

THE SEA HUT
Palmetto, Florida

It was December 19, 1979, and I was in my Berkshire farmhouse, with about four inches of snow in the woods and meadows, enjoying one of my favorite pastimes: reading menus. This time it was the dinner menu from the Sea Hut Restaurant at Pelican Point in Palmetto, Florida.

The first interesting point to make is that the Sea Hut is a spinoff from the Red Inn in Provincetown, Massachusetts, both owned by the Barker family.

The cover of the menu caught my eye immediately with its beautiful photograph of a very proud pelican who is one of the feathery denizens of the Sea Hut.

However, inside the menu is where everything really starts happening, with many different kinds of sea food chowder listed among the appetizers. One of them is New England clam chowder — a specialty of the Red Inn. Also listed are old-time crab specialties, including Chesapeake Bay crab cakes, crab Norfolk, crab imperial, and stone crab claws. These are freshly caught every day by their own fishermen and are prepared in the Sea Hut "crab shack," which is next to the canal connecting the Terra Ceia Bay with the Manatee River.

The snapper, grouper, scamp, and pompano are bought fresh from the fishing fleet which ties up at Cortez just a few miles away.

The shellfish section of the menu includes baked stuffed shrimp with fresh crabmeat dressing, fried shrimp, shrimp Dijon, fried oysters, scallops Pierre, and fried scallops. These can also be put together in various types of seafood platters.

There are also meat dishes such as sirloin steak, filet mignon, chicken Baltimore and frogs' legs.

The dessert menu (which has always been a great feature at the Red Inn) includes key lime pie, cheesecake, chocolate Bavarian pie, and all kinds of ice creams and parfaits.

Visiting the Sea Hut is like getting together with old friends, because Ted and Marce's oldest son Alan, and his wife Deb, are now living in Florida year-round, along with Deb's brother Bruce, Ted's nephew Eric, and brother Dave, all of whom are involved at the restaurant. Adding to the "family" presence are Ted and Marce, along with Bobby Souza and Peter Meads, who are also from the Red Inn.

The Sea Hut is located on Pelican Point, so named because of the pelicans that line the docks and pilings—there are usually at least a half dozen of these majestic birds in evidence. The Sea Hut boasts two exotic pets, "Pete," a great blue heron, and "Penny," a very tame egret. Pete and Penny are always in demand by photographers.

I'm delighted to welcome the Sea Hut Restaurant in this edition of *CIBR*. Our many readers who have visited the Red Inn in Provincetown through the years will be equally delighted to visit the Barkers in Florida.

SEA HUT RESTAURANT, Snead Island Road, Palmetto, Fla. 33561, 813-746-3355. A waterside marina-restaurant (no lodgings available). Luncheon and dinner (separate menus) are served from 11:30 a.m. to 10 p.m. daily. The Barker Family, Innkeepers.

Directions: From north: Follow Bus. 41 to 10th W., turn right, follow to Snead's Island. From south: Follow Bus. 41 to 10th St. W., turn left, follow to Snead's Island.

CHALET SUZANNE
Lake Wales, Florida

Chalet Suzanne started with the Great Depression of the 30s. At that time Bertha Hinshaw was a new widow with two children, $1700 from a cancelled insurance policy, two old cars, and a six-room house about a mile and a half from the main highway. She decided to open a restaurant. For ten days no one came, and then finally a family of five arrived and stayed for Christmas. Chalet Suzanne was in business.

A fire in 1943 turned out to be a blessing because Bertha started all over again—this time with some pretty unique ideas. She created an atmosphere that looked like a set from a movie. There is a conglomeration of little houses, lodges, and chalets that could belong in nearby Disney World. It's Oriental, Persian, Bavarian, Swiss, and chocolate layer cake. There are little bridges, penthouses, cupolas, balconies, minarettes, peaked roofs, flat roofs, and here and there little tiny windows that lack only a Snow White peeking through them. Just to make it more fun, these strange places contain lodging rooms!

These are all connected by brick walls and cobblestone paths.

Guests can choose accommodations for their moods — Byzantine or medieval, carpenter Gothic or *Erewhon.*

Truly exceptional food is served at Chalet Suzanne in five different dining rooms, all in a sort of Hans Christian Andersen setting. The late Clementine Paddleford tasted the soups and wrote in her column in the *New York Herald Tribune,* "It's good! good! good!" In fact, the soups led to still another business and now Chalet Suzanne Soups, including at least nineteen different kinds, are available in food specialty shops and supermarkets all over the country.

Besides the soup, the cannery in 1977 added six new citrus sauces which are delicious as an accompaniment to all meats, poultry, and hot or cold entrees. Chalet Suzanne products are available in the gourmet pantries of local supermarkets, and in gourmet-type shops.

Bertha's son, Carl, is the major-domo of the kitchen, and the opening course for dinner at Chalet Suzanne is always an invention by Carl's wife, Vita. One such concoction is a chicken liver canapé centered in the original Chalet baked grapefruit. Among other specialties is their famous Chicken Suzanne, glazed with its own natural juices to a beautiful amber color. Other main courses are lobster Newburg, lump crab and shrimp curry. Crêpes Suzanne are served just before the dessert. These are rolled-up tiny pancakes topped with one of the new sauces.

In 1979, the big news was the wedding of Carl and Vita's daughter Tina to Bob Farewell. Unfortunately, it came at a time when I was in England, but Vita's letter included a glowing account. "Of course, we held a reception here at Chalet Suzanne and our guests were seated in all five dining rooms, the living room, on the patio, and around the swimming pool. After dancing to an orchestra on the patio, the bridal couple took off for the Bahamas from our airstrip, with father Carl at the controls and brother Eric flying co-pilot. After flying north for a few minutes, they returned to the Lake Wales airport, and to the Chalet to spend their wedding night in the balcony suite overlooking the Swiss room! The next morning they reciprocated the bird feed thrown at them for their send-off by throwing more at our houseguests below at breakfast, and *really* left for the Bahamas later that day. I do wish you could have been here!"

Chalet Suzanne has been in *CIBR* since 1973.

CHALET SUZANNE, P.O. Box AC, Lake Wales, Fla. 33853; 813-676-1477. A 30-room phantasmagoric country inn and gourmet restaurant, 4 mi. north of Lake Wales, between Cypress Gardens and the Bok Singing Tower near Disney World. European plan. Dining room open from 8 a.m. to 9:30 p.m. daily. Closed Mondays June through October. Pool on grounds. Golf, tennis, riding nearby. Not inexpensive. The Hinshaw Family, Innkeepers.

Directions: From Interstate 4 turn south on U.S. 27 toward Lake Wales. From Sunshine State Pkwy. exit at Yeehaw Junction and head west on Rte. 60 to U.S. 27 (60 mi.). Proceed north on U.S. 27 at Lake Wales. Inn is 4 mi. north of Lake Wales on County Road 17A.

LAKESIDE INN
Mount Dora, Florida

"You're as young as you want to be." These words were firmly spoken to me by a white-haired lady wearing tennis shoes and visor out in front of the Lakeside Inn.

"Young man, I'm on my way over to the tennis courts right now," she continued. "Why don't you get your racquet and join me? Mr. Edgerton told me you were a tennis player. I'm 70 years old and I play tennis every day."

While I didn't find too many senior citizens ready to challenge me on the courts at 8 a.m., I will say that the collection of grandmothers and grandfathers at the Lakeside Inn had a great deal more pep than one might ordinarily expect. I asked Dick Edgerton about this.

"We've always been popular with retired people. However, in the past few years there has been a steady increase in the number of younger guests who come with their children. I think part of this is because we have so many facilities for everyone. There is a swimming pool and a wide variety of outdoor games. We have excellent fishing and boating, and we're not far from Disney World.

"One of the diversions which people of every age like is lawn bowling. Mount Dora has the third largest lawn bowling club in the United States, and there is nothing like good outdoor activity to keep people lively and in good spirits."

Dick could have included the fact that there are five golf courses within a twenty-minute drive of the Lakeside, including one right in the community of Mount Dora.

One of the pleasurable aspects of visiting the Lakeside is the opportunity to turn winter into summer. There are palm trees standing side by side with oaks, pines, and cedars. One of the most beautiful trees in this part of the country is the serinam cherry and there are also golden raintrees and kumquat trees. The fragrance from the trees, flowers and shrubs is heavenly. This is also where migrating and resident birds meet and flit from tree to tree.

Just before press time, Dick sent me the following newspaper clipping with the headline: "Movie Magnates Focus On Mount Dora." According to the clipping, the working title for a planned film comedy is, "Honky Tonk Freeway." Dick said that it is a comedy about a tourist-oriented town (Mount Dora) that is shut off from the world after a new freeway bypasses them. The outdoor scenes will be shot in Mount Dora. "It's ironic that they should pick Mount Dora after our fight to keep the highways *out*," said Dick.

This isn't the first time that a *CIBR* inn has been used for filming a motion picture. The Heritage House in Little River, California, was used for some scenes in *Same Time Next Year*.

Lakeside Inn has been in *CIBR* since 1973.

LAKESIDE INN, P.O. Box 175, Mount Dora, Fla. 32757; 904-383-2151. A 110-room resort-inn on Lake Dora in central Florida, 30 mi. northwest of Orlando. American plan. Breakfast, lunch, and dinner served to travelers daily. Open from Dec. 20 to April 6. Swimming

pool, fishing, waterskiing, putting green, and shuffleboard on grounds. Golf, tennis, bicycles, lawn bowling, and sailing nearby.
Dick Lee, Innkeeper

Directions: Follow I-95 south to Daytona Beach, then I-4 to Rte. 46 west to Mount Dora. Or, follow I-75 south to Wildwood, then Rte. 44 east to Rte. 441. Proceed on Rte. 441 to Mount Dora. After passing Lakeside Inn billboard on Rte. 441, turn south at first paved road (Donnelly St.) and proceed to Lakeside Inn.

BRAZILIAN COURT HOTEL
Palm Beach, Florida

I had found the other side of Palm Beach—not the glittering social facade, but the side with more genuine people. Furthermore, I was amazed to find a Palm Beach hotel with the simplicity and good taste that appealed to such people. It is called the Brazilian Court although most everyone refers to it as the "BC."

It was built back in the 1920s, and the Palm Beach residential area with sedate homes and beautifully landscaped gardens grew up around it. The building is a two-story Palm Beach Mission design with two completely enclosed patios. One patio, with several varieties of palm trees, begonias, and poinsettias, is a marvelous place to catch the morning sun.

The other patio really sets the tone for this discreet hotel. Dispersed among the royal palms, orange, banana, and African tulip trees are dining tables, many with umbrellas. Weather permitting, all three meals are served here, and each time of day has its own captivating mood.

In the evening, small lights twinkle on the inside of each umbrella and indirect colored lighting dramatically underscores the trees and exotic tropical plants. As night falls the lights become more brilliant against the dark blue sky. Now add a three-piece orchestra playing softly in the background and you have the complete picture.

The BC is reminiscent of the Black Point and the Asticou in Maine. And the climate brings to mind the Inn at Rancho Santa Fe, California.

Because there are many long-staying guests, the selections on the menu are numerous and varied. The broiled pompano amandine is delicious. The red snapper and Florida lobster Newburg are very appetizing also. There are several dishes prepared with Florida fresh fruit offered at each meal.

The big news from the Brazilian Court is that a beautiful new third court has been added at the center of which is a swimming pool and a pool patio. Several of the lodging rooms looking over that

scene now have sliding glass doors and private terraces. This means that BC guests can now enjoy not only the ocean bathing a few blocks away, but also the advantages of a new pool.

The lodging rooms and suites are furnished with quiet elegance. They overlook the residential area of town or the attractive inner patios.

The BC is basically a conservative resort-inn with quite a few of the amenities that guests find enjoyable. Great emphasis is placed on both the food and the service. The famous Worth Avenue shops of Palm Beach are just a few minutes away.

The Brazilian Court is part of my select group of inns and hotels in larger cities including the Algonquin in New York, the Botsford on the Detroit city line, the Cheshire in St. Louis and Lamothe House in New Orleans. I think they meet a need for personal hospitality.

Brazilian Court Hotel has been in *CIBR* since 1973.

BRAZILIAN COURT HOTEL, 300 Brazilian Ave., Palm Beach, Fla. 33480; 305-655-7740. A 125-room hotel in the heart of Palm Beach. A secluded patioed garden spot just a short walk from the ocean and Worth Avenue shops. European plan (includes breakfast) and Mod. American plan available to houseguests. Breakfast, lunch, and dinner served to travelers daily. Open from December to April. No pets. Swimming pool on grounds. Ocean swimming, boating, fishing, tennis, golf, and bicycles nearby. James Ponce, Innkeeper.

Directions: From Sunshine State Pkwy., take Exit 40 to Okeechobee Blvd. Turn left and proceed 6 mi. to Royal Palmway Bridge. Cross bridge and take first right, then turn left after 1 block on to Brazilian Ave. Hotel is two blocks east on Brazilian Ave.

Louisiana

LAMOTHE HOUSE
New Orleans, Louisiana

There are special sections in many cities and towns in North America that still reflect some of the grace and style of earlier times. Fortunately, some of these have been declared Historic Districts to preserve them for generations to come. Some which come to mind are the old sections of Charleston (South Carolina), Newport (Rhode Island), Alexandria (Virginia), Sistersville (West Virginia), Marshall (Michigan), Boston (Massachusetts), and Cape May (New Jersey). And certainly high on everyone's list is the French Quarter in New Orleans.

That's why it has been a source of constant joy to me to have found, a number of years ago, the Lamothe House which sits on the very edge of the French Quarter and is typical of old-fashioned New Orleans hospitality.

The Lamothe House was built by two brothers from Santo Domingo who came to the United States to escape an uprising. They established a sugar plantation and built the house in 1800. It has the same floor plans on both sides of the center hall which divides the three floors of the house completely in half. There are two lovely winding staircases to the upper floors. The old formal parlors on the first floor have been converted into handsome suites with elegant antique furnishings. Rooms with balconies surround the flagstone courtyard on the back of the house.

A couple of my readers wrote me a short note about their recent visit to the Lamothe House: "As we entered, we walked along the center hall and emerged into the courtyard with its flowers, fish pond, and banana plants. Mimi Langguth, the innkeeper, greeted us as old friends because we have been stopping at the Lamothe House for 15 years. She showed us the Scarlett O'Hara and Rhett Butler suites. They have five beds and are great for families, or can be divided for separate sleeping accommodations.

"During our three-day stay," the letter continued, "I had a chance to see many of the rooms and was delighted to see the redecoration, new bedspreads and other touches which combine so well with the collection of antiques. I heard one couple say that the

antique furniture of the Lamothe House rivals any they have seen in New Orleans.

"The warm, personal charm of this inn comes through at *petit dejeuner* around the dining room table each morning where everyone has a chance to meet. This tradition was started by Mrs. Gertrude Munson and is being carried on by her daughter, Mimi.

"I have not seen the Lamothe House or the garden patio in better condition and this fine gem of an inn is continuing its warm and personal traditions."

The canopy beds found in most rooms appeal to honeymooners and also to people returning on their anniversaries.

An old-fashioned family Christmas Eve party for the guests of the house features Mrs. Munson's old plantation punch recipe. The Lamothe House is a favorite for families at Thanksgiving and Christmas holidays because of its history, tradition, and family warmth.

In the paragraphs above, I have mentioned Mrs. Gertrude Munson, who was the founder of the Lamothe House and the mother of the present innkeeper, Mimi Langguth. Mrs. Munson, whom I met in the fall of 1972 on the occasion of my first visit, was certainly a most remarkable individual, filled with *joi de vivre* and was a subject of an earlier article in *Readers Digest*. She passed away during 1979, but a letter from Mimi indicates that the spirit of hospitality and good will at the Lamothe House continues, even to the third generation, because Gertrude's granddaughter Cynthia is now helping at the inn. "She and her grandmother were very close and I'm sure that she caught the real feeling from her," writes Mimi.

The letter goes on to say that the opening of the United States Mint as a Museum and Visitors' Center, just two blocks from the Lamothe House, is creating much interest. There was a Christmas bazaar there in November complete with jazz bands and Cajun cuisine."

Lamothe House has been in *CIBR* since 1973.

LAMOTHE HOUSE, 621 Esplanade Ave., New Orleans, La. 70116; 504-947-1161. A small, elegant, 14-room inn in the French Quarter within walking distance of many fascinating New Orleans restaurants and attractions. European plan with complimentary petit dejeuner. No other meals served. Closed mid-July to Sept. 1. No pets. Near Lake Pontchartrain, Mississippi River, bayou and river cruises, plantations and mansions on the Great River Road. Golf, tennis, fishing, and bicycles nearby. Mrs. Kenneth ("Mimi") Langguth, Innkeeper.

Directions: From the west or east on I-10, take the Orleans Ave. exit to Claiborne Ave. which runs under I-10 at that point. Proceed east for 7 blocks or until the intersection of Esplanade Ave. Turn right on Esplanade and proceed 10 blocks. Or take Esplanade Ave. exit from I-10.

South Carolina

THE SWORDGATE INN
Charleston, South Carolina

Suzanne and David Redd, innkeepers at the Swordgate, were telling me about the pleasures of keeping an inn in the historic city of Charleston.

"We try to run the inn as a family. Our daughter Martha Sue, age thirteen, is really a young lady and makes reservations, checks guests in, and enjoys telling the history of this old house, especially the part about the ghost.

"Our son David, Jr., is ten, and is chief of the coke machine. The only problem so far is that little David likes to pass cokes out to his friends. He assumes more duties every year.

"We're very excited about our collection of French antiques in the French ballroom. This is a splendid room and very refreshing here in Charleston where many of the houses have only English furniture. The ballroom is included in the historic Charleston

Foundation spring and fall tours sponsored by the Preservation Society."

David is a native Charlestonian and a professional organist. He is minister of music at the First Baptist Church of Charleston, which is a beautiful building just a few squares away from the inn. It is one of the oldest Baptist churches in the South. He's also organist for the Citadel Military College, located in Charleston.

In speaking of the breakfasts, Suzanne said, "I think this is one of the most enjoyable times for our guests. In most of the months of the year they can sit out in our garden and before you know it, they are getting acquainted and planning to do things with each other.

"Our muffins are hot from the oven and we have Charleston grits. The secret with grits is to cook both yellow and white grits together and add real butter. There's jam and homemade bread as well. It's the only meal we serve."

The five guest rooms of the Swordgate Inn are individually decorated. Each has its own distinctive sheets, pillowcases, bed-spreads, and ruffles. Two of the bedrooms have tester beds, and another has a brass bed. Fresh fruits and flowers are placed in the guest rooms daily, and there is a newspaper at the door each morning. Four of the rooms are on the first floor of the old mansion. The fifth room on the third floor has a canopy bed and a view of the fascinating rooftops of the old city.

All of the guests are invited to view the grand ballroom on the second floor and this is an opportunity to see a stately old Charleston mansion. It has a handsome marble carved fireplace on one end and at the opposite end, a gold-leaf classic mirror that runs from the floor to the ceiling. I can imagine what great parties were held there during the nineteenth century. The gentle Charleston climate encourages azaleas, camellias, and gardenias which are in profusion in the courtyard as well as magnolias and holly trees.

Charleston seems to have something going on almost continually and one of the highlights is the Spoleto Festival which is held in May and June. It is a real outpouring of music and art. Early reservations at the Swordgate would be highly advisable.

Old Charleston is a place of balustrades, cupolas, dormers, fences, walls, scrollwork, cobblestones, old street lamps, trees that bend over the roads, gorgeous mellowed red brick walls, overhanging galleries, and even a gazebo in the park. Ruby Allen, also one of the innkeepers, says there are seventy-three pre-Revolutionary homes in the area. But actually, the architecture reflects different stages of American architectural taste.

The Swordgate Inn is a fitting complement to such well-preserved, quiet elegance.

SWORDGATE INN, 111 Tradd St., Charleston, S.C. 29401; 803-723-8518. A quiet 5-room elegant inn located in the center of an historic area of the city, amidst distinguished 18th and 19th century homes. Within walking and biking distance of most of Charleston's cultural and historic landmarks. Bicycles furnished without charge to guests. Lodgings include informal breakfast. No other meal served. Open every day of the year. No children or pets. Beaches, sailing, and fresh water and deep sea fishing nearby. David and Suzanne Redd, Ruby Allen, Innkeepers.

Directions: Take I-26 to Meeting St. South Exit. Turn right on Meeting St., 12 blocks to Broad St.; turn right on Broad, two blocks to Legare St. Turn left on Legare for one block; turn left on Tradd St. Look for small sign on right that says Swordgate Inn.

Mississippi

NATCHEZ
Natchez, one of the oldest cities on the North American continent, is built on the site of an ancient Indian village which was once the home of the sun-worshipping tribe for which it is named. It

is believed that De Soto's men came to the area as early as 1642; in 1682, the explorers La Salle and Tonti visited Natchez. The French made it a permanent settlement in 1716. However, like other places in the new North American continent, Natchez became a pawn in the power plays of the European monarchs, and it passed to Great Britain in 1763. This was a short-lived era, because the Spaniards arrived in 1779 and laid out most of the old town as it is seen today. The new American government, seeking to establish its boundaries more firmly, negotiated with Spain for more than a year, and finally on March 27, 1798, Natchez became a part of the United States of America.

These were the great days of Natchez. At one time, at least half of the twenty millionaires of the United States called Natchez their home. It was during these affluent times that the Natchezians built and furnished their homes with the very finest appointments. Many traveled to Europe to purchase Italian marble mantels, French mirrors and chandeliers, fine furniture and cabinets, and even paintings by such masters as Rubens. These showplaces were lavish with porcelain, Dresden and Sèvres china, Waterford and Venetian crystal, and Sheffield and Georgian silk. Henry Clay, Lafayette, Jenny Lind, Mark Twain, and Stephen Foster were entertained in Natchez homes. Andrew Jackson was married at "Springfield," and Jefferson Davis was married at "The Briars."

Meanwhile, Natchez-Under-the-Hill, as the section along the Mississippi River was known, grew in notoriety. Fortunes were won and lost in a night; men disappeared, only to be found floating down river; tales of its high women and riverboat gamblers spread to courts throughout the world.

The Civil War found Natchez virtually defenseless as Vicksburg, seventy-two miles north, had to be defended by the Confederates at all costs. Union forces occupied the city, and Grant plotted Vicksburg's end here. Natchez suffered but little under Yankee occupation, and when the War Between the States ended, she led a dormant life through Reconstruction days and the Great Depression.

However, in 1932, the Natchez Pilgrimage started a new way of life for the city. During the month of March, some forty thousand visitors make their way to Natchez, and this is repeated again in the fall. Today, many of the ante-bellum homes, along with the art museum, the early churches, the Emerald Mound, are open year around. The Natchez Trace, which is a parkway that follows the route of the original frontier road, is a great tourist attraction. During my short visit, I discovered that Natchez-Under-the-Hill is also being restored with interesting shops and restaurants.

To La Salle, it was the most desirable site on the river. To some, Natchez may appear to be just a town in the southwest corner of Mississippi nestled on the bluffs overlooking the river, but to those who know and love her, Natchez is a way of life, one which its inhabitants are happy to share with travelers.

THE BURN
Natchez, Mississippi

I was walking in the terraced garden of The Burn, truly a most remarkable guest house in Natchez, enjoying the extraordinary experience of seeing the moon rise, while at the same time catching the pink tinge on the clouds created by the setting sun. Each passing moment brought the Mississippi night into a deeper shade of velvet blue. Around me, the marvelous scent of the gardens . . . the sweet olive trees, the live oaks, the pecans, the magnolia bushes, and late roses pervaded the atmosphere. By now, the terra cotta statues in the garden representing the four seasons were just barely visible in the gathering dark.

In all of my experience, while traveling to many parts of the world, I have never found an inn and a community more closely wedded than is the Burn to Natchez. They belong together.

The building was constructed in 1832 by John P. Walworth, a Scotsman who came down the river from Ohio at the early age of twenty-one with a fortune in his pockets. Designed in the pure Greek

Revival style and fashioned from cypress timbers, this mansion typifies Natchez at the height of its cultural and intellectual development. Incidentally, it is named for a brook that flows through the property. The word *burn* means brook in Scotland. During the American War Between the States, General Grant (a distant relative of mine), occupied the house as hospital and headquarters, and horses were stabled in what is now the breakfast room.

Today, The Burn is not only an exquisite accommodation for those fortunate travelers who are able to make reservations, but it is also the personal home of Buzz and Bobbie Harper, for whom this house is a temple of grace and beauty. Everywhere I could see the evidence of their love of beautiful things.

Just as are all the other guests, I was taken on a tour of the house which began at the front entrance between the pure Doric columns. As my hoop-skirted guide Mary Louise Burley (who is thoroughly acquainted with all of the handsome antiques of this lovely mansion) led me through the front hallway, I noted the most interesting architectural feature of the house— a free-standing, semi-spiral staircase, which still retains its original cypress treads and mahogany bannister.

The tour included the music room with a priceless piano and harp, the dining room, and the "gentlemen's parlor" where the gas chandeliers provide just the right touch. At one end of an informal dining room is a guest lounge where I saw a portrait of Bobbie and Buzz painted by their daughter, Mrs. Robin Johnson. There were also some photographs of General Grant taken during his occupation of the house.

Each of the four bedrooms provided for overnight guests were furnished with handsome antiques, and had elaborately carved four-poster beds with wooden canopies. These and all the other antiques were part of Buzz's and Bobbie's personal collection.

Later, on the terrace overlooking the swimming pool, we enjoyed tea and cakes served by the white-uniformed maid and butler. Breakfast is the only meal served at The Burn and there are always homemade breads, hot biscuits, cinnamon rolls, homemade jellies, jams, grits, ham and very special baked eggs. Everybody sits at the same table and, as might be expected, most of the conversation deals with Natchez and The Burn.

This is The Burn's first year in *CIBR*.

THE BURN, 712 No. Union, Natchez, Miss. 39120; 601-442-1344, 601-445-8566. A 4-room mansion-guest house in the quiet residential section of this historic Mississippi town. Breakfast served only to houseguests. No other meals. Open year-round except Christmas. The Natchez Trace and many famous houses and buildings are within a short distance. Swimming pool on grounds. No facilities for preschool children. No pets. Mr. & Mrs. Buzz Harper, Innkeepers.

Directions: From Jackson: take I-55 south to Exit 18 and then Hwy. 28 to Fayette and Hwy. 61 south to Natchez. From New Orleans: take I-10 west to Baton Rouge, turn right on I-12 east to Hwy. 61 and north to Natchez.

I do not include lodging rates in the descriptions, for the very nature of an inn means that there are lodgings of various sizes, with and without baths, in and out of season, and with plain and fancy decoration. Travelers should call ahead and inquire about the availability and rates of the many different types of rooms.

Rates are comparable to those at hotels, motels, and resorts in the same geographic area. To me, this represents a travel bargain, for there is so much more offered at a country inn.

"European Plan" means that rates for rooms and meals are separate. "American Plan" means that meals are included in the cost of the room. "Modified American Plan" means that breakfast and dinner are included in the cost of the room. Some inns include a Continental breakfast with the lodging.

WHAT IS INNKEEPING REALLY LIKE? *(con't)*

". . . Of course, we're changing the inn all of the time, subtracting and adding different ideas. It's been a pleasure completing the guest rooms because of not having to accomplish this in a given short time. Each of our guest rooms is so different from the other. Instead of numbers, we have given them names to fit their personalities." —New York State

"Another winter season is about to commence. Considering the gas situation in early July, we made it through the summer with another good record. Luckily for us, there seems to be a growing interest in country inns." —Vermont

". . . In the fall as we sit in front of the fire, reading notes from guests and their comments in the log book, one of the most rewarding things is to realize that we have a whole family of people that belong to our inn. The photos and personal letters we get from our guests are so heartwarming. Now finishing our third year as an inn, I can best sum us up as a place where it's possible to 'just be.'" —Maine

". . . To sum it all up, I can only say it's been a satisfactory year. Oh, we've goofed, we've been tired through *to the bones; but! we've laughed, made changes (of progress, we hope!) found new friends and kept the old ones. So on to the next year with new sights set and new hopes, and we hope that we'll not make the same mistakes, but we do know that we'll make new ones, and pray we do a better job all the way around."* —Pennsylvania

". . . A big restoration project was the installation of private baths in two of our nicest guest rooms. We all are working this winter on yet another guest room which will be open for reservations May 1. We also did mundane things like wiring, paint, etc. Our guest rooms are really elegant now, all done with Victorian antiques." —Wisconsin

"We will be carrying on some restoration work including painting the exterior, a new roof, some landscaping, and anything else we can afford, that will bring back more of the original character of the inn . . ." —Canada

Oak Bay Beach Hotel, *Victoria, British Columbia*

James House,
The Farmhouse,
Port Townsend

Captain Whidbey, *Coupeville*

■ SEATTLE

Lake Quinault Lodge, *Quinault*

WASHINGTON

Partridge Inn, *Underwood*

■ PORTLAND

Far West

Pacific Time Zone

● Benbow Inn,
Garberville
● Grey Whale Inn, *Ft. Bragg*

● Heritage House, *Little River*
● Harbor House, *Elk*

● Red Castle, *Nevada City*

ARIZONA

Rancho de los Caballeros,
● *Wickenburg*

■ PHOENIX
● Hermosa Inn, *Paradise Valley*
Lodge on the Desert,
Tanque Verde,
● *Tucson*

Wine Country Inn,
St. Helena   ■ SACRAMENTO

SAN FRANCISCO ■

Sutter Creek Inn, *Sutter Creek*

Bed and Breakfast Inn, *San Francisco*

CALIFORNIA

● Vagabond House,
Rosita Lodge, *Carmel*

● Ojai Valley Inn, *Ojai*

LOS ANGELES ■

The Inn, *Rancho Santa Fe*

■ SAN DIEGO

Arizona

HERMOSA INN
Paradise Valley, Arizona

I had actually fallen asleep while floating on a rubber mattress in the pool at the Hermosa Inn.

It had been a most interesting day beginning early in the morning in my snow-covered Berkshire farmhouse and ending here in the wonderfully warm and inviting atmosphere of Paradise Valley. I knew that I already had a faint touch of suntan from playing a couple of sets of tennis here at the inn, and I fell asleep contemplating dinner which, that evening, would feature tournedos Hermosa.

I'd been picked up at the Phoenix Airport by the limousine and transported directly to the front entrance of the inn, which was dominated by two splendid royal palm trees amidst a lavish cactus garden. An energetic Ike Bauer was on hand to greet me and we walked through the living room and dining room out to the swimming pool area and barbeque pit.

He described the various types of accommodations: "There are villas that have a living room with a fireplace and beamed ceilings, a kitchen, two bedrooms, a bath and dressing room, and an enclosed private patio," he said. "The *casitas* have one bedroom and are similar to the villas; there are also *hacienda* rooms. All of them have combination tub-showers, color TV, direct-dial telephone lines, and a private patio."

At this resort-inn in the land of almost perpetual sunshine, tennis is the game. There are five private tournament-type courts. "One of the attractive aspects," said Ike, as we crossed over an *arroyo* (which, he explained, is a dry water course that fills up during the sudden southwest rainstorms), "is the fact that it's almost always possible for our houseguests to obtain a court. We also have a full-time tennis professional on the staff, as well as ball-throwing machines and a practice backboard."

My *casita,* like all the rest of the buildings, was constructed in the pueblo style with white walls and dark, painted beams. I could have prepared my own breakfast at the little kitchenette, but preferred instead to share the full breakfast which features *huevos revueltos à la Mexicana.* "These are eggs that truly underwent a revolution and became scrambled," said Ike. "We add the appropriate southwestern touches."

My swimming pool reverie was gently awakened by the arrival of a very attractive woman with two small boys. "Hi," she said, "I'm Angy Bauer, and this is Andrew and Jason. Ike said you were here, so I thought it would be fun to come over and get acquainted." It was from Angy that I learned some of the fascinating history of the Hermosa—the fact that it was started in 1930 by the famous cowboy artist, Lonn Megargee. "The original structure," she said, "contains beehive fireplaces, secret passages, thick adobe walls, and a fabulous ceiling whose heavy beams came from an old railroad trestle near Globe, Arizona. It's been a resort since 1947."

Angy continued, "Actually, the Hermosa is really carved out of the desert, and considering the fact that it takes many of our cacti so long to grow, we know they were here long before the house was built. We have hedgehog, barrel, saguaro, prickly pear, cholla, and ocotillo cacti, plus oleanders, date palms, lemon, orange, and lime trees, and many other beautiful plantings.

"I wish you were going to be here on Sunday," she said, "because that's when many of the valley residents drop by for Sunday brunch. It's always a good time."

HERMOSA INN, 5532 N. Palo Cristi Road (36 St. at Stanford Drive), Paradise Valley (Scottsdale) Az. 85253; 602-955-8660. A 30-room resort-inn with special emphasis on tennis, located within a few minutes of the Phoenix Airport. Breakfast, lunch, and dinner served daily to travelers. Open Sept. 30 to May 31. Within a convenient distance of many of the area's cultural, historic, and recreational attractions. Five tennis courts, Jaccuzzi swimming pool on grounds. Golf, horseback riding nearby. European plan. No pets. Lodging rate includes Continental breakfast. Eckard (Ike) and Angy Bauer, Innkeepers.

Directions: Use 40th St. exit on Maricopa Freeway (I-10, I-17), north 9 mi. to Stanford Dr. Left on Stanford for 1 stop sign to Palo Cristi Road. Hermosa is on the corner of Palo Cristi and Stanford Dr.

RANCHO de los CABALLEROS
Wickenburg, Arizona

I found myself with an interesting group, among which was a gentleman and his wife from Illinois who had been coming to the Rancho for at least ten years. They had become so attached to the high desert country in Wickenburg that, during the previous year, they had purchased one of the beautiful houses adjacent to the ranch property and were now part-time residents. Sometime during the last two or three years, they had met a second couple also staying at the ranch and found that they all liked tennis. This was actually a reunion for them.

We were all sitting in the lounge overlooking the tennis courts, swimming pool, and the Bradshaw Mountains, which seemed no farther than 25 miles distant in the clear air. I was surprised to learn that they were at least 50 miles away! The sun was going down behind Vulture Peak, and the convolutions and gradations of the mountains across the valley were constantly changing until they melted into one black silhouette against the night sky.

More people joined our circle and we talked about the day's activities. The newcomers who had been out on one of the trail rides were being kidded about feeling a bit stiff. The "old hands" enjoying their third or fourth day were comparing the personalities of the different horses. All of this "horsey" talk caused me to change my mind, and instead of more tennis the next morning, I told the head wrangler that I would be on the slow ride, at ten o'clock.

Rancho de los Caballeros is a most impressive ranch-inn. A great deal of care is taken with plantings, gardens, and lawns around the main house and the beautiful cacti and trees are filled with birds (at least 45 varieties), particularly in early morning.

The decor and furnishings are those of a luxurious, large *hacienda* and the individual lodgings are all done in an Arizona-Indian motif.

Many families have been returning for years, and there is a children's counselor to keep young people entertained. I'm always amazed at how the children take immediately to ranch life. They are the first ones out and the last to come in.

The big news at Rancho de los Caballeros is that in January 1980 the first nine holes of Los Caballeros Club's eighteen-hole golf course was ready to play. Actually, it will be 7,025 yards par 72 and will surround ranch facilities and offer challenging play for the most avid golfers. "We have natural desert rough which contrasts with the lush Bermuda fairways," explained Rusty Gant, the innkeeper-pilot-owner of the ranch. "The original nine holes play 3,520 yards par 36 from the back of the championship tees."

Rancho de los Caballeros has been included in *CIBR* since 1970.

RANCHO de los CABALLEROS, Wickenburg, Ariz. 85358; 602-684-5484. A luxury 62-room ranch-resort, 60 mi. from Phoenix in the sunny dry desert. American plan. Breakfast, lunch, dinner served to travelers daily. Open from mid-October to early May. Swimming pool, horseback riding, hiking, skeet shooting, air strip, putting, tennis and golf on grounds. Special children's program. No pets, no credit cards. Dallas P. Gant, Jr., Innkeeper.

Directions: Rtes 60, 89, and 93 lead to Wickenburg. Ranch is 2 mi. west of town on Rte. 60 and 2 mi. south on Vulture Mine Road.

THE LODGE ON THE DESERT
Tucson, Arizona

The slanting rays of the western sun, providing spectacular backlighting for the great banks of clouds which seemed to skim the jagged peaks of the Santa Catalina Mountains, streamed through the casement window and lit up the interior of my spacious studio bedroom at the Lodge on the Desert.

Even though the afternoon temperature in September reached 85, I knew that later that evening I would want a fire in my fireplace to ease the chill of the cool desert night.

My bedroom was really most impressive, with three windows on two sides and a patio facing north. The two double beds had rich bedspreads that complemented the orange curtains, and an armful of freshly picked flowers lent an air of gaiety to the dark tones of the

315

carved wooden tables and chests. The full-sized closet reminded me that many people come here to spend weeks at a time, enjoying the benefits of a friendly climate in both summer and winter, plus the many opportunities for outdoor recreation, as well as the pursuit of the arts.

Tucson is one of the most sophisticated cities in the Southwest with many fine homes and good shops in the downtown area. The University of Arizona is an active cultural center with a continuing program of music, drama, and art and craft exhibitions.

"My father built the Lodge on the Desert outside Tucson in 1936," explained Schuyler Lininger, the *patron grande* of this resort inn. (I found that in the Southwest innkeepers adopted this rather impressive Spanish title.) "Now the city has grown up around us; fortunately, we have no tall buildings to disrupt our guests' view of the mountains, and yet we are set apart by the hedges around the property. However, many of our guests find nearness to the center of things in the city most desirable, even though it seems we are way out in the country."

Here in the Southwest desert during the outdoor weather everybody gathers around the swimming pool, and here is where many conversations and lasting friendships start.

For cooler days, the Lodge has a very spacious and inviting living room with lots of books which guests are free to take to their rooms, a chess game, a jigsaw puzzle, and many opportunities just to sit and relax.

The lodging rooms of the inn have been designed after the manner of Pueblo Indian farmhouses, the beige adobe color frequently relieved by very colorful Mexican tiles.

Although the dining room features many dishes of the Southwest, I found there were also such favorites as Chateaubriand for two, roast rack of lamb, and several veal dishes. Schuyler explained that he and Helen have gone to great lengths to bring milk-fed Wisconsin veal to the table in different versions. Incidentally, one of the most popular features of the inn is breakfast served on the guest room patios in the beautiful early morning sunshine.

I believe another guest succinctly summed up my feelings about the Lodge on the Desert while we were both taking advantage of that bright September sun to get a few more degrees of tan.

"What I like about it here," she said, "is the really endless variety of things that are going on in Tucson—the Art Center, the many different theaters, the new museum, the exhibition of Indian arts, the opera company, the ballet, the Tucson Symphony, the golf courses, the racetrack, and all kinds of sports events—it's so *civilized!*"

The Lodge on the Desert has been included in *CIBR* since 1976.

THE LODGE ON THE DESERT, 306 N. Alvernon Way, Tucson, Ariz. 85733; 602-325-3366. A 35-room luxury inn within the city limits. Near several historic, cultural, and recreational attractions. American and European plans available in winter; European plan in summer. Breakfast, lunch, and dinner served to travelers every day of the year. Attended, leashed pets allowed. Swimming pool and lawn games on grounds. Tennis and golf nearby. Schuyler and Helen Lininger, Innkeepers.

Directions: Take Speedway exit from I-10. Travel about 5 mi. east to Alvernon Way, turn right (south) onto Alvernon (¾ mi.). Lodge is on left side between 5th St. and Broadway.

TANQUE VERDE
Tucson, Arizona

With a practiced flick of the wrist, Bob Cote sent the flapjack spinning into the air where it somersaulted and landed on the hot griddle.

We were all watching in awe—children, parents, fast riders, medium riders and slow riders. This was the meeting point of the Tanque Verde breakfast ride.

About 8 a.m. we had gathered at the corral, the wranglers paired us off with our horses. The head wrangler explained that the slow ride doesn't involve cantering or loping, but the intermediate and fast rides use more rapid gaits.

On the slow ride, about ten of us followed a leisurely pace around the hummocks and past the beautiful giant saguaros.

Morning on the desert was cool and quiet. Shortly, the sun would be peeking over the mountains, and we would be ready to remove our heavier jackets. Our leader pointed out various plants and birds as we rode.

After an hour of desert riding, all of the riders met at the Old Homestead where a camp breakfast of pancakes, scrambled eggs, bacon, sausage, warm biscuits, and hot coffee was waiting. We all waited our turn for Bob's pancakes and many went back for seconds.

Horseback riding is an important part of vacation life at Tanque Verde. There are three rides a day, and day-long rides and overnight rides are also available. Children have their own riding program. The indoor pool, outdoor pool, whirlpool bath and sauna are welcomed by the riders, tennis players, and hikers.

In the evening, there is usually something planned—movies, slides, square dancing, or other organized activities if guests wish to participate.

On a recent trip I met Dr. David Sellman of London, England, his wife Ingrid, and their two children who were spending their second Christmas at Tanque Verde. He explained that everything was so casual that it was easy to get acquainted and that both his children were enthusiastic about their vacation. "They're busy from breakfast to bedtime," he said. "Children have their own dining room, but we can also eat together."

Accommodations are in almost luxurious individual *casitas,* all of which have their own Spanish-style corner fireplaces. Meals are served at long tables in the vaulted dining room, and there's nothing like the desert air to encourage healthy appetites.

One further point: Tanque Verde is open throughout the entire year, and during the summer there are many guests from Europe and Asia enjoying the full holiday in the desert. As innkeeper Bob Cote says, "We have so many guests speaking different languages, we could almost advertise that it's a good place for children to get some language tutoring."

Tanque Verde has been included in *CIBR* since 1970.

TANQUE VERDE RANCH, Box 66, Rte. 8, Tucson, Ariz. 85710; 602-296-6275. A 65-room ranch-inn, 10 mi. from Tucson. American plan. Breakfast, lunch, and dinner served to travelers by reservation. Open year-round. Riding, indoor and outdoor pool, tennis, sauna, exercise room, and whirlpool bath on grounds. Robert and Dee Dee Cote, Innkeepers.

Directions: From U.S. 10, exit at Speedway Blvd. and travel east to dead end.

California

RED CASTLE INN
Nevada City, California

"We are, I believe, one of the prime examples of Gothic Revival architecture in California." Jerry Ames, Chris Dickman, and I were seated in the pleasant garden of the Red Castle Inn high above Nevada City, discussing the history and other fascinating features of the inn. Chris, who is extremely knowledgeable about such things, asserted that, as far as he knows, the Red Castle is one of two examples of genuine Gothic Revival design on the West Coast, and this should not be confused with "carpenter Gothic," which is quite common. "It's particularly identifiable by the arched windows on the top floor and the double brick walls. The house has never been altered since it was built in 1860 by Judge John Williams, a mine owner and civic leader who, with his family, crossed the plains in 1849.

"In near-ruins, the house was restored by James W. Scharr in 1963. I think it stands today as a proud reminder of the part that the 'Argonauts' played in the heritage of California. It's a registered point of historical interest and recognized as such by the Daughters of the Golden West."

The house tour included one fascinating feature after another.

On that particularly warm day, I was delightfully impressed by the fact that the temperature inside the house was at least twenty degrees cooler than it was outdoors. Jerry said that was because of the double brick walls. I saw all seven bedrooms, five of which have private baths, and all are furnished with very handsome antiques. Each one has its own individuality. "By the time we bought it, the house had been through several different careers." commented Chris. "Fortunately, it has never been altered, which is wonderful because some of these old buildings have been butchered over the years." Chris proved to be rather adamant on the subject of preservation, undoubtedly because of his background in interior design.

We started from the very top floor and worked our way down, and it was on the small balcony way up in the treetops that I learned about one of the early inhabitants, Judge William's son and his penchant for playing the cornet from this vantage point. I believe it had something to do with communicating with the ladies of the town. There's a photograph of him in the hallway sporting a very fierce mustache.

Throughout the house there are wonderful collections of wall hangings and such decorative pieces as beautiful fans and theatrical masks from all over the world, including a Japanese *"No"* mask made about 1870 and signed by the actors. I've never seen an inn with a collection of masks before. Much interesting reading is available with a wide selection of magazines and books.

We tarried for awhile in the main living room where I felt the sense of buoyancy that fresh flowers give to a room. On an antique

desk there was an old-fashioned brass telephone with a separate earpiece, as well as stereoscopic photographs and a special viewer. Fascinating bric-a-brac filled almost every corner. "We've tried to keep everything as authentically 'period' as possible," Jerry said.

In Nevada City, California, where gold strikes were a way of life a hundred years ago, I found one of my own: the Red Castle Inn. This is the first year for the Red Castle to be included in *CIBR*.

RED CASTLE INN, 109 Prospect St., Nevada City, Ca. 95959; 916-265-5135. A 7-room inn located on a hill overlooking one of the great gold rush communities in the foothills of the Sierra Nevada Mountains. Approximately 2800 ft. altitude. Lodgings include Continental breakfast (the only meal served). There are numerous historic, cultural, and recreational attractions, all within a very short distance. Open from mid-February to mid-January. No recreation on grounds. Hiking, golf, xc-skiing nearby. No diversions for small children. German and Spanish are spoken. Jerry Ames and Chris Dickman, Innkeepers.

Directions: Nevada City is on Rte. 49, the Gold Rush Highway. Eastbound: When arriving in town, take Broad St. turnoff. Turn right, and then right again up the hill to the Exxon station. Take a hard left into Prospect St. Westbound: Take Coyote St. turnoff. Turn left down the hill, and left on Broad St., right on Sacramento; up the hill to the Exxon station and a hard left into Prospect.

THE GREY WHALE INN
Fort Bragg, California

Ever since the first edition of this book in 1966, I have visited inns that were formerly gristmills, poorhouses, majestic mansions, carriage houses, stagecoach taverns, farmhouses, and log cabins. However, the Grey Whale is the first inn that began life as a hospital!

"The inn was built in 1915," explained John Bailey who, with his wife Colette, acquired it in 1978. "It was the Redwood Coast Hospital before it was transformed into an inn in 1974."

John, Colette, and I were browsing through the thirteen guest rooms, eleven of which have private baths. Its early life as a hospital created a distinct advantage for the present-day inn guests, because the rooms are quite large, with many generous windows.

The Grey Whale features an unusual variety of textures and colors, ranging from the marvelous weather-beaten exterior boards to the brilliant colors of the interior carpeting and the wide selection of original contemporary paintings. The lodging rooms have comforters with matching pillow covers, bright decorator sheets, and one has a working fireplace.

Each contains a folder which describes all of the sights and attractions of Fort Bragg and the Mendocino Coast, including the redwood forest, art galleries, the Botanical Gardens, the beautiful Pacific Ocean beaches, the Skunk Railroad, and a brief summary of some of the restaurants. (The Grey Whale offers bed and breakfast.)

When we passed through the little second-floor kitchen, Colette explained that she bakes all the breads and coffee cakes that are served on the Continental breakfast. "These can be enjoyed right here, or the tray may be taken to the bedroom. Many guests like to eat breakfast in bed," she said.

Motorists passing through Fort Bragg on Highway #1 just can't miss the Grey Whale, because it stands at the north end of town surrounded by a large grass and turf area with some very colorful plantings of marguerite, California poppies, amaryllis, African daisies, and geraniums.

"Whale watching is one of our great pastimes," said John. "The whale watch starts in mid-December and from then on through March there are programs planned at various points along the coast."

It was from John that I learned of the many activities and attractions in this section of northern California. "We have theater, craft shows, scuba diving, fishing, hiking, and many museums," he reported. "We appeal to the art buff, the whale watcher, the beachcomber, and anyone who wants to have some unhurried hours away from pressures."

Whether the traveler is headed north or south south along the Mendocino Coast, or bent on staying a few days, the Grey Whale provides a unique country inn experience.

This is the first year The Grey Whale Inn has been included in *CIBR*.

THE GREY WHALE INN, 615 No. Main St., Fort Bragg, Ca. 95437; 707-964-0640. A 13-room inn located on Hwy. #1 at the north end of Fort Bragg. Continental breakfast included in room rates. (Only meal served.) Open every day in the year. Many natural, historic, and recreational attractions within a short distance. Available by Greyhound Bus and Skunk Train. Ocean swimming, scuba diving, fishing, and hiking nearby. John and Colette Bailey, Innkeepers.

Directions: From the south, follow Hwy. 101 to Cloverdale, take Rte. 128 west to Hwy. #1, and follow north to Fort Bragg. Alternate route: Exit Hwy. 101 at Willits, then west on Rte. 20 to Fort Bragg. Driving time from San Francisco: 4 hrs. Another alternate: Hwy. 1 along the coast. Driving time from San Francisco: 6 hrs.

BENBOW INN
Garberville, California

Because this book is revised, enlarged, and rewritten *every* year, it's possible for me to keep readers completely up-to-date on the progress and improvements being made at the inns.

The Benbow Inn is a case in point. For the benefit of our new readers, I first visited the Benbow Inn in 1973 and was immediately intrigued not only with its location in the glorious redwood country of northern California, but also with its design, which shows definite influences of the Art Deco of the early 1920s. There are also some touches of an English Tudor manor house found in the half-timbers, carved dark wood paneling, solid oak furniture, bookcases, hardwood floors, a truly massive fireplace in the main living room and handsome oriental rugs.

Eleanor Roosevelt visited there, Herbert Hoover fished the Eel River outside the door, and John Barrymore was an overnight guest.

Even in the short time that I've been acquainted with the Benbow, it has accumulated some latter-day history of its own. As I pointed out in the fourteenth edition (1979), Chuck, Patsy, and Muffin Watts, who had owned the Vagabond House in Carmel, California, exchanged inns in 1978 with Dennis Levitt, who had previously been the owner of the Benbow.

"Ever since day one," said Chuck Watts, during my visit there in September of 1979, "we have been very happy and have had a really

tremendous time. It's a continuing challenge and we've gotten a great deal accomplished, but I like the idea that the future is big with plans."

"We feel that we are a destination resort-inn, able to accommodate and provide amusement and diversion for all our guests of any age," chimed in Patsy. "We are designing a new wing and this will include a newer, warmer lounge area, a library, a projection room for films, and a banquet room for about eighty people.

"If all goes well, we would like this to be complete by about 1981, and wouldn't it be wonderful if all of the innkeepers from *Country Inns and Back Roads* could gather here for our big national meeting!"

(Patsy was referring to the fact that all of the innkeepers in *CIBR* have ample opportunity to meet at a large meeting which is held every fall. During my last visit to the Benbow, there was a regional meeting for *CIBR* innkeepers on the West Coast and we all had a wonderful time talking shop, strolling in the woods and along the Eel River, and enjoying some of the Benbow's delicious food.)

The Benbow is, indeed, a destination resort-inn—in addition to swimming, it now offers tennis on two new tennis courts, a good golf course within walking distance, hiking, and magnificent back-roading. By the way, it's very accessible by public transportation since the Route 101 buses stop almost at the front door.

A most impressive sight during the dinner hour is the main living room. In one quiet corner there is a chess set, the fireplace is burning with a display of beautiful candles on each side of the mantel. Over the fireplace is an oil painting of the inn, and in various corners are arrangements of big comfortable chairs and sofas inviting conversation, rest, and relaxation. Several clocks that are part of Chuck and Patsy's collection and pictures of some early settlers decorate the walls. A big jigsaw puzzle always has five or six people hovering. A honeymooning couple is looking at one of the big picture books that are scattered around on the library tables. This living room is big enough for two rooms, but the furniture is arranged in a way that makes it possible to be off in a corner by oneself.

Patsy, Chuck, and Muffin (their gorgeous Afghan hound, the most photographed canine in northern California) are having a wonderful time greeting guests, sharing their enthusiasm, and providing their own bubbling brand of warmth and hospitality. In short, they're model innkeepers. I'm glad they and the Benbow Inn found each other.

Benbow Inn has been included in *CIBR* since 1974.

BENBOW INN, 2675 Benbow Drive, Garberville, Ca. 95440; 707-923-2124. A 70-room English Tudor inn in the redwood country of northern California. On Rte. 101 near the Benbow State Park. European plan. Breakfast, lunch, and dinner served to travelers daily. Open March 15 to Dec. 1. Swimming, tennis on grounds; golf adjacent. Hiking, magnificent backroading, and tennis nearby. Chuck, Patsy, and Muffin Watts, Innkeepers.

Directions: From San Francisco follow Rte. 101 north 200 mi. and exit at Benbow.

HERITAGE HOUSE
Little River, California

"To Don and Hazel Dennen, the deans of northern California innkeeping!"

We all rose as one, glasses raised high, and Don Dennen, the innkeeper of Heritage House, modestly raised his hand acknowledging the well-deserved compliments from other innkeepers who had gathered here for a day of good conversation and exchange of ideas and a lovely dinner at this truly original inn on the spectacular northern California coast.

"It doesn't seem possible that it was 1949 when Hazel and I came through here, saw the location and remembered that the farmhouse was built in 1877 by my grandfather, John Dennen. We decided to open a quiet country inn. Actually the arrangements were made within an hour. In just a few months, we built the first guest cottages."

"Well, I'm certainly glad you did," said Jane Way of the Sutter Creek Inn. "I'm sure you remember the day I came up here and you encouraged me to open my inn over in the gold country."

Patricia Corcoran from nearby Harbor House in Elk, chimed in, "I don't think we could have made it if it hadn't been for Don and Hazel. They were tremendously encouraging."

Jim Smith from the Wine Country Inn in St. Helena said, "I know that my mother and father came here many times to talk to the Dennens about innkeeping. This is my first visit, but I've never seen anything quite like it."

That particular comment, "I've never seen anything quite like it," is typical of the compliments that I receive in great numbers from readers who visit Heritage House. Here's an excerpt from a lady who had been using *CIBR* to tour California: "We drove to Heritage House which is just a lovely dream. The chicken tarragon and corned beef with ginger glaze was incredible. We stayed in one of the little cottages you mentioned back in the 1971 edition, because it was on a point overlooking both the inlet and the ocean. We set our alarm so we would be sure to see the sunrise."

"Oh, I believe I remember them," said Hazel Dennen, her eyes lighting up with a nice smile. "They sent us a long letter and said they were going to write you."

The Heritage House is about a three-hour drive up the coast from San Francisco. Although there are a few guest rooms in the main building, most of the accommodations are in the cottages tucked unobtrusively into the landscape with an unobstructed view of the ocean. They have names inspired by early-day buildings of the area. For example, "Scott's Opera House" was the center of entertainment on the coast with traveling minstrel shows and, later, a hand-cranked moving picture operation. It was moved to its present location overlooking the ocean. Other cottages are named "Country Store," "Bonnet Shop," "Ice Cream Parlor," "Barber Pole," "Stable," and the like. Most of the furnishings have come from the area.

"We never advertise," said Don. "All of our guests come to us because some former guest has recommended us. Frankly, we like it that way, because the place attracts the kind of people we like and many of them have become warm friends. We keep our atmosphere informal and relaxed. We don't arrange any games or activities, because we feel our guests would prefer not to be regimented. There are numerous walks along the beaches and through the forest, and we can provide our guests with ample information about circle tours along the coast and into the great redwoods."

He smiled, pulled on his earlobe, then with a twinkle in his eye said, "I can honestly say, I have never known a guest to be bored."

Heritage House has been included in *CIBR* since 1971.

HERITAGE HOUSE, Little River, Ca. 95456; 707-937-5885. An elegant oceanside inn with 52 accommodations on Coast Highway #1, 144 mi. north of San Francisco, 6 mi. south of Mendocino. Modified American plan omits lunch. Breakfast and dinner served to travelers daily by reservation. Open from February through November. No pets. No credit cards. No amusements or special facilities for children. Don Dennen, Innkeeper.

Directions: From San Francisco (a 3-hr. drive); follow Rte. 101 to Cloverdale then Rte. 128 to Coast Highway #1. Inn is 5 mi. north of this junction on Hwy. #1.

HARBOR HOUSE
Elk, California

Patricia Corcoran, looking attractively svelte in a full-length flowered skirt and a harmonizing wine-colored top, poured me another glass of orange juice, and we continued our breakfast in the dining room of the Harbor House which has such a striking view of Greenwood landing, once a busy port for lumber schooners plying the Mendocino coast.

"We've discovered that many of our guests are coming in what used to be called the 'off season!' For one thing, the Pacific waves crashing on the rocks are very spectacular in January, February, and March. It never gets very cold. Another awesome sight is the whales

on their way south early in December until late February, when they go north again. We also have many sea otters."

The Harbor House was built in 1916 by a lumber company as an executive residence. The construction is entirely of redwood taken from nearby forests. Four of the five rooms of the inn have fireplaces and there are four additional cottages on the south side, all with private baths. The hand-carved and hand-fitted redwood ceiling and walls in the living room were coated with hot beeswax in 1916, which has preserved the quality and color of the wood for over sixty years.

From the front of the inn there is a winding path and steps which lead down the bluff to the caverns in the rocks along the seashore below. Patricia pointed out the Victorian benches that have now been added at intervals. Many guests welcome the opportunity to "sit a spell."

Guests enjoy ocean wading, abalone and shell hunting, fishing, hiking, biking, and some beautiful backroading along the coast and in the forest. There are also many opportunities to sit in front of the big living room fireplace for an evening of guitar-playing and poetry reading.

Patricia and I strolled around the outside of the inn and I admired the unusual number of brilliantly colored flowers, including fuchsia, old-fashioned geraniums, and nasturtiums. A source of great pride for Patricia is the rapidly growing kitchen garden where many of the menu items can be freshly picked every day.

Once again, I peeked into the room I had occupied on my previous trip, which has the four-poster bed, an old-fashioned cast iron stove, and a collection of watercolors. It has an unobstructed view of the massive rock formations with their tunnels which extend out into the blue Pacific.

Passing by the open kitchen window, I detected the intriguing aroma of freshly baked bread and rolls. "We have fresh broiled salmon on the menu most of the time." she said. "Also, unusual things like Iberian pork chops, and a unique Moroccan chicken. We make homemade soups like broccoli and mushroom, and two of the most popular desserts are mocha coffee pie and the Bavarian layered dessert."

Under Patricia Corcoran the Harbor House, which I first visited in 1976, has now earned a reputation as one of the most successful and sought-after inns in northern California. It is one of the rapidly growing number of inns with women innkeepers. I'm very proud of them all.

Harbor House has been included in *CIBR* since 1976.

HARBOR HOUSE BY THE SEA, Hwy. #1, Elk, Ca. 95432; 707-877-3203. An 8-room seaside inn, 16 mi. south of Mendocino, overlooking the Pacific. Modified American plan omits lunch. Breakfast and dinner to houseguests served daily. Open year-round. Ocean wading, abalone and shell hunting, fishing, and hiking on grounds. Biking, boating, deep sea fishing, golf, canoeing nearby. No credit cards. Patricia Corcoran, Innkeeper.

Directions: Take Rte. 128 from I-101 to Coast. Turn south on Hwy. #1, 6 mi. to Harbor House.

SUTTER CREEK INN
Sutter Creek, California

It was breakfast time at the Sutter Creek Inn. We were all sitting around the three harvest tables in the old-fashioned kitchen where everyone passes the platters of fresh eggs, miners' hash, and wonderful, light baking powder biscuits which taste so good with the homemade jam. The talk was about the gold country and how history seems so recent out here. Innkeeper Jane Way was telling us about an old native of the town with whom she had had a recent conversation.

"He could remember sitting around the dinner table when he was a child, and his father saying that the gold was running out. 'We would all hold hands,' he said, 'and pray that the gold would go on. The next day more gold would be found. We depended upon God to feed us.'"

Ever since 1967 when I opened the gate in the white picket fence and strode up the narrow walk of this New Hampshire inn in

northern California, I've been intrigued by gold rush country. On that first visit, Jane and I drove to many of the fascinating towns in the area including Jackson, Volcano, Murphy's Angels' Camp and Sonora—all names prominent in the living history of this area, which today still has tremendous deposits of gold underneath the verdant hills.

After breakfast, most of us decided to continue our conversation in the front parlor of the inn where bookshelves cover one wall. The titles include everything from late novels to bound copies of *American Heritage* magazines. The room is a glowing testament to Jane Way's eclectic interests. There are many plants, much comfortable furniture, and a large center table loaded with different kinds of magazines. I noted reproductions of Brueghel, Cezanne, Manet, Rubens, and El Greco. There's also a most handsome collection of pewter spoons, a corner cupboard with an arrangement of beautiful old glassware, an unusual chess set in one corner, and a cribbage set in the other. Some guests ask Jane to read their palms or teacups.

Jane's lifelong devotion to beauty and the arts continues in the highly individualistic designs and furnishings in the inn bedrooms. For example, my room was the Garden Cottage, one of several outbuildings that have been converted into guest rooms. It had a fireplace, a canopied bed, cathedral ceiling, windows with tinted glass, and its own porch with a vine-covered trellis. There were two comfortable chairs and a shelf with dozens of books right next to the bed.

The bathroom had reproductions of Flemish prints and a print of a typical New Hampshire house. A special feature in all the rooms is the decorator sheets and towels.

The only meal served at this inn is breakfast, which is really an experience. When the bell rings at nine o'clock everyone troops in for a hearty mother lode repast and, incidentally, there is no smoking in the dining room.

Because the inn is rather intimate in nature, children are not encouraged as guests. Reservations in advance are almost always necessary. There's a two-day minimum stay on weekends, whether Friday and Saturday or Saturday and Sunday.

"Once in a while," explained Jane, "we do have last minute cancellations."

For many of her guests, Jane Way and the Sutter Creek Inn are the "first" country inn experience. "People frequently ask me," she said, "about the essential qualities for successful country innkeeping.

"I reply that there are three things that are most important: First unlimited love for people."

Sutter Creek Inn has been in *CIBR* since 1968.

SUTTER CREEK INN, 75 Main St., Sutter Creek, Ca. 95685; 209-267-5606. A 16-room New England village inn on the main street of a historic mother lode town, 35 mi. from Sacramento. Lodgings include breakfast. No meals served to travelers. Closed all of January. No children under 10. No pets. Water skiing, riding, fishing, and boating nearby. Mrs. Jane Way, Innkeeper.

Directions: From Sacramento, travel on the Freeway (50) toward Placerville and exit at Power Inn Rd. Turn right and drive one block, note signs for Rte. 16 and Jackson. Turn left on Fulsom Rd., approximately ¼ mi., follow Rte. 16 signs to right for Jackson. Rte. 16 joins Rte. 49. Turn right to Sutter Creek. From San Francisco, follow Freeway (80) to Sacramento and take previous directions or drive via Stockton to Rte. 49.

THE WINE COUNTRY INN
St. Helena, California

The story of this inn is inspirational. It goes back a few years when Ned and Marge Smith visited me in Stockbridge, Massachusetts, and we talked about the ideals and objectives of innkeeping. They live in St. Helena, in the beautiful Napa Valley, where Ned is a prominent real estate broker. They were looking for the qualities that they most admired in country inns because they were interested in having an inn of their own. I was delighted that they stopped off to share some of their experiences with me.

After visiting about fifteen New England inns they returned to California and began to give form to their ideas. A perfect site was found and the Smith family, all of them, began to work on building their inn.

In June of 1975, I called them to say that I was planning to come to California in late August. "Wonderful," said Marge. "We'll be open by that time for certain." The day arrived and I drove down from Elk on the coast and approached St. Helena from the north on Rte. 128. At the outskirts of St. Helena, following directions, I turned down Lodi Lane and in about thirty seconds I saw a spanking new sign, "The Wine Country Inn."

After our reunion, we set off on a complete tour of every nook and cranny of the new inn. Ned explained that the building was carefully designed to fit the site which overlooks the upper part of the Napa valley in full view of Glass Mountain.

"We tried to arrange for every room to have a view, so some have intimate balconies and others have patios leading to the lawn. The natural wild mustard, lupin, poppies, and live oak trees have been blended with plantings of oleanders, petunias, and Chinese pistachios to accent the scenery."

Each room is individually decorated with country antique furnishings refinished and reconstructed by members of the family. Many of the rooms have fireplaces, canopied beds, tufted bed-spreads, and handmade quilts. There are no televisions or radios, but a generous supply of magazines and books and big, comfortable, fluffy pillows encourage the lost art of reading.

To top everything off, there is a generous Continental breakfast served every day with fresh California fruit and muffins or delicious caramel-pecan rolls served warm. When it comes to the evening meal the Smiths can make many helpful suggestions for they know every restaurant in the valley.

In 1979, ten new rooms were completed in two separate buildings, both built in the same style. They've all been handsomely landscaped with many flowers and bushes.

Marge and Ned's son Jim, about whom I wrote in the 1979 edition, has decided to make a career of innkeeping and has returned to college to get his degree in hotel and restaurant management at the City College in San Francisco.

Ned points out that the interest in fine wines seems to be growing steadily and that there are now over eighty wineries within ten miles of the inn. "Besides that," he says, "at least six new superb restaurants have opened in the Napa Valley in the past eighteen months, so this once sleepy little area has become an interesting gourmet's delight, with emphasis on good food, good wine, and good lodging. Would

you believe that even with all of these good things, Marge's nineteen quilts, made over the past seven years, are still the highlights of our little inn?"

The Wine Country Inn has been included in *CIBR* since 1976.

THE WINE COUNTRY INN, 1152 Lodi Lane, St. Helena, Ca. 94574; 707-963-7077. A newly built 25-room country inn in the Napa Wine Valley of California, about 70 mi. from San Francisco. Continental breakfast served to houseguests, no other meals served. Open daily except December 22-27. No children; no pets. This inn is within driving distance of a great many wineries and also the Robert Louis Stevenson Museum. Golf and tennis nearby. Ned and Marge Smith, Innkeepers.

Directions: From San Francisco take the Oakland Bay Bridge to Hwy. 80. Travel north to the Napa cutoff. Stay on Hwy. 29 through the town of St. Helena, go 1¾ mi. north to Lodi Lane, then turn east ¼ mi. to inn.

THE BED AND BREAKFAST INN
San Francisco, California

It was a wonderfully warm morning in mid-September. The sun shone down from a completely cloudless sky, and happy San Franciscans moved briskly up and down the many hills of the city pursuing the day's occupations—the kind of a day in which I knew everything would go right, and it did.

I had walked a few blocks on Union Street, then turned on

Charlton Court, and I was standing in front of one of San Francisco's Victorian houses, painted light green; wooden stairs ascended the front of the building to the very top floor. There were beautiful golden marigolds in boxes and pots placed around the porches, and a birdhouse with a very chipper occupant. The sign said, "The Bed and Breakfast Inn."

The reception room apparently was used as one of the breakfast areas. It had a very light and airy feeling, enhanced by white wicker furniture, many flower arrangements, and light touches everywhere. The enticing aroma of fresh coffee filled the room, and some guests were just finishing delicious-looking croissants.

There followed in delightful order my first meeting with Marily Kavanaugh and her husband, Bob; a tour of all of the eight rooms in the inn; a leisurely chat on the garden deck, and a wonderful realization that I had at last found my country inn in San Francisco!

First the lodging rooms: some of them are named after various parts of London. There's Covent Garden, Chelsea, Green Park, and Kensington Garden. Other rooms are called The Library, Autumn Sun, The Willows, Mandalay, and The Celebration. When I was there, Bob and Marily were moving out of their apartment on the top floor, which was soon to be available for guests.

Each room provides an entirely different experience. For example, many have completely different sets of sheets, pillowcases, and towels. There are all varieties of beds, from those with carved Victorian headboards to traditional shiny brass bedsteads. There are flowers everywhere, thermos jugs of ice-water, many books, baskets of fruit, an electric clock with an alarm, down pillows and gorgeous coverlets and spreads. Three of the bedrooms have their own bathrooms, and the others share. Three rooms have the garden view. I saw old-fashioned British ceiling fans in some of the rooms. "They're hard to find outside of Bombay," said Marily.

The location of the Bed and Breakfast is another virtue. Charlton Court is a little dead end street off Union, between Buchanan and Laguna. It's within easy walking distance of Fisherman's Wharf. In fact, San Francisco is such a "walking place" that it's convenient to everything. The nicest part of it is that when people get tired of walking, they can always take the cable cars!

Marily and Bob are very proud and happy to be located in San Francisco, and they take great pleasure in providing guests with information about all of the things to do and restaurants to visit. However, one of their guests had this word of admonition for me: "You'd better warn your readers to reserve a room here as far ahead as possible."

The Bed and Breakfast Inn has been included in *CIBR* since 1979.

THE BED AND BREAKFAST INN, Four Charlton Court, San Francisco, Ca. 94123; 415-921-9784. A 9-room European-style pension in downtown San Francisco. Convenient to all of the Bay area recreational, cultural, and gustatory attractions. Continental breakfast is the only meal offered. Open daily except late December and early January. Not comfortable for small children. No pets. No credit cards. Robert and Marily Kavanaugh, Innkeepers.

Directions: Take the Van Ness Exit from route 101 and proceed to Union Street. Turn left on Laguna. Charlton Court is a small courtyard street halfway between Laguna and Buchanan, off Union.

VAGABOND HOUSE
Carmel, California

Once again, I was at the corner of Fourth and Dolores Street in Carmel. I smiled, remembering back to 1975 and my first visit to the Vagabond House. On that occasion, I stood for at least a full minute thinking that I had come to the wrong place. There was no indication of an inn being anywhere in this verdant residential area.

I walked up the stone steps and entered an atmosphere that seemed almost magical. It was a three-sided courtyard enhanced by many trees, including mock orange, magnolia, and live oak. There were camellias, primroses, tulips, and daffodils in great profusion, along with impatiens, rhododendrons, fuchsias, and many other varieties of flowers.

There have been a few changes in this hideaway inn since 1975. There are still twelve lodging areas, many with woodburning fireplaces, lining the three sides of the courtyard-square, but as I pointed out in the 1979 edition, the *dramatis-personae* has changed.

One of the principal new characters now appeared on the scene — Festus, a canine of some undefinable background, but with a proclivity for friendliness. I swear he almost spoke to me.

I sat down and he put his head on my knee; then we were joined by two new members, Siamese cats whom I later learned were called Suki and Fibi.

"Oh, I see that the cats have discovered you already." This was Julie Brown, my dear friend, whom I first met at the Benbow Inn in northern California a few years ago. Through an interesting switch, she and Dennis Levett are now the owners of the Vagabond House, and Chuck, Patsy, and Muffin Watts, the previous proprietors of the Vagabond House, are now owners of the Benbow Inn!

Julie extricated me from the well-meaning attentions of the animal crew and drew me through the entrance of what she proudly announced was the new lobby of the inn. A small fire burned at one end, and two guests were seated in very comfortable chairs musing over several of the menus from restaurants in Carmel, Monterey, and Pacific Grove.

"This has been a wonderful change," she said, "making this living room into an area for all of our guests to meet, and Dennis has hung his large collection of hunt and coach scenes. With the assistance of Bruce, I have added a new flower garden in the rear, and we have two new flower gardens in the front, and a new one across the street next to the parking lot. Dennis says we're beginning to look like *Green Mansions*. He swears he saw Johnny Weissmuller and Chita eating bananas on the limb of one of our trees the other day."

At this point Dennis came bounding up the steps and there was another gladsome reunion. Julie excused herself to greet some new guests and Denny picked up where she left off. To my obvious question about the change of scene from the Benbow in northern California to the totally different atmosphere of Carmel, he replied: "It's terrific here. Of course, a part of me will always be with Chuck and Patsy at the Benbow, but both Julie and I love keeping this smaller inn. I'll be here for life."

We made plans to have dinner with Joan and Jeff Stanford from the Rosita Lodge, and decided to take a stroll on Ocean Avenue just to look at the shops. "Although there's always something to be done here," he said as we moved down Fourth Street, "the person who keeps all of this running so smoothly and so beautifully is Julie. She just loves the guests, and they love her."

VAGABOND HOUSE, Fourth & Dolores Streets, P.O. Box 2747, Carmel, Ca. 93921; 408-624-7738 or 408-624-7403. A 12-room village inn serving Continental breakfasts to houseguests only. No other meals served. Open every day of the year. Not ideal for children. Attended, leashed pets allowed. Bike renting, golf, natural beauty nearby, enchanting shops. Dennis Levett, Jewell Brown, Innkeepers.

Directions: Turn off Hwy. 1 onto Ocean Avenue; turn right from Ocean Avenue onto Dolores, continue 2½ blocks. Parking provided for guests.

THE ROSITA LODGE
Carmel-by-the-Sea, California

"I absolutely don't believe it," Joan Stanford laughed gaily as she hung up the telephone. "Can you imagine, you're sitting right here, and the woman on the telephone wanted to know if this was the inn with the black cat and the dog with the Canadian name! It looks as if some of our guests forget us, but remember our pets!"

It was good to be back talking with the Stanfords in Carmel once again. It had been about a year since we first met, and meanwhile I had included their story in *CIBR, 1979*. "Oh, we've had a lovely year," exclaimed Jeff. "Quite a few people have come from your book and of those, there's been a considerable percentage from the East Coast. A surprising number have come in January and February which is a pleasant time to be here in Carmel, without the crowds.

"We feel that Rosita Lodge is most typically Californian," said Jeff. "We have many plants in the rooms, and as you can see, the low, ranch-style buildings with the shake roofs are traditional California architecture. We've furnished the lodging rooms with antique pine furniture and paintings and serigraphs by local artists."

"This has been a very busy year," said Joan. "The major undertaking was the installation of five additional fireplaces, so that now every room has one and we no longer have to disappoint our guests. They are all woodburning and we supply lots of oak firewood. While we were doing it, there were a lot of other things that happened too, such as new paneling and tiling. It was fun to change the pictures, the furniture, and the plants."

"My grandmother visited us last winter," Jeff said. "It was a real working holiday for her because she sewed new curtains for all the rooms, which she does professionally—at age 86! It certainly makes a marvelous difference in the rooms."

Joan picked up where he left off: "We've replaced bedspreads with comforters, shams, and dust ruffles, and we have been very busy wallpapering the kitchens and baths, and searching out good prints and having them framed. The most recent acquistions are humorous golf cartoons produced originally for Perrier, the French sparkling water company."

Meanwhile, Toronto, the Labrador, joined us on the deck in a corner of the garden where we were literally surrounded by fuchsia, begonias, bougainvillaea, jasmine, cyclamen, azaleas, camellias, and rhododendrons. Several strategically placed bird feeders provided treats for many different humming birds and an occasional finch darted from branch to branch. This floral-paradise feeling was enhanced by a trellis-covered brick walkway between the lodging rooms.

The Rosita Lodge is at Fourth and Torres in Carmel which, as I recall, is right across the street from the police station. There is a carved sign in front with gold letters that say, "The Rosita Lodge, Private Garden Patios, Kitchens, Fireplaces." There was an addenda to the sign the day I was there that said: "Sorry, No Vacancy."

Lodgings are in generously sized rooms some of which have their own private patios and six of them also have fully equipped kitchens so that guests can prepare their own meals if they desire. "I think this is one of the reasons why returning guests book longer stays." said Joan. "We provide tasty Continental breakfasts, including hot Danish rolls, and orange juice, if they prefer."

Conversation is one of the big pluses at the Rosita. Both Joan and Jeff seem to have things under control and appear to be able to spend lots of time talking with their guests about everything from Aardvarks to Zanzibar. Their intellectual curiousity is reflected by the hundreds of books and magazines I found everywhere, including copies of the *National Geographic.* "We feel that no room *anywhere* should be without a *National Geographic.*"

The Rosita Lodge was first included in *CIBR* in 1979.

THE ROSITA LODGE, P.O. Box 2077, 4th and Torres, Carmel-by-the-Sea, Ca. 93921; 408-624-6926. A 9-room bed-and-breakfast inn within a two-minute walk of the shops, galleries, and restaurants of Carmel. European plan includes Continental breakfast served to inn guests only. No other meals served. Open year-round. Please check in advance for the regulations on pets. Tennis, golf, fishing, swimming, and all the Monterey peninsula recreational delights are nearby. Jeff and Joan Stanford, Innkeepers.

Directions: Turn off U.S. Rte. 1 at Ocean Ave. and proceed west to Junipero. Turn right and continue three blocks to 4th Ave. Turn right to Rosita Lodge.

OJAI VALLEY INN
Ojai, California

It was early March in Ojai, which is springtime in southern California. The robins were nesting in the oak trees. The plantings on the patio of the Ojai Valley Inn were in early bloom, and the golf course and tennis courts were in readiness. The putting green had already been swept free of the dew, and the air was so clear and dry I felt as though I could drive every green or ace every serve.

The native Indians named this sunny valley, which is pronounced "o-hi." It means "the nest." It is most aptly named, for it sits in the center of a vast amphitheater of towering mountains. These mountains create an ideal climate year-round, and I understand that the average summer temperature is between 70 and 90 degrees. Winter daytime temperatures range from 60 to 85 degrees. There is no fog or smog or dampness because everything is 1000 feet up in the dry, invigorating air. The days are warm and brilliant with sunshine and the nights are cool. I've slept under a blanket even after the warmest days.

This inn is one of the very few American resorts where guests can enjoy the four major outdoor playtime activities — golf, tennis, riding, and swimming throughout the year.

The championship golf course, designed by Billy Bell, is 6,800 yards. "Tricky, but fair" is one description. There's a heated swimming pool with cabanas and terraces for sun bathing, and luncheon and refreshments are served at poolside. There are hundreds of miles of riding trails in the mountains, valleys, and canyons surrounding Ojai. Horses are available at the inn stable. The tennis pro is always glad to arrange games, and I've already made quite a few tennis friends among the regular residents of this attractive town.

One other important feature that delights me at this inn is the playground for children and other possibilities for their having fun; and babysitters can be arranged.

The architecture of Ojai Valley Inn is in Spanish mission style. It is surrounded by beautiful oaks, evergreens, eucalyptus and an occasional palm tree. There are more varieties of birds than I could possibly count.

Innkeeper Bill Briggs, a Massachusetts native who has been here at the inn for many, many years explained that because of its many sporting and recreational facilities, the inn is now quite popular for business meetings and small conventions.

The Ojai Valley Inn is somewhat larger than the average inn listed in *CIBR*. I first visited in the late 1960s, and on each visit since I have found it to be a very pleasurable resort experience, where there are certain obvious dress requirements such as gentlemen wearing jackets and ties for dinner. However, there is no attempt "to put on airs." It's the most natural thing in the world to dress for dinner here and ladies wearing long gowns like the party feeling.

Golfers were already getting ready for the morning round. As two of them passed on their way to the first tee, I heard one say, "Do you realize that we're only an hour and a half from L.A.?"

Ojai Valley Inn has been included in *CIBR* since 1970.

OJAI VALLEY INN & COUNTRY CLUB, Ojai, Ca. 93023; 805-646-5511. A 100-room resort-inn with its own championship golf course, 12 mi. northeast of Ventura on U.S. 33. American plan. Breakfast, lunch, and dinner served to travelers daily. Open year-round. No pets. Tennis, riding, heated pool, golf, and bicycles on the grounds. Bill Briggs, Innkeeper.

Directions: From the Ventura Freeway, exit at Hwy. 33.

THE INN
Rancho Santa Fe, California

The town of Rancho Santa Fe, California, is one of the most attractively designed that I have ever visited. It has been well-described as a "civilized planned community." The homes and estates have been created in perfect harmony with nature's generous endowment of climate and scenery. One of the dominating factors is the presence of the gigantic eucalyptus trees.

Innkeeper Dan Royce told me the story. "It's hard to imagine this place without these great trees, but back in 1906 it was nothing but an area of sand and occasional low trees and brush. At that time the Santa Fe Railroad purchased the land for the purpose of growing eucalyptus trees for railroad ties. About three million seedlings were planted, but the project failed when it was discovered that the wood was not suitable. Fortunately, the trees were left to flourish and today we have glorious shade and beauty. They provide homes for literally thousands of birds.

"The first building of The Inn was constructed in 1923 and is now a part of the main building of today's Inn. Beginning in 1941 it was expanded into a quiet resort where guests could enjoy the truly beautiful surroundings.

"In 1958, my father Steve acquired the property, and it's been a family operation ever since."

At this mention of Steve Royce, who was dean of southern California hotelmen for many years, I was reminded of my first visit to Rancho Santa Fe.

Steve had given me the pleasure of a tour of the entire community with its beautiful homes and orange groves. When I mentioned it to Danny, he smiled and said, "Yes, my father certainly made a great contribution to innkeeping. One thing I learned from him that will never leave me is to make a point of meeting personally every guest in The Inn during his or her stay. I think in the true definition of the word, dad was a real innkeeper."

Although Dan may not be able to greet every newly-arrived guest, the chances are that Peggy Beatty, who has been associated with the Royce family for many years, will be on hand to extend best wishes for an enjoyable stay. Peggy has an incredible memory for names that is possibly unmatched by anyone I've ever met in the innkeeping business. "She certainly amazes me," said Dan.

This "family" feeling is extended even further when guests learn that the stunning framed needlepoints very much in evidence through the main lobby and living rooms of The Inn, have been done by Danny's mother. For example, there is one very large, extremely handsome piece showing a large eucalyptus tree. It has become the symbol of The Inn and is found on all of the stationery used. My favorite is a needlepoint clock located on one wall of the cathedral-ceilinged living room.

Cottages are scattered among the towering trees, and there's recreation for everyone here, including the younger set. The Inn has membership in nearby private 18-hole golf courses, and there are three tennis courts and a putting green on the grounds. The swimming pool has an outdoor terrace where luncheons and refreshments are available. Also, The Inn has a beach cottage at nearby Del Mar for use during the summer months.

Part of the pleasure of staying at The Inn is the opportunity to

visit the shops in the village. They are all designed to be attractive, but unobtrusive. I stood in front of one building for three minutes without realizing that it was a supermarket!

All of this is happening today at Rancho Santa Fe because eucalyptus trees could not be used for railroad ties!

The Inn at Rancho Santa Fe has been included in *CIBR* since 1973.

THE INN, Rancho Santa Fe, Ca. 92067; 714-756-1131. A 75-room resort-inn, 27 mi. north of San Diego Freeway #5, 5 mi. inland from Solana Beach, Del Mar. European plan. Breakfast, lunch, and dinner served to travelers daily. Open year-round. Pool, tennis, putting green, and bicycles on grounds. Golf and ocean nearby. Airport transportation provided. Daniel Royce, Innkeeper.

Directions: From I-5, take Exit S8 and drive inland about 6 mi.

Washington

THE CAPTAIN WHIDBEY INN
Coupeville, Washington

Let's go back in time a little to 1972, and my first visit to the Captain Whidbey; in fact, my first trip to the Northwest. I've been there several times since.

I remember walking through the big front door of this inn which is on the shores of Penn Cove, and there, greeting me in broad New England accents, stood innkeeper Steve Stone, complete with tweeds, white hair, and a corncob pipe. Steve, a Nantucket Island

man, was the last thing I expected to see here in Coupeville, Washington, 3,000 miles away from the "grey lady of the sea."

I had seen a postcard of the Captain Whidbey which showed its rustic exterior, but I was completely surprised at the extensive collection of antiques, bric-a-brac, original oil paintings, pewter, silver, ship models, spinning wheels, books, and memorabilia which greeted me inside.

I had lunch in the Chart Room that day, and although it was a busy Saturday, Steve and Shirlie were both able to join me. It wasn't long before we found we had several friends in common, including David Wood, another Nantucketer, who is the curator of the Norman Rockwell museum in Stockbridge.

It was on that occasion that I had my first taste of the world-renowned Dungeness crab, the specialty of the inn, which was baked in its shell with butter and herbs. Since that time I've enjoyed almost all of the menu choices from filet mignon, to grilled halibut steak, and salmon.

Steve and Shirlie had explained that Coupeville is one of the oldest towns in Washington, and that the inn was built in 1907 of madrona logs, which are found in quantities on Whidbey Island. It's been a family inn for most of the past sixty years and has had surprisingly few innkeepers. I took a tour of the lodging rooms, and on the second floor, the first things that greeted me were a huge wall of books, an old spinning wheel, a marble-top music cabinet, and a long hall filled with all kinds of pieces to delight collectors. Most of these things came from the Stones' own collection.

Then, as now, some of the lodging rooms in the main house of the inn share a common gentlemen's and ladies' room which includes bath facilities. However, since my first visit, other rustic buildings have been built overlooking the lagoon—all of these have private baths.

The terrace facing the cove is highlighted with plantings of holly, Oregon grape, fir trees, Indian paintbrush, Scotch broom, English ivy, junipers, and fig trees.

The natural center of the inn is the living room with a very big fireplace made out of round stones. Here, everybody—houseguests and dinner guests alike—sit around talking and leafing through the dozens of various magazines. There's a fire almost every evening because, as Steve told me that first time, "It really draws people together."

That was many visits ago. Since then I have been a yearly visitor to this bit of New England on Puget Sound. Few things have changed, but there is one notable exception. Steve and Shirley's son John, who was a student at Western Washington State College when I first met him, has become the manager of the inn and furthermore, was married in the fall of 1978 to Mendy, a very pretty young lady whom I had the pleasure of meeting at our innkeepers' conference at Annapolis, Maryland, in November.

Now there is a new grandson, Andrew Grant Stone.

As we see, the Captain Whidbey family is growing.

THE CAPTAIN WHIDBEY INN, Rte. 1, Box 32, Coupeville, Wash. 98239; 206-678-4097. A 25-room country inn, 50 mi. north of Seattle, 3 mi. north of Coupeville. European plan. 4 cottages with private bath; 12 rooms with private bath. Breakfast, lunch, and dinner served daily to travelers. Open year-round. Pets allowed in cottages only. Boating and fishing on grounds. Golf nearby. Steve, Shirlie, and John Stone, Innkeepers.

Directions: Whidbey Island is reached year-round from the south by the Columbia Beach-Mukilteo Ferry, and during the summer and on weekends by the Port Townsend-Keystone Ferry. From the north (Vancouver, B.C. and Bellingham), take the Deception Pass Bridge to Whidbey Island.

JAMES HOUSE
Port Townsend, Washington

"You can't stay here without talking to someone before breakfast." Barbara Bogart was busy setting the breakfast table, toasting toast, and putting out pots of jam, while at the same time introducing guests in the wonderful, old-fashioned kitchen in The James House, where we were all gathered for breakfast.

The James House is a Queen Anne mansion built in 1891 overlooking Port Townsend Bay with the Cascade Mountains to the east, and the Olympic Mountains to the west. There's no television. Only the ticking of the old clock, the sound of the wind, and the whistle of the ferris disturb the peace and quiet. There are ten immaculate lodging rooms, each with its own color scheme, genuine antique furnishings and personality. Best of all it has plenty of books.

"Without so-called modern diversions," said Barbara, "guests can do what their ancestors did, use their imagination. I grew up in a front porch society. We touched each other both physically and emotionally, and I think that's what people miss now, and so that's what we are trying to bring back here at The James House."

In autumn 1979, the exterior of the handsome building was restored, and Barbara said that she could hardly wait for the job to be finished and the workmen to go home. "The house is far more beautiful than I ever imagined," she continued. "This restoration has been Lowell's dream for some time. It's really been very exciting. We've ended up doing a complete restoration and removed the dark lower shingles which were put on over the original horizontal siding in the 1930s. The original shingles have been painted, and the badly weathered ones in front, replaced.

"The entire house is much more pleasing to the eye now. Incidentally, the removal of these lower shingles revealed a doorway off the back of the house which we are going to replace.

"The most exciting thing that has happened to us is the arrival of our oldest daughter Marty to be our third innkeeper. Jennifer is still here, but is much more involved in high school activities than in innkeeping, Port Townsend is a wonderful place for children to grow up in."

First-time visitors to Port Townsend are quite surprised to find that this town has a very unusual history of its own. It was once slated to be the greatest seaport on the West Coast, only to have its dreams come to naught because Seattle replaced it as the railroad terminal. At the turn of the century, many very impressive Victorian mansions were built to house the consulates of many countries. Fortunately, these well-preserved beauties are still in use today and enhance Port Townsend considerably.

The Bogart family moved to this part of the world from their farm in Oklahoma, and they are having a wonderful time, not only restoring this lovely old house, but also providing a warm, beautiful haven for guests, including quite a few honeymooners.

"Oh yes," said Barbara, "We're quite popular with guests who are celebrating birthdays, anniversaries, marriages, divorces, or what-have-you. On one evening last June we had seven newlyweds staying here at the same time."

The James House has been included in *CIBR* since 1976.

JAMES HOUSE, 1238 Washington St., Port Townsend, Wash. 98368; 206-385-1238. A 10-room village inn, 50 mi. from Seattle on the Olympic Peninsula. Some rooms with shared baths. European plan with sit-down breakfast served to houseguests. No other meals served. Open year-round. No children under 12; no pets. State parks and beaches nearby. Lowell and Barbara Bogart, Innkeepers.

Directions: See Farmhouse.

THE FARMHOUSE
Port Townsend, Washington

My life is considerably enriched, not only for my visits to Dorothy and John Ashby Conway at their restaurant located on the Straits of Juan de Fuca in Port Townsend, but for the lively and entertaining correspondence I have enjoyed with them over the years. Fortunately, their yearly newsletter (available on request) also has flashes of John's literary *hors d'oeuvres* which are sometimes as spicy as his Greek and Hungarian dishes.

Here is one amusing tidbit from a letter I must share with you: "A Canadian couple told us that they had recommended The Farmhouse to a friend who was coming to the area for her honeymoon. After a suitable interval, they called to see how she had

enjoyed it. 'Enjoyed it! It was the highlight of my honeymoon!'"
John commented that this reminded him of Oscar Wilde's great line
to the effect that "Niagara Falls must certainly be the second greatest
disappointment to American brides."

The Farmhouse is a genuinely gourmet restaurant, and John
and Dorothy have a couple of ground rules which I would like to
explain: There is one set menu each month, and reservations are
imperative. (I hope that all of our readers will telephone in advance.)
Please do not "drop in" on The Farmhouse. The trip from Seattle is
somewhat different now that the bridge has been destroyed, and it
might be convenient to reserve rooms overnight at the nearby James
House.

Here are the monthly specialties for 1980: February - Mandarin
food from North China; March - a German menu; April - classic
Greek food; May - curry and sambales from northern India.

In June, July, and August, there's a summer schedule for
Thursday, Friday, Saturday, and Sunday. Thursday's entrée is
marinated leg of lamb; Friday's is seafood; Saturday's is usually roast
beef; and Sunday the entrée is fowl served in a Persian style with
pomegranate syrup from Damascus.

September, the inn is open weekends, including Friday, with an
Italian menu. In October, it's Hungarian; November is classic
Japanese, and the inn is closed in December and January.

I was pleased when The Farmhouse received the prestigious
Travel-Holiday award. They were the fourth recipients in the five
northwestern states. John says it's the equivalent of the "Ph.D." in
the restaurant business.

Remember: one menu at a time, limited seating means reservations in advance, and *please* telephone if your plans change. Guests

are asked not to bring young children. The food is too sophisticated for them, and as John says, "an unhappy or unruly child can discommode an entire dining room." Short shorts are out, but campers are invited, and it is suggested that they wear their best camping clothes.

The Farmhouse has been included in *CIBR* since 1973.

THE FARMHOUSE, North Beach, Port Townsend, Wash. 98368; 206-385-1411. A unique gourmet country restaurant, 50 mi. from Seattle. Meals by reservation only. Dinner served Thursdays through Sundays in June, July, and August; dinner served Fridays, Saturdays, and Sundays from September through May. Closed months of December and January. Dorothy and John Ashby Conway, Innkeepers.

Directions: The Hood Canal Floating Bridge between Kitsap and the Olympic Peninsula was partially destroyed during a windstorm February 13, 1979. To compensate for the loss of the bridge, a new temporary ferry route has been established between Edmonds and Port Townsend. Edmonds is approximately 15 mi. north of Seattle. Take Exit 177 from I-5 to Edmonds. Allow 30 min. driving time from Seattle. Crossing time to Port Townsend is 9 min. Motorists southbound on I-5 may turn off at Burlington and take Hwy. 20 to the Olympic Peninsula via Whidbey Island and the Keystone-Port Townsend Ferry. Driving distance from I-5 to Keystone, 47 mi. Crossing time 30 min.

LAKE QUINAULT LODGE
Quinault, Washington

"A rain forest?" I asked. "I always associated the term with the Amazon River." Marge Lesley smiled and said, "Even though we're within a very short distance of snowcapped mountains, here in the Quinault rain forest, the temperature runs between forty and seventy degrees year around and we have an annual rainfall of between one-hundred-ten and one-hundred-sixty inches. These conditions produce the ideal growing environment of a greenhouse and there's a wide variety of plants from three-hundred-foot, centuries-old Douglas firs, to tiny mosses and delicate ferns."

Marge and I were driving up Route 101 which leads from Aberdeen to Port Angeles on the extreme western coast of Washington. Great stretches of the road are cut between avenues of majestic trees, and it reminded me of northern California and the redwood country.

We were going to visit Marge and Larry Lesley's Kalaloch Lodge, which overlooks the beautiful Pacific Ocean in the Olympic National Park.

"The two places are quite different," she said. "The Lake Quinault Lodge overlooks the placid waters of the lake and is surrounded by mountains with great fir forests. Our guests spend the days walking or driving in the woods.

"Kalaloch, on the other hand, is by the ocean and there people enjoy beachcombing, clamming, and fishing. At Kalaloch, we have hotel, motel, and cabin accommodations, whereas at the Lake Quinault Lodge, it's more like a traditional country inn."

I nodded in agreement remembering that late the previous afternoon I had walked through the big front door of the Lodge into a most welcome living room with a fire crackling in the fireplace. There was a fresh supply of wood stacked up on either side of the massive chimney. On one side, great glass doors provided a view of the spacious lawns of the Lodge which lead down to the lake. I could see some children playing croquet.

There was a chess game going on in front of the fireplace, and other guests were reading magazines and taking a few moments of respite after what I presume was a busy, pleasant day in the forests.

Fran Still, at the reception desk, gave me a warm greeting and assured me that I had time for a quick swim in the indoor pool before dinner. "Marge and Larry will join you a little later on," she said. "They're all excited about going over to Europe again this year as representatives of the State of Washington Committee on Tourism."

She pointed out that the Lesleys have been adding considerably to their collection of Indian objects, including wall hangings, rugs, and similar crafts. "We're all very proud of the Indian heritage of this section, and the Lesleys have really gone out of their way to preserve as many as possible of the old things and the old ways."

Most of the bedrooms at the Lodge are very colorful and comfortable, ranging from rustic to modern. Many have individual fireplaces, Tiffany-style lamps, and panoramic views of the lakes and the mountains.

One thing that always impresses me about this place is the number of ways devoted to keeping children happily occupied. Besides some lakeside playground equipment such as swings and slides, there is a fully equipped game room in the basement with all kinds of electronic games and pinball machines, Ping-Pong, and billiards.

Naturally, one of the things that keeps all guests occupied for part of every day is eating. Marge spoke at length on this subject: "We're primarily known for seafood and steak. Our principal seafood dish is lobster. Everybody loves the salmon, too — either poached or grilled — which is caught fresh nearby."

By this time we were within sight of Kalaloch Lodge, and I could see the numerous oceanside cabins. There was a grocery store, gasoline station, and restaurant. Rollers from the Pacific were majestically parading in, and I couldn't help but remark to Marge that, indeed, it was quite different from the Lake Quinault Lodge.

Lake Quinault Lodge has been included in *CIBR* since 1976.

LAKE QUINAULT LODGE, Southshore Rd., Quinault, Wash. 98575; 206-288-2571. A 55-room resort-inn in the Olympic National Forest of the State of Washington, about 40 mi. from Aberdeen. European plan. Breakfast, lunch, and dinner served daily to travelers. Open every day of the year. Fee for pets; must be attended. Indoor swimming pool, chipping green on grounds. Hiking, mountain climbing, fishing, nature walks nearby. Marge and Larry Lesley, Innkeepers.

Directions: Use Quinault exit from Rte. 101. Proceed 2 mi. on south shore of Lake Quinault to inn.

PARTRIDGE INN
Underwood, Washington

The most exciting thing that happened at the Partridge Inn in 1979 was the publication in the October *McCall's* magazine of Nora McNabb's article on how she found a career after retirement. It tells the story of the Partridge Inn, and how Nora met the problem of the many changes in her lifestyle during recent years.

I imagine that there will be other writing efforts from Nora in the years to come if this excerpt from a letter to me is any example: "I love innkeeping. Occasionally, on a very busy Sunday afternoon when I have a moment to stand unobtrusively and survey the dining room, I'm filled with so much joy with what I see and am able to provide. In one corner is a couple who dine out once a month. At the table next to them might be a minister and his wife relaxing after their busy morning. In the far corner, a group of ladies, longtime friends, plus a newcomer, chatting happily after their church service.

"At the big table, there's a family group celebrating the mother's seventieth birthday. Nearby is a middle-aged couple treating their mother to a dinner away from the nursing home. She has so much reminiscing to do she forgets to eat.

"Now I see the 'full-of-life-and-love' young couple who came in from a hike. Some are from many miles away and some are from closeby.

"For all of these people I am able to provide good food and a pleasant, scenic atmosphere, with all the warm homemade bread and pear butter they want.

"For desserts, I surprise them with such pies as Dutch apple, lemon crunch, or maple nut, as well as banana cream and chocolate."

The Partridge Inn is a modest restaurant with two unassuming lodging rooms available for overnight guests. From Nora's front lawn a view to the south and east is up the glistening Columbia River to Hood River, Oregon, and well beyond to the hills near The Dalles, Oregon. There are also spectacular views of Mount Hood and the Hood River Valley from vantage points nearby.

Friday night is barbeque night at the Partridge Inn, and the menu might include partridges and sirloin steaks, among others. The smoked flavor from the pearwood is most tantalizing. The barbecue is set up right outside the window, so guests can watch their dinner cooking from their tables, or as they wander about the grounds. Other specialties of the Partridge Inn are Swiss steak, homemade tamales, seafood thermador, Underwood Mountain meat loaf, and usually, roast beef and roast pork with bread dressing.

"Many of our dinner guests come from Vancouver and Portland, but people from other parts of the country are usually very much surprised at the number of attractions in our area," explains Nora. "Here at Underwood, we have the unique nine-mile-long lumber flume that speeds rough-cut lumber down the mountain to be finished. It crosses over the highway at several points. Our little towns of Bingham and White Salmon resemble German towns along the Rhine River. Many of our guests come to visit the Dalles Dam with the fish ladders which allow migrating fish to continue their accustomed journey from the upper rivers to the sea, and back again.

"When I look out the back window on a warm sunny afternoon and see our guests enjoying themselves and visiting with other guests,

for this kind of life I say, 'Thank you.'"

Partridge Inn has been included in *CIBR* since 1978.

THE PARTRIDGE INN, Box 100, Underwood, Washington 98651; 509-493-2381. A country restaurant with two lodging rooms located 60 miles east of Portland, Oregon, or Vancouver, Washington. Restaurant open for dinner Wednesdays through Saturdays at 5 p.m.; Sundays and holidays at noon. Breakfast served to houseguests only. Hiking trails and camping nearby. Free huckleberry-picking in season. Pears and apples for sale most of the year. No credit cards. Nora McNab, Innkeeper.

Directions: On Washington Highway 14, 60 miles east of Ft. Vancouver turn left on to Cook-Underwood Road at the confluence of the Columbia and White Salmon Rivers. (This road has 2 ends, do not turn off at Cook.) Follow yellow line up the hill for 2 miles. When the Columbia River is on the left begin to look for inn sign on the right. Coming from the Oregon side along Interstate 80N, 60 miles east of Portland cross the interstate bridge at the town of Hood River. Turn left and drive 2 miles to Cook-Underwood Road directly after crossing the White Salmon River. Follow directions up the hill as above. From coastal region take any highway leading to Portland, Oregon, then pick up 80N going east.

British Columbia

OAK BAY BEACH HOTEL
Victoria, British Columbia

My host, during my first visit at the Oak Bay Beach Hotel in Victoria, was Kevin Walker who, at the age of 21, has already had eight years' experience in the inn business. "I think it's wonderful," he

said. "I just can't imagine being involved in anything else. I have worked in almost every department, but I guess because my father is the owner, I've had to work that much harder."

Kevin and I were enjoying high tea in the beamed, low-ceilinged living room overlooking the Straits of Juan de Fuca. A fire crackled in the fireplace.

"We're the only seaside hotel in the area," he said. "Very often we can see killer whales, seals, and salmon. In fact, we have our own friendly neighborhood sea serpent who is a part of Indian legend and mythology.

"Right in front of us are the Straits of Haro with the United States-Canadian border running right at mid-channel." He pointed toward a small island, "That is Discovery Island named for Captain Vancouver's ship, and those are the San Juan Islands across the Strait. Mount Baker is to the east and it's more than 10,000 feet high. You ought to see it when the sun catches the snow-clad peaks and glaciers in the early morning or evening. We are a combination of water and mountains."

Even while we were watching, a cruise ship glided through the Straits, disdainfully ignoring a stubby tugboat towing one of British Columbia's most abundant resources: logs.

"We have a front seat for the annual Swiftsure race," he remarked. "Boats come from all parts of the world."

Kevin and I had just finished a tour of the hotel lodgings. Each room has a character of its own. For example, there's a group on the

third floor with names like "Georgian Suite" and "Samuel Pepys" room. "These accommodations are inspired by English history and literature," he explained. "In fact, most of the antique furnishings were acquired in England."
Still another very handsome room was called "Prince Albert." One suite overlooked the Oak Bay Marina.
"English" is indeed the word to describe the Oak Bay Beach Hotel. I've often remarked that Victoria was the most English of all Canadian cities, and this inn in many ways resembles several inns and country houses I have visited in England. One that comes to mind is the Mermaid in Rye, which also has the handsome Tudor-style half-timbers.
"May I offer you some more tea?" Kevin said, picking up the Spode teapot. I acquiesced immediately, and helped myself to more crumpets and jam, refraining momentarily from the selection of English Wensleydale, Cheshire, and Stilton cheeses.
There were other reminders of England here at this British Columbia inn. One was a public room with a water view known as "The Snug." Kevin explained that this was the Canadian equivalent of the Englishman's local." "Some people have been coming here for a long time as you can see from their names on the mugs hanging there. It's an English tradition."
Long before my visit to the Oak Bay Beach Hotel, I had heard from John Stone of Captain Whidbey's Inn, and Marge and Larry Lesley of the Lake Quinault Lodge, that it was indeed the kind of place I would like. Now, sitting here enjoying high tea with Kevin Walker, looking over the dinner menu which included beef Wellington, Juan de Fuca filet of sole and veal Oscar served with sauce Bernaise, I knew that they were entirely correct.
Oak Bay Beach Hotel was first included in *CIBR* in 1979.

OAK BAY BEACH HOTEL, 1175 Beach Drive, Victoria, B.C. V8S2N2; 604-598-4556. A 48-room seaside inn located in one of the quiet suburbs of Victoria. A short distance from the spectacular scenery and recreational resources of British Columbia. European plan. Breakfast, lunch, and dinner served to travelers. Open every day in the year. Swimming on grounds. Golf, tennis, fishing, sailing available nearby. No pets. Bruce R. Walker, Innkeeper.

Directions: Take Johnson St. or Fort St. from downtown Victoria east to Oak Bay Ave., which leads into Newport Ave. Turn left into Windsor Ave. to Beach Dr. Turn right and continue to 1175 Beach Dr. If arriving by air at Victoria Airport, I suggest you take public transportation to the center of the city and then take a taxi to the hotel.

Important: *Many of the inns can be reached by public transportation, and arrangements can frequently be made to be picked up at bus and train stations, as well as airports.*

I do not include lodging rates in the descriptions, for the very nature of an inn means that there are lodgings of various sizes, with and without baths, in and out of season, and with plain and fancy decoration. Travelers should call ahead and inquire about the availability and rates of the many different types of rooms.

Rates are comparable to those at hotels, motels, and resorts in the same geographic area. To me, this represents a travel bargain, for there is so much more offered at a country inn.

"European Plan" means that rates for rooms and meals are separate. "American Plan" means that meals are included in the cost of the room. "Modified American Plan" means that breakfast and dinner are included in the cost of the room. Some inns include a Continental breakfast with the lodging.

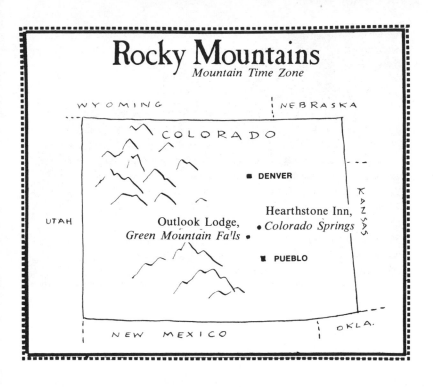

Colorado

COLORADO SPRINGS

I asked Dorothy Williams of the Hearthstone Inn how Colorado Springs came to be. "It was founded by General William Jackson Palmer, the promoter of the Denver and Rio Grande Western Railroad, when he decided in 1871 to make Colorado Springs a railroad terminus.

"Palmer created a proper city of parks, wide tree-shaded streets, a college, schools, churches, and a health resort. Writers and artists came because it is such a paintable and free place. At one time there was more wealth here per capita then in any other place in the country.

"We are actually a gateway to the mountains. Summer weather is really very nice. We have a few hot days but most of the homes are not air conditioned. Our snow is so dry that it is more like powdered sugar. There are probably only two or three days in the winter when it is difficult to get around. Even on cold days the sun is good. Skiers ski in their cut-offs and short sleeves. Most of our parks have cross-country ski trails."

THE OUTLOOK LODGE
Green Mountain Falls, Colorado

"This is a rather historical bathroom because it was supposedly the first one in Green Mountain Falls and people would line up to pay fifty cents to take a bath!"

Don, Anna, and Impy Ahern were showing me through the Outlook Lodge and we were now on the second floor. Impy is Don's mother; Anna is his wife.

"We call ourselves country Victorian," said Anna, "We do a few things that are a little different. For example, if guests leave their shoes outside the door before 10 p.m., they'll find them shined when they wake up in the morning. I'll bet you don't find many inns in your book that do that, do you?"

"The fact is that nostalgia is a very heavy theme here," said Don, who is an instructor in English at the nearby Air Force Academy. "We try to entertain our guests in the old-fashioned ways with plenty of opportunity to sit around the table and talk, and even roast marshmallows over the fire."

We wended our way back downstairs to the sitting rooms where Anna pointed to a piano. "Impy plays and Don holds forth on the guitar," she said. "We've got tons of sheet music and guests love to gather around and have informal sing-alongs."

The dining room has an adjoining kitchen with an old propane oven. "One of the other things that makes us popular is the fact that our guests have refrigerator and stove privileges. It's a sort of old mountain custom that for the most part has died out, but we think it's important. Lots of people prepare their own dinner in our kitchen and then remain here for the evening. You know, Impy is a great mixer and many guests have made lots of new friends while they were staying with us."

Outlook Lodge is literally on the lower slopes of Pike's Peak. It's only eight miles from Colorado Springs, but worlds apart in a great many other ways. The village is located at an altitude of almost 8,000 feet and dates from the 1880s. The inn is located next to the historic "Church in the Wildwood." In other days, the Lodge was a parsonage for the church. Today, it consists of two buildings with a total of twelve rooms. Lodgings include a complimentary Continental breakfast which features homemade breads, such as cranberry and banana-nut, squash bread, and gumdrop bread.

Besides all of the nostalgia and the really homelike feeling, the Outlook Lodge is also very convenient to a really awesome collection of sightseeing attractions. Those that come readily to my mind are Pike's Peak, the Cog Railway which runs to the top, the old gold mining town of Cripple Creek, and the Air Force Academy. Energetic guests can go horseback riding or hiking; enjoy tennis, swimming or other vigorous pursuits. The backroads have magnificent pine-scented views of the impressive mountain scenery. Colorado Springs with its many restaurants, its theater, and symphony concerts, and the Broadmoor with all of its activities, is just a few miles away.

"Outlook is close to big city entertainment and yet very much a part of the Rockies . . . rustic and homelike," concluded Impy. "In fact, eight of our twelve rooms have shared baths. However, one thing has changed: We don't charge fifty cents anymore for the use of the historic bathtub!"

OUTLOOK LODGE, 6975 Howard, Green Mountain Falls, Colo. 80819; 303-684-2303. A 12-room rustic lodge on the slopes of Pike's Peak, 8 mi. from Colorado Springs. Immediately adjacent to all the copious mountain recreational activities as well as the U.S. Air Force Academy; Colorado Springs Fine Arts Center; Cripple Creek Gold Camp. European plan. All lodgings include Continental breakfast. No other meals served. 8 rooms with shared baths. Open from June 1st through Labor Day weekend. Tennis, swimming, horseback riding, hiking, backroading, all nearby. Don, Anna, and Impy Ahern, Innkeepers.

Directions: Green Mountain Falls is 8 mi. west of Colorado Springs on U.S. 24. Outlook Lodge is located next to the historic Church in the Wildwood.

359

THE HEARTHSTONE INN
Colorado Springs, Colorado

The Hearthstone is becoming one of the showplaces of Colorado Springs. This Queen Anne-style house was bought by Ruth Williams and Dot Williams in 1977, and they have redecorated and furnished it as it would have been in 1885. The fifteen lodging rooms, plus the sitting and dining rooms have all been furnished with many authentic nineteenth-century pieces.

The lodging rooms have unique names such as The Library, The Drawing Room, The Peak View, and The Garden Room. Thirteen of the fifteen have their own bathrooms, and all have colorful handmade quilts.

I want to share a letter I have from Ruth and Dot, which reads in part: "We are enjoying a beautiful fall here. Our guests have been taking trips to the mountains nearby to view the breathtaking aspen in their changing colors. The yellow leaves contrast beautifully with the dark green of the pine and spruce. We've been lighting a fire in our dining room fireplace in the mornings as we serve breakfast, so I guess winter will be along here soon." (Winter did come to Colorado quite early in 1979!)

"We always look forward to winter as it brings our month-long Victorian Christmas. The Hearthstone is decorated inside and out, and the center of attraction is our twenty-two-foot tree trimmed in handmade ornaments and strings of popcorn. We are already hosting groups from all over the country for whom it has become a tradition to spend the Christmas holidays with us.

"We love being in a part of the country where each season is enjoyed to the fullest and has certain traditions and tasks. Spring is the season for us to begin working outside again, and last year we received an award from the Colorado Springs Area Beautification Association for restoring our house and beautifying our grounds. We're proud of our new fence which a friend of ours from eastern Colorado made by hand in the style of cast iron fences of the 1880s. We've been in correspondence with the Jackson and Perkins rose people in order to choose a special variety of rose bush to complement our exterior color scheme, and outline our entire house.

"Summer brings with it our annual Fourth of July celebration. We gather our guests into the van and head for the memorial park to enjoy a picnic and listen to the Colorado Springs Symphony. Summer also brings with it state and country fairs. We had fun entering our homemade pastries and jams, and took home an assortment of ribbons this past summer.

"By the way, Norman, the Hearthstone was recently listed on the National Register of Historic Places and we're grateful for the honor."

The Hearthstone, with its delightful Victorian atmosphere, is being run with admirable *esprit* and true concern for guests' comfort and convenience. Although breakfast is the only meal served, both Dorothy and Ruth, who have the same last name but are not related, love good food and are happy to talk about the restaurants in Colorado Springs.

THE HEARTHSTONE INN, 506 N. Cascade Ave., Colorado Springs, Co. 80903; 303-473-4413. A 15-room bed-and-breakfast inn within sight of Pike's Peak, located in the residential section of Colorado Springs. A full breakfast is included in the price of the room; only meal served. Open every day all year. Convenient to spectacular Colorado mountain scenery as well as the Air Force Academy, Garden of the Gods, Cave of the Winds, the McAllister House Museum, Fine Arts Center and Broadmoor Resort. Golf, tennis, swimming, hiking, backroading nearby. Check innkeepers for pet policy. Dorothy Williams and Ruth Williams, Innkeepers.

Directions: From I-25 (the major North/South Hwy.) use Exit 143 (Uintah St.) travel east (opposite direction from mountains) to third stop light. (Cascade Ave.) Turn right for 7 blocks. The inn will be on the right at the corner of St. Vrain and Cascade. A big Victorian house, grey with lilac trim.

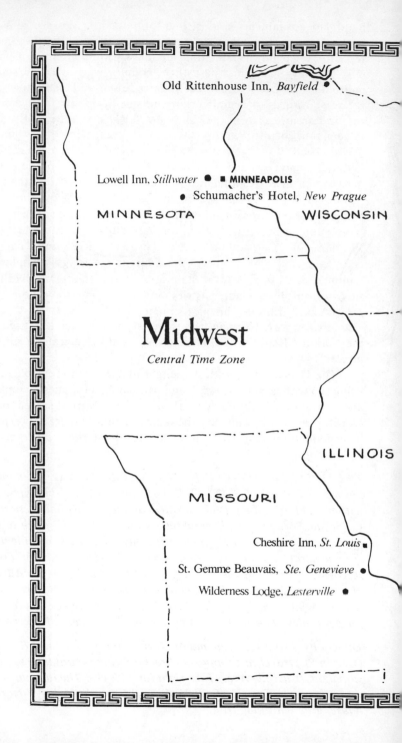

Old Rittenhouse Inn, *Bayfield*

Lowell Inn, *Stillwater* ● ■ **MINNEAPOLIS**
● Schumacher's Hotel, *New Prague*

MINNESOTA   WISCONSIN

Midwest
Central Time Zone

ILLINOIS

MISSOURI

Cheshire Inn, *St. Louis* ■

St. Gemme Beauvais, *Ste. Genevieve* ●

Wilderness Lodge, *Lesterville* ●

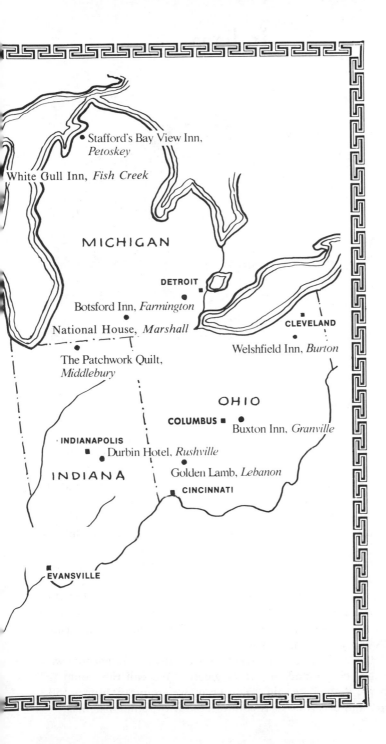

Stafford's Bay View Inn, *Petoskey*

White Gull Inn, *Fish Creek*

MICHIGAN

DETROIT

Botsford Inn, *Farmington*

National House, *Marshall*

CLEVELAND

Welshfield Inn, *Burton*

The Patchwork Quilt, *Middlebury*

OHIO

COLUMBUS

Buxton Inn, *Granville*

INDIANAPOLIS

Durbin Hotel, *Rushville*

INDIANA

Golden Lamb, *Lebanon*

CINCINNATI

EVANSVILLE

Indiana

DURBIN HOTEL
Rushville, Indiana

The Durbin Hotel is the essence of Midwest America. It is like corn on the cob, fried chicken, and James Whitcomb Riley's poetry. The Durbin family tradition of innkeeping has been going on for over fifty years. It began many years ago when Leo Durbin, a traveling salesman from Ohio, and Mary Cain of Indianapolis, were married and went into the hotel business. They had seven children, a great many of whom, inspired by their upbringing in the hotel, went into the business in other places. The present innkeeper, their son David, has continued in Rushville and many of *his* seven children have been employed at various times in the family hotel.

When I arrived on my most recent visit, David immediately took me in tow to see some of the interesting changes that had been made recently. "We used to call this room the Gay Nineties Room, but after we uncovered the brick walls, exposing the beams, and made it into a reproduction of an old taproom, the rest of my family began to call it 'David's Folly'—the name has apparently stuck."

I followed him into a newly decorated corner dining room with very bright colors and an air of gaiety. "We call this room the Strawberry Patch," he said. "You know we are pretty homey folks out here, and everyone feels comfortable with familiar names."

Our tour continued through many of the newly decorated and refurnished bedrooms. Each of them has its own theme, and all are very attractive. I asked him whether or not some of the beds still had the "Magic Fingers" mattresses. He smiled and said, "Well, you don't find them in very many hotels or inns, but our guests tell us that they love them."

We returned to the lobby again, and while David went to get a menu, I sat down and just enjoyed being here in this friendly atmosphere. There is a main counter with all kinds of postcards, old-fashioned stick candy in jars, books, maps, and even some crafts from the section of Indiana. The grandfather clock tolls every fifteen minutes, and the penny scale still works. There is an arrangement of comfortable furniture in one corner, which is appropriately decorated with many photographs of Mr. Wendell Willkie, the Republican presidential candidate during the early 1940s, who made the Durbin Hotel his campaign headquarters.

David returned and we immediately launched into a discussion of the hotel's home-cooking which is noted far and wide.

"To begin with," he said, "everything is made from scratch. We make our own pies, cakes, and breads right here in the kitchen. The menu is just good farm food, things like scalloped chicken, noodle casseroles, fried chicken, candied yams, baked beans, Danish lobster tails, filet mignon.

"Our menu changes with the season and, of course, we have fresh vegetables whenever they are available. One of our most popular dishes is a homemade ham loaf. We also serve lots of liver, either broiled or pan fried. Do you know that we serve 700 for dinner on many Sundays? By the way, in this part of Indiana when someone says 'dinner' it usually refers to the midday meal. Supper is served at night."

Vistors during 1980 will find some major face-lifting in progress.

DURBIN HOTEL, 137 W. Second St., Rushville, Ind. 46173; 317-932-4161. A 28-room country hotel in a bustling town, about one hour from Indianapolis. European plan. Breakfast, lunch, dinner served daily except Christmas and New Year's. Leashed pets allowed. Rushville is the home of Wendell Willkie, the 1940 Presidential candidate. Several round barns and covered bridges in the area. David Durbin, Innkeeper.

Directions: From the Indianpolis Beltway take I-74 south to Rushville-Shelbyville exit. Or follow Rte. 52 from the Beltway directly to Rushville. Located on Rtes. 52 and 43, one block from Rte. 3.

PATCHWORK QUILT
Middlebury, Indiana

It is now ten years since I first visited the Patchwork Quilt restaurant, and I thought it might be fun if we all looked at the 1971 edition of *CIBR* which tells of that first visit:

"Imagine winning a five-thousand-dollar first prize for having the best recipe for chicken in the U.S.A.!" I exclaimed. I asked Arletta Lovejoy just how she had arrived at the winning combination of ingredients.

"My recipe was for Buttermilk Pecan Chicken. It's like the one I've been using for some time, but one Christmas I was preparing it for thirty-five members of our family, and found that I was out of one of the ingredients—fresh milk. I had some buttermilk in the house, substituted this, and found that it made a better batter for the chicken and made the breading stick on better, so I incorporated it into the recipe and that's what won the prize."

Arletta Lovejoy handed me a glass of mulled cider and introduced me to the other guests awaiting the dinner bell. We were indeed a mixed bag; there were quite a few people from such nearby Indiana towns as Elkhart and South Bend, as well as Chicagoans, people from Cleveland, and a sprinkling from New England.

The signal was given and we all took our places in the Keeping Room. I was seated so that I could see into the remarkable kitchen with its Danish oak cabinets. The women of the neighborhood, many with cooking specialties, were each busy with some phase of preparing our meal.

Now Treva Swarm came out with the salad-and-relish buffet

table and announced the relishes for that evening: apple sauce, kidney bean salad, potato salad, pecan cheese roll, a five-bean salad, corn relish, pickle relish, ham salad, and she went on listing several more. An "ah" went through the room.

Shortly thereafter, Treva returned and recited the main dishes which were all to be served family-style. They change almost every day. That evening there was ham, steak Robert, and the famous buttermilk chicken. The plate with the meats was garnished with parsley and small red tomatoes. There were also green beans with mushrooms and almonds, and corn with bits of red pimentoes.

On that first visit, by eating carefully and slowly, I was able to enjoy three pieces of the chicken and a generous helping of the ham and steak. This was followed by a large serving cart with blueberry pie, pecan pie, candied violet cake, grasshopper pie, apricot chiffon pie, cherry cake, and cherry walnut torte.

Things have not changed very much at the Patchwork Quilt restaurant since 1970. The meals are still served in exactly the same way, except that a great many menu items have been added and replaced over the years. Furthermore, the reputation of the Patchwork Quilt has gone around the world several times, and people from some rather remote places on the globe go out of their way to enjoy dinner at this farmhouse-cum-restaurant. Even with all this, Milton Lovejoy and Herb Swarm continue to work the farm, raising a good crop every year.

Herb and Treva's daughter Marcia is now the roll-baker and is learning much about the business from her mother. As Arletta says, "Treva has been doing a wonderful job of taking over the reins here, and I am taking it easier as time goes on. Milton and I became grandparents again in December, when our daughter Penny gave birth to Luke Anton Hoskam in Concord, Massachusetts."

The last ten years of my life have been greatly enriched for my friendship with Milton and Arletta Lovejoy and visits to the Patchwork Quilt.

PATCHWORK QUILT COUNTRY INN, 11748 C.R. #2, Middlebury, Ind. 46450; 219-825-2417. A working farm restaurant in the tradition of midwestern hospitality, about 20 mi. east of Elkhart. No lodgings. Dinner served daily by reservation only. Closed Sundays, Mondays, Thanksgiving, Christmas, and New Year's. No credit cards. Arletta Lovejoy, Innkeeper.

Directions: From east or west, exit Indiana Toll Road at Middlebury (Exit 10) and go north ¼ mi. to County Rd. #2 and proceed west 1 mi. to inn. From Middlebury follow Indiana Rte. 13 for 8 mi. north to County Rd. #2 and west 1 mi.

Michigan

THE BOTSFORD INN
Farmington Hills, Michigan

John Anhut, the innkeeper, and I were standing in the attractive fully paneled private dining room of the Botsford, and I commented on the unusual patina of the walls.

"That's an interesting story," replied John. "Under Henry Ford's direction, these panels were installed carefully by expert cabinetmakers and the entire room was then sealed off. The fireplace was filled with corncobs and then lighted. Can you imagine this room filled with corncob smoke? Well, the fire burned for a long time and the wood was allowed to cure. The result is an antique finish which can only be obtained by this type of treatment. By the way, the colonial sideboard is supposed to have come from General Lee's home in Virginia."

The Botsford Inn has a fascinating history which began 141 years ago when it was a stagecoach stop on the road between Detroit and Lansing. Like other country and village inns of the 19th century (and even today), the public room was the scene for lots of stories and jokes and probably a great deal of business. Incidentally, the doors have remained open continuously since the first day. It is Michigan's oldest inn.

The late Henry Ford became interested in its preservation in 1924 and, upon purchasing it, placed a great many of his own 19th-century antiques and treasures in it. Among them are furnishings from his country home, including a beautiful little inlaid spinet, a handsome horsehair sofa, his music boxes, a Simon Willard clock, an exquisitely inlaid mahogany table, and an attractive oil painting of the Botsford Inn showing people in costumes of the late 19th century.

I walked through the other rooms including one with very low ceilings and huge beams. The fireplace had mammoth andirons and there was a cross section of the wall left bare by Mr. Ford in order to show the split laths of 150 years ago.

John had a few words to say about the menu: "We believe in serving predominantly American food; we aren't a French restaurant and we have never tried to be one. Consequently, we have a lot of things on the menu that people come to associate with country living here in the Midwest. We have a salad bowl with lettuce, pea beans, celery, carrots, and tomato sections." There are lots of casserole dishes, and on that particular night I enjoyed short ribs. "As far as I know," John added, "now we're going to have dinner theater each week with an emphasis on light comedy."

He continued, "I think that we have many elements of a New England country inn here, but we're really a big city inn. We attempt to compensate for bucolic charm in other ways."

In 1979, John received the most welcome news that the Botsford Inn has been listed in the National Register of Historic Places. This is a recognition of the historical significance of the inn to the country and to the community. "It is the culmination of years of hard work and great cooperation from the local citizenry," said John.

Later, while dressing in my room after a welcome swim, I was grateful for some modern conveniences in the Botsford Inn such as air conditioning on an afternoon of record heat. The throb of the Motor City had almost entirely receded. So near, and yet so far.

The Botsford Inn has been included in *CIBR* since 1969.

BOTSFORD INN, 28000 Grand River Avenue, Farmington Hills, Mich. 48024; 313-474-4800. A 62-room village inn on the city line of Detroit. European plan. Dinner served daily except Monday. Breakfast and lunch Tuesday thru Saturday. Sunday brunch. Closed Christmas and New Year's Day. Pool on grounds. Greenfield Village, skiing, and state parks nearby. John Anhut, Innkeeper.

Directions: Located in Farmington Hills on I-96 which is easily accessible from major highways in Michigan.

MARSHALL, MICHIGAN

Marshall should certainly take its place, along with Cape May, New Jersey, and Port Townsend, Washington, as one of the most significant centers of Victorian restoration in the world. There are dozens and dozens of gorgeous Victorian homes being lived in by the good people of Marshall today. Fifteen have been designated as State historic sites and six are in the National Register.

The most significant individual in Marshall's restoration and revival is Mr. Harold C. Brooks, a former mayor and true benefactor of the community. He became involved in the preservation more than fifty years ago. He bought several of the important vacant Victorian homes in Marshall and held them until an owner arrived on the scene who was interested in preserving and restoring the building.

The highlight of Marshall's year comes on the first weekend after Labor Day. It is the Annual Historic Home Tour in which Marshall homes are open for visitors. Over 35 organizations and 1400 volunteers work on this project and this is astonishing when we consider that the city has a population of only 7400. Thousands of people are in Marshall during these two days.

THE NATIONAL HOUSE
Marshall, Michigan

Norman Kinney, the innkeeper at the National House Inn, was helping me to assimilate the experience of this unusual town. "Mr. Brooks was the most important factor," he said. "He was the man who had the vision of Marshall. But everybody in town has joined in. We are proud of the homes and the museums and we all work together. I am sure that we could not have restored the National House if it hadn't been a community effort. People helped out in so many ways.

"This is probably the oldest remaining hotel building in Michigan," he pointed out. "We learned that it was open in 1835 and undoubtedly was the first brick building of any kind in our county.

"At one time it was a windmill and wagon factory, and more recently an apartment building," Norman continued. "My good friend, Hal Minick and I, along with his wife Jacqueline and my wife Kathryn, decided to restore the building and return it to its original purpose.

"It has really been hard work, but underneath the dirt and grime of dozens of years, we found the solid, beautiful structure of the original brick as well as the irreplaceable woodwork. We converted the apartments into sixteen bedrooms and baths.

"As you can see, Marshall is very much a Victorian restoration. We searched everywhere—culled all the antique shops and removed furniture from our own homes. Many of our friends contributed some of their beloved pieces in order to help us recreate the atmosphere of Marshall before the turn of the century."

One of the most striking features of the National House is the passionate attention to detail. For example, each bedroom has its own ambience and there are colorful comforters, old trunks, marble top tables, bureaus, dried flower arrangements, electric lamps that are reproductions of gas lamps, candle sconces with reflectors, little corner sofas, special care with door knobs, and special attention is given to the linens. The bedroom windows overlook either the residential part of town, or a beautiful fountain in the town center park.

Breakfast is the only meal served, and is offered every morning in the dining room which has a most fetching collection of chairs and tables from great-grandfather's day. The color tones are warm brown and beige. The breakfast offerings include homebaked coffee cakes and muffins, nut breads, and the like. I spent an hour and a half at breakfast talking with many different people.

The Kinneys and Minicks have devoted a great deal of loving care, pride, and considerable investment in restoring this beautiful building to its original state. The people of Marshall can well be proud of the National House Inn.

THE NATIONAL HOUSE INN, 102 South Parkview, Marshall, Mi. 49068; 616-781-7374. An elegantly restored 16-room Victorian-period village inn. Marshall is the finest example of 19th-century architecture in the Midwest. It has 15 State Historic Sites and 6 National Register Sites. European plan includes Continental breakfast. No other meals served. Open year-round. Closed Christmas Eve and Christmas Day. Tennis, golf, swimming, boating, xc skiing nearby. Norman D. Kinney, Steve Poole, Innkeepers.

Directions: From I-69 exit at Michigan Ave. in Marshall and go straight 1½ mi. to inn. From I-94 use exit 110, follow old 27 south 1½ mi. to inn.

STAFFORD'S BAY VIEW INN
Petoskey, Michigan

Janice Smith and I were rocking in the red rockers with the yellow cushions on the porch at Stafford's Bay View Inn. While we were gazing over Little Traverse Bay, she said, "Oh look, there's a sailboat race—and they're setting their spinnakers." Sure enough, while we watched, the boats came about, and for this leg of the race they broke out their colorful balloon-like sails.

It had been a very interesting day—Jan and I had gone to Petoskey, particularly so that I could see the famous Gaslight district with its branches of many smart stores which I have also seen in Chicago, Naples, Fort Lauderdale, and Palm Beach. It's part of the reason why Petoskey is known as Michigan's Cote d'Azur.

I asked her how the inn happened to be built. "It was a part of the Bay View section of Petoskey," she replied. "Bay View is a summer resort community with a program of music and drama along with religious lectures and services. The community began in the late 1880s, when people rode on the Grand Rapids and Indiana Railroad or on the lake steamers to reach Petoskey."

She laughed for a moment, saying, "It must have required a bit of faith to see the future glory of the area, because there were nearly two hundred miles of unbroken forest to the south.

"However," she went on, "the early residents built the fine

Victorian homes which are scattered throughout Bay View today. The cultural and religious programs which started then are still going on, providing our guests with the additional opportunity for summertime enlightenment and enjoyment.

"Duffer (Stafford) and I met here at the inn in 1960 when I was the hostess and he was the assistant manager. We fell in love with each other and the inn, and a year later had scraped up enough money to make a down payment on it and also to get married. The inn has been a major part of our life.

"Our children have really grown up with the inn. Our 17-year-old son Reg attends school in Beaver Dam, Wisconsin, and serves as quite an assistant. He'd like to attend a hotel school. Mary Kathryn is beginning to learn the waitress service ropes, and Dean pours a mean cup of punch. Grandma Johnson fixed him up with a pint-sized tuxedo uniform like Duff's and he's become quite a little host."

I suggested a walk on the shore of the lake, and as we crossed the country railroad tracks which go around the bay, she said, "It's great fun to cross-country ski up these tracks—there are lots of trails up around the bend."

We strolled along the lake, and I realized it provided a striking view of the inn—a white building, three stories high, with a green mansard on the third story. Many of the rooms look out over Little Traverse Bay.

"We are most interested in the afternoon tea and hors d' oeuvres idea which we picked up at the Pleasant Hill meeting last fall," Jan remarked. "We think that the program is a natural for our unlicensed inn and we plan to be off and running with afternoon teas during July and August of 1980. By the way, it was wonderful to meet those British innkeepers. We're looking forward to the 1980 meeting at the Red Lion Inn in Stockbridge!"

Stafford's Bay View has been included in *CIBR* since 1972.

STAFFORD'S BAY VIEW INN, Box 3, Petoskey, Mich. 49770; 616-347-2771. A 23-room resort-inn on Little Traverse Bay in the Bay View section of Petoskey. Modified American plan omits lunch. Breakfast, lunch and dinner served daily to travelers. Open daily Memorial Day to mid-October, Christmas week and long weekends during the winter sports season. Lake swimming and xc skiing on grounds. Golfing, boating, fishing, hiking, and Alpine ski trails nearby. Pickup service provided from Pellston Airport on request. Stafford and Janice Smith; Kathy Hart, Innkeepers.

Directions: From Detroit, take Gaylord Exit from I-75 and follow Mich. Rte. 32 to Rte. 131, north to Petoskey. From Chicago, use U.S. 131 north to Petoskey.

Minnesota

LOWELL INN
Stillwater, Minnesota

The plane made a wide circle around the Minneapolis-St. Paul Airport and obligingly dipped a wing so that I could get a full view of the golden grain country of Minnesota. I asked my seat-mate to point out the St. Croix River and the little town of Stillwater. "If you're going to visit the Lowell Inn," he said, "you're bound to like it."

A short time later, I drove to Stillwater from the airport and soon the Mount Vernon exterior of the inn with its tall white pillars and beautiful red brick walls came into view.

I stepped inside and it was like being in a rather large home. As Innkeeper Arthur Palmer explained to me, "We really consider the inn a home, and the lobby is our living room." Everything was decorated with an eye toward comfortable elegance. The large Colonial fireplace was surrounded with quilted couches, blue leather chairs, and a grandfather's clock. The side parlor's furniture had summer slipcovers with flower designs and a beautiful breakfront with Dresden china on display.

Maureen Palmer explained that many of the fine furnishings were collected by Arthur's parents, Nelle and Arthur, Sr., during the 1930s. Nelle was an actress and talented cornet player and Arthur, a pianist. They met and married when both worked with Nelle's sisters' traveling troupe "The Obrecht Sisters." When the opportunity arose to manage the Lowell Inn, they decided it was time to settle down and become innkeepers, something they had always wanted to do. After leasing the inn for a number of years, their final dream came true when they purchased the inn in 1945.

I found the originality of this Midwestern inn most exceptional. For example, there are three dining rooms, each with its own theme. The George Washington Room shows appreciation and love for antiques of the Williamsburg Colonial period. The Garden Room was originally conceived as an outdoor garden court and even has an indoor fish pool from which guests may select their own fish.

Probably the most striking experience of all is to dine in the Matterhorn Room which would be unique even in Switzerland. It reflects the Palmers' Swiss family background. The room is filled from floor to ceiling with authentic Swiss woodcarvings. The staff is dressed in Swiss costume and the feature of the five-course, fixed-price dinner is fondue Bourguignonne, which offers cubes of select prime beef which each person cooks to his own taste in individual fondue pots.

Weather permitting, the front terrace of the inn is now used as a sidewalk cafe. The menu includes French crêpes and a light, modestly priced lunch. There are petunias under the front window and there's a very gay atmosphere with yellow umbrellas, trees, and plants.

Lodging rooms at the Lowell Inn are quite elegant. Many have leaded glass doors to the hallway, and several of the rooms have French telephones. Each room is decorated separately with its own set of sheets and pillow cases. A clock radio eliminates the necessity for wake-up calls. There are fresh flowers everywhere.

Something new and exciting is always happening at the Lowell Inn, and I find several pleasant surprises on each visit. "I think that's because I've inherited my mother's and father's love of show business," explained Arthur.

THE LOWELL INN, 102 N. Second St., Stillwater, Minn. 55082; 612-439-1100. A 22-room village inn 18 mi. from St. Paul, near all the cultural attractions of the Twin Cities. European plan. Lunch and dinner served daily except Christmas Eve and Christmas Day. Open year-round. No pets. Canoeing, tennis, hiking, skiing, and swimming nearby, including 4 ski resorts within 15 mi. Arthur and Maureen Palmer, Innkeepers.

Directions: Stillwater is on the St. Croix River at the junction of Minn. 95 (north and south) and Minn. 36 (east and west). It is 7 mi. north of I-94 on Hwy. 95.

SCHUMACHER'S NEW PRAGUE HOTEL
New Prague, Minnesota

John and Nancy Schumacher are representative of a dedicated genre of new younger innkeepers who gain great satisfaction and personal fulfillment in running a country inn. "For John and myself," said Nancy, tossing her golden mane, "it's been a wonderful experience since 1974 when we first discovered New Prague and the hotel. It's been hard work, but so much fun and certainly a wonderful future."

Perhaps the best way to tell the story of this inn is to share some of John's comments about Nancy, and vice versa: "Nancy is an artist. She writes the menu, designs the brochures, decorates the rooms, buys the furniture, and when we need a hostess, she can fill in. She also does all of the bookkeeping. This operation is fifty percent Nancy Schumacher!"

Nancy says of John: "The food is John's department; even though he seems young, he's been a cook and a baker since 1964. He has a great flair for creating new dishes. He went to the Culinary Institute of America and graduated at the top of his class. Each of the dinners is prepared as ordered. It may take a bit longer, but it tastes so much better. We bake our own breads and pastries. All side dishes, main courses, and desserts are made from fresh vegetables, fresh fruit, and fresh meats. Recipes are from John and the little Czechoslovakian ladies of the village."

Nancy has decorated the twelve lodging rooms, named after each month, and they greatly resemble inns and hotels I have visited in Bavaria and Austria. Each room is almost totally different. One of the most welcome features are the eiderdown-filled comforters on all of the beds, a custom I found throughout northern and central

Europe. Each room is minutely described in the colorful brochure of the inn.

The menu has approximately fifty-five main dishes, most of them having Central European origins. The fish, poultry, and game courses all have Czechoslovakian names. These include boneless breast of chicken topped with blue cheese; roast duck cooked in caraway seeds served with dumplings and red cabbage, and two of the house specialties: creamed rabbit and bock beer batter shrimp. There are also several different types of schnitzels served with dumplings, red cabbage, and German potato salad.

The staff is dressed in central European costumes with colorful vests and dirndl dresses. "More of Nancy's designs," said John.

John and Nancy visited both Czechoslovakia and Germany in late fall 1978 in order to get a more intimate feeling for both the culture and cuisine of the regions. Through Jens Deikmann, they visited many of the Romantik Hotels in Germany (see *CIBR-Europe*). As a result of this trip, Schumacher's New Prague Hotel is the first Romantik Hotel in North America. "I'm sure we're going to have many visitors from Europe in the coming years." said John.

The exciting things that happened in 1979 included the restoration of the lobby and the addition of a Bavarian bar. Several ideas from the German and Austrian trip have been incorporated. Hand-painted stained glass was custom-built into the windows and cabinets. The bar stools, hand carved in Massachusetts, were custom designed by Nancy.

Schumacher's has many of the important touches that make a difference in anyone's stay, including candies under pillows, fresh arrangements of flowers and live plants scattered about the hotel and rooms, complimentary local newspapers, and perhaps most important of all, a genuine, warm, personal sense of involvement with all of the guests. "After all," said Nancy, "this is our home, too."

SHUMACHER'S NEW PRAGUE HOTEL, 212 West Main St., New Prague, Mn. 56071; 612-758-2133. (Metro line: 612-445-7285.) A 12-room Czechoslovakian and German inn located in a small country town approximately 35 mi. south of Minneapolis and St. Paul in the verdant Minnesota countryside. European plan. Breakfast, lunch, and dinner served to travelers all year except three days at Christmas. No pets. No credit cards. No entertainment available to amuse children. Good bicycling and backroading nearby; also xc skiing, tennis, and golf. John and Nancy Schumacher, Innkeepers.

Directions: From Minneapolis, take 494 west to 169 south to Jordan exit. Turn south on Rte. 21 for 9 mi. to New Prague. Turn left to Main St. at the stop sign, and the hotel is in the second block on the right.

Missouri

CHESHIRE INN
St. Louis, Missouri

Although the Cheshire Inn is hardly a small inn in the country, it is as British as anything one might find this side of London's Piccadilly Circus. Imagine finding two red double-deck London buses and a Tudor-style building with half timbers just a few miles from the Mississippi River!

For the most part, furnishings and decorations of the inn are the result of a passion for collecting shared by proprietors Steve and Barbara Apted, and this passion extends to the lodging rooms, some of which are named for prominent English literary figures such as Johnson, Galsworthy, Dickens, and Tennyson.

I stayed in the Richard the Lionhearted Room which had a canopied bed with curtains around it, reminding me of several country house hotels in Britain. When the sun came up, the matching rich red curtains at the windows created a marvelous red glow. The television set was hidden in an old oak chest.

Houseguests enjoy a breakfast buffet which offers an endless array of eggs (poached, scrambled, fried, soft boiled and hard boiled), bacon, and several different kinds of fresh breads, delicious hot chocolate, and a very pleasant and accommodating morning staff which makes even the dullest days seem bright.

The first page of the very extensive dinner menu explains why the Cheshire Inn has been created in an English atmosphere. It says in part: "Times were hard in 'Merrie Olde England'. People worked hard for long hours and to compensate, learned how to live and live well on the simple pleasures of everyday life. At sundown they would repair to their hearthsides for a warming bowl of soup followed by rich roast beef.

"At Cheshire we try to recreate this jolly period with costumes, recipes from old books, music, and a general air of 'hail stranger, hail friend, sit down and rest yourself, partake of what we offer!'"

The descriptions of the main courses are enough to give one the appetite of Henry VIII. One of the specialties of the house is roast prime rib of beef served with Yorkshire pudding and horseradish sauce. The meat is roasted on a slowly turning spit to keep in the natural juices and flavor.

Another specialty is roast duck which, according to the menu, is prepared, "in the manner preferred by Charles Dickens." The glazed pork chops Buckingham are brushed with a sweet-sour sauce and topped with a grilled pineapple ring. There are many, many more selections on the menu, including trout stuffed with crabmeat, short ribs of beef, fish, lobster tails, and many types of steaks. The most popular dessert is the English trifle; or perhaps it is the Missouri apple pie served warm with cheese or ice cream; or maybe it's both.

I enjoy staying at the Cheshire Inn when visiting St. Louis because it's right across the street from the park where there's so much happening in both summer and winter. There are plans to have horse and carriage rides available for guests' pleasure.

CHESHIRE INN and LODGE, 6300 Clayton Rd., St. Louis, Mo. 63117; 314-647-7300. A 110-room English style inn, 1 block off Hwy. 40 near Forest Park. European plan only. Breakfast lunch, and dinner served to travelers daily. Accommodations available every day of the year. Restaurant closed on New Year's Day, Memorial Day, July 4th, Labor Day, and Christmas Day. Pool, bicycles on grounds. Boating, golf, tennis, carriage rides, and riding nearby. St. Louis Art Museum, zoo, Gateway Arch, and opera nearby. Jim Prentice, Innkeeper.

Directions: Just off Hwy. 40 at Clayton Rd. and Skinker Blvd. on southwest corner of Forest Park. From the east, take Clayton Rd. exit. From the west, take McCausland Ave. exit, north two blocks to Clayton Rd.

ST. GEMME BEAUVAIS INN
Ste. Genevieve, Missouri

The magazine was called *Missouri Life* and Boats Donze handed it to me with a twinkle in his eye, "I think you'll find something interesting on the inside."

I leafed through the rather handsomely designed pages and came to a full-page color photograph of the St. Gemme Beauvais Inn

framed by a tree and a beautiful wrought iron fence in the foreground. On the opposite page was a smaller photograph of a man in a very elegant-looking yellow brocaded coat and a ruffled shirt standing at the top of the four brick steps that lead to the entrance of the inn. I peered at it closely and said, "Why Boats, that's you!" He smiled somewhat deprecatingly and admitted that it was.

It is perfectly natural for Boats Donze to be wearing an antebellum French costume while standing in front of his inn, because the inn is his boyhood home. "My father bought it in 1923," he said. "It was the property of the daughter of Felix Rozier who built it in 1848. Before that, the property was owned by first families of the village, including St. Gemmes and Beauvais — hence its name."

The inn is really a showcase for the Mississippi River village of Ste. Genevieve, which is fifty miles south of St. Louis. The people of the village have lived under three different flags. Settled by the French in the latter part of the seventeenth century, in 1763, the treaty of Fontainebleau gave the territory west of the Mississippi to Spain, which then returned it to France in 1800. As part of the Louisiana Purchase in 1803, Ste. Genevieve became a part of the United States.

It is to its French heritage, however, that the town addresses most of itself. It is the only place in Missouri where so much of the state's French culture has been preserved. Thirty buildings were built before 1800 and almost all of them remain the same as they were two hundred years ago. Quite a few are open to the public, and a complete walking tour is available.

The Donzes have furnished the inn mainly with 19th-century regional pieces. There are six-foot-high carved headboards, marble top dressers, floral wallpapers, and bright carpets. Most of the lodgings are two bedroom suites. Each of these little suites has its own bathroom.

A favorite room is on the top floor where the windows overlook the uppermost branches of a Douglas fir tree. "They are quite rare in this part of the country," explained Frankye.

My lunch that day consisted of a tasty quiche Lorraine (most appropriate for a French inn), carrots with a distinctive herbal touch, string beans cooked with bacon bits, and a salad. The dessert was a homemade cobbler. One of the house specialties is chicken-filled crêpes.

Frankye and Boats have lovingly restored three other old buildings of Ste. Genevieve including the Amoureaux House, the Beauvais House, and the Green Tree Tavern which was built about 1790. It was the first inn in Ste. Genevieve. "All of this restoration was done with private funds and not supported by any foundation money," asserted Boats.

ST. GEMME BEAUVAIS, 78 N. Main St., Ste. Genevieve, Mo. 63670; 314-883-5744. An 8-room village inn about 1½ hrs. from St. Louis. Modified American plan includes breakfast only. Breakfast served daily. Lunch served Mon.— Sat. Open year-round. Closed Thanksgiving and Christmas Day. No pets. Golf, hunting, and fishing nearby. Frankye and Boats Donze, Innkeepers.

Directions: From St. Louis, south on I-55 to Hwy. 32. Exit east on 32 to Hwy. 61 to the Ste. Genevieve exit.

WILDERNESS LODGE
Lesterville, Missouri

"We're having a wonderful time here, I wish we could stay forever." I was having breakfast at Wilderness Lodge and making the acquaintance of a young honeymoon couple who were kind enough to say that they had chosen this Ozark resort-inn because they read about it in *CIBR*.

"Aside from being on our honeymoon," said Sue, her eyes dancing, "we're having a beautiful time here because we love the floating." Tom joined in, never relinquishing a loving hold on his wife's hand. "Yes, I like to fish, but I hate to paddle, and Sue doesn't like to fish, but loves to paddle, so I think we're off to a great start!"

As the waitress served the pancakes, Tom said, "It seems to me that we've been eating every minute since we got here, and every meal is better than the last."

For people who love horseback riding, floating, platform tennis, canoeing, hiking, fishing, and other outdoor activities that encourage hearty appetites, the Wilderness Lodge in the Missouri Ozarks is ideal.

There is a wide variety of accommodations. My hillside room in a rustic cabin made of native wood had a big fireplace with the wood already laid in the grate. A rear balcony was perched high in the trees overlooking the river. The furniture was all country-made. This is not an ordinary hunting lodge, but something very special with conveniences built right in. Even the air conditioners are tucked out of sight.

The buildings of the Lodge are spread out on a hill that slopes down to the banks of the Black River. Their basic construction is of horizontal logs with the bark stripped off and white mortar in between.

The center of activities is the dining hall which is also a gathering place for the guests at the beginning and the end of the day.

Besides being a great place for honeymooners, Wilderness Lodge provides a super vacation for kids. It has just about everything in the world for them to do.

I mentioned "floating." This is a wonderful outdoor experience enjoyed on the Black River. Guests and canoes are taken upriver anywhere from five to fifteen miles. The canoe is put in the water and then begins to float with the current down the river, returning to the Lodge. Paddles help out here and there. Box lunches are provided. It's great fun to drift slowly underneath the trees on the riverbank or perhaps lift the canoe up on the sandy shore and stretch out on the grass in the warm sunshine.

WILDERNESS LODGE, P.O. Box 87, Lesterville, Mo. 63654; 314-637-2295. A 24-room resort-inn located in the heart of the scenic Ozarks approximately 2½ hrs. from St. Louis. Modified American plan. Breakfast and dinner to travelers. Closed from Christmas to the day before New Year's. Box lunches available. No pets. Tennis, platform tennis, bocci, horseback riding, canoeing, float trips, walking and nature trails, fishing, archery, and many other sports on grounds. Stephen and Barbara Apted, Innkeepers.

Directions: From I-244 take Hwy. 55 south and just past Festus, take Hwy. 67 south. After the junction of Hwy. 32, Hwy. 67 becomes two lanes only. Follow 67 and very shortly look for a sign: "W," Farmington. Take this exit and turn right. You'll be on W west. Remain on W for approximately 8 mi. and there will be a sign, Jct. V. Turn left onto V for 9 mi. and it ends at Hwy. 21 in Ironton, where you turn left. Follow 21 and 1 mi. past town of Hogan be careful. This is Jct. of 21 and Hwy. 49. 49 will continue straight ahead and 21 will swerve to the right. No big thing if you look for it, just be sure to go right, toward Lesterville. As you approach Lesterville, you'll pass Lake Taum Sauk signs; 1/4 mi. further, on the left, are a Dairy Queen and an old package store (both small white buildings), and a group of resort signs. Turn left, before the signs, follow the hard surface road. You'll cross over the Black River bridge and follow the road turning left at the next set of signs, and just a little farther, on the right, is Wilderness Lodge.

Ohio

THE BUXTON INN
Granville, Ohio

The faces of two beautiful young ladies were both smiling at me from photographs which proved unmistakably that Melanie and Amy Orr, whom I first met in 1975 on my first visit to The Buxton Inn, are now growing up.

On my original visit, Amy was 9½ years old and Melanie was going on 13. Amy was wearing a most charming 1812 costume and a big smile. As it developed, she was my principal guide through the inn.

Amy's parents are Orville and Audrey Orr who acquired The Buxton Inn in 1972 and then spent two years researching, planning, designing, and restoring it. The origins of the inn have been traced back to 1812, when Orrin Granger, a pioneer from Granville, Massachusetts (not far from Stockbridge), built "The Tavern" on land purchased in 1806. The Buxton Inn is now on the National Register of Historic Places.

On my first visit, all of the Orrs, including older daughter Melanie, took me on an excursion through all of the bedrooms, dining rooms, courtyard, and the basement—where Amy said, "You know those stairs we just walked down? Well, President William Henry Harrison actually rode his horse on those stairs!"

The basement, where the drovers and stagecoach drivers used to cook their own food and sleep, was attractively decorated with

handsome wooden tables, old pewter, and an old fireplace. Upstairs, on the first floor, there were several dining areas, all of them furnished in antiques.

We were joined on our tour by Major Buxton. "A very smart cat," exclaimed Amy. "He strolls about like he owns everything, and we like him so much we put him on our sign outside."

My first dinner at The Buxton Inn was roast duckling with wild cherry sauce, and I see that it is on the menu today, along with a quiche of the day, grilled ham steak with Cumberland sauce, and other country offerings, such as sautéed baby beef liver a l'orange and French pepper steak.

Today, the tempo at The Buxton Inn has, if anything, increased. Melanie, now going on seventeen, is a desk clerk and chef's assistant on weekends. Amy, who is going on fourteen, washes windows, dishes, and helps make up rooms. All of the family and the staff members still dress in the costumes of 1812.

The ballroom on the second floor has been restored to its 19th-century opulence, and the Lincoln Lounge opened early in 1980. Besides being used for businessmen's lunches at noon, it's a rather plush, authentic Victorian lounge after five p.m.

Now, with Amy and Melanie really growing up, I'll have to hurry out to The Buxton Inn again — before they "fly the coop!"

THE BUXTON INN, 313 E. Broadway, Granville, Ohio 43023; 614-587-0001. A 3-room inn in a college town in central Ohio near Denison University, the Indian Mounds Museum and the Heisey Glass Museum. European plan. Lunch and dinner served daily. Closed Christmas Day. No pets. Golf, tennis, horseback riding, cultural activities nearby. Orville and Audrey Orr, Innkeepers.

Directions: Take Granville exit from I-70. Travel north 8 mi. on Rte. 37 into Granville.

THE GOLDEN LAMB
Lebanon, Ohio

Sandra Reynolds and I were seated in the lobby of the Golden Lamb waiting for Jack Reynolds to finish a telephone call, and then we were all going to walk up the street to the Warren County Museum.

Just to be in this lobby is to partake of a generous helping of the American past. Among other things, there was a lamp, the base of which was made out of a candle mold, and a curly maple table. An old coal stove that was used 100 years or more ago is still in use today. Always on hand is a big punch bowl where guests and friends may enjoy a modicum of refreshment. There are quite a few examples of Shaker crafts in the lobby and elsewhere in the inn, including Shaker boxes, dowels, chests, and Shaker-style furniture in the dining room.

"The Shakers came to this section of Ohio during the 19th century and attracted buyers from all over the country for their fine farm stock, medicinal herbs, furniture, and other household essentials," explained Sandra. "Their community Union Village was sold by them over a half-century ago, but we have a lot of local interest in their culture, and the Warren County Museum has a considerable area devoted to Shaker memorabilia."

If Ohio could be called the "mother of presidents," the Golden Lamb might be called the "mother of country inns," because it is a significant force in providing inspiration for many innkeepers to preserve the best of the old, and at the same time to back it up with good innkeeping. Throughout the inn are found artifacts, furniture, and furnishings that have been collected from America's past which in a sense give us a real feeling of appreciation for what our forebears thought was beautiful, useful, and promising.

The building dates back to 1815 and was built on the site of an original log cabin erected by Jonas Seaman, who was granted a license in 1803 to operate "a house of public entertainment." Even before roads were built many guests came on foot or horseback to the inn. Here in the warmth of the tavern's public rooms they exchanged news of the world and related their own experiences. Many famous people have stopped here, including ten United States presidents as well as Henry Clay, Mark Twain, and Charles Dickens. Overnight guests may stay in rooms that are named for some of the great and near-great, both national and international, who have enjoyed accommodations here in the past.

"This section of Ohio is really quite a holiday and vacation focal point," said Sandra. "We have the Little Miami, Ohio's first scenic river, with fishing, canoeing, hiking, and riding, as well as the Glendower State Museum which is in a restored Greek Revival

mansion. I think one of our most popular things, however, is King's Island, which is a fantastic place for everyone in the family to enjoy lots of fun. It is centered around a 33-story replica of the Eiffel Tower and has a variety of rides, attractions, and entertainment. Jack Nicklaus has a golf center there too."

Jack came out of his office and handed me a letter. "Here is something I think you will enjoy reading," he said. "It's a letter from a lady who said she enjoyed having Sunday dinner here and makes a point that no matter how busy it may seem, it never loses its special feeling of friendliness. She said she also enjoys the gift shop, and all of the reproductions of 19th-century rooms on the third floor."

We had a very pleasant visit at the museum and a lovely dinner at the Golden Lamb. I remained all night and joined Jack the next morning at the village ice cream parlor, since the inn does not serve breakfast. It is a kind of morning village meeting place and nicely augments the Golden Lamb, which has been included in *CIBR* since 1971.

THE GOLDEN LAMB INN, 27 S. Broadway, Lebanon, Ohio 45036: 513-932-5065. A historic 20-room village inn in the heart of Ohio farming country on U.S. Hwys. 63, 42, and 48. European plan. 19 rooms with private bath. No pets. Breakfast served only on Sundays. Lunch and dinner served daily except Christmas. Golf and tennis nearby. Jackson Reynolds, Innkeeper.

Directions: From I-71, exit Rte. 48 N, 3 mi. west to Lebanon. From I-75, exit Rte. 63 E, 7 mi. east to Lebanon.

WELSHFIELD INN
Burton, Ohio

"It's a funny thing," I said, "I tried your recipe for skillet-fried chicken back home in the Berkshires, doing everything just as you told me. I even got the right kind of iron skillet, but somehow mine doesn't taste as good as yours. What's the problem?"

Brian Holmes pushed his chef's hat farther back on his head and said, "Well, I understand that you have some great chickens in Massachusetts, but I have a feeling they can't compare with the kind we raise here in Ohio."

I was standing in the extremely neat kitchen of the Welshfield Inn watching Brian put together different ingredients needed for dinner that evening. In addition to the skillet-fried chicken, there was a raisin sauce for the baked ham bubbling on the stove, and the wonderful aroma of the apple pies already in the oven was filling the room. Brian paused long enough to call my attention to the pans of sole and salmon. "Even though we are 500 miles from the nearest ocean, we never serve any frozen fish here. Everything is absolutely fresh. The seafoods are some of our most popular menu choices."

There were pans filled with baked acorn squash, stuffed zucchini, and the makings of fresh strawberry shortcake. "Our recipe for Indian pudding came from Cape Cod," he said. "We took it as a compliment when one of our customers said it tasted exactly like the pudding at the Red Inn in Provincetown."

One of the waitresses, dressed in an attractive early American costume, complete with a white duster cap, rushed into the kitchen and apologized for being a little late. Brian said he understood and popped some freshly made rolls into the oven. "That's another thing," he said, "we never use mixes. Our rolls and bread are made from scratch."

At this point Brian said that he had time for a short break, so we went out to the dining room which has a collection of 19th-century antiques and bric-a-brac. The center of interest is the old nickelodeon. I dropped a coin in, and the machine started playing "Three O'Clock in the Morning." The music had a nostalgic flavor and sounded like a combination of mandolin, flute, violin, and

piano. The machine never played a song that I didn't know, and as I hummed along, Brian remarked that my record was unbroken.

Brian pointed to a seat in the corner and said, "That's where Van Johnson sits every time he's here, and over there is Vivian Vance's table. We had Lucille Ball here for a week. You know, we have a very good theatre nearby where all of the big names appear."

Guests started coming in, so Polly went out to greet them, and Brian went back to the kitchen. I was left alone with the nickelodeon. I dropped in another coin, and this time the machine played, "She Was Only a Bird in a Gilded Cage."

My record is still unbroken.

Welshfield Inn has been in *CIBR* since 1973.

WELSHFIELD INN, Rte. 422, Burton, Ohio 44021; 216-834-4164. A country restaurant on Rte. 422, 28 mi. east of Cleveland. No lodgings. Lunch and dinner served weekdays. Dinner only served on Sundays and holidays. Closed the week of July 4th and three weeks after Jan. 1. Closed Mondays except Labor Day. Near Sea World and Holden Arboretum. Brian and Polly Holmes, Innkeepers.

Directions: On U.S. 422 at intersection of Ohio 700, midway between Cleveland and Youngstown, Ohio.

Wisconsin

OLD RITTENHOUSE INN
Bayfield, Wisconsin

In the midsummer of 1978, I arrived in Bayfield to the accompaniment of a thunder and lightning storm of positively Wagnerian proportions. the electrical display lit up the shoreline of Lake Superior, providing spectacular but "eye-blink" views of the Apostle Islands lying offshore.

I came in on Route 13 and easily identified an impressive Victorian mansion as the Old Rittenhouse Inn. It is located on a tree-shaded street on a high bank considerably above the road. It has four stories with a white porch around the front and side.

I waited a few moments for the deluge to abate, and then, dodging raindrops, hurried through the front door into a world of delicate Victoriana. The first person I saw was Jerry Phillips, a handsome bearded gentleman wearing a white, turn-of-the-century suit with a double-breasted vest, a red shirt with ruffles at the cuff, and a black, oversized butterfly tie.

"Welcome to the Old Rittenhouse Inn," he said. "We've tried to turn out for you in real style."

"Style" was exactly what I found in great abundance during that visit with innkeepers Jerry and Mary Phillips. Jerry showed me to my table and explained that he and Mary, who does all the cooking (with the exception of the desserts, which are Jerry's province), would join me for a long after-dinner talk.

I was served at a round oak table with a single candle. The cream and sugar and salt and pepper were a silver set. There was a green napkin on my plate in the middle of which was placed a small red blossom. Jerry presented the spoken menu, explaining very carefully the details concerning every individual course and the delicate content of each recipe. That evening, my first course was a mushroom Burgundy soup. The second course was a fruit salad made with fresh wild blackberries, raspberries, blueberries, peaches, and apples.

The six main courses included Lake Superior whitefish baked in wine, garnished with almonds, and served in a champagne butter sauce; ham baked in a spiced orange glaze and garnished with fresh fruits; ocean scallops sautéed in a very delicate curried drawn butter; leg of lamb roasted with fresh rosemary, garlic, and lemon served in its own sauce. There were four freshly baked breads available that evening, as well.

After dinner, when Jerry and Mary joined me, they explained that the house had been built in 1890 as a summer home. When they bought it, much restoring and redecorating were needed. "Furnishing it with Victorian furniture was fun," said Mary. "We've met every antique dealer between Duluth and Milwaukee getting the right furniture for five bedrooms and three dining rooms."

During the holiday season of 1979, the inn presented a series of traditional English wassail dinners, complete with musicians, carols, flowers, and flaming pudding. They were sold out in October. In January, February, and March of 1980, the second annual Sunday concert series was offered, something which delights both Phillipses, because they are also professional musicians. "These are always successful, and reservations are most necessary," Mary cautioned.

Yes, the word for the Old Rittenhouse Inn is *style,* to which I must inevitably add the word *grace.* I found them both in abundant quantities at this inn in Bayfield, Wisconsin on the shores of Lake Superior.

OLD RITTENHOUSE INN, 301 Rittenhouse Ave., Bayfield, Wis. 54814; 715-779-5765. A 5-room Victorian inn in an area of historic and natural beauty, 70 mi. east of Duluth, Minn., on the shores of Lake Superior. European plan. Breakfast and dinner served to travelers. Open all year except the first three weeks in November; Christmas Eve and Christmas Day. Advance reservations most desirable. No pets. Not comfortable for small children. Extensive recreational activity of all kinds available throughout the year, including tours, hiking and cycling on the nearby Apostle and Madeline Islands. Jerry and Mary Phillips, Innkeepers.

Directions: From the Duluth Airport, follow Rte. 53-S through the city of Duluth over the bridge to Superior, Wisconsin. Turn east on Rte. 2 near Ashland (1½ hrs.), turn north on 13-N to Bayfield.

THE WHITE GULL INN
Fish Creek, Wisconsin

For me, the story of The White Gull Inn began one summer morning in 1978 when Jan and Andy Coulson, and their now two-year-old daughter Meredith, and I enjoyed a breakfast of cherry pancakes and Door County maple syrup.

Andy told me about their plans to add another dining room and expand the kitchen; all of which took place during the winter of '78 and '79. The principal reason for this expansion was to increase the seating capacity for the White Gull's Fish Boils.

The Fish Boil itself is reason enough to visit this inn in Door County, and was featured on the front page of the food sections of the *Chicago Tribune* and the *New York Times.* It features freshly

caught lake fish, homemade cole slaw, fresh-baked bread, and cherry pie.

Center stage is outdoors at the rear of the inn, where Russ, the master boiler, has built a roaring fire under two huge cauldrons in which the fish is boiled. This wood-smoke fire, combined with the aroma of the Lake Michigan fish, creates gargantuan appetites. In addition, Russ plays the accordion and leads everybody in lots of singing and clapping of hands. The White Gull has a Fish Boil every Wednesday, Friday, Saturday, and Sunday evening.

On Monday and Thursday nights, from mid-June through September, an early American buffet is served, including a selection of old-fashioned prepared dishes and fresh-baked goods. The menu includes turkey dumpling soup, glazed baked ham, corn and clam pie, maple-baked carrots, Boston baked beans, scalloped potatoes, and lots of homemade breads. During the summer, 1979, these evenings were enlivened by a recorder ensemble and other professional classical music groups who literally played "for their suppers."

The inn is a white clapboard three-story building dating back to 1896. It doesn't "put on airs," and there's a definite open informality among the owners, the staff, and the guests. The rooms are tidy and neat, and some of them in the main house share a bath. There are also spacious cottages in the rear.

"All of this started more then 75 years ago," said Jan, "when The White Gull was part of a large resort area consisting of several of the present-day hotels in Fish Creek."

"I think we're still very much of a resort area," joined in Andy. "Fish Creek is still basically an unspoiled village, but there are dozens of ways for our guests to enjoy themselves. For example, we have Peninsula Park which has thousands of acres of forests, majestic cliffs, caves, and a rugged coast line. There are bridle paths and bathing beaches. We have more miles (250) of shore line in Door County than in any other county in the United States."

Jan pointed out that not only were there all of these wonderful outdoor activities, but there were also professional companies of singers and actors, including the Peninsula Players who have been delighting audiences in this area for the past 44 years. "There's also the Birch Creek Farm Performing Arts Academy, as well as the Peninsula Music Festival," she said.

Although The White Gull is basically a hotel and restaurant and not a complete resort, it is, nonetheless, a very pleasant place for children. The cottage are ideal for young families, and there are lots of beach and playground facilities nearby.

THE WHITE GULL INN, Fish Creek, Wis. 54212; 414-868-3517. A 9-room inn in a most scenic area in Door County, 23 mi. north of Sturgeon Bay. Considerable outdoor and cultural attractions nearby. Rooms with and without private baths. Open mid-May through late October. There are plans to be open during winter '80 and '81. Please confirm with inn. European plan. Breakfast daily throughout the season. Lunches mid-June to Labor Day. Fish Boils: Wednesday, Friday, Saturday, Sunday nights throughout the season. Early American buffet: Monday and Thursday. Dining room closed Tuesday nights. All meals open to travelers. Reservations requested for evening meals. Golf, tennis, swimming, fishing, biking, sailing, and other summer and winter sports nearby. Excellent for children of all ages. Pets allowed in cottages but not in main lodge. Andy and Jan Coulson, Innkeepers.

Directions: From Chicago: take I-94 to Milwaukee. Follow Rte. I-43 (141) from Milwaukee to Manitowoc; Rte. 42 from Manitowoc to Fish Creek. Turn left at stop sign at the bottom of the hill, go 2½ blocks to inn. From Green Bay: take Rte. 57 to Sturgeon Bay; Rte. 42 to Fish Creek.

INDEX

To our readers in Great Britain and other countries in Europe:
Welcome to North America! Many of you are making your first visit and we're delighted that you'll be experiencing some of the *real* United States and Canada by visiting these country inns. Incidentally, all of them will be very happy to help you make arrangements and reservations at other inns in the book.

For your further convenience, automobile rental reservations for the United States can be made before your departure through a world-wide rental corporation: AutoEurope.

Here are some AutoEurope telephone numbers in major European cities to make easy contact before departing: London- 017-27-0123; Paris- 227-4649; Amsterdam- 722-874; Munich- 089-22-3333; Madrid- 91-401-7510; Rome- 06-475-6412; Lisbon- 884-257.

Once in North America, the toll-free telephone number for AutoEurope is 1-800-223-5555.

In addition to books on North American and European inns, the Berkshire Traveller Press also publishes books on other types of travel, history, cookbooks, country living, Shaker lifestyles, and Shaker furniture design; works of fiction: juvenile, adult, and historical.

Author's inquiries are invited; please send a two- to four-page outline of the work. Unsolicited manuscripts are not accepted.

The Last Word . . .
Remember, to avoid disappointment, telephone ahead to all inns for reservations.

Country Inns and Back Roads, North America is completely rewritten each year. The new edition is available every March. Your bookstore will be happy to reserve your copy in advance. For a complete catalogue on Berkshire Traveller Books write to: The Berkshire Traveller Press, Pine Street, Stockbridge, Massachusetts 01262.